Peru

England

Russia

Syd Browne

A PROFESSOR AT LARGE

THE MACMILLAN COMPANY
NEW YORK · BOSTON · CHICAGO
DALLAS · ATLANTA · SAN FRANCISCO

MACMILLAN AND CO., LIMITED
LONDON · BOMBAY · CALCUTTA
MADRAS · MELBOURNE

THE MACMILLAN COMPANY
OF CANADA, LIMITED
TORONTO

STEPHEN DUGGAN

A Professor at Large

by

STEPHEN DUGGAN

NEW YORK

THE MACMILLAN COMPANY

1943

To

The Men and Women of the United Nations
Whose Lives Were Sacrificed
In the Cause of Freedom
During the Second World War

This Book Is Reverently Dedicated

THE AUTHOR

Stephen Duggan, Ph.D., LL.D., Litt.D., L.H.D. (to give him all his degrees), has been Director of the Institute of International Education since it was founded, February 1, 1919. Previous to that he was Professor of Political Science at the College of the City of New York. His duties as Director of the Institute have brought him into every state in our Union, almost all the countries of Europe, all of the countries of South America, and a number of those of Asia. In nearly all the foreign countries he has delivered lectures at many of the important universities and addresses to scholarly organizations. In recognition of his services to the cause of international culture he has received honorary degrees from several institutions of higher education in the United States and decorations from several of the European governments. He has written the following books on foreign affairs and international educational relations: *The Eastern Question, a Study in Diplomacy*, 1902; *A Student's Textbook in the History of Education*, 1916; *The League of Nations, The Principle and the Practice*, 1920; *The Two Americas, An Interpretation*, 1933. He has also been a contributor to numerous periodicals.

FOREWORD

THIS is not a war book, although the content is brought up to date. The book was begun before the war broke out. Nor is it an autobiography, though incidents of a personal nature are described in each chapter. It is autobiographical only with respect to my activities as Director of the Institute of International Education. I believe that intelligent Americans may be interested in the story of the recent expansion of international cultural relations in which the Institute of International Education was a pioneer and which has had a real influence in making the peoples of different countries better understand one another and one another's culture and problems. Though the book is primarily devoted to cultural affairs it also considers the political, economic, and social conditions of countries I visited, because these largely determine cultural attitudes. In only the first two chapters are my experiences in the United States considered in any detail. Not all the countries I visited are discussed, but virtually all those of crucial importance in the present world crisis come within this purview.

The experiences described are those of a plain American who was brought into contact with ordinary foreigners, though his mission, which was of a cultural nature, resulted in his meeting with many prominent people especially among scholars, publicists, and university professors. The book is written from the standpoint of democratic liberalism and has an underlying objective, namely, to interpret the transition from the period of United States dependence on foreign cultural influences to the more recent period when American culture has penetrated throughout the world. The objective of the book naturally requires some repetition but I earnestly believe it has been reduced to a minimum.

By permission of D. Appleton and Company I have used in this volume a small amount of material from my *History of Education*, and by permission of Charles Scribner and Sons a somewhat greater amount from my book on *The Two Americas*. By permission of the Editors of *Foreign Affairs*, *Harper's Magazine*, *The Yale Review*, *The Political Science Quarterly*, and the *New York Times*, I have also used some material taken from my articles that appeared in these publications.

Several friends read chapters with whose subjects they were particularly familiar and gave me the benefit of their criticism. This is not true of the first two chapters which are the most autobiographical. The third chapter, "Foreign Influences upon American Culture and Education", was read by Professor Marjorie Nicolson of Columbia, Professor Howard Mumford Jones of Harvard and Professor I. L. Kandel of Teachers College. The chapter on England was read by Sir Angus Fletcher, formerly Director of the British Library of Information; Dr. Henry Allen Moe, Secretary General of the John Simon Guggenheim Memorial Foundation; Mr. Willard Connely, Director of the American University Union in London; and Sir Norman Angell. The chapter on France was read by the late Professor Henri Focillon of the Sorbonne, Albert Guérard of Stanford University, and Dr. Horatio S. Krans, Director of the American University Union in Paris. The chapter on Germany was read by Professor Carl Friedrich of Harvard, Professor Robert Fife of Columbia, and Professor Walter Kotschnig of Smith College. The chapter on Italy was read by Count Sforza, formerly Italian Under Secretary of State for Foreign Affairs, and Professor Dino Bigongiari of Columbia. The chapter on Russia was read by Boris Bakhmeteff, formerly Russian Ambassador to the United

States; Michael Karpovich of Harvard; and Joseph Barnes, expert on Russia for the *New York Herald Tribune*. The chapters on Latin America were read by Professor Ernesto Montenegro, the Chilean journalist; Professor Dana G. Munro of Princeton; Professor Clarence H. Haring of Harvard; John I. B. McCollouch, Editor and Publisher of *The Inter-American Monthly;* and Dr. Samuel Guy Inman. The chapter on the Philippines was read by Major General Frank Ross McCoy, President of the Foreign Policy Association. And the chapter on China by Mr. Chih Meng, Director of the China Institute in America; Professor L. Carrington Goodrich of Columbia, and Mr. Eugene E. Barnett, Secretary of the International Committee of Young Men's Christian Associations. Dean Carleton Brownson of the College of the City of New York read the chapters on the Philippines, China, and Russia; and Professors Nelson P. Mead and J. Salwyn Schapiro of the same institution, most of the chapters. President Paul Klapper of Queens College advised with reference to objectives. To all these friends I am greatly indebted. Their criticisms were very valuable. They are not, however, responsible for the contents of the book or the opinions expressed. Those are my own. Also the inevitable mistakes.

To two friends I wish to express particular gratitude: Philip Curoe, Professor of Education at Hunter College, and Randle Elliott, my associate at the Institute. They read the entire manuscript and I profited greatly by their frank criticism concerning content and structure. Mr. Elliott made invaluable suggestions as to the organization and arrangement of materials and also read the proof. Finally, to my secretary, Miss Agnes Dowd, who typed the entire manuscript, checked the accuracy of many statements, and read all the proof, no words can express too warmly my great indebtedness.

STEPHEN DUGGAN

INTRODUCTION

THE one immutable problem that has always confronted mankind, whether he was organized into aboriginal tribes like the Australian bushmen or into complicated societies like the United States, is: "How much freedom should be allowed the individual and how much control should be retained by the social whole?" Each people of the past and of the present has had a solution of this problem, but the extremes of difference in the solutions are to be found in the East and the West. In the later nineteenth century the idea of the unity of society was tenaciously held in the Far East, where the individual was suppressed because his destiny was controlled by some force external to himself, such as ancestor worship in China or the caste system in India. Society in the East, therefore, was conservative. The farther one moved westward, the more the individual was exalted and the more progressive society became. There was more individualism in Russia than in India, more in Germany than in Russia, more in England than in Germany, and most of all in the United States. The recent development of totalitarianism in Europe is a throwback, a retrogression.

There are two factors in the education of the individual: namely, heredity and environment. The Nazis emphasize heredity and make much of blood and race; the democracies emphasize environment. We know almost nothing with certainty about the part heredity plays; we know a great deal about the part environment plays. When the term "education" is mentioned the mind almost instinctively thinks of an institution, the school, and of a period of life between the ages of six and twenty-one during which the individual attends school. But the school is only one institution of many which mold the individual. Others are the home, the church, the library, the newspaper, the radio, and the theatre. The education of a person is not condensed into a definite period of years; it is a life process. He is never free from the transforming influences of these institutions. This fact has been recognized only recently and adult education has become a necessary supplementary influence in society.

Of all the institutions which educate, the school is the one which the collective whole, the state, deliberately employs to make sure that the individual will be readily absorbed into the body politic and not become an irritant within it. Throughout history there have been liberating states and enslaving states. Today the United States represents, among others, the liberating state; Germany, the enslaving state. The state transmits to the individual the traditions and ideals which have enabled it to survive in the past and the objectives it hopes to attain in the future. The liberating state does this by allowing and providing access to all sources of information and maintaining methods of teaching which permit the individual to question acts of the state. The enslaving state demands unquestioning acceptance of its viewpoint. In this case the teaching is direct indoctrination and the resulting product is a man who is not free. The educational value of the traditions and ideals held by the different nations of which I write in this book, and the degree of indoctrination pursued by them, have had much to do in determining the conclusions I have drawn. I regard education in its narrow as well as its broad sense as the most important function of the state and the chief determinant of its way of life. This view is held with great conviction by the modern totalitarian states, and they have pursued ruthlessly and relentlessly their objective of regimenting the minds of their citizens. The attitude of the democracies as typified by the United States has been one of *laissez-faire,* and they have only just now awakened to the values of their own liberalism and the dangers inherent in the methods of indoctrination.

Human progress has never been a continuous evolution forward. It has usually been a matter of two steps forward and then one back. We took two long steps forward when we undertook the crusade to make the world safe for democracy and put an end to war. And then we took a long step to the rear by turning our backs upon the rest of mankind and refusing to enter the cooperative scheme to accomplish the very ends for which we entered the war. We isolated ourselves from other nations and gave complete vent to the acquisitive instinct in a wild speculative scramble for riches. The result was inevitable. Few countries suffered more than the United States in the world economic depression after the speculative house of cards crashed upon the sands of Wall Street.

The experience of Americans since the founding of their government has made of them intense individualists. In Europe necessary reforms in social conditions have come from the government. In the United States they have come from individuals or organizations of individuals. Here the government takes over a reform usually after it becomes a demonstrated success. From the beginning of our national history practically all Americans—farmers, business men and others— have resented interference upon the part of government. But the new situation occasioned by the depression of 1929 was unprecedented. We had sustained economic crises in the past but they were minor and affected only those living on the economic fringe of society. In this depression our whole population suffered: banks suspended operations, factories shut up, unemployment among the skilled as well as the unskilled increased by leaps and bounds. If absolute destitution was not to be forced upon millions of our people, there was only one recourse, the federal government. But interference and control by the federal government would be in conflict with all our political instincts and traditions, with states' rights and individual enterprise. Nevertheless if our way of life was to be preserved with its focus upon the human being whose life, liberty and happiness were to be maintained, a campaign for the re-education of the American mind would be necessary.

The re-education of our people at home, having as its objective the development of a more humane interpretation of the "general welfare", was carried on at the same time with their re-education in their relations with other nations. The objective in the latter case was to convince our people that science and technology had reduced the world to so small a compass that no nation could live alone in isolation, that all nations had been made neighbors dependent upon one another for their very living, that all might live together in harmony as good neighbors or in strife as bad neighbors. It is unfortunate that before the process of re-education in this matter was complete we were compelled to enter World War II. The New Deal at home required but little interference in the life of the average individual; the war demands a daily increasing interference which will probably result in an almost total control of the individual by the state before the war is over. That will almost without question leave behind a residue of greater control by the state in peacetime and a change in the status of individual liberty. In both domestic and international affairs a "new order" is inevitable. We shall not as individuals or as nations return to the conditions of life that prevailed in the pre-war days.

The history of the United States is the story of the widening of the domain of freedom, of interpreting the phrase "the general welfare" to include more and more individuals and groups in the enjoyment of increased opportunity for material and spiritual advancement. This has unquestionably been an inspiration to peoples in other lands. Millions of immigrants have written home to describe their higher standard of living, their freedom from police espionage and government interference, and their participation by means of the ballot in making decisions on questions that would determine their future way of life in the New World. This was a great educational activity of a spontaneous nature, not directed by any person or group, devoid of the element of premeditation.

Even when Americans deliberately engaged in educational work in other lands it was wholly without any tinge of cultural imperialism such as was true of similar activities on the part of practically all the other Great Powers. The schools and colleges established by Americans in China and the Near East were not spearheads for political and economic exploitation. Our government had nothing to do with their organization or support. That is why today they are practically the only foreign educational institutions in those countries not regarded with suspicion by the native peoples. It is true, they taught our way of life and unquestionably stimulated a desire for greater individual freedom, democratic institutions, and national independence. But when the world beheld that one generation of American control in the Philippines had to a great extent converted the Islands to comparatively speaking a modern democracy after three and a half centuries of Spanish medieval feudalism there, it is natural that in the unprecedented crisis which confronts mankind today it should turn to the dynamic civilization which resides in the United States for leadership in finding the way out.

When this war is finally ended by the defeat of the Axis powers, all the combatants will be in a state of exhaustion, many in chaos. The campaign of relief, rehabilitation, and reconstruction that must of necessity be undertaken will strain the resources of philanthropy and statesmanship of the

United Nations. Reconstruction cannot this time be confined to material things as it was at the close of World War I. Reconstruction of attitudes toward all human problems—political, economic, social, and international—will be necessary if this holocaust is not to occur again. The people who have had most experience in the change of attitudes resulting from educational reconstruction are the American people. For their own welfare as well as the welfare of all mankind, Americans must participate in this great work of reconstruction. We must, moreover, participate as leaders—not to impose our view of life upon any people but to inspire in all peoples an understanding of our common destiny, to place our experience at their service in the hope that they, like us, will want to help build the better world in which liberty and security and justice shall prevail.

It is to the story of the more recent world-wide expansion of American cultural influence, in which the Institute of International Education has played a pioneer part, that this book is devoted. The chapters which follow recount the reflections of an exponent of liberalism, a former college professor, whose work as Director of the Institute brought him around the world and into contact with many men and women who were shaping world policies.

CONTENTS

A PROFESSOR AT LARGE

CHAPTER I

THE MAKING OF AN AMERICAN INTERNATIONALIST

I HAVE often been asked when I first became interested in international affairs. I usually answered that I was born interested. When I was at school my favorite studies were geography and history. When I went to college, economics, political science, world history, and foreign languages were added to those subjects. My college education was obtained at the College of the City of New York, from which I was graduated in 1890. The student body would, in England, be termed "middle-class", made up chiefly of the sons of tradesmen, though sons of professional people were also represented. For example Gano Dunn and Bernard Baruch, whom I afterward grew to know very well, were members of the class of 1889, which preceded mine by a year. Gano Dunn was one of the handsomest men I ever met. He was a brilliant undergraduate, afterward studied engineering, and eventually became President of the White Engineering Corporation. He was a typical successful businessman and became one of the government's dollar-a-year men in World War I. I have known Bernard Baruch as a man of the keenest vision, with a fine imagination for great realizable enterprises. He was always ready to spend his money for spiritual causes. During World War I he rendered splendid service to our government as a member of different commissions but probably most service as Chairman of the War Industries Board. He afterward became an Elder Statesman and the government has profited by his advice in this war.

The great majority of the students were native born but of foreign parentage. There were many German Americans, some Irish Americans and a few of scattered ancestry. I was sometimes invited to the homes of my colleagues and was naturally influenced by the atmosphere of those homes. I heard much German spoken and learned to speak it quite well myself, much better than French, with which I had but little practice. Music was nearly always an element in the home life of these colleagues, which helped to develop in me a natural fondness for it. After graduation, when I became a teacher, I subscribed annually to a seat in the top gallery of the Metropolitan Opera House. All the operas presented in those days were foreign; none was American. These German families had a liberal view of social life. Wine and beer were beverages in constant use and there was much singing of *Studenten Lieder* and *Volkslieder,* and other harmless conviviality. These people were part of the cosmopolitan element in a city which was constantly growing more cosmopolitan, and I was naturally affected by the life about me.

The College had not become so predominately proletarian and Jewish as it did later, after the immigration of poor Jews from Eastern Europe. A large part of the students of German parentage were Jews, however, and I made many friendships among them. I was unconsciously impressed by their studious character, by their more serious view of life and particularly by the attitude of tolerance that characterized them. I found them very analytically minded, and I discovered later in life that this was true of their people generally. As this was a time that antedated the great influx of Jews from the countries in which the persecutions and restrictions upon them were especially harsh, these students, like their fellow students of native parentage, were conservative. More of them were Republicans than Democrats, none was a Socialist, and probably nobody among them even knew what a Communist was.

One of the agencies that played a part in making me an internationalist had been founded a few years before my graduation from college, namely, the Lecture Bureau of the Board of Education of New York City. It was organized and administered by Dr. Henry M. Leipziger, a fine spirit who was always on the lookout for what he considered "good material" as lecturers. The Lecture Bureau was one of the earliest efforts at adult education in New York. At a time when neither the radio nor the movies existed, it rendered a significant service to the spiritual welfare of the city. A lecturer might be asked to give a single lecture or a series of half a dozen or more. If he turned out to be an interesting expositor in his field, he was sent to another part of the city to repeat his talks. Lectures were given in many fields of knowledge, such as history, geography, literature, science, and government. Someone had told Dr. Leipziger that I was good at making clear some of the difficulties in the field of political science, and he invited me to organize a course of six lectures on American government. I repeated the course many times in different parts of the city.

Early in my career I learned the difficulties of making clear to foreigners the intricacies and anomalies of our government, a lesson which stood me in good stead in my later work in foreign countries. The first of my six lectures was an attempt to explain how our federal government came into being. I laid great stress on the divided condition of the country after the Revolution and the difficulty of getting the states to form a union because of the jealousy of the large states by the small states, the boundary disputes that almost caused open conflict, the imposition of tariffs by some states against products from other states, and similar obstacles. I emphasized the point that if there were anomalies in the structure of our government they resulted from the necessity of making compromises when the full demands of each side were not accepted by the other.

The first school in which I delivered my series was in a district on the lower East Side, inhabited almost exclusively by recently arrived Jewish immigrants. The lectures were given at night when people were free from work. When I arrived at the scheduled time the lecture hall was quite full, the audience made up almost wholly of men. The audience was very attentive and warmly applauded at the close of the lecture. I felt the lecture had been a success and was putting on my coat when an old Jew with a long beard and wearing a gaberdine that almost reached his ankles approached. "Teacher, pleeze," he said, "dot wass a gut lesson und I learnt much. But vot I don't understand is vy dose states didn't vant to come in dot union." "Neither do I," I answered, and stalked out vowing to myself that obviously generous applause was no criterion of the degree of comprehension. Many candidates for public office have learned the same lesson. During my lifetime William Jennings Bryan and Alfred E. Smith attracted immense and enthusiastic crowds to their meetings when campaigning for the Presidency. They were misled into believing they would be successful but each of them lost the election.

After graduation from college I was able, with the money earned by teaching, to enter Columbia University as a graduate student. The remarkable School of Political Science, the equal of which had never existed before in the United States, had been established at Columbia University a few years previously, and graduate students flocked to it from all parts of the country. It is seldom that such a galaxy of scholars in one field of study is assembled in a single university. Among them were Mayo Smith and John Bates Clarke in economics, Seligman in finance, Giddings in sociology, Dunning and Osgood in American history, Robinson in European history, and Munroe Smith in jurisprudence. I became acquainted with all of them and the personal friend of some of them, and I always felt a deep sense of gratitude for having enjoyed such a privilege with men whom I held in high honor and deep admiration. Because I specialized in public law, my teachers included John Bassett Moore in international law and diplomacy, John W. Burgess in comparative constitutional law, and Frank Goodnow in comparative administrative law. The subject of my thesis, for which I was later granted the Doctor's degree, was "The Eastern Question, a Study in Diplomacy." I found real satisfaction in its being that year one of the three which the School selected annually for publication in its series in History, Economics, and Public Law. While it was of service to students as late as World War I, the changes that took place after 1919 rendered it entirely out of date. The studies in my chosen field enabled me to obtain a fairly thorough knowledge of the political systems of Great Britain, France, Germany, and the United States, and to a less extent of some other countries. My major professor was Judge Moore, then Professor Moore, a man of keen penetration, of unusual ability to organize knowledge and synthesize ideas— in a word, a man of profound and original scholarship. He was deeply interested in the welfare of the eleven young men who constituted his seminar. I became a reverent admirer, as in fact we all did, and later because of my continued residence in New York City, I had the opportunity of more intimate association. Judge Moore admitted me to his friendship, a highly prized possession, and his sound advice was of invaluable assistance in later days in helping to solve certain personal problems.

The School was a tribute to its dean, Professor Burgess, who sought original scholars everywhere. Though a man of great mental power, unusual analyzing ability, and positive and dogmatic views, he was infected by what would be called today the "Nordic myth". He advocated an alliance of some kind between Great Britain, the United States, and Germany, which was to be the guarantor of order, security, and civilization generally. Burgess was a strong advocate of the Austinian theory of the State, which in essence maintained that the rights of the individual proceed from the State and therefore could be withdrawn by the State, a theory which I believe is wholly incompatible with the existence of a democratic way of life and with sound ethical thinking. Burgess was later selected to be the first Theodore Roosevelt Exchange Professor at the University of Berlin, and became a great friend of the Kaiser. When the first World War broke out, it became apparent that like some other American professors who had done their research work in Germany, he was a strong pro-German and he lost influence and friends. Despite his great scholarship, he was a man of prejudices. At the time I was a graduate student at Columbia, a delegation of three women students visited him to request permission to enroll in the School, which at the time was not open to women. He denied the request. One of the women said, "But, Professor Burgess, women can enroll in the graduate school of political science in Chicago." "So much the better," said Dean Burgess, "let them all go there and let the men come here." Although the splendid teachers of the School were detached and objective in presenting the facts of their subjects, I found that they were not without biases on various aspects of life. Unlike scholars in the natural sciences, they were dealing with human beings individually or collectively, and it is the unusual mind, indeed, that resists predilections when dealing with human beings.

Character of the College of the City of New York

In 1896 I accepted an offer to teach in my Alma Mater while continuing with my studies at Columbia. I began as an instructor to teach international and constitutional law. Since my own undergraduate days, the student body of the College had been rapidly changing. The proportion of Jews had been constantly increasing until, by the time Dr. John H. Finley was called to the Presidency in 1903, they numbered about seventy-five per cent of the total. Moreover, the majority were themselves either recent arrivals from Eastern Europe or were the sons of recent arrivals. They were practically all poor and many of them had been badly persecuted in Russia, Poland, Rumania, and in Central Europe generally, and some of them naturally looked upon government with suspicion. But few foreigners absorbed democratic views more readily and became better Americans than the Jews of that time. Moreover, President Finley was a man of such broad and tolerant views, and was so deeply interested in helping students make a happy orientation into American life, that he was a powerful influence in a true Americanization program. He made a great impression upon me personally, having made a confidant of me early in his career as President.

Dr. Finley's forte was not administration but he had one quality that every great administrator has. He selected a group of men to help him administer the College, gave them his confidence, and then practically allowed them *carte blanche* to carry on their activities. Among them he chose Carleton Brownson as Dean. Brownson had been invited to the College from Yale. He was a splendid classical scholar and in addition a man of fine ideals whom everyone trusted. I have never met a man more fair and just. Dr. Finley himself was so fine a personality, with such noble ideals of life, and exuded so much actual goodness that no one intimately associated with him could fail to become a better person by contact with him. Many of the graduates of the College have in later years told me of the profound impression he made upon their lives. As time elapsed that impression was extended first throughout the city and then throughout the country. Dr. Finley became generally recognized as a great force for everything that was best in our national life.

Dr. Finley took an action concerning myself which had a great influence on my later career. I had been offered a place in a western institution at a higher salary and at his request I declined it. A year later the State Board of Regents raised the qualifications for a teacher's license in such a way as to require the establishment of a Department of Education in the College. Dr. Finley said to me, "Your way to be made professor of political science is blocked by the fact that a good man holds the position. I want to promote you and suggest making you professor of education." "But," I answered, "I am not qualified to teach the courses in the new department." "One of them," he answered, "is the history of education. You have been trained in history and I know that you have always been interested in the history of civilization. The history of education is the history of civilization. You can give the course in the history of education and secure assistants in psychology and methodology." I followed his advice and invited Dr. Paul Klapper, now the President of Queens College, to be my first assistant. The success of the new department was very much due to the services of Dr. Klapper. He was untiring in his attention to his duties and never faltered in his loyalty to his fine ideals. He became very influential in the educational system of the city. The chief importance of Dr. Finley's action on my own career was that it kept me in New York.

The Meaning of Education

The necessity of organizing the course in the history of education caused a clarification in my own mind of the meaning of civilization and of the place of the individual and of the collective whole, the state, in each civilization. Because of the limited time given to the course—three hours a week for one semester—and also because of my own ignorance of other civilizations, the course was confined to Western civilization. As described in the Introduction, I adopted as the two fundamental concepts of the course, first, that the chief problem of the state is the reconciliation of individual liberty with social security and, second, that the chief problem of education is to develop the capacities of the individual to increase his own happiness while rendering the greatest service to society. As there was no textbook that conformed to my own view of the problem, in the course of time I wrote my own textbook, founded upon my experience in the classroom discussions with my students and also with school teachers to whom I gave the course in the late afternoons. The book, which was published in 1916 and is still in use, was adopted by a considerable number of colleges.

A number of years passed before Professor Walter Clarke, the incumbent of the chair of political science, resigned to become president of a western institution and I succeeded him, Dr. Klapper following me as Dean of the School of Education. During those years, as a strong advocate of adult education, I had established the Extension Courses for Teachers with a view to providing them with a wider and deeper knowledge in the fields of history, literature, science, art, and music. Sixteen hundred teachers matriculated the first year, a number which in the course of time reached five thousand. I also founded the first Night College in the United States. I believed that there must be in the city thousands of graduates

of high schools and young men who had completed only a
partial college course who would be glad to work toward a
college degree. The Night College opened in 1907 with 208
enrolled students fulfilling the requirements for admission.
It has 11,700 today, but not all of them are candidates for a
degree. Both these enterprises were opposed by the conservative members of the Board of Trustees and of the Faculty.
They would have been impossible of realization save for the
hearty and persistent support of Dr. Finley and the loyal cooperation and hard work of Dr. Klapper.

The Student Body at the City College

While organizing and administering these new activities I
continued my regular courses with the undergraduates. No
teacher could have had a finer student body to work with.
They were studious, keen and forthright. They did not hesitate to analyze any subject to its fundamentals regardless of
tradition or age. The reverence paid to the Constitution did
not prevent them from questioning the continuance of the
anomaly of New York and Nevada each having two Senators
despite their enormous disparity in population, or whether
the Supreme Court was a better judge of the "general welfare" than Congress, e.g. in deciding the first federal income
tax unconstitutional. I allowed the freest discussion in my
classroom and placed no restrictions upon a student putting forward views that were radical or unpopular. I did
this from preference but I also discovered that untenable
views were frequently demolished by the students themselves.
I usually closed the discussion by presenting my own attitude
on the subject, which ordinarily carried weight possibly because of the greater experience behind it. I do not hesitate to
say that I learned a great deal as the result of the keen ques-

tioning of these young men. It was fatal to evade; one had always to be on the *qui vive*.

I found these students, like students everywhere, very grateful for an evident interest in their personal welfare. In those days few colleges had counselors to advise students on personal matters. Before my marriage and removal to one of the suburbs of the city I frequently invited a group of students to spend an evening with me at home. I listened with great interest to their views on the problems of life that confront all of us, such as earning a living, the relation of youth to age, the right political attitude to take toward the community and the country, marriage, and many others. Some of these views were quite different from those held by students in a college situated in a less cosmopolitan environment. A number of these students remain my firm friends to this day and I am very proud of their success in "making good" in the finest sense of the word. I do not remember one of them with whom I was on intimate terms who did not become an outstanding figure in the life of the city and did not make some constructive contribution to its welfare. They formed the most socially minded group of young people that I know. Many of them had become members of the University Settlement, then one of the finest agencies for good government in the city. It still is.

In later years, especially after the disillusionment following the close of World War I, the College acquired the unjust reputation of being "red". Unquestionably some of the students were allured by the promises of the "Bolshevik heaven" established in 1917 in Russia, as was true at the time of the universities in most of the countries of Western civilization. Some of them became members of the Communist party and followed the "party line" dictated at Moscow. I feel confident that the number of such students was decidedly less than ten per cent of the student body. But they were there for the definite purpose which they followed in every country: as agents of Communism to bring about confusion, to arouse hatreds between economic classes, and to destroy confidence in the institutions of the country. They carried out a definite, organized program. When a mass meeting of students was called for any purpose whatever the Communists were always ready to assume control and to propose able party men as chairman and secretary. They were usually trained as skilled debaters and adepts at parliamentary law and were generally able to prolong the meeting until all the sincere students had left. Then the Communist rump would adopt resolutions favoring their own program, which in no way represented the real views of the mass of the students. Such meetings were given much publicity in the local press as were various incidents like clashes on the campus between Communists and their opponents.

As the great majority of the students were Jews, reds and Jews became synonymous in the minds of many unthinking people. All this contributed to the growing anti-Semitism in New York, which was a characteristic of the two decades following World War I. This became all the more true when a legislative investigating committee, the Rapp-Coudert Committee, in 1940 disclosed the existence of a small group of Communists in the teaching staff of the College among the leaders of which were some Jewish teachers. I cannot express too strongly my detestation of anti-Semitism. That a man's value should be determined not by merit nor character but by such an adventitious matter as race or religion is to me outrageous. There will be considered in later chapters the extent of the phenomenon in advanced form that I met in many European countries. Among Jews, as among all other people, there are all degrees of desirable and undesirable individuals. If, as Edmund Burke said, we cannot indict a whole nation, certainly we cannot indict a whole race. Anti-Semitism in New York is typical of the attitude practically always aroused among the members of a community when it is invaded by a large number of aliens of distinctly different ways of life. The Irish peasant immigrants were regarded with much disfavor in many American communities after the Civil War and have never overcome that disfavor in Boston, because of their almost continuous control of its recent political life. Such epithets as Dago, Hunkey, Mick, and similar words show that prejudice has not been aimed exclusively at Jews. But the Jews in New York and its suburbs now number more than 2,000,000—more than in all Germany—and because of their number they influence all aspects of the city's life. Economic competition explains much of anti-Semitism.

The First World War Breaks In

During these years I had watched with growing anxiety the constantly increasing friction between Great Britain and Germany, and the positions that were being taken by the Great Powers on the diplomatic battleground. When World War I finally broke out it was like a bombshell to the American people. They had for nearly a generation devoted themselves almost exclusively to domestic affairs and they were woefully ignorant of the background of the war and the issues involved. A group of fine spirits and forward-looking patriots in New York—Paul Kellogg, Norman Hapgood, Charles A. Beard, Charles P. Howland, Joseph P. Chamberlain, and some others—determined to do all they could by means of the spoken and written word to provide factual information concerning those issues. This group of which I was a member finally organized the League of Free Nations Association, and I became its Secretary. Later, as described below, it was transformed into the Foreign Policy Association.

Joseph Chamberlain is the most selfless man I have ever met. Modest, retiring, and without ambition to appear in the headlines, his life has been devoted to hard work for many civic causes, to which he contributed liberally. Paul Kellogg, as Editor of the *Survey-Graphic,* has never failed to espouse the cause of the alien and the underprivileged despite open and secret opposition. Norman Hapgood, Charles Howland and Charles Beard were among the liberals who could always be relied upon to rally to the defense of individuals and groups who were unjustly attacked. We held luncheons every Saturday at which one of the issues of the war or one of the problems that would have to be settled at the peace was discussed. The luncheons took place at the Café Boulevard on Broadway and I usually presided. The gatherings were sometimes difficult of control for tempers were on edge.

The luncheons were not our only meetings. The United States soon became the home of propagandists for practically all the Powers big and small that had a stake in the war. We frequently held special smaller meetings to listen to one of them expound his cause and to question him as to its justification. I grew well acquainted with several of these propagandists, some of them newspaper men, some scholars, some government officials. The finest of such expositors was unquestionably Thomas Masaryk, who fled from Austria-Hungary to plead the cause in the United States of a free *Czech* people. He was so obviously sincere and upright that I conceived a great respect and friendship for him. Before he returned to Europe toward the close of the war I was very pleased to have him say that I had rendered him a great service while he was in the United States by inviting him to speak at meetings of various organizations. The next time I saw him was upon his invitation to the Hradcany palace in Prague.

As the war progressed, it became obvious that our country would be drawn in. The Carnegie Endowment for International Peace determined to hold a conference in the spring of 1917 to consider the various aspects of the question of war and peace. Dr. Nicholas Murray Butler, the Director of the Division of Intercourse and Education of the Endowment, sought a man to organize the sessions of the conference and Professor Samuel McCune Lindsay, one of his confidants, and Judge Moore recommended me. I already knew Dr. Butler slightly. I was appointed to the very difficult job, Dr. Butler saying that a man trained in international relations and functioning as an educator ought to make a success of it. He made me chairman of a committee to draw up a program which provided for a thorough discussion of all aspects of the problem of whether we should enter the war. It was decided to hold the conference May 28th-June 1st at the Hotel Nassau at Long Beach on Long Island away from the distractions of New York City. Despite the fact that Congress declared war on April 7th, the conference was held and the discussions were wholly free and very illuminating. I enjoyed the sessions where attitudes were presented by men varying in views from the extreme pacifism of Oswald Garrison Villard, Editor of *The Nation,* to the comparative militarism of General Charles H. Sherrill, afterward our Ambassador to Turkey. The conference was a success in that it attained the purpose for which it was organized. It had a marked effect upon my later career.

When we entered the war in April, 1917, President Wilson established the Committee of Inquiry under the chairmanship of Colonel House, his *alter ego.* The Inquiry was to be composed primarily of men who were considered to be experts on some one of the many problems that would confront the peace conference at the end of the war. It was their duty to study the problems and to provide, in reports to the men who would compose the American delegation, accurate information which would be serviceable to the delegation in the formulation of policies at the conference. Colonel House was too busily engaged in learning something of foreign affairs, by visits to the European combatant capitals in order to secure immediate peace, to supervise the Inquiry. He appointed his brother-in-law, Dr. Sidney E. Mezes, who had become the President of the College of the City of New York three years previously, to do the real directing of the Inquiry. Dr. Mezes, whose field of scholarship was philosophy, was a fine gentleman but was wholly unqualified to do this by training, experience and temperament. The direction of the Inquiry fell of necessity but most fortunately to Dr. Isaiah Bowman, then the Director of the American Geographical Society of New York. He was ably assisted by Dr. James T. Shotwell, Professor of History at Columbia University. Dr. Mezes invited me to become a member of the Committee as one who was supposed to know something about the Eastern Question. I had submitted one report on the Balkan situation to Dr. Bowman when I became a victim of the influenza epidemic, which swept over the entire world in 1917–1918 and resulted in the death of more people than the total number of combatants and civilians who lost their lives through military action in World War I.

The Committee of Inquiry did an excellent job despite the fact that Dr. Mezes appears to have understood so little of its work that the organization would have been disrupted, I believe, but for the great influence David Hunter Miller had with Colonel House, who definitely curbed the interference of Dr. Mezes. As the result of the knowledge that afterward became available, it was evident that some of those who composed the Inquiry did not maintain the objectivity that is supposed to characterize scholars. Professor Charles H. Haskins of Harvard was an eminent historian, but at Paris he was too pro-French. Professor Robert H. Lord also of Har-

vard, who afterward became a Jesuit priest, was actively pro-
Polish and was apparently more interested in the erection of
a strong Roman Catholic Poland than in the establishment
of a viable state. Professor Douglas Johnson of Columbia was
rigidly statistical and demographic and apparently understood too little the political forces of old Europe.

The Institute of International Education Is Born

Almost immediately upon the signing of the armistice the
Carnegie Endowment decided to establish an organization
which should help develop good will between the American
people and the citizens of other countries by promoting the
study and understanding of our civilization and culture by
them and of their civilization and culture by us. The prime
movers in the plan were Elihu Root and Dr. Butler, and I
was invited to become the Director of the new organization.
I was requested to suggest a name for it and did suggest calling it the Institute of International Relations. My idea was
that the Institute should study all aspects of the life of a country—its political, economic, social, and cultural conditions—
and distribute the results of these studies widely among the
agencies of information in the United States for subsequent
dissemination among our people. I then hoped to secure
cooperation in the European countries looking to the adoption of a similar program. Mr. Root was an unusually able
statesman but a very conservative and cautious man. He ve-
toed the plan and the name on the ground that it would be
encroaching upon the domain of the State Department, of
which he had been Secretary only a few years before. Moreover, he stated that such an organization would cost too
much. As the Endowment had plenty of money at the time, I
had counted on a liberal expenditure to do a first class job.

It is interesting to reflect that today Institutes of International Relations are scattered all over our country, some doing excellent work.

The new organization was given the name of the Institute of International Education, and its activities in realizing its objectives were restricted to the use of educational agencies in the narrow academic sense. But I was promised *carte blanche* in its organization and administration. The Institute was opened with a good-sized office near Columbia University, and as staff an Executive Secretary, a stenographer and typist. I then determined to visit the chief univerities and colleges of our own country to acquaint them with my plans in order, if possible, to secure their cooperation. I found practically all enthusiastic about the idea and eager to assist in its realization, for all knew the ignorance of our people in international affairs. To my amazement, the institution where I found students best informed on foreign affairs was on neither the Atlantic nor the Pacific seaboard but in the far interior, at the University of Utah. At that time, 1919, the University though non-sectarian was still controlled by the Mormons, and it was customary for the Mormon students before graduating to spend a year abroad as missionaries.

With the assurance of university support at home, I determined to visit the chief European countries with a similar purpose. Now the accomplishment of the United States in World War I had been sufficiently striking to open the eyes of European statesmen and scholars to its significance as a world power. My program, therefore, was welcomed in every country I visited. I was able to make this visit, and even more prolonged ones later, because in Miss Mary L. Waite, the Executive Secretary, I was fortunate in having selected an assistant of sound judgment, remarkable efficiency, and unquestioned loyalty. As the years passed the staff of the Insti-

tute became much enlarged but Miss Waite remained in her
position until she voluntarily retired in 1938, much to my
regret.

Reverberations from Versailles

While the peace negotiations were taking place at Versailles rumors reached home that our delegation was showing
a willingness to accept policies not at all in conformity with
President Wilson's Fourteen Points, for which the League
of Free Nations Association had made a positive stand. The
President had decided to interrupt his stay at Paris in order
to return to the United States to be present at the opening of
the session of Congress in March, 1919. The Executive Committee of the League of Free Nations Association determined
to request the President to receive a small committee to discuss the rumors. Upon being informed that he would be
willing to do so, Norman Hapgood, Thomas Chadbourne,
and I were selected to go to the White House for the interview. The President spoke freely of the difficulties he was
encountering. For example, he mentioned how Marshal Foch
frequently sat on the opposite side of the table insisting that
France be given the control of the German territory on the
left bank of the Rhine. "Foch is a fine general but a damned
poor statesman," was the President's remark. In the light of
recent events that characterization of the Marshal as a statesman has become more doubtful, but there can be no question that the Marshal's demand would not have received acceptance by our Congress nor by our people.

We returned from our visit to the White House with the
feeling that the President had become convinced that in
order to achieve his objectives compromises would be necessary. When the Treaty was finally signed, the extent to which
he had compromised became evident. The Covenant of the

League of Nations was always his primary consideration, and to retain the Covenant as the first part of the Treaty he accepted compromises that aroused much opposition in our country. I was seated one day at luncheon at the long table in the Century Club with Herbert Croly, the Editor of the *New Republic,* on my right and I was deeply concerned at the degree of his indignation at what he termed the "sell out" at Versailles.

The League became a partisan political issue. Senator Lodge was the leader of the bitter opponents of the Treaty, but he could not have prevented its passage in the Senate as his associates did not control one-third of the votes. There was a group of real statesmen among the Senators called "Mild Reservationists" who asked the President to accept certain changes in the Treaty, which many citizens regarded as necessary to safeguard American interests. But the Treaty and the League had become a matter of personal antagonism between Senator Lodge and the President. The President refused to accept any reservations. That grand citizen of New York, Charles Burlingham, called a meeting of the friends of the President and of the League to consider what action should be adopted. We all signed a letter to the President, requesting him to accept the suggestions of the Mild Reservationists. But despite his strength of character, President Wilson was an obstinate man. As I remember it, he never acknowledged receipt of the letter. When the Senate finally voted on the Treaty, it was rejected by only seven votes. A change of four votes would have saved it.

Although personally opposed to some of the provisions of the Treaty of Versailles, I believed that our country ought to have accepted it and relied upon subsequent modifications being accepted in practice or adopted under Article XIX of the Covenant, which provided for the reconsideration of out-moded treaties. The Covenant would give us a world organization much better than the international anarchy that had existed before the war. It was not possible then to foresee that the new League of Nations would become to too great an extent primarily an instrument for the enforcement of the Treaty of Versailles and for the realization of the international policies of the two chief members, France and Great Britain. I felt justified in my view, however, because of the personnel of the early national delegations to the Assembly and the Council, and particularly because of the staff of the Secretariat. The members who first composed the Secretariat were devoted adherents of the League and had a real vision of its possibilities as a great institution for peace and international understanding. As the years elapsed, however, the delegates and the Secretariat became more and more composed of persons influenced by the national needs and ambitions of their home countries rather than international welfare. To be sure, all that could not be foreseen in 1920, and in the Presidential campaign of that year I took the stump in favor of our membership in the League. As I went about the country speaking in favor of our entrance into the League, I soon became convinced that the voters would reject it. I talked with all kinds of people and found the general sentiment well expressed by an elevator man in a hotel in a mid-western city, who said to me, "To hell with Europe, we've done too much for them."

Unfortunately, the American people were not given an opportunity to vote for or against the League. The issue was confused during the electoral campaign because thirty-one prominent pro-League Republicans, headed by Messrs. Root, Taft, Lowell, and Butler, issued a public statement to the effect that the election of Mr. Harding would result in the adoption of a better League of Nations, and consequently many people voted for Harding, thinking they were voting for the League.

After the election, the friends of the League formed the

League of Nations Association in the hope that a strong campaign of education on the value of the League might lead our people to demand active United States support of the League. Among them were Hamilton Holt, George W. Wickersham, Justice John H. Clarke, Raymond Fosdick, and James T. Shotwell, the last two succeeding each other as Presidents of the Association. I became one of the trustees and remained so for fifteen years. The educational work of the Association, which was largely directed to publicizing the excellent non-political accomplishments of the Secretariat and the International Labor Organization, did result in a happier attitude toward the League. In the first few months after the formation of the League, our State Department did not even acknowledge letters from it, but with the passage of time a very cooperative attitude on non-political activities was adopted by our government. The political activities of the League, however, were often at such variance with the purposes of its founders that it became evident to me that there was little hope of the United States ever becoming a member. For that reason and because I was quite overwhelmed with other work, I reluctantly resigned from the Board of Trustees of the League of Nations Association in 1935.

Europe after Versailles

My first visit to Europe in my new job was just after the signature of the Versailles Treaty. Almost immediately upon my arrival in Paris, I visited the battlefields and was horrified at the scene of desolation. As far as the eye could reach there was not a sign of a living thing, man, beast or bird. Stumps of trees without a leaf, miles of barbed wire, broken camions and wagons, gaping shell holes and destroyed trenches met one's view on every side. I resolved then and there that I would permit nothing personal to interfere with the attempt to realize the objective of the Institute as my small contribution toward the understanding that might lead to a more durable peace. I could not foresee that twenty years later the course of events would compel me to advocate another resort to force in order to save mankind from a new form of slavery. It did not take long to impress upon me the immense difficulties in the way of a durable peace. I returned from the battlefields to the atmosphere of suspicion, resentment and hate that prevailed in Paris, where I became the object of attention by propagandists. This was true of nearly every American, for our prestige was very high just then.

Shortly after my arrival in Paris, I was walking across the Place de la Concorde when I was hailed by a friend, Homer Johnson of Cleveland, Ohio. I had not been aware that he was in France. He told me that President Wilson had appointed a commission of three to go to Poland and report upon the very difficult question of the status of the Jewish minority in new Poland. The Commission was composed of General Jadwyn, Henry Morgenthau, and Mr. Johnson. Mr. Johnson said that they needed an adviser upon the international-legal aspects of the problem and asked permission to nominate me to serve in that capacity. I answered that I would cable to Dr. Butler, the Chairman of my Board of Trustees. Dr. Butler replied promptly that I should render any service to our government that I could. The Commission, which was probably created to satisfy insistent demands of American Jews that some form of protection be guaranteed to their coreligionists in Poland, was to go to Poland in a week. In the meantime I was to move to the Hotel Crillon, the American headquarters, and prepare for the mission. I was given an orderly to do my errands, a soldier, who put his hand to his forehead and gave me a very jerky salute every time he entered my room. I sent for all the documents in the case, the telegrams and reports, and held conversations with the members of the Commission. It was obvious that General Jadwyn and Mr. Johnson held a view about the place of a minority people in a national state wholly at variance with that maintained by Mr. Morgenthau. I was soon convinced that the visit to Poland would not result in reconciling the two views but only in a majority and a minority report. Under the circumstances I did not believe my remaining in the position of political adviser would serve any useful purpose. As I was eager to start my visit to the educational authorities of the different countries, I resigned before the week was up and was succeeded by another adviser. The visit of the Commission to Poland did result, as I had anticipated, in a majority and a minority report.

After resigning as political adviser to the Commission to Poland, I visited the various countries with which I hoped to establish cultural relations. My odyssey brought me as far as the Balkans and, as I observed, my program was everywhere heartily welcomed. In the twenty years between 1919 and the outbreak of the present war in September 1939, I visited the European countries five times at intervals of about four years each and was greatly impressed by the steady demoralization that was taking place in European life. No discerning visitor could fail to be amazed by the determination of the British conservative classes to return to pre-war conditions as soon as possible, despite the great changes in views about economic and social problems brought about by the war itself; nor could he fail to be impressed by the smug attitude that prevailed toward those great changes. In France the constant increase in political factionalism with its accompanying impotence, and the repeated evidence of corruption in France's political and social life, gradually but inevitably led her allies of the Little Entente to lose confidence in her ability to dominate the international situation in Europe. I happened to be in Paris in February 1934, when the attempt was made by the Rightist mob to cross the Pont de la Concorde and charge upon the Chamber of Deputies which was in session. This fracas resulted in the loss of the lives of seventeen Frenchmen and lowered French prestige because it revealed a socially divided and weakened country.

As the years elapsed the increasing resentment against the Treaty of Versailles in Germany, the growing belief that the Allies were determined to keep Germany in an inferior international position, the antagonistic attitude adopted by influential classes in Germany toward the Weimar Republic and its inability to control them, made way for the comparatively easy advent of National Socialism. The growth of extreme nationalism in the new and revived countries of Central and Southeastern Europe, their determination to be self-sufficient militarily and economically resulted in the adoption of tariff policies and autarchic devices generally that hastened the economic demoralization of the continent. The effect of all these changes was a disintegration of standards—moral, political, economic, social, and religious.

The Council on Foreign Relations

Upon returning from my first visit to post-war Europe, I found that a group of forward-looking persons, some of whom had been associated with various branches of government work during the war, were considering the formation of an organization with the following plans: to engage in research in foreign affairs, to hold evening meetings restricted to its own membership in order to listen to discussions by statesmen and scholars in the field of international relations, and to publish a quarterly magazine devoted to problems in that field. The organization was to be the American counterpart of the Royal Institute of International Affairs in London. Both were simultaneously organized at Paris after the close of the war, under the chairmanship of General Tasker H. Bliss. The American organization took the name of the Council on Foreign Relations in 1921 and elected to membership a carefully selected group of scholars, financiers, industrialists, and military authorities whose activities gave evidence of a deep interest in our international relations. This careful selection of the membership has been maintained ever since. The organization elected a Board of Directors of which I became one, to represent international education. The Board was largely made up of men of distinction in their fields: Frank Polk, John W. Davis, Paul Cravath, George W. Wickersham and Norman Davis in law; Otto Kahn, Paul Warburg, Russell Leffingwell and Owen Young in finance and industry; John H. Finley, Isaiah Bowman, Edwin F. Gay, Archibald Coolidge, and Whitney Shepardson in scholarship and letters. Hamilton Fish Armstrong was appointed Executive Director.

In almost every organization, the active control is soon assumed by a small group. Partly because of ability, partly as the result of knowledge and experience, and partly because of willingness to give the necessary time and attention to detailed affairs, the Council's administration gradually fell into the hands of the group of scholars—Bowman, Gay, Coolidge, Armstrong, and Shepardson. Despite the composition of the Board, the majority of which was conservatively inclined in domestic affairs, its discussions and decisions were distinctly liberal in foreign affairs. I have served on many boards and committees and I have not known any whose members were more faithful in attendance at meetings. The man who in course of time showed the greatest ability and acquired the most influence in the affairs of the Council was Hamilton Fish Armstrong. This was most fortunate because he is a man of unusual executive capacity, financial insight, and tolerance of view. John W. Davis was elected first President of the

Council on Foreign Relations. He is a man of culture and distinction, a delightful toastmaster and an excellent chairman. He became the Presidential candidate of the Democratic party in 1924. Mr. Wickersham succeeded Mr. Davis. He was a most lovable as well as capable colleague, simple, objective, and tolerant. He was followed by Norman Davis, slow and deliberate of speech but very conscientious and competent. Possibly it was the possession of these latter qualifications that suggested to President Roosevelt that he appoint Mr. Davis his traveling ambassador before the second World War.

The Research Committee of the Council has done impressive work in carrying on its investigations and has issued excellent books and monographs. The evening meetings were either of the whole membership to listen to outstanding political figures in foreign affairs or of smaller groups interested in some particular field such as our stakes in the Far East, debts and loans to Latin American countries, or our policy toward the Soviet government. Every Secretary of State since the formation of the Council, foreign premiers and cabinet ministers such as Clemenceau, Ramsay MacDonald, Bruening, Sforza, and Matsuoka, and eminent foreign scholars and distinguished figures in our own public life have been invited to present views on international problems. Only American citizens were eligible for membership in the Council and admitted to its meetings; no reporters were present at meetings held at the Council House; no resolutions were adopted. The policy of the Council on Foreign Relations was to exert influence in American life through personal relationships, through its published monographs, and especially through its quarterly journal, *Foreign Affairs*. In the last few years it has fostered the establishment of groups in a number of other cities scattered about the country, which have conducted their activities in a manner similar to that pursued by the New York organization.

The Council began the publication of *Foreign Affairs* in 1922. Its first editor was Archibald Coolidge of Harvard, who laid down the general outlines of policy that have since been followed. Professor Coolidge died in 1928 and was succeeded as editor by Hamilton Fish Armstrong, who had been his assistant. This succession was most fortunate, for under Mr. Armstrong's editorship the magazine became without question the most authoritative periodical in the world in the field of international relations. Mr. Armstrong welcomed to the pages of *Foreign Affairs* opinions of all kinds provided they met his high standards of content and form. He visited Europe every summer to interview prospective contributors. He organized an Advisory Editorial Board, which met twice a year to discuss the subjects that ought to receive attention and the persons best qualified to write the articles on the subject. At the present time (1942) Dr. Lowell, President Emeritus of Harvard; President Seymour of Yale; President Bowman of Johns Hopkins; Professor George A. Blakeslee of Clark University, our foremost authority on diplomacy of the Far East; the economist, Professor John H. Williams of Harvard, and myself form the group. *Foreign Affairs* became so distinguished in its field that the most eminent statesmen and scholars were pleased to be invited to contribute to its pages. When Mr. Armstrong became editor he was relieved of the detailed administration of the Council as Executive Director and a most competent substitute was found in Walter Mallory, who, in addition, edited the Council's *Political Handbook of the World,* which has become a standard work of reference for the large press associations, government bureaus, and educational institutions.

The Foreign Policy Association

Meanwhile a transformation was taking place in the League of Free Nations Association. The Board of Trustees, of which

I was a member, decided immediately after the war that it must unquestionably remain in existence and continue its educational work in the field of international relations. In order to emphasize the fact that it was interested in the international relations of all countries and not merely free nations, it adopted the name of the Foreign Policy Association in 1921. It became known as the chief liberal, democratic agency in that field and did yeoman service in spreading a knowledge of foreign affairs among the mass of intelligent people throughout the country. Its Saturday luncheons, given over usually to the discussion of some current problem, were generally in the nature of debates between representatives of the two or more sides of a vital current question. The luncheons were open to the public generally and were frequently attended by as many as five hundred people. Similar discussion luncheons were held by the many branches of the Foreign Policy Association scattered about the country and now numbering nineteen. As a number of these discussions were locally broadcast, the educative influence of the Association can be readily appreciated.

In the course of time, as the result of increased financial resources, the Association established a research division, which furnished the public with the weekly Foreign Policy *Bulletin* and the fortnightly *Foreign Policy Reports*. Its *Headline Books* are of particular value for popularizing the study of international affairs. All these publications contain accurate information and excellent interpretations of the current international problems that were arousing people's anxieties. Most of the splendid body of forward-looking men, who formed the original group of founders, remained for many years in control but when one fell out for any reason he was always replaced by someone of equal ability and similar sympathies. The Foreign Policy Association has been fortunate in its successive presidents. The first was James G. McDonald, a most attractive personality who made friends for the Association among people who could help to support it. He was a delightful toastmaster at the Saturday luncheons and very popular with the general public. When he resigned to become High Commissioner for Refugees (Jewish and Other) Coming from Germany, he was followed by Mr. Raymond Leslie Buell, with undisputed reputation as a scholar. It was during his administration that the research department of the Association became active and influential. When he resigned in 1939 to become associated with *Fortune* magazine, he was succeeded by Major General Frank Ross McCoy, one of the most distinguished figures in our military and diplomatic life. General McCoy took office at a most opportune time for a military man, just before the outbreak of the present war. He is as much a statesman as an authority on things military.

Necessity compelled me to make a decision in the mid-1920's which I deeply regretted. Partly because of the ambitious program that I had outlined for the Institute of International Education, of which I had become Director, and partly because of a scarcity of assistants due to lack of necessary funds, I was pretty heavily worked. My attendance at the meetings of the governing bodies of the Council on Foreign Relations and the Foreign Policy Association, and the attention I gave to the problems presented at the sessions of their boards, when added to my Institute labors, resulted in a great deal of work at night. I felt I had to give up my place on one of the two boards and while I retained my membership in the Foreign Policy Association, I resigned as a member of the Board of Trustees. An event in 1924 which I could not foresee at the time, really rendered this decision unnecessary. I was in that year provided with more funds, which enabled me to have additional assistants and relieved me of some of the pressure under which I had worked. I doubt that the

Board of Trustees of the Foreign Policy Association lost any great amount of wisdom by my withdrawal, but I have ever since missed the illuminating discussions on foreign affairs that took place at its meetings and also the delightful companionship of a splendid group of forward-looking, internationally minded men and women.

The World Peace Foundation

The leisure I secured in 1924 was afterward absorbed by my becoming a member of the Board of Trustees of the World Peace Foundation. The Chairman of the Board at the time was Dr. William H. P. Faunce, the President of Brown University, with whom I was well acquainted. He and Dr. George Blakeslee, another member, urged me to accept an invitation to membership on the Board and I did so. The Board was made up of a distinguished group of scholarly men deeply interested in and familiar with international affairs. It has maintained that standard of membership ever since and has had a great influence upon public opinion. The publications of the World Peace Foundation have been of unusual value in supplying teachers in our colleges and high schools with accurate and authoritative information about problems in foreign affairs that were of current interest and importance.

The members of the World Peace Foundation Board concerning whom I was most interested were Newton D. Baker and A. Lawrence Lowell. Mr. Baker was a liberal of fine vision and sound judgment. He had been Secretary of War during World War I and his judgments on personalities and events during that conflict were most illuminating. His views on current international problems were equally clarifying. He was a mild and sweet-tempered man, but that characteristic did not interfere with earnest presentation of the positive views that he usually held. Living in Cleveland, Ohio, he could present to the Board the views on foreign affairs held by various groups in the Middle West.

But it was Dr. Lowell who intrigued me most. I have met few men in my career for whose mentality I have had a greater admiration. His reasoning was convincing and his memory remarkable. His knowledge concerning international politics was profound and had great influence upon the Board's conclusions. Though a conservative in his attitude toward life, he was very tolerant of other people's opinions and during his entire administration as President of Harvard University, he was a bulwark of academic freedom. Dr. Lowell was always at the service of the community and in 1927 he was appointed by the Governor of Massachusetts as a member of a commission of three to advise upon the staying of the execution of Sacco and Vanzetti. There can be no question that he tried to arrive at a just conclusion and it is not for me to criticize the decision. But when friends of such legal acumen as Charles Burlingham and Felix Frankfurter drew a contrary conclusion from the same evidence, I felt that there might exist the doubt which in our legal system is expected to go to the benefit of the accused. Certainly the execution of Sacco and Vanzetti aroused bitter criticism of the United States among the working classes of the entire world. I met this hostility almost everywhere in my various journeys.

President Lowell sometimes invited me to his home for lunch and even to stay overnight preceding a meeting of the Board, a privilege which I greatly prized. On one such evening during the Hoover administration we remained until midnight discussing national and international problems. It was then more than at any other time that I became aware of his conservatism. Among other questions that we were considering was the immigration problem and its influence upon our foreign policy. Dr. Lowell incidentally remarked, "There is no reason why a native American should not be a success in our country." I understood him to mean a success in a material sense. At that very time a considerable number of native Americans were losing their farms through mortgage foreclosures in the North. Native American share croppers in the South did not lose theirs for the simple reason that they did not have any to lose. And only one half of all Americans had an annual income of $870. I believe that the truth was that Dr. Lowell, like some others whose ancestry dates back to the colonial period, unconsciously used the term "native Americans" as synonymous with those "older Americans."

The Williamstown Institute of Politics

One of the most potent agencies in arousing interest in international affairs among our people after the first World War was the Williamstown Institute of Politics. It was founded in 1921 as the result of the success of the President of Williams College, Dr. Harry Garfield, in interesting Bernard Baruch in financing the experiment. Dr. Garfield visited Europe each winter to invite distinguished statesmen and scholars to become the guests of the Institute for the month during the summer when the sessions were held, and to deliver a series of addresses upon some particular aspect of international affairs about which they were known to be real experts. Such men as Count Sforza, Arnold Toynbee, William Rappard, Sir Arthur Salter, and Boris Bakhmeteff attended. Equally representative American scholars such as Raymond Buell, Foster Bain, and Arthur Holcombe also lectured at the Institute. The sessions were open to anyone interested in foreign affairs upon the payment of a reasonable fee and it was expected that a good many research scholars as well as journalists, magazine writers, and college professors would attend. This was quite true in the beginning of the Institute's career, but it became less so with the passage of time. Williamstown is beautifully located in the Berkshire Hills, one of America's favorite summer resorts. Everyone was enamored of the locality and gradually the sessions of the Institute were decreasingly attended by research scholars and experts in the field of foreign affairs and increasingly by elderly ladies and gentlemen, unquestionably refined and intelligent but not particularly valuable for the purposes originally intended for the Institute.

All members of the Institute had to enroll in one of the Round Tables, each of which was devoted to some specific study such as the Allied Debts, the Soviet Union, the League of Nations. When I returned from a six months' visit to South America in 1932, I was invited to succeed Dr. Rowe, the Director of the Pan American Union, as the leader of the Round Table on Latin America. A Round Table was usually limited to about twenty persons. My own Round Table was composed chiefly of teachers of history and politics, a few journalists and a considerable number of the general public. They were all intelligent men and women but they had little real knowledge of Latin American affairs. As the years elapsed Dr. Garfield had grown tired of the burden of administering the Institute of Politics and it did not reopen after the 1932 session. It had, however, performed a great service. It had been widely publicized and had been attended by men and women from all over the United States. The result was that when the Institute finally closed, other institutes under a variety of names sprang up in different parts of the country to continue the discussion of national and international problems.

European vs. American Way of Life

The organizations which I have described above are by no means the only ones with which my work as Director of the Institute of International Education brought me into personal contact. In later pages I shall of necessity describe others, such as the Institute of Pacific Relations. Those I have discussed illustrate one typical characteristic of Americans and, to a lesser extent, of the British. Americans have been pioneers from the beginning of their history. The pioneer necessarily is an individualist. He has to rely upon himself to work out his own salvation. In frontier days there was always a good deal of united effort among neighbors and in an emergency that cooperation was essential, for government was often far away. The uniting of individuals in organizations for a desirable objective became a tradition. Therefore, when Americans discovered their ignorance of international affairs during World War I it was most natural that they should found organizations in various parts of the country to study foreign relations. I had learned the extent to which the characteristic I am describing was lacking in the countries of continental Europe. I was soon to have it impressed upon me many times by personal experience. Perhaps one illustration will suffice. One of the early activities of the Institute of International Education was the exchange of students on scholarships between the United States and other countries. On the American side of the exchange all the scholarships were provided by the individual colleges and universities. On the side of the continental European countries they were everywhere provided by the government.

To what extent the principle and practice of individualism—for which my experience abroad strengthened my affection—will survive this present war is an open question. The impetus toward state control inaugurated by the Bolsheviks at Moscow in 1917 left no country unaffected. Its influence is not confined to the totalitarian states but has greatly affected Great Britain and has crossed the Atlantic to the United States. There can be no doubt that state control and state regulation are practically everywhere throughout the world the order of the day. But for the state to undertake activities on a large scale, greatly enlarged revenues and more numerous officials are required. Hence increased taxation and bureaucratization. In all probability with the increasing trend toward state control will come the increased need for carrying on large-scale enterprises resulting from a finer concept of government "to promote the general welfare" of people who through no fault of their own lead lives of material poverty and spiritual monotony. What Americans must be watchful of is that the liberties of the individual, of speech, of worship, of assembly, of the press, and of free enterprise shall not be lost. This is particularly true in war, as at the present time. It will be hardly less true after the war. Unless the immense sums spent now on destructive purposes throughout the world are followed by the expenditures of equally large sums on constructive purposes throughout the world, the effects of another period of disillusionment may be fatal to our democracy.

The European countries are old; government is omnipresent, watchful, and often distrustful of the activities of its citizens. In most European countries the church, the school, the railroad—in fact most human activities on a large scale—are either state activities or under state control. The tradition, therefore, is not that of self-help nor of union of individuals to realize a desirable objective, but to look to the state for enterprise. Where continental Europeans colonized, as in Latin America, that tradition was carried with them. Where the English colonized, the emphasis was upon individualism.

My Relations with Government Officials

Most of my relationships with the European countries excepting Great Britain have been with governmental officials. Most of them in the United States have been with private agencies. But naturally anyone continuously engaged in international activities will sooner or later come into contact with the State Department. And because of the Institute's cultural cooperation with the Latin American countries, it has entered into intimate relationships with the Pan American Union whose distinguished Director, Dr. Leo Rowe, has been at the head of the Union ever since the Institute has existed.

Intelligent Americans are fairly familiar with the history of the Pan American Union. It was a conception of Secretary of State James G. Blaine, and was founded in 1889 in Washington where its seat has been located ever since. Mr. Blaine's purpose was to strengthen commercial relations with the Latin American countries. At the Pan American conferences held in different Latin American countries at five-year intervals, until the conference at Montevideo in 1933, the United States delegation had tried to confine discussions to noncontroversial subjects such as patents, copyrights and trade conventions. The Latin American delegates on the contrary have desired more and more to discuss the controversial subjects, especially those of a political nature like American intervention in the Caribbean countries. In drawing up the agenda and making arrangements for these conferences the Pan American Union had an important part to play, and it can be readily understood how difficult a position Dr. Rowe has filled. The Latin Americans have in the past frankly considered the Pan American Union an appendage of our State Department, which, they maintained, controlled its policies despite the fact that each American republic had its ambas-

sador or minister at Washington as a representative on the
Union's governing board. The attitude of the Latin Americans did not diminish their fondness for Dr. Rowe who, they
had reason to believe, despite his diplomatic reserve did not
always approve our official position. The Good Neighbor policy was not only a relief to all the Latin American nations
but a source of joy to Dr. Rowe and the staff of the Pan
American Union. In accordance with it they could work
heartily for objectives which they had always hoped might be
pursued. The Good Neighbor policy was equally acceptable
to the Institute of International Education, whose cooperation with the Pan American Union in developing cultural
relations with the Latin American countries had been very
intimate and harmonious. Both organizations participated in
the incident described in the following paragraph.

My admiration for Charles E. Hughes as a citizen and
statesman developed into a much-prized friendship before he
left New York for Washington. His autographed photograph
is one of those which hang on my office wall. Mr. Hughes became Secretary of State in 1921 at a time when our relations
with the Latin American countries were anything but happy.
He was not greatly admired by the Latin Americans for the
policies he pursued toward their countries and particularly
for his attitude on the Monroe Doctrine, which he said was
a principle of self-defense of the United States that "reserved
to itself its definition, its interpretation, and its application."
The fifth Pan American conference held at Santiago, Chile,
in 1923 was particularly obnoxious to the Latin Americans
because of the obvious determination of the United States
delegation to prevent discussion of subjects that the Latin
Americans had close to their hearts. Shortly after the conference I wrote to Dr. Rowe, expressing my concern over what
I termed the growing dislike by the Latin American peoples
of the policy that the United States maintained toward their

countries. Whether Dr. Rowe may have mentioned my letter to Mr. Hughes or showed it to someone who in turn mentioned it to him, I do not know. But some time later I had occasion to visit the State Department upon another matter. I had hardly entered the door when Mr. Hughes said, "Dr. Duggan, how do you know the relations of the United States with the Latin American countries are bad and growing worse? I want to tell you we have never had happier relations with them." I explained to Mr. Hughes that my informants were teachers, students, and men of affairs who passed through my office. He insisted that his sources of information were better than mine. I did not dispute the fact with him but his information came chiefly from official sources and sometimes official sources are not the best sources. Officials are sometimes not in close and direct contact with the people. When the next Pan American conference was held in 1928 at Havana, Mr. Hughes confronted an aroused phalanx of resentful Latin American delegates who did not hesitate to criticize freely and adversely the Latin American policy of the United States. It required all his skill to secure an adjournment without an open break.

It was natural that my work should bring me into contact with the foreign embassies and consulates, and I grew to know well many of the representatives of foreign countries. I was acquainted with Lord Bryce before becoming Director of the Institute. He apparently never wasted a moment. I was tolled off once to look after him when he came to New York from Washington to make a luncheon address at the Commodore Hotel. After greeting me he asked how much time would elapse before lunch. I told him a little less than half an hour. "Will you excuse me, then. I will have just enough time to write a letter which I should have sent before leaving Washington." We had a delightful talk after the luncheon. I asked him how he came by the remarkably intimate views of American life that he expressed in *The American Commonwealth*. He answered that he tried to enter into conversation with almost everybody he met and added that his best knowledge of American conditions and opinions came from talking with men in the smoking rooms of Pullman cars, especially with commercial travelers.

I was not greatly impressed with the alleged ability of most of the British ambassadors. Sir Esme Howard became a good friend whom I afterward visited at Ulleswater in the Lake country. The British representative whom I have most admired is Sir Gerald Campbell, then the Consul General at New York. He knows American life and conditions as few foreigners ever did, having been Consul General at San Francisco before coming to New York. He is one of the wittiest men I ever met and he became very much sought after as an after-dinner speaker. When Lord Lothian died, to the great loss of British-American friendship, I wrote to influential friends in England expressing the hope that Sir Gerald Campbell might succeed him as the best qualified man at that crucial time. He was appointed to the second place as Minister. Because the British wanted to show honor to the government of the United States, they sent as ambassador Lord Halifax, some-time Viceroy of India and, at the time of his appointment, Minister for Foreign Affairs. Shortly after his arrival I listened to him make an excellent address on the radio on Britain's aims in the war. The next week he was invited to speak at the Council on Foreign Relations and gave an uninspiring talk on the background of the war, which seemed to me something in the nature of a defense of Chamberlain's appeasement policy. I had a few words with him and was impressed by his evident sincerity.

I greatly admired Jusserand, who remained here so many years as French Ambassador and did yeoman service for his country during World War I. He was a distinguished scholar,

an indefatigable worker, and soon became thoroughly familiar with our problems and conditions. He was greatly admired and loved by hosts of Americans for his simplicity and
integrity. I could not understand why he should have been
recalled in 1925 at so critical a time, but was later told in
France that it was the result of low political trickery. I was
sometimes a luncheon guest at the French embassy and, as in
the case of Great Britain, I did not consider the French ambassadors a strong body of men. The poet, Paul Claudel, simply did not know what politics was all about, and I do not
believe he ever accomplished a single worthwhile thing for
his country. The last ambassador before Vichy, Count René
de St. Quentin, is a man of thought and ability. I once accompanied him on the train to a college where he was to
receive an honorary degree and I was to make an address on
French culture. We had an excellent discussion on the internal problems of the United States. I was interested in his
statement of belief that ours was an undisciplined democracy.
I thought he was to some extent right, but in the light of
events in France two years later the degree to which an ambassador was mistaken about conditions in his own country
is startling. Again, as in the case of Great Britain, it was not
the ranking man who impressed me as the strong man at the
French embassy but Jules Henry, the Counselor of the Embassy. He had been at the embassy many years, knew our
people thoroughly, spoke English like a native—something
unusual in the French embassy—and generally knew what was
the best policy to follow in an emergency. He was made
French Ambassador to Spain just before the war broke out
and left our shores with the admiration and good will of all
who knew him.

Of all the German ambassadors I met, I liked Dr. Luther
most. He was a short, stout, bald-headed man with twinkling
eyes and an agreeable countenance. He spoke English very

precisely but with a decided German accent. He was quite jovial and I believe was really liked by our politicians. Of course, after Hitler came into power, Germans were very cautious concerning things at home and I was never able to discover whether he was a Nazi at heart. He did, however, have one of Goebbels' chief men present when he invited me to lunch in Berlin after his retirement. He read American books omnivorously and could discuss them very intelligently. He once asked me whether I ever thought about what became of the chief figures of *Gone with the Wind*. I answered that I had not. "Well," he said, "Scarlett O'Hara continued to bedevil everybody as she had always done. Rhett Butler went from bad to worse in his course of evil, but always dominating a situation. Ashley Wilkes remained the boob that he appears in the book."

No two ambassadors differed more than Mr. Horinouchi, who represented Japan, and Dr. Hu Shih, who represented China. I came to know them both intimately. Mr. Horinouchi was essentially an aristocrat, very formal but always trying to put himself on a level with his hearer. He was a trained diplomat of the old-fashioned school, but I always found him honest and sincere and very eager to understand our ways of thinking and acting. His wife was one of the most beautiful Orientals I ever met, like a lovely cameo. Mr. Horinouchi was finally recalled for not being able to perform a wholly impossible task, namely, to make the American people like Japan despite her wholly unjustified policy of aggression against China. Dr. Hu Shih is the very opposite of Mr. Horinouchi. He is a splendid scholar, a great philosopher, and a thorough democrat. A fascinating talker and very approachable, he became a prime favorite with the American people and in great demand to make Commencement addresses and after-dinner speeches. His popularity is evidenced by the fact that he has today some fourteen honorary degrees, most of them from our outstanding institutions.

Some of the ministers of the smaller countries like Dr. Peter, who represented Switzerland for many years, were excellent representatives of the civilization and culture of their countries. I shall speak, however, of only one, John Pelenyi, Minister from Hungary, who succeeded Count Szechenyi. He visited all parts of our country to learn of conditions and paid especial attention to our universities. When Hungary joined the Axis in November 1940, Mr. Pelenyi resigned from his position as Minister. He had always been eager to develop cultural relations between Hungary and the United States, particularly by means of the exchange of students. We had grown to know each other well and it was natural that he should ask my advice about the possibility of securing a professorship of international law and diplomacy or of international relations in one of our universities. His scholarship and diplomatic experience received recognition in his receiving a call to Dartmouth.

I have mentioned by name some of the men with whom I had personal and professional relations as Director of the Institute. I must not forget to speak of some of the women who contributed significantly to international education. In the early history of the Institute, Jane Addams was deeply interested in our ideal of international amity through mutual understanding. It was natural that the angel of the homeless and forlorn should extend her hospitality to a heartsick refugee scholar, as she did. Mary E. Woolley, President of Mount Holyoke College, and Virginia Gildersleeve, Dean of Barnard—both members of the Board of Trustees of the Institute —became two of the most distinguished women internationalists in our country and performed a great service in securing the expansion of the study of international affairs in the women's colleges. Mrs. Aurelia Reinhardt, President of Mills College, rendered a similar service on the Pacific coast.

All of these women were leaders in organizing the American Association of University Women, which has been a foremost agency in international education. Mrs. Esther Caukins Brunauer, Associate in International Education of the Association, has done yeoman service in organizing groups of alumnae throughout the country for the study of international affairs. Miss Gildersleeve asked me what I thought of the projected Association before its organization had been completed. I answered that I did not favor it, that I thought that in the field of scholarship there should be no distinctions based on sex. "Dr. Duggan," Miss Gildersleeve said, "you have a liberal view with reference to women's education, and you are frequently asked to recommend people to fill vacancies in colleges. If you were asked tomorrow to recommend someone to fill a vacancy, let us say, in history, would you think of recommending a woman?" I had to admit I would not. "Now you know one reason why we need an American Association of University Women," she added. Its many branches scattered about the country became study clubs throughout the winter for the discussion of problems of national and international importance. This was also true of the branches of the League of Women Voters, which has been non-partisan but distinctly progressive in its approach to the political and economic questions of the day.

Mrs. Dave Hennen Morris, the founder of the International Auxiliary Language Association, of which I became president in 1940, was another of many significant figures in international affairs. None of the women whom I have known exerted a greater influence upon the development of knowledge in that field than Carrie Chapman Catt, the distinguished President of the International League for Peace and Freedom. In more recent days when I became a member of the Executive Committee of the International Student Service I formed a great admiration for Mrs. Roosevelt, one of the Committee with whom I was already slightly acquainted. Her ideals were of the finest and she was very sincere in her efforts to realize them. Incidentally, I never heard her make an ungenerous statement about the most unfriendly critic. Of course there were women's organizations as well as men's which were of a purely propagandist character in their consideration of international problems. But the women of the United States through their various organizations have performed unusual service in educating our people, young and old, in foreign affairs.

CHAPTER II

THE INSTITUTE OF INTERNATIONAL EDUCATION

The Institute as a Center for Information and Advice

IF THE Institute of International Education were to be made an effective agency in realizing its objectives, it would of necessity become a center of information and advice on all aspects of international educational relations. As time elapsed and the work of the Institute became widely known in our own country and among foreign peoples, its correspondence became very large. Letters came in from all kinds of people: scholars, administrators, journalists, teachers, and ordinary citizens. Though they were primarily devoted to matters educational, they were by no means confined to such matters. The letters now average 3,000 a month, and reading the second class mail consisting of pamphlets and magazines from all parts of the world taxes the resources of our staff. Every letter is promptly acknowledged and the attempt is made to provide the desired assistance. Visitors to the Institute seldom number less than about twenty-five persons a day seeking information and advice on the greatest variety of subjects. I have often had, during a single morning, a succession of callers such as an American, a Japanese, a Frenchman, and a Chilean, each with his especial problem; and it sometimes has required a good deal of mental agility to pass from the problem of one to the problem of another.

On one occasion early in the history of the Institute, a representative of the White Engineering Corporation came in with a tall, dark-skinned Ethiopian dressed in flowing garments of several colors. The White Corporation had secured a concession from the Ethiopian government to build a dam on one of the branches of the Nile. Its representative acted as interpreter for I was absolutely ignorant of Amharic. The Ethiopian wanted me to secure some twenty American teachers to return home with him to help establish an educational system, which was very badly needed in his country. When I asked him the subjects in which he wanted teachers, he enumerated first of all a bandmaster as he had been much impressed by a band in Cairo. But he did want some teachers of practical subjects. It would have cost quite a sum of money to take twenty American teachers all the way to Addis Ababa; and when they got there they would have found conditions of life exceedingly primitive. Now the students of the American University of Beirut come from all over the Near East and its teachers are well acquainted with the needs and conditions of the different countries of that area. I told the Ethiopian that he could get the best-qualified teachers from that progressive university and that it would cost him very much less to bring them to Ethiopia from there. He took my advice and when he arrived at Beirut his teachers were ready for him, as I had written ahead to the President describing his needs.

The Institute and Student Exchange

There are few more fascinating subjects of study than the wandering students of the Middle Ages. They came from all parts of Europe to study under a particular teacher like Abelard at Paris or to pursue a particular subject like law at Bologna. Usually before returning home they wandered to other centers of learning to listen to other great masters. This was not difficult because all studies and discussions everywhere were conducted in the same language, Latin. The lives of the wandering students were not always exemplary, but they did bequeath to us the delightful student songs which were descriptive of their life. Contact with peoples of different lands, with their different customs and viewpoints, almost inevitably mitigated the prejudices with which they started from home. When they finally returned home they nearly always became as lighthouses in a surrounding sea of ignorance. With the establishment of national states following the Renaissance, the movement of students from one country to another gradually decreased and finally almost ceased. It was not revived until the latter half of the eighteenth century when foreign students began to go to German universities. A few American students went to German universities before the Civil War, but the movement became something in the nature of a hegira after the War. This was chiefly due to the fact that the American college was essentially a teaching institution in which research was not an important feature.

It was not until toward the close of the nineteenth century that the influence of the first real American university, Johns Hopkins, which opened its doors to students in 1876 and was imitated at other centers, reduced the number of students going to Germany. Nevertheless, until the first World War there were far more Americans who went to European universities to study, especially to German universities, than there were Europeans who came to American universities. The accomplishment of the United States in the war amazed the peoples, the statesmen, and the scholars of the European countries. They wanted to court this new Great Power. They wanted to know more of American civilization and culture, which up to the war they had practically ignored. The British and French realized during the war the great influence exerted in favor of Germany by some of the professors in our colleges who had done their graduate work in Germany. Oxford and Cambridge introduced the degree of Doctor of Philosophy, which had never existed there before, in order to lure American students to their halls. The French *doctorat d'Etat* could only be obtained after many years of research and publication. The French educational authorities had already established for the benefit of foreign students the *doctorat de l'université,* which might be obtained in two or three years. It was now emphasized especially for American students. Nevertheless, the United States rapidly became the Mecca of foreign students. By 1930 there were almost 10,000 studying in our colleges and universities, twice as many as the number of American students studying abroad.

But I was anxious that the best of our students should have the opportunity to study in foreign universities and that the best foreign students study in our institutions of higher education. This was frequently impossible because of impoverishment resulting from the war. Moreover, I judged that if an exchange of such students could be established we should probably have the best possible agency for developing international understanding. The young usually differ from older people in not yet having fixed ideas which are difficult to change. I decided that exchanges should be limited to students who had already secured their national education, that is, had their baccalaureate degree. I did not want any American exchange students to become denationalized or expatriates. If they were thoroughly grounded in their own civilization and culture they could absorb the best in a foreign system without danger as the result of comparing the best in the foreign system with the worst in our own. I am a strong advocate of students' going abroad to study only for graduate work.

The Institute was not provided with funds to enable me

to realize this plan so I appealed to our colleges and universities. A young Frenchman with his *baccalaureat* could easily fit into the junior or senior class of an American college, or if more advanced, do graduate work in an American university. The same is true of almost any other young student from Western Europe. Our institutions responded most happily and by 1938 more than one hundred allotted one or more scholarships to the Institute for exchange purposes. What this means financially should be clearly understood. If Vassar College gives a scholarship covering tuition and maintenance for a foreign student it must budget itself $1200 because that is the fee it charges an American student. If Williams College grants a similar scholarship it must charge, on the average, $1000 against itself. Since the inception of this plan and down to the opening of the war in 1939 American colleges and universities granted, through the Institute, scholarships to more than 2500 foreign students, with a value of $1,970,000. Whenever I hear American civilization decried as devoid of spiritual elements—a charge I have often heard in foreign countries—I cite this magnificent tribute to the generosity and idealism of our institutions of higher education. Most of them have usually felt that the influence of the foreign student on the campus was a partial *quid pro quo* for the financial expenditure they made. As mentioned before, the scholarships for American students studying abroad were almost always given by the governments of the foreign countries. The number of these scholarships is less than for foreign students coming to the United States, for although the student exchange with the European countries is nearly always equal, the Latin American countries have only just begun to reciprocate. Altogether the Institute has been responsible for having sent some 2357 students to study abroad upon exchange scholarships. The value of these scholarships is in the neighborhood of $917,040. This is proportionately lower than the evaluation of the opportunities arranged for foreign students in this country, owing to the lower cost of living in almost all foreign countries and to the fact that tuition fees in foreign institutions are practically negligible. The Americans who receive awards are chosen by committees of selection appointed by the Institute from the teaching staffs of our institutions of higher education. National committees in the European and Latin American countries pass upon the credentials submitted by the applicants and the final decision by the Institute is based entirely upon merit. The European and Latin American method, however, occasionally permits of the infusion of political considerations at the source.

Consider for a moment the splendid opportunity given to an exchange scholarship student to become acquainted with the civilization and culture of a foreign country. He has been selected because he measures up to the standards of scholarship, adjustability, and working knowledge of the language of the country to which he goes. The exchange student in an American college lives with native students in the dormitory, eats with them in the commons, exercises with them in the gymnasium, plays with them on the athletic fields, recites with them in the classroom, and discusses all kinds of national and international problems with them in the lounges. The sense of humor of the American student sometimes, alas, causes embarrassment to the foreign student! This was well illustrated in the case of an attractive Austrian student who went on exchange to a New England college. Having been invited to Sunday evening supper at an American home, he consulted his American fellow students as to the proper way of entrance and exit. At the close of the evening he shook hands with the hostess saying, "Thank you for inviting me. I have had a hell of a time."

Many first-class colleges today have appointed a professor or committee to facilitate the orientation of the foreign student in the college—in his matriculation, choice of subjects, and advice on personal matters. The counselor committee usually secures invitations for the foreign student to visit typical American homes, to attend political rallies or public debates on current problems, and recommends the best journals and magazines to help the visitor secure an understanding of American life. At the Christmas and Easter vacations the foreign student is often invited to the home of one of his fellow students or joins with two or three of them in buying a second-hand auto to travel to other parts of our country and familiarize himself with its geography and its historic places. Few of the universities in continental Europe have dormitories, and American exchange students are placed in typical homes where their respective universities are located. But the influences I have described operate upon them also, though to a lesser degree.

With such an experience it can be readily understood that the exchange scholarship holder usually returns to his own country not only with a fair understanding of the civilization of the people among whom he has sojourned but with a real admiration for them. I know of exceedingly few exchange students of which that is not true. My work has brought me to most of the countries of Europe, some in Asia, and nearly all in the Western Hemisphere, and I have invariably been sought out by former exchange students who have assured me that their year at Oberlin or Stanford, or wherever it may have been, was one of the happiest of their lives. Exchange students are generally selected because they have evident elements of leadership and in the course of time they nearly always become leaders. In most cases I have found them occupying positions of influence in government service, in industrial life or teaching in a university. I was never visited by one who was not pro-American and using his influence to make our country better appreciated by his own people. It may be objected that it was the ambitious young men who rallied to the banners of the dictators. That is certainly not true of the majority of these young men and women. They had become too impregnated with the free spirit of our life. It must not be forgotten that I have been speaking of the carefully selected exchange students coming here on Institute scholarships. They usually numbered about two hundred a year. It is true, however, that in a few of our institutions of higher education the foreign students who came here on their own were left to shift for themselves, felt deeply their isolation and the indifference of the American students, and did not return home in a happy frame of mind toward the United States. But I am confident that they represent a minority of all our foreign students.

The exchange students repay the Institute most handsomely in one respect. Each one of them is required to write two confidential reports of his experience, one at the close of each semester. The second is written after his return home so that he can evaluate his experience more objectively. These reports not only describe the career of the student in the university but the life of the community and public opinion on the current problems of the country. It is largely from these reports that the Institute staff secures fairly unbiased information concerning conditions in the foreign countries. The only other persons permitted to read the reports, in general, are exchange students of later years who go to the same university. It is of the greatest help to an exchange student who is awarded a scholarship to Grenoble, Göttingen, Naples or elsewhere to be able to read the reports of the American students who have preceded him in the university where he will study.

Were I to enumerate all the industrial, commercial and financial corporations, the learned societies, and the interested individuals who also have provided the Institute with scholarships the list would be interesting but too long for inclusion here. I feel I must select one organization for purposes of illustration:

General John J. Carty was President of the General Electric Company in 1920. He was deeply interested in securing memorials of a proper kind to honor the 126 American ambulance drivers who lost their lives in the service of France before the United States entered World War I. The Committee which he formed and of which I was a member decided to solicit funds with which to establish memorial fellowships, each to be named after one of the deceased ambulance drivers. Unfortunately when only half of the large sum necessary to carry out the project had been secured General Carty died. As the Committee did not have sufficient funds to provide a fellowship in honor of each of the ambulance drivers and did not want to discriminate among them, the fellowships were given the title, "American Field Service Fellowships for French Universities." Since their establishment in 1921, 161 American graduate students have been enabled to study in French universities on them. In the spring of 1942, the Institute sent a questionnaire to all these students and the returns from it were published in a booklet. The degree of success secured by the students in their vocations and the splendid literary output mentioned in their replies, which were usually attributed to the possession of the scholarship, have given great satisfaction to the Committee. No grants for fellowships for study in France have been made by the Committee since France entered the war on September 3, 1939. But they will be resumed when France is freed of the invader.

One of the most successful and profitable experiments undertaken by the Institute to realize its objective was the "summer school" organized for Latin American students at the University of North Carolina in January 1941. Held for a six-weeks period in mid-winter, it was called "summer school" because it took place during the summer of the South American countries from which the students came, and while their regular studies were interrupted for vacation. For the 108 young men and women who attended, the University of North Carolina organized special courses in American history, geography, literature, government and institutions, to give the Latin American students some knowledge of American civilization. Advanced courses were also offered in the professions because many of the students were of graduate quality. Although all the students were supposed to know English, their ability to converse freely in this language was frail in some cases.

Some of the students were housed in homes of persons who knew Spanish, but the great majority were accommodated in the Carolina Inn. The University organized admirable extra-curricular activities in the form of musicales, theatricals and dances, and invited the Latin Americans to the football games where they became great rooters for the North Carolina team. Not only the teachers and students of the University but the residents of Chapel Hill outdid themselves in their hospitality. Indeed, the entire state was enthusiastic and the State Legislature held one of its regular sessions at the University in order that the Latin American students might learn something of our methods of making law.

At the close of the special courses the Institute, in conjunction with the Grace Line and the Pan American Union, organized a tour for the students to enable them to become acquainted with other parts of the United States. In every city visited they were entertained by committees of distinguished citizens, and sometimes by their mayors and common councils. They were also received by Mrs. Roosevelt at the White House and by a group of members of Congress. The tour ended with five days of sight-seeing in New York City and a final banquet tendered by the Institute of International Education.

The results of the "summer session" were most fortunate. Living for six weeks in a typical American environment populated almost exclusively by native Americans, the visiting students lost some of the prejudices which a few of them confessed they had held before this experience. The United States students at the University similarly learned to admire the fine qualities of the visiting students. One of the unforeseen benefits much appreciated by the Latin Americans was the intermingling of the students themselves, few of whom had ever visited Latin American countries other than their own. The students were thoroughly enthusiastic over their experience and the repercussions in their home countries were most happy. The following winter our nation was at war and the "summer schools" organized by the Institute at the University of North Carolina, the University of Pennsylvania, and Columbia University—while very successful—were each attended by smaller numbers. Since then no "summer school" organized especially for Latin American students has been held, but this splendid method of developing understanding between ourselves and our neighbors to the South should certainly be revived when this war is over.

Before leaving the subject of student exchange one incident of national significance as well as international interest should be mentioned. Among the various institutions of our own country which I visited in the course of my travels were Hampton and Tuskegee. Dr. Moton, who at the time was President of Tuskegee, expressed great interest in the plan of student exchange. Some time after my visit he wrote to me suggesting that I take up with the French educational authorities the possibility of sending six Tuskegee graduates to study in French institutions in exchange for six Senegalese Negroes, preferably men who had fought in World War I, to study at Tuskegee. I was quite delighted at the prospect and felt much let down when informed from France that the Senegalese were citizens of France and could not be subjected to the discrimination against Negroes that existed in Alabama. I regretfully informed Dr. Moton that the Senegalese students were not available.

Two amusing incidents occurred in the early days of our student exchanges. The Institute cooperated immediately after the war with the Association of American Colleges in bringing to this country some two hundred French girls, who already had their *baccalaureat,* to enable them to continue their studies in our colleges. Shortly after the conclusion of peace, the fine French officer in charge of the activity expressed the hope that the girls might remain and even be increased in number. I answered that we would like to have some young men also. "Ah, Dr. Duggan," he replied, "keep the girls. We have a big surplus and some of them may marry here. And we need our young men at home." On another occasion, one of the officers attached to the Italian Commission expressed to me the hope that some Italian professors might be invited to lecture in our universities. "Certainly," I answered, "in what fields of study would you recommend?" "In medicine," he replied. "But," I said, "we are plentifully supplied with good teachers of medicine. What I think we need are Italian professors who could explain various aspects of Italian civilization." "You know, Dr. Duggan," he replied, "our professors do not speak English well and you do not need to speak much in cutting up bodies before students."

Institute Conferences

One method of realizing the ideals of the Institute was by the holding of conferences on important problems of international education. This can be well illustrated by the Conference on the Returned Chinese Student held in 1924. The previous year my attention had been called to an unfortunate result of the large number of Chinese undergraduate students studying in the colleges and universities of the United States. These students frequently stayed a considerable length of time to complete their education. The number often rose in a single year to 2,500. Many came upon national and provincial scholarships, some were sent by American missionaries, and a large number came at the expense of their parents. These students became accustomed to our high standard of living and upon their return to China in some cases found difficulty adjusting themselves to the more primitive environment of their home country. This resulted in discontent and sometimes in their actually becoming liabilities rather than assets to their country at the very time that China was in the greatest need of trained intelligence. The Chinese themselves, moreover, had been engaged in founding institutions of higher education after the establishment of the Republic in 1912, and—though they did not have the reputation of our colleges—in many instances they had developed into strong institutions which gave a good undergraduate education.

On January 8, 1924 I called a conference at the Faculty Club of Columbia University to consider the general problem of the Chinese student in the American college. The men and women best qualified by experience in China attended. They included President Burton of the University of Chicago, President Goodnow of Johns Hopkins, President Pendleton of Wellesley, President Comstock of Radcliffe, President Stuart of Yenching, Professor Paul Monroe, the American representative on the Boxer Indemnity Fund, and Professors Porter and Carter, representing the Department of Chinese at Columbia University. The resolutions adopted by the conference expressed strong approval of the policy of Chinese students' securing their national education before coming to the United States and recommended that to an increasing degree the advent of Chinese students here be confined to graduate research students. These resolutions were sent to the principal educators in China and were very well received. In the following year all students granted Boxer Indemnity fellowships were graduate students. Though some Chinese undergraduates still come to study in our institutions, the number has decreased and a much larger proportion consists now of graduate students.

More than a thousand Chinese students enrolled in the colleges and universities of the United States became stranded here as one result of the Pearl Harbor débâcle of December 1941. They were unable to return to China and they could get no funds from home. Under the circumstances the Department of State set apart a considerable sum of money to assist them and placed the distribution of the fund in a committee of two persons: Mr. Chih Meng, Director of the China Institute in America, and myself. The Chinese government arranged for a similar fund to help the students. Mr. Howland Shaw, the Assistant Secretary of State in charge of personnel, suggested three principles to be followed in the selection of the students to be given a grant: first and most important, that they be engaged in study and research that would be of immediate service to China in reconstruction after the war; second, that they have good scholastic standing; and third, that they be really in need. Nearly all the students were engaged in graduate work and of high standing, and most were in need.

Despite my own desire to favor the humanities as much as possible in these days of the exaltation of the technical studies, I realized that for China's welfare preference should unquestionably be given to students in the various fields of engineering, medicine, public health and sanitation, education, and the technical subjects generally rather than to philosophy, literature and the arts. As soon as possible we transferred students to self-sustaining jobs in industrial establishments which allowed us to spread our funds to a larger group of students. The whole enterprise was of the greatest benefit to the students and will undoubtedly be of immense service to China in the time of reconstruction. The letters the Committee received expressing the gratitude of the students helped, moreover, augurs well for good understanding between China and the United States in the post-war period.

In 1941 the Turkish government transferred ninety-two students who had been studying technical subjects, particularly engineering, in institutions in Great Britain and Germany to similar institutions in the United States where there would be no danger of having their studies interrupted by military developments. They were to be accompanied by a leader who was to supervise their orientation in our universities and keep track of their progress. Apparently the plan did not work out well because a year later one of the Embassy Secretaries visited the Institute of International Education with the request that we undertake the same supervision of Turkish students as we give to other foreign students. As this would require considerable correspondence and travel the Embassy agreed to bear the expense of the activity. It is gratifying to state that the records of the Turkish students have shown them to be serious and studious young men who measure up well to the standards attained by our own students.

The Institute and the Visiting Professor

In the years immediately preceding World War I there had been a few, a very few, exchange professorships between such large and important institutions as Harvard and Columbia on our side, and the universities of Paris and Berlin on the European side. The exchange naturally died during the war. It was obvious to me that owing to the impoverishment of Europe its revival would be difficult even for the large institutions, and would be wholly impossible for small and remote colleges. And yet it was those latter institutions and the surrounding communities, which sometimes had never been visited by any foreigner, that needed foreign visitors most. Hence I suggested to our United States colleges and universities the institution of the Visiting Professor. I agreed to invite a distinguished scholar or man of affairs to come to the United States and to organize a circuit for him among the colleges and universities that could afford to pay an honorarium for a lecture or series of lectures. He would stay a day, a week, or longer as the guest of the institution, depending upon the number of lectures he was to deliver. Each lecture would be followed by questions from the students and general discussion. The visitor would also be a source of information and interest among the professors, at the faculty club dinner table and lounge.

It can be readily understood what a source of inspiration it has been for professors and students to have the Right Honorable Herbert A. L. Fisher, the English Minister of Education, or Harold Laski of the London School of Economics describe the problems confronting Great Britain; or have André Siegfried or Emile Légouis of the Sorbonne discuss cultural conditions in France; or have Ernst Jäckh, President of the Hochschule für Politik at Berlin, or Carl Becker, the Prussian Minister of Education, describe internal conditions of Germany. One can also realize the advantage I myself enjoyed as their host in acquiring knowledge of international affairs. During the existence of the Institute more than 260 eminent scholars, teachers, men of affairs, and statesmen from all the countries of Europe have been circuited by the Institute among our institutions of higher education.

But this activity, excellent in itself, did not conform to my objective in undertaking it. These distinguished men lectured only at institutions that could afford to pay an honorarium, and those institutions were more or less familiar with foreign visitors. What I was most anxious to do was to select a few able scholars in international affairs to send on a prolonged circuit to the smaller and remote institutions of the South and West. In 1935 I appealed to Dr. Frederick P. Keppel, the President of the Carnegie Corporation, who was always alive to the wisdom of supporting a worthwhile enterprise. I found him enthusiastic about the plan and he agreed to approve a grant of $4,000 a year for two years to realize it, with the understanding that thereafter it should become self-supporting. I wrote to the presidents of the institutions I had in mind, to secure their cooperation and in each case suggested that they entertain the lecturer while he was visiting their institutions and invite in the people of the neighborhood to some of the lectures. They were unanimous in expressing a delighted desire to cooperate. The young foreign scholars I had selected were not only specialists in their fields but were in every case able and experienced expositors. The letters I received, not only from the presidents but from persons among the public who attended the lectures, all expressed the earnest hope that the activity be maintained. We were able to continue the third year, but on a reduced scale because some of the colleges could not afford the small honorarium of $50. When the fourth year arrived the plan had to be dropped. But I commend this fine activity to any unappropriated millionaire who is anxious to enhance the spiritual welfare of large numbers of our people.

Among the men of affairs whom the Institute circuited among our universities was Dr. Hjalmar Schacht, President of the Reichsbank. In 1930 I agreed to arrange an itinerary for him so that the students in our universities, especially students of economics, might hear his views. It was a most successful tour, for as soon as bankers in a university city heard he was coming they wanted to invite him to luncheon or dinner meetings of Chambers of Commerce to hear him talk upon world monetary and financial problems.

Dr. Schacht was one of the most hard-boiled, dogmatic and ambitious men I ever met. The German American Chamber of Commerce of New York had arranged a luncheon in his honor on the day after he arrived and I was asked to act as toastmaster. The night before, he had given an interview to reporters in which he outlined quite specifically what the United States ought to do in the economic emergency. The interview had brought forth sharp criticism in some of the New York papers the next morning. Naturally, Dr. Schacht sat on my right at the luncheon. Paul Warburg sat on my left. At an opportune moment Mr. Warburg whispered to me, "Schacht is really here to raise a loan for Germany. If he goes about our country talking to reporters as he did last night he won't raise a cent. Do you think you could give him a hint?" I answered that I would try, and at an unoccupied moment I said to Schacht, "Dr. Schacht, ours is a very large country whose diverse sections differ very much in their points of view on nearly all matters of national concern. I think you will be interested in listening to the representatives of the different sections before deciding what the general American viewpoint really is." Schacht reddened at once and blurted, "Dr. Duggan, if you want to dictate what I shall say in my lectures, I shall take the next boat home." I assured him I had never attempted to dictate to any of our lecturers but that I did always try to inform them of the conditions that they would probably meet in different parts of our country so that they might be better prepared to face their audiences. He was not then mollified but the next time I visited Germany he gave a luncheon in my honor at the Reichsbank. Incidentally, he did not "raise a cent."

Not all the Germans who visited the Institute were like Dr. Schacht. I never enjoyed a visit more than that made in 1930 by Dr. Carl Becker. He had been invited by Teachers College to give lectures on current views in Germany on education. I attended some of them. He not only spoke realistically but with great wisdom. Any criticism he made of American education was by inference only and was, I thought, deserved. My personal talks with him on conditions in Germany, especially among the youth and in the universities, were most clarifying. Even then he was much disturbed by the divisions existing among the German people. Another fine German who lectured under Institute auspices in 1932 was Dr. Julius Curtius, former Minister of Foreign Affairs of Germany. He was a very lovable and scholarly gentleman and his wife was a delightful lady. They were accompanied by their twenty-year-old son, a fine frank young man of splendid physique. As all four of us were going down in the elevator of the building on our way to lunch, the son stood in front of us facing the door of the elevator. Dr. Curtius pointed to him and whispered, "He'll make a great soldier." If a man like Curtius made such a remark, I wondered whether it might not be expected from practically all Germans.

On the occasion of his first visit to America, André Siegfried toured the country under the auspices of the Institute and there resulted the volume *Les Etats-Unis d'Aujourd'hui,* translated into English as *America Comes of Age.* M. Siegfried intended to make a prolonged visit in the various parts of the United States and to meet persons in many vocations and stations in life in order to familiarize himself with all aspects of our civilization. He was a most meticulous person and a very systematic worker. Almost immediately after any interview he typed the results. When he first arrived I brought together at lunch some of the best authorities at Columbia University in the various fields of scholarship. He asked a great many questions and they spoke very frankly about the elements of weakness as well as of strength of our social system. I have no doubt that *America Comes of Age* contains some, possibly most, of M. Siegfried's real views of our civilization and culture, but I do not think it contains all his views. I later heard him deliver a lecture in Paris on the subject. He spoke admiringly of many aspects of our life, but he said that he decidedly did not want to see France become Americanized. There was still too much of the primitive and crude, and too little of the gentle and refined in our life. It was the view of the typical French intellectual who has always regarded France as *le pays le plus civilisé*. It would be interesting to learn whether M. Siegfried holds the same view today (1943) of the relative values of French and American civilization.

American Lecturers to Foreign Universities

Most of the European belligerent countries in World War I were so stricken financially at its close that it was hopeless to expect them to invite American scholars to lecture in Europe in anything like the extent to which European scholars were invited to the United States. I recommended, therefore, at the beginning of the Institute's career that we take advantage of our admirable institution of sabbatical leave to overcome the difficulty. Most of my readers will probably know that it is the custom among our first-class colleges to give a professor, who has served the institution seven years, a year's leave of absence with half pay or a half year's leave of absence with full pay. The professor can use the sabbatical leave to do research, to write a book, to travel, or simply to rest. My plan provided that a distinguished professor on sabbatical leave be allotted traveling expenses to and from a country which he wished to visit with the understanding that he deliver some lectures at the universities of the country and report on his experiences to the Institute. The amount of the grant would depend upon the distance and cost of transportation. Professor Paul Monroe of Teachers College lectured in Chinese universities in the field of education. Dana C. Munro of Princeton University lectured at Robert College and the Constantinople Women's College in the field of history. Charles D. Hazen of Columbia lectured at the University of Strasbourg on American history and civilization. Similar grants were made to other scholars for lecturing in various countries.

The scheme was a great success. The American scholars, who were usually well known in the foreign universities which they visited, received a most cordial welcome and unquestionably left behind a more favorable impression as to the standards of American scholarship than had previously prevailed. The reports which they made were usually very illuminating not only upon scholastic conditions in the university visited but also upon political, economic, and social conditions of the foreign country in which they resided. The reports were afterward distributed to other scholars in the same field of study. A sum of $12,500 a year had been assigned for the Sabbatical Year Plan but unfortunately when the support of the Institute was transferred in 1923 from the Carnegie Endowment for International Peace to the Carnegie Corporation, the appropriation for the Plan was not continued. Europe will be utterly exhausted at the close of this second World War. It is to be hoped that something similar to the Sabbatical Year Plan may then be revived in the interest of intellectual cooperation.

Institute Publications

Another method of realizing the fundamental objective of the Institute was to influence public opinion by means of publications of various kinds. Probably the most important of all the publications is *The Guide Book for Foreign Students in the United States*. This contains a very brief history of higher education in the United States, of the cost of education in different parts of the country, of the American college curriculum, of life in the dormitories and commons, of our unique system of credits to secure a degree, and most of the other peculiar aspects of our educational system. The idea underlying the booklet was to provide the foreign student with information concerning our colleges and universities before his advent here so that he would not be wholly ignorant of conditions upon arrival. The booklet is very popular in foreign countries and has gone through several editions. Under the title of *Guía del Estudiante Hispanoamericano en los Estados Unidos,* it has recently been revised and enlarged and translated into Spanish for the benefit of the many students coming from the Latin American countries. The Institute has published for the benefit of American students similar booklets on the French, English, and Italian systems of education because a large number of American students have gone to those countries for purposes of study. It also issues occasional brief pamphlets on significant subjects from time to time.

However, it is the monthly bulletin of the Institute of International Education which probably exerts greatest influence. The *News Bulletin* is issued on the first day of each month of the academic year, October to May. It contains notices of the meetings of international educational and scholarly associations that will be held anywhere throughout the world, announcements of changes in the organization or administration of education, especially of higher education, that have been made in the various national systems, notes about the alumni of the Institute—that is, its former scholarship holders—and an editorial by the Director of the Institute. The editorial is not always on an educational subject but is often devoted to expressing the views of the Director on American policy in international affairs. That it has had an effect in influencing opinion in our colleges is made evident by the number of letters received from professors and students nearly all expressing approval. The Director is aware that readers who do not approve seldom send notice of their disapproval, but he has reason to believe that the editorials have had a real effect. The *News Bulletin* is sent to the president, librarian and some of the professors in all our colleges and universities, to the many correspondents of the Institute in foreign countries, and to some of the American newspapers which give much attention to foreign affairs. Each issue numbers about 5,000. It is frequently quoted in student magazines and sometimes in the daily press. Reprints of special articles are made for distribution.

In addition to the monthly bulletin, the Institute issues on October 1st the *Annual Report of the Director,* describing the activities of the Institute during the previous year and giving his opinion upon educational prospects in the different countries in the immediate future. In order to enable the Director to plan for a long-term constructive program, in 1924 the Carnegie Corporation was requested to make its grant of funds for the support of the Institute for a five-year period instead of annually. The request was granted, with the result that the Director's annual report at the close of each five-year period is much more complete than other annual reports. A complete report is being issued this year.

Some Outstanding Visitors to the Institute

In 1927 a commission headed by Senator Honnorat of France came to the Institute for advice. Associated with M. Honnorat was M. Auguste Desclos, the distinguished Assistant Director of the *Office national des universités et écoles françaises,* and an architect whose name I have forgotten. Senator Honnorat was one of the most attractive Frenchmen that ever visited the Institute—thoughtful, courteous and quick to perceive. M. Desclos was a scholar who spoke English admirably and had been a frequent visitor to our country. The commission wanted to learn as much as it could concerning the dormitory life of our colleges, including provision for lounges and recreation. Its report was to be the guide for the erection of the American House at the Cité Universitaire in Paris, of which I shall write more fully in the chapter on France. Before it started upon a circuit among our universities, I took the commission to Columbia University to visit one of the men's dormitories and to Barnard College to visit one of the women's. Miss Gildersleeve, the Dean of Barnard, accompanied us about the College. She showed us small rooms for individual students and suites containing bedrooms with a central room for study to accommodate two or more students. "I can understand the possibility of two men students living in harmony for a year," said Senator Honnorat, "but I can't conceive of that's happening with two women students." He probably learned a great deal about such matters upon his tour, for the American House at the Cité Universitaire is a splendid institution with rooms for men students and women students, some of them for two men and others for two women.

One of the most attractive persons to visit the office was Colonel Lindbergh, who came in one day with a letter of introduction. He wore no hat, had clothes which certainly were not those of a dandy, had a tousled head of hair, and a frank open face. I liked him at once. He said he wanted to fly with his wife to the South American countries to learn as much as he could of their civilization and culture. He wanted particularly to visit universities and become acquainted with students and professors. He was not going as the agent of the Pan American Airways with which he had been connected, nor upon any commercial errand. He asked whether I would be willing to help him arrange his itinerary especially among the universities and to recommend books on South America that he might read before going. I told him I would gladly do so and would give him letters of introduction to scholars and personal friends who would be of service. I suggested, however, that I invite Mrs. Lindbergh and himself to dinner, at which I would have a group of people all of whom knew South America by personal experience and each of whom represented a different activity. He gladly agreed.

The dinner was held in March 1931 at the Cosmopolitan Club. I do not remember all who were there but Waldo Frank represented the American literary figures that are admired by Latin Americans; General Palmer E. Pierce, attorney for the Standard Oil Company of New Jersey, and Mr. James S. Carson of the Electric Bond and Share, represented business; Dr. Samuel Guy Inman, the missionary interests; Dr. Charles Burlingame represented medicine, and Professor William R. Shepherd, scholarship. I invited Mrs. M. C. Migel, a Chilean who was a Trustee of Santiago College, and Miss Edna Duge, the Secretary of the Latin American Division of the Institute, so that Mrs. Lindbergh would not be the sole lady present. After dinner I asked Colonel Lindbergh to explain the purpose of his intended visit. When he finished I suggested that we go around the table and call upon each one present to tell, in the light of his or her personal experience, the aspects of Latin American civilization that Colonel Lindbergh must unquestionably come into contact with and the questions and considerations that he had better avoid. It was a most valuable symposium for any prospective traveler to South America. Colonel Lindbergh told us he wanted to start as soon as possible, but I said he could not possibly do so for at least six months. The Prince of Wales (afterward Edward VIII) had just returned to England after such a tour, and were Colonel Lindbergh to start at once upon a similar tour the British might consider that he went in order to diminish the prestige of the Prince in the eyes of the South Americans. Colonel Lindbergh reluctantly agreed to this view, in which all concurred. He and Mrs. Lindbergh stated that they would study Latin American affairs in the meantime. Before leaving they assured me that they had seldom spent a more interesting and profitable evening, and a few days after the dinner I received an autographed photograph of the Colonel and Mrs. Lindbergh.

That visit to South America never took place. About two months later, John Barrett, the predecessor of Dr. Leo Rowe, as Director of the Pan American Union, gave an interview to representatives of the press in which he said that it was about time that our Prince, Colonel Lindbergh, ought to tour South America in the same capacity as the Prince of Wales, namely, as our chief salesman. Colonel Lindbergh and I agreed that the visit would have to be indefinitely postponed. In my last interview with him I suggested he visit the Far East instead of Latin America and I gave him a letter of introduction to Edward Carter, the Director of the Institute of Pacific Relations. I feel, therefore, that I am slightly even if remotely responsible for the writing of that fine volume, *North to the Orient*.

At the time of which I am writing Colonel Lindbergh was one of the most popular men in the United States. Today that popularity has almost vanished as the result of his attitude upon the present war. He became a leader of the "isolationists" who were primarily responsible for our lack of preparedness when we entered this war. Although I hold a view upon that subject the very opposite of that held by Colonel Lindbergh, I do not doubt his sincerity. But his judgment was bad and had bad consequences. I wonder sometimes whether he has not been influenced by others whose sincerity is more open to question. And I deeply regret Mrs. Lindbergh's *The Wave of the Future,* which might readily influence readers to be willing to accept conditions leading to totalitarianism.

In the fall of 1930, Dr. Einstein visited the United States and lectured at a number of our institutions of higher education. I went to hear him at the City College—or rather to see him—for he spoke on relativity and he spoke in German. I knew nothing of relativity and I could not understand his very technical German. However, I soon discovered that most of the audience, which filled every seat of the amphitheatre, was there for the same reason that I was. I recognized many persons who knew no German and I doubted the knowledge of many others concerning relativity. We all went to see the scholar who had revolutionized our concepts concerning the physical universe. He was a splendid figure with his magnificent head surrounded by masses of grey-white hair that bristled in every direction.

I later became acquainted with Dr. Einstein under rather unusual and amusing circumstances. Toward the close of his second visit to the United States in the spring of 1934 he was invited by Mr. and Mrs. Dave Hennen Morris (Mr. Morris afterward became United States Ambassador to Belgium) to meet a small group of friends at dinner. I was not one of them but was informed afterward of the incident I am about to mention. Among those at the dinner was Dr. Ludwig Kast, the President of the Josiah Macy Foundation, well known in New York philanthropic circles. After dinner Dr. Kast asked Dr. Einstein whether there was any way in which his American admirers could serve him. Dr. Einstein answered that he was compelled to devote a great deal of his time and energy in working out his mathematical formulae—a task which a mathematical scholar could do just as well—but that he could not afford to engage one. Dr. Kast stated that his American friends would be very glad to pay the mathematical scholar's salary, a statement which naturally delighted Dr. Einstein.

When Dr. Einstein came in the following fall he at first lived on the ship that brought him, I believe for economy's sake. At that time Mrs. Einstein expressed her gratitude to Dr. Kast for the projected gift and asked him when they might expect it. Dr. Kast exclaimed, "Why, it went immediately following your visit last spring." "We never received it," answered Mrs. Einstein. Dr. Kast said he would cable to the bank in Berlin the following morning. He did so and received the answer that the money had arrived at the stated time, that the bank had notified Dr. Einstein of its arrival but that no answer had been received from the notice and that the money was still awaiting Dr. Einstein's order. Dr. Kast called me up the following morning to say that he had a sore throat and asked me whether I would be willing to accompany Mrs. Kast to the boat and notify Dr. Einstein of the answer from the Berlin bank. I gladly agreed.

I telegraphed to the captain of the boat, which was docked at Hoboken, to find out when Dr. Einstein might receive us. The captain told me that Dr. Einstein returned at different hours from his daily excursions to New York. It might be at five or six or even seven o'clock in the evening. Despite his profound scholarship, Dr. Einstein was a simple, even naïve, soul who took the greatest delight in visiting the sights of New York. Mrs. Kast and I decided that we would risk seeing Dr. Einstein at six o'clock, and he did arrive shortly after. When we informed him that the money to employ the mathematician had been in the bank since the previous spring he exclaimed, "Oh, I think I can explain this matter. You see the world is full of kind people and many of them write to me to get my autograph, which is very nice of them. But I can't answer them all at once so I have a basket and put the letters in it until I have time. I'm afraid I thought the notice from the bank was a request for my autograph and put it in the basket."

One of the activities undertaken by the Institute which has had a lasting influence was to bring groups of English debaters to the United States. The first invitation was extended in 1922 to the Oxford Union to send a team to the United States to undertake debates on international problems with similar teams in our universities. College debating in our institutions was a stereotyped affair, very rigid in its organization with an allotted time for presentation and refutation and with only one objective, namely, to win. I had been much impressed by the debates at the Oxford Union, which were not debates but discussions having as an aim the enlightenment of the audience. The American debaters were simply flabbergasted by the attitude of the Oxford men who did not hesitate to make admissions such as "I fully agree with my opponent on this point which he has so admirably presented." The Institute sent the Oxford teams—and later Cambridge teams—all over our country. The result was a great change in the character of college debating in the direction of informality, factuality, and humor. After a few years' experience, the Institute turned over international debating to the National Student Federation of America as a proper student enterprise.

The Russian Student Fund

Among the important activities undertaken by the Institute has been the receiving and placing of refugee students and professors in our institutions of higher education. Among the million persons who fled to foreign parts from the Bolshevik terror after the Russian Revolution were several thousand professors, students and scholars of all kinds. Few of the professors and scholars reached this country. Because of their scant knowledge of English and of conditions in the United States, or their insufficient power of adaptability, few were able to adjust themselves to life in this country. Within a few years after its establishment, the Institute published a booklet containing the name, field of work, former university connection and ability to use English of several hundred of these men. Only a very few found places in our institutions.

Not so with the students. The Russian Student Fund, covering one of the finest activities in which the Institute ever engaged, was formed in my office in 1921. The moving spirit was Alexis Wiren, son of Admiral Wiren who was shot in the early part of the Revolution. We formed a committee of well-known men whose names would be a guarantee of the worthiness of the activity, who would use their influence in securing funds, and who would actually attend meetings and help the movement with advice and supervision. Frank Polk, Allen Wardwell, Francis Robbins, General William Haskell, Reeve Schley, Boris Bakhmeteff, E. T. Colton, and Edwin Merrill were the chief members of the Board of Trustees. I was a member also and Chairman of the Committee of Selection to choose the exiled students who were to receive grants to enable them to continue their education in American universities. I have since become the Chairman of the Board, and have felt more than amply repaid for the time and attention I have given to the Fund. The Fund made a strong appeal to all generous minds but especially to the wealthy and conservative who abhorred communism. Somewhat more than $600,000 was contributed and more than 600 students were assisted. The assistance was in the form of a loan contract by which each student agreed to pay back over a term of years the total sum that had been loaned to him. Despite the great depression and resulting unemployment and the difficulty of adjustment to the new environment, in no year did less than ninety-five per cent of the students receive a college report lower than "very good". To date $220,000 or thirty-five per cent of the total loan has been repaid. Twenty-seven per cent of those assisted have repaid the advances in full. I know of no college loan fund that surpasses this record. These students have studied in 84 different colleges and universities throughout the country, chiefly in practical fields such as engineering, agriculture, library economy, and teaching, in order to become self-supporting at as early a time as possible.

The young men and women helped by the Russian Student Fund founded an alumni association and edited a monthly magazine, *The Russian Student,* which kept each informed of the whereabouts and activities of the others. At the time of writing nearly all have become American citizens and are very loyal to their adopted country. So true is this that it is doubtful that any will ever return to Russia whatever social system it may have. The purpose of the Fund, to assist young Russians to continue their education, which was interrupted by the Revolution, has been accomplished; and the diminished resources now available will be used to assist in the education of the children of the original recipients many of whom have become married. This whole enterprise is a remarkable tribute to the sublime faith, untiring devotion and attractive personality of Alexis Wiren.

The Emergency Committee in Aid of Displaced
Foreign Scholars

Splendid as is the record of the Russian Student Fund, it is surpassed in importance and accomplishment by that of the Emergency Committee in Aid of Displaced Foreign Scholars. In the early months of 1933, Franklin Roosevelt and Adolf Hitler each came into power. Roosevelt almost immediately launched the Good Neighbor policy as the chief American principle in international relations, emphasizing a determination to observe international law, to honor treaties and to refrain from interference in the domestic affairs of other nations. Hitler initiated a policy of sabre rattling, of determination to secure a place in the sun for Germany and of threats to any nation putting obstacles in the way of accomplishing his purpose. The philosophy of Nazism is based upon the myth of race, soil, and blood. The Germans are said to be the *Herrenvolk* of the world, while others are to be given subordinate status, and some are to be outcasts. Chief among the latter are the Jews. Immediately upon his accession to power Hitler began a ruthless persecution of the Jews, making no distinction between rich and poor, learned and ignorant, worker and professional, refined and vulgar. Among the most scholarly men in all Germany were to be found Jewish professors, who were at once ousted from their universities. As many of them as could do so fled to neighboring countries which accorded them a generous welcome.

It was soon evident, however, that this problem was not merely a Jewish problem but a great human problem, for the Nazis did not confine their persecution to Jews, but extended it to all liberals and others of suspicious political opinions whether Jew or Gentile. In early June of 1933 there came to my office Messrs. Bernard Flexner, Alfred Cohn, and Fred M. Stein to discuss the problem of forming some kind of organization to assist the refugee professors in continuing their research and teaching in their chosen fields of scholarship. Then and there was founded the Emergency Committee in Aid of Displaced German Scholars, the word "German" being changed to "Foreign" when the Nazis began the subjugation of non-German countries, commencing with Czechoslovakia. A body of distinguished presidents of colleges and universities and eminent scholars in many fields of learning were invited to form the General Committee, and in every case accepted the invitation. President Livingston Farrand of Cornell University became the Chairman of the Executive Committee and I became the Secretary. President Farrand was seldom able to attend the numerous meetings of the Executive Committee and I served in his stead, succeeding him as Chairman when to our great sorrow he died in 1939. The other members of the Executive Committee consisted of Messrs. Flexner, Cohn, and Stein, mentioned above, to whom were added Professor L. C. Dunn of Columbia University and Professor Nelson P. Mead of the College of the City of New York.

The Committee set for itself a threefold objective: to serve the personal needs of the refugees, to preserve their great attainments for the benefit of scholarship in the United States, and particularly to assist the institutions of education to absorb the refugee scholars without disturbance in administration or conflict with personnel—a courtesy due the institutions as a simple return for the splendid attitude of hospitality adopted by them upon the publication of the Committee's appeal and maintained by them ever since.

To realize the objectives of the Committee, three guiding principles of action were adopted. The first was to receive applications for assistance only from institutions of learning and not from individual scholars. The reasons for the adoption of this principle are not far to seek. The Committee was not long in existence before it was overwhelmed with requests from dismissed scholars in Europe for positions in institutions in the United States. Moreover, the Committee believed that the departments of learning of an institution were better qualified to select the men they wanted than was the Committee, which, however, always placed its lists in any field at the disposal of an institution.

The Committee stipulated, however—and this was its second guiding principle—that its assistance be confined to mature scholars of distinction who had already made their reputations. There were many fine young American scholars who had finished their graduate work and were seeking positions in our colleges. Were encouragement given to young foreign scholars, resentment would have unquestionably arisen among our own teachers. The Committee believes that in all cases, but especially among young scholars, preference should be given in cases of equal merit to Americans. Only where there is exceptional ability have grants been made to scholars under thirty-five years of age or, at the other end of the scale, to scholars over fifty-eight years of age. This did not prevent refugee scholars younger than thirty-five from attempting to secure posts and sometimes succeeding—but not through the instrumentality of the Committee.

The Committee's third guiding principle was that it would grant preference to applications from institutions which could give reason to believe that after a year or possibly two years of experience with a scholar, he would be absorbed by the institution into its faculty. No commitment was asked of an institution but the hope for the absorption of the scholar was always expressed and in the majority of cases fulfilled.

Because of the early exhibition of Nazi hatred of Jews, the first refugee scholars were of that race. Their coreligionists in the United States rallied to their assistance and the financial support of the Committee came at first exclusively from

Jewish foundations and individuals. To date these Jewish sources of aid have contributed more than $600,000. The fact that the financial support of the Committee was almost exclusively Jewish had no effect upon the Committee's decisions. Applications from Catholic and Protestant institutions received the same attention as did those from non-denominational institutions. The minority of Jewish members on the Executive Committee were particularly insistent upon that point.

In the early days of its existence, the Committee was able to make grants of $2,000 a year for two years to institutions which gave promise of absorbing distinguished scholars. In practically every one of these cases, the Rockefeller Foundation duplicated the grant, and in some cases gave more. As time elapsed, however, and demands upon the Committee's resources increased due to the conquest of Austria and Czechoslovakia, and later of Norway, Belgium, the Netherlands, and France, the Committee was compelled to cut down on the amount which it could give. In the majority of cases the Committee's grant is now in the neighborhood of $1,000. The Oberlaender Trust cooperated with the Committee wherever possible.

With the aid of the Rockefeller Foundation and the Oberlaender Trust, the Emergency Committee has helped to support 323 refugee scholars in our institutions of higher education. Of these scholars about 175 have already been absorbed into the staffs of the colleges and universities. The Committee has confined its activities to work on behalf of those men and women who had held teaching posts—usually as professors or Privatdozenten—in foreign universities before their flight from Europe. The Committee has not taken under its sponsorship physicians, lawyers or engineers. Among those aided have been scholars of unusual distinction, including two Nobel Prize winners. The great majority have made rapid and happy adjustment to their new and unfamiliar environment.

It is surely unnecessary to enlarge upon the contribution to scholarship that may be expected from these mature teachers and research scholars. As soon as sufficient time elapses they practically always become American citizens. If space permitted it would be of unusual interest to describe the manner in which these men and women have contributed to the literary, artistic and musical culture of the college communities in which they have found refuge.

In an attempt to coordinate the work of all the principal agencies in the United States engaged in assisting refugee scholars, from time to time new members were added to the Executive Committee which had functioned so well since the Committee's work started. Among these additions are Dr. Frank Aydelotte, Director of the Institute for Advanced Study at Princeton; Dr. Alvin Johnson, Director of the New School for Social Research; Mr. Charles J. Liebman, President of the Refugee Economic Corporation; Dr. Henry Allen Moe, a Trustee of the Oberlaender Trust; Professor Harlow Shapley, the eminent astronomer who had organized at Harvard financial aid for superannuated refugee scholars, and Miss Hertha Kraus of the American Friends Service Committee.

The enlarged and strengthened Committee is engaged in a great enterprise to help save for the people of the world the immense fund of talent and ability possessed by the thousands of displaced scholars. As a result of the destruction that has taken place in the European countries which are at war, it is to the nations of the Western Hemisphere that the fleeing scholar must look for a haven to continue his work and research. The generous hospitality already shown by the colleges and universities of the United States gives assurance that our country is aware of the opportunity to render a service comparable to that shown the Greek scholars by Western

Europe when Constantinople fell to the invading Turks in 1453. The Emergency Committee has accomplished a remarkable work. It has done it quietly, without dramatic publicity methods. Its members have felt a great joy in performing the task; none more than its Chairman.

The refugee scholar might reasonably look forward to being absorbed in time by our institutions of learning. It probably never occurred to him that he would contribute to the war effort of the American government. But upon our entrance into the war so many professors of mathematics, physics, medicine, chemistry, statistics, psychology, and economics were absorbed by the government that many of our institutions of higher education were glad to avail themselves of the reservoir of teachers supplied by the displaced scholars. Soon that reservoir was exhausted. Nevertheless the armed services called upon the Emergency Committee for distinguished research men who might render special service to the war effort, even though they were not citizens. Among many, one such scholar was employed in the mathematics of aeronautics, another in research on military explosives, another on climatology and meteorology, another on crank-mechanism motions. A distinguished economist, now a citizen of the United States, was absorbed by the Social Security Board, while another refugee citizen was taken over by the Bureau of the Census. These are but a few typical illustrations. In all probability no soldier at the front has worked more enthusiastically to assist in bringing victory to the Allied cause than these refugee scholars who in so many cases were driven from their homelands because of their devotion to the cause of freedom.

The Friends, Trustees, and Staff of the Institute

The Carnegie Endowment for International Peace founded the Institute in 1919 and supported it until 1923 when it was turned over to the Carnegie Corporation for support. During those four years I naturally consulted Dr. Nicholas Murray Butler, the President of the Board of Trustees of the Institute, on matters of policy and administration. He retired from the Board when the Carnegie Corporation undertook the support of the Institute. In the same year Dr. Frederick P. Keppel became President of the Carnegie Corporation and at once showed his confidence in the work of the Institute. He secured an enlarged annual grant from the Corporation, to be made at five-year intervals. As long as Dr. Keppel remained President of the Corporation my relations with him were of the happiest. He never once suggested a modification in any of the policies of the Institute nor interfered in the slightest with any of its activities, and he unhesitatingly recommended at the end of every five-year period that the Corporation renew the grant. He is a man of fine vision and broad sympathies, and under his administration the Carnegie Corporation rendered American society an enduring service. All the happy relations between the Institute and the Corporation have continued unmodified since Dr. Walter A. Jessup succeeded Dr. Keppel as President. He is a scholar and gentleman of similar calibre.

A description of the work of the Institute would be very incomplete were no mention made concerning the fine attitude of the Board of Trustees toward myself and the staff. The Board is composed of an unusual group of high-minded men and women devoted to the cause incarnated in the Institute. Some of them have been members of the Board since its founding twenty-four years ago: Judge John Bassett Moore, formerly of the World Court; Henry Morgenthau, Sr., formerly Ambassador to Turkey; Leo Baekeland, the distinguished scientist; and Virginia Gildersleeve, Dean of Barnard College. Some have passed on: Walter James, the eminent physician; Livingston Farrand, President of Cornell University; Henry Pritchett, President of the Carnegie Foundation. Their places have been taken by men and women equally representative. Never have I known a body more devoted to the cause for which the Board was formed despite the fact that they varied in their attitude toward social problems. Sometimes, as in the case of the Rettig affair described in the chapter on Germany, there was pronounced difference of opinion as to the procedure to be undertaken. Never has there been a divided vote. When difference of opinion existed, the action to be followed was usually referred to the Director with power to act. Few administrators have had as happy an experience with a governing board.

The staff of the Institute has been equally cooperative. They have been hard-working, efficient and loyal, ready in any emergency to assume added burdens that the strain might be overcome. The Institute has been very fortunate in its five Assistant Directors, the first four of whom were young men, who left the Institute because of invitations to occupy higher positions elsewhere at increased salaries. One became a college president; another, Secretary General of the League of Red Cross Societies; a third, Director of the Davison Fund; and a fourth, the Director of the European Division of the Columbia Broadcasting System. In order to add young blood to the Board, the last two, Arthur Packard and Edward Murrow, became Trustees upon my recommendation. Mr. Packard was Assistant Director but a short time; Mr. Murrow the longest time of all. I found him an attractive and a brilliant young man endowed with initiative, imagination and sound judgment. When he resigned from the Institute, I determined to secure a more mature man who would be more likely to remain with it. The present incumbent, Dr. Edgar J. Fisher, was Dean of Robert College in Constantinople; his experience in administration and in education has thoroughly justified the selection.

It was natural that as the Institute became widely known and respected in its field, its Director should be invited more and more to join the governing boards of all kinds of organizations interested in international affairs—some of a permanent character, others of a propagandist nature. It was gratifying to be invited every year to deliver Commencement addresses, nearly always on a subject of international interest. This was particularly true of the invitation extended to address such organizations as the Association of American Colleges and the American Association of University Professors because it gave splendid opportunity to widen the interest in the purpose for which the Institute existed. I feel I ought to mention one relevant incident.

In 1937 I was invited by the Dean of the School of Education of the University of Minnesota to deliver three lectures on "Aspects of International Education." At the end of my week's stay, Dr. Lotus Coffman, the President of the University—one of the most able university presidents in the United States—told me that he had invited about forty of his outstanding teachers to a farewell luncheon in my honor. At the close of the luncheon, President Coffman turned to me and said, "Dr. Duggan, you have been working on this job of developing international understanding and good will for almost twenty years and there is today more misunderstanding and ill will among the nations than there has been for a generation. You have the floor to defend your position."

I had assumed that I would be called upon to speak but had not at all anticipated that kind of introduction. However, the challenge of President Coffman was not new to me. I was talking to a friendly and intelligent group of men and, judging from the generous response at the close of my brief address, they did not seem to be unconvinced. In addition to presenting some of the facts given in this chapter, I emphasized another aspect of the problem: I maintained that neither statesmen, diplomatists, industrialists, financiers nor others having international relationships had been any more successful in bringing about understanding among peoples than educators. They were all continuing their efforts. I saw no reason why I should not continue mine. In the light of subsequent events I still believe that it is chiefly upon educators in every nation that reliance must be placed to substitute for the doubts, suspicions, and jealousies that divide peoples, an understanding of their interdependence and necessity for cooperation. This is why there is still need for organizations like the Institute of International Education.

The influence of education is seldom direct. When an individual is prepared for a vocation, the process is one of training rather than of education. I had always realized that the influence of the student exchange upon the individual student, while lasting, would be neither immediate nor definite. I was delighted, therefore, when a condition arose where the exchange could render a decided, immediate and specific contribution to the American government. The occasion was the appointment by President Roosevelt on November 21, 1942 of the Governor of New York State, Herbert Lehman, as Director of the Office of Foreign Relief and Rehabilitation Operations in reoccupied territories.

I immediately informed Governor Lehman, with whom I was acquainted, that in the previous twenty years the Institute of International Education had sent more than 2000 American students to study upon scholarships in the universities of the European countries. They were all college graduates when they went, knew the language of the country in which they studied, and remained for a year or more accustoming themselves to its civilization and the psychology of its people. Moreover, the Institute had brought to our colleges and universities more than 2500 students from European countries, who learned English, something of American history and government, and much of our way of life. If the enterprise of which he was the head was to succeed, the greatest care would have to be taken that those engaged in it would understand the languages, psychology and institutions of the peoples among whom they worked. Various universities had already established courses for the training of administrators to work in the different occupied countries. I pointed out to Governor Lehman that the Institute provided a reservoir of competent persons who were already prepared for the service he required.

At the time I wrote, Governor Lehman was in great need of able men to go to North Africa and immediately asked whether I could supply a dozen "star" administrators. I sent him the names of 27 who had studied in French universities, 14 of whom had taught in lycées in different parts of Algeria. This list was followed by the names and addresses of our former students, and comments as to their comparative competency for the work to be done. When it became known that we were recommending to Governor Lehman's organization men and women well prepared to undertake administrative work in the reoccupied areas, we were asked to render a similar service to the Red Cross, the State Department, and the Office of Strategic Services of the War Department.

Many of these men and women will undoubtedly render unique service to the United Nations in the important tasks for which they are peculiarly fitted. Thus, for almost a quarter of a century the Institute of International Education has been actively serving the cause of international understanding through its varied program, and at the same time passively preparing—by accumulating a wealth of highly trained "alumni"—for what may prove to be its most direct contribution to human welfare. By seizing this opportunity for service, the Institute hopes to have justified the faith of its friends.

CHAPTER III

FOREIGN INFLUENCES ON AMERICAN CULTURE AND EDUCATION

PRIOR to the turn of the twentieth century, even prior to the first World War, the participation of the United States in European cultural and educational developments was not very significant. The number of students who came from Europe to study in our universities was negligible. On the other hand, the number of American students who studied in European universities, especially those of Germany, was quite large. While it is true that a few exchange professorships existed between American and European universities, they carried little influence, and visiting professorships existed to an even less degree. Though the contributions of Americans to scholarly periodicals of an international character were increasing in number, they were relatively few compared with the number from Europeans. American contributions to art, music, and the drama were not impressive. Cooper and Poe had been widely read in Europe as had Emerson, Whitman and Mark Twain at a later time, but in general American writers exerted comparatively little influence on European literature. Recognition, however, was given to American accomplishment in science, especially applied science. Our democratic system of education generally was regarded with small favor as leading to mediocrity. In fact, it is but slight exaggeration to say that most cultured Europeans looked upon Americans in the days previous to World

War I somewhat as Greeks looked upon Macedonians in the days previous to Alexander the Great. They were regarded as a strong and virile people but largely devoid of culture. The development of an American culture and its reaction upon the rest of the world provide a fascinating study.

The Anglo-Saxon civilization which developed in the American colonies during the seventeenth and eighteenth centuries has in the course of time been modified in almost every respect. This has been due to a great variety of causes, but unquestionably one of the most influential has been the absorption into the body politic since 1790 of almost 40 millions of immigrants coming from almost every country of Europe. These immigrants brought with them their own attitudes toward life, and in the resulting conflict with the native attitude there took place a disintegration of some of the old American ideals of life, especially since the Spanish-American War. All foreign elements have contributed to the building up of the dynamic civilization which exists in the United States today and which is characterized by a perennial state of change so rapid that it is impossible to foresee the outcome. In general, culture and education in the United States before the first World War were subject to three great foreign influences: British, French, and German.

British Cultural Influence

During the colonial period the culture of the United States was fundamentally British. Because of kinship in language, moreover, British culture has continued to exercise a great influence upon Americans. Few Americans read foreign works of literature other than British because few Americans are familiar with foreign languages. The classics of British literature are as much classics for Americans as for Britons, and new works in British literature are widely read in the

United States and exert a large influence not only upon the thought of our people but upon the style and technique of our own writers. The British stage sends its best plays to the United States, and a playwright like George Bernard Shaw has a far greater clientele in the United States than in Britain. Unity of language is also responsible for a continuous exchange of teachers, clergymen, and scientists. British ideas on political, social, and economic subjects as published in British newspapers, magazines and books have wide currency in the United States. The legal system of the United States, moreover, is founded upon the common law of England, and the Puritan ideas inherited from the English Reformation still wield a potent influence.

The American Revolution was essentially a political, not an economic or a social revolution. After independence had been won the colonists resumed all their former relationships with England, save those of the political tie. England continued to be the well from which they drew most of their spiritual nourishment. It is true that some Englishmen were familiar with the works of the New England School. But in our own country Dickens was more popular than Hawthorne, Tennyson more highly appreciated than Whitman, and Herbert Spencer wielded almost as much influence upon our thinking as did Emerson. Despite the "Flowering of New England", the United States retained culturally somewhat of a colonial status almost down to the Civil War. After the Civil War our industrialists enthusiastically embraced the philosophy of *laissez-faire,* which had had such a profound influence in Britain. This helped in the enormous development of our industries but brought in its train social evils that resulted in the rise in the early years of the twentieth century of the radical school of literature which emphasized reforms in social conditions and relationships. The United States has slowly evolved its own civilization and culture which are different from those of Britain, but in its own civilization there are still many more elements derived from Britain than from any other foreign country.

Until after the Revolution, education in America was confined to the higher and middle classes. In the southern colonies organized on the plantation system, where schools were difficult of access, the English system of employing tutors in the family was followed. The middle colonies were settled by Dutch, Germans, Swedes, and French as well as by English. They all brought their evangelical beliefs with them and, while insisting that everybody be taught how to read the Bible, they also insisted upon the school's being an adjunct of the church; hence the parochial type of school flourished. This was also true wherever the Roman Catholics settled. Only in New England, settled by a homogeneous people holding Calvinistic beliefs, did the people establish town elementary schools, partly supported by tuition fees and partly by taxation. This system held true also in the establishment of the "academies" which in the late colonial period provided an excellent secondary education preparatory to entrance into college. The religious motive prevailed everywhere and indirect religious supervision continued well into the nineteenth century. But the unity of religious belief that characterized early New England gradually gave way to divergence of belief and toleration of other sects, and in 1827 publicly supported and controlled non-sectarian schools became a reality. This was at the height of the movement across the Alleghenies and at the beginning of the movement that put control of the federal government in the Jacksonian democracy. In the pioneer civilization that developed, there took root and flourished the fundamental idea of American life that had been latent in New England, equality of opportunity—wholly alien to the English way of life. Wherever New Englanders settled in the West, the "little red schoolhouse" was established to provide elementary education for all children. Except for Friday afternoon declamations and singing classes, in most cases there was not a great deal of education beyond that. The demands of a pioneer civilization consumed men's time and efforts and little attention could be given to the amenities and refinements of life embodied in literature, music, and the arts.

British influence remained longer in higher education. When the first institution of higher education, Harvard College, was founded in 1636, it was almost a replica of Emmanuel College in Cambridge University where many Dissenting clergymen had studied. The curriculum consisted of Latin, Greek, mathematics, and philosophy; the teachers were all clergymen; the discipline was rigid; and the chief objective was to provide leading pillars of the community, especially ministers, for the church. Other colleges founded during the colonial period were nearly always organized for the same purpose. The curriculum of the college, inherited from England, remained practically the same almost to the Civil War, though some institutions broadened it by introducing a foreign language and some natural science, and a few substituted English for Hebrew or Greek. The professions, as in England, were filled by means of the apprentice system. Almost to the twentieth century, moreover, the English system of testing ability exclusively by final examinations prevailed with us. English influence upon American higher education has recently been made manifest in the introduction of the preceptorial or tutorial system at a few Eastern colleges such as Harvard and Princeton and of the residential colleges at Harvard and Yale. Those systems will probably spread elsewhere.

The American college, though inherited from England, has had a peculiar development and is today a unique institution. The development of education in England has been similar to that of education in continental countries in its threefold division into elementary, secondary, and university education. With us the division is fourfold, the liberal arts college being interposed between the high school and the university. This evolution has been due to a number of causes, the chief of which was the late development of universities in our country. As already mentioned, the first institution to fulfill the pattern of a modern university was Johns Hopkins, opened to students less than seventy years ago, in 1876. By that time the liberal arts college, which had spread across the country as a companion movement of the religious denominations, had become a strongly entrenched part of our educational system.

While continental European countries had considerable influence on the organization and administration of the American university, they had practically none on the college whose *raison d'être* is not understood in those countries. But British influence has been very great. After the Renaissance the English adopted as their educational ideal the old Athenian objective of a "sound mind in a sound body" and we inherited it from them and carried it to excess in the football team. It is only in Oxford and Cambridge, moreover, that is found the combination of intellectual, extra-curricular, and social influences that characterize our colleges. They, too, believe that "a college is a place to grow up in" socially as well as academically. The result of this evolution has been to make the liberal arts college one of the most potent influences in shaping American life. As soon as the frontier became stabilized, the liberal arts college was established to provide the rudiments of higher education and to emphasize democracy as the form of political and social organization that was American. It is to be hoped that the reduced enrollment of students, interest on investments, and contributions to endowments, which characterize this war period, may not endanger the college's existence.

When the state universities began to be founded the influence of Scottish universities upon them was considerable. Democracy in education, so uncommon at Oxford and Cambridge, had always characterized Scottish institutions. One of our oldest state universities and one having a most enviable record is the University of Michigan. Many of the ideas concerning organization and curriculum which were developed in Michigan and several of the older institutions of higher education were the result of the infiltration of Scottish professors who, when they came to this country, found greater opportunity to develop their own theories at the state university rather than at the endowed university. The great President of the University of Michigan, James Burrill Angell, had received his education at Brown University and later became President of the University of Vermont, when it was the exemplar of the Transcendental movement in this country. Vermont Transcendentalism was a peculiar combination of English and German idealism, and the graduates of Vermont carried that philosophy to many of the older state universities of the Middle West. During President Angell's administration, Scottish influence at Michigan was quite pronounced.

French Influence

Most Americans are unaware of the extent to which the French contributed to the racial make-up and cultural development of our country. By 1656 so many French and Walloon Protestants had settled in New Amsterdam that it was necessary to issue all government and town proclamations in French as well as Dutch. When the British seized New Amsterdam in 1664 one quarter of the population was made up of French Huguenots, who also formed a considerable part of the population of South Carolina. The first large and important French addition to the population of the colonies was made when the persecution of the Huguenots in France drove many of them to our shores, especially after the Revocation of the Edict of Nantes by Louis XIV in 1685. Wherever the Huguenots settled they taught the colonists how to live. They spread a knowledge of gentle manners and of the arts and accomplishments of a polished civilization. Their homes were usually attractive and they softened the hardships of existence with their good humor and gaiety. Although their influence was not widespread, their contribution to American life was important.

The next addition of French-speaking people to the population of the colonies was made up of the 10,000 Acadians whose unhappy story is given in Longfellow's *Evangeline*. They were scattered among the colonies from New England to Georgia but especially large numbers went to Louisiana. They were followed by an even larger number of émigrés from Haiti and Santo Domingo when the slaves rose against their masters after the French Revolution. These émigrés were in turn joined by others from France itself, first by royalists including Louis Philippe, who remained throughout his life a staunch friend of the United States and greatly eased the difficulty over spoliation claims in the administration of Andrew Jackson. After the Restoration of Louis XVIII came the Bonapartist émigrés, including Joseph and Jerome Bonaparte, whose son remained to raise a family here. But the greatest addition to the population of French-speaking people was made by the purchase of Louisiana in 1803, when some 50,000 became citizens of the United States. It was not merely that it added to our territory the enormous area between the Mississippi and the Rockies, but in New Orleans it annexed a remarkable center of culture which led a life peculiarly its own. In the early nineteenth century, New Orleans—where music, literature, art, and manners held sway as well as business—was the most European city on this continent. Place names like St. Louis, Vincennes, Detroit and many others illustrate the widespread geography of early French influence. Small groups of French were added to the population annually thereafter, but it is impossible to say what proportion they bore to the entire population. A far more important question to consider is what kind of people they were and what influence they had upon the civilization and culture of the United States.

During the colonial period when the French were installed in Canada and in the country west of the Alleghenies, and when conflicts between them and the colonists were frequent, the attitude of the American colonists toward the French was distinctly hostile. When the French military menace on the frontier was removed after the Seven Years' War by the cession to Great Britain in 1763 of Canada and the western country, a different attitude toward things French began to prevail in the colonies. That was the period of the Enlightenment, the age of the *philosophes* and *encyclopédistes* whose teachings made a great appeal to the upper classes in American society. Their insistence upon intellectual freedom, their ridicule of religious dogmatism, their appeal for a more enlightened humanitarianism had a profound effect upon leaders of public opinion, especially Franklin and Jefferson. A skepticism as to the value of the prevailing ecclesiastical establishments which in France had led to the growth of deism prevailed among many of the intellectuals in the United States down to the outbreak of the American Revolution. During the long military struggle which ensued, the officers of the French army exerted a refining influence upon the social life of the upper class in America, an influence which was greatly strengthened later by the influx of émigrés after the French Revolution.

It has seldom been the fate of one book to influence the historical development of a people to the extent that Montesquieu's *L'Esprit des Lois* has influenced the historical development of the American people. Montesquieu, who greatly admired the British constitution, believed that the liberties of Great Britain resulted from the division of powers between the executive and the legislative. The *Esprit des Lois* was published in 1748 just at the time when the legislature of Great Britain was absorbing all the powers of government and developing the parliamentary system as it functioned in Great Britain during the nineteenth century. But the men of the Constitutional Convention of 1787 believed that the liberties of the colonies had been preserved during the colonial period by the division of powers between the British royal governors and the colonial legislatures and were glad to call upon the *Esprit des Lois* for arguments to support their views. In fact, the book became a kind of political bible in which exponents of most unpopular views found justification for their positions.

When the French Revolution broke out in 1789 the similarity of ideas expressed in the Declaration of the Rights of Man to those expressed in our own Declaration of Independence won the hearty sympathy of Americans and that sympathy continued until the excesses of the Terror alienated the good will toward France which had been so pronounced a few years before. Moreover, the average American looked upon Napoleon as a tyrant, a view which was sedulously propagated by the many royalist émigrés who settled in our country. The reaction was greatly augmented by the remarkable renaissance of the Protestant spirit in the United States which characterized the latter half of the eighteenth century. The Great Revival, led by the Englishman, George Whitefield, burst forth almost simultaneously in all parts of the country and what is today called Fundamentalism became the generally accepted religious doctrine among the common people. It was in deadly antagonism to the deism which had appealed to many in the ranks of our upper classes. With the passing of the years, the influence of the adherents of the revivalists increased. The old suspicion of France revived and even after the restoration of Louis XVIII it was a question in the minds of the average American whether in exchanging Robespierre and the Goddess of Reason for the Pope and the Jesuits, the French had not gone from bad to worse. Nevertheless, it was to the French *philosophes* that the friends of freedom of thought turned to find weapons with which to fight the growing obscurantism. They were a tower of strength to the liberals during that period.

After the close of our War of 1812, the United States definitively turned its back upon Europe and entered a period of comparative isolation. It faced the West and gave its thought and energy to the upbuilding of the empire spread before it, and to the development of its natural resources. The attention of the people was directed to domestic problems, such as state rights, internal improvements and, to a growing extent, slavery. There were few controversies with European countries and the people were but slightly interested in what was taking place on the other side of the Atlantic. Yet foreign cultural influence, and at that time this meant primarily French influence, was not by any means extinguished. Chairs for the study of the French language were established in many of our colleges. French journals, magazines and books were found in our book stores and were quite widely read. The Positivism of Auguste Comte had a profound influence on historical thinking in our country as shown in its emphasis upon environmental and biological factors. American students of art studied in the ateliers of France.

During this period French science enjoyed a real hegemony. The French were supreme in mathematics, astronomy, physics, and chemistry, and they revolutionized the old ideas and introduced new methods in medicine. This influence on the scientific development of the United States lasted until it was superseded by the development of German science in the middle of the century. In our political life every president of the United States down to Andrew Jackson read French and some of them, notably Jefferson and Monroe, spoke it fluently. But with the triumph of Jacksonian democracy and the development of Whig nationalism under the leadership of Henry Clay, all foreign influence in the changing civilization of the United States waned. Relatively few people realized the extent of French collaboration during the two preceding generations in establishing the political doctrines of the sovereignty of the people, the liberty of the individual, and political and social equality.

German Influence

As America entered into the frontier period of its cultural development, Germany was the spring from which it drew inspiration. When Edward Everett, afterward Governor of Massachusetts, Ambassador to Great Britain, President of Harvard College, United States Senator, and Secretary of State, matriculated at Göttingen in 1815, he became the precursor of several thousand Americans who studied at German universities during the nineteenth century and who upon their return made an indelible impression upon American education and culture. This movement was greatly needed in American life as a necessary correction in American values then current. Americans have been prone—and still are—to exalt the man of action, the man who *does* things, especially above all others the successful business man. The American students who went to Germany, particularly after the Civil War, lived for a while in a country where scholarship was highly prized and university teachers held in the greatest esteem. A large percentage of these students became teachers in our own colleges and universities and brought the reverence for true learning with them. Moreover, there has been a steady stream of German-born scholars to the United States, beginning with Francis Lieber, the great authority on political science who began his teaching career in the United States in 1827 in South Carolina College, and continuing down to Michelson, the great physicist who was awarded the Nobel Prize in 1907 and who taught until his death at the University of Chicago. More than three hundred German scholars have been called to chairs in the institutions of higher education in the United States and they have done a great deal to enhance the position of the university teacher in public esteem. It would be hard to overestimate the influence at the present time of the 400 university teachers driven from Germany by the Nazi terror who have already been absorbed by our colleges and universities. The subject is discussed at length in Chapter II.

Upon the life and spirit of the university itself German influence has been enormous. Its greatest contribution is probably its insistence upon thoroughness in thinking and accuracy in research. Americans value more highly the discussion method in classroom work than the lecture system which prevails in German and French universities, but they regard the seminar system which they learned in the German universities as one of the most potent instruments of higher education. The seminar tests the patience of the student in following clues which may lead nowhere, his willingness to work hard to get the facts justifying a conclusion, and his ability to draw the correct conclusion from the premises he discovers. This thoroughness has been particularly valuable in a country like the United States where people are in a hurry to have things done. Associated with this research was the belief that the work of the advanced student should result in a real contribution to the sum of human knowledge. Though it is doubtful whether the great majority of the theses turned out annually by the Doctors of Philosophy in American universities accomplish this, some do. Certainly it is the only justifiable ideal to hold.

Another characteristic of German higher education in the nineteenth century which has had much influence in the United States was its emphasis upon *Lehrfreiheit* and *Lernfreiheit*. It must never be forgotten that the American college originated during the colonial period partly in the need to provide clergy for the churches. Clerical influence has, therefore, been pronounced and has often been used to try to muzzle professors. In recent years legislatures in some of the more backward states have also attempted to control the opinions of teachers in the domain of biology. All these attempts have met with the determined opposition of the German-trained teachers in our colleges and universities; they have insisted upon the right of the scholar freely to seek the truth and fearlessly to announce it when he has found it. In the midst of the movement of American students to German universities another movement having influence upon American life was the advent of the German liberals led by such men as Carl Schurz and Franz Sigel after the Revolution of 1848 in Germany. This splendid group of Germans were unlike the ordinary immigrants who came to the United States to better their economic status. The German liberals were people of education and culture who brought with them not only high ideals of life but a practice of its amenities and refinements, especially a love of music and literature. Fortunately, the majority moved to the Middle West, the newer region of our country, where their influence was particularly valuable.

Another influence of Germany upon our higher education was in the organization of our universities. Up to the establishment of Johns Hopkins, American higher education seldom extended beyond the college, which was essentially devoted to teaching. German influence upon our institutions of higher learning was not unknown before that time but its influence on the organization of Johns Hopkins was profound. For many years Johns Hopkins had no undergraduate college. It was devoted primarily to work of a research character and college graduation was a pre-requisite for admission. In addition it incorporated schools for training in the professions of law, medicine, and engineering, which hitherto had usually maintained independent existences.

The founding of Johns Hopkins spelled the doom of the predominant influence of Germany and in fact the influence of all foreign countries in American higher education. The number of American students in German universities reached its maximum in the decade 1890–1900. After that it steadily declined. This decline was due primarily to the fact that all the great privately endowed and large state universities were reorganized so as to provide the training for which students had formerly felt they had to go to Germany. Eminent scholars were appointed as professors, magnificent libraries founded, splendidly equipped laboratories erected for advanced research, and liberal fellowships provided for the maintenance of mature students. American students continued to go to Germany to study in certain fields in which it was believed Germany had pre-eminence, but it was increasingly felt that American institutions could provide sound training just as well in most fields and better in some.

Then came the first World War, during which American-

German cultural relations ceased entirely. But the war had a more significant influence than the cessation of American-German relations. The tide of students going abroad for purposes of study was reversed. Foreign students came from practically every country of Europe, Asia, and Latin America. Moreover, as already mentioned, France and Great Britain had learned how great had been the influence of Germany upon the United States as the result of the study of American students in German universities. Those countries had not shown before the first World War the same degree of cordiality toward American students that had characterized the German universities. After the war they adopted a very different attitude.

German influence has been even greater in our elementary school system than in our institutions of higher education. In the early nineteenth century a new spirit was brought into our schools by the introduction of Pestalozzian methods from Germany. Most important of all was the inspiration Horace Mann received, as the result of a visit to Germany in 1843, for the establishment of institutions for the training of teachers, none of which existed at the time in the United States. The Normal School became a distinctive element in our system of education. Later through the initiative of one of our great educators, the Federal Commissioner of Education, Dr. William T. Harris, the Froebel kindergarten spread throughout the United States. Finally, in the last decade of the nineteenth century the theory of Hebart became the prevailing one in American elementary education, producing most important changes in its purposes and methods and maintaining influence almost until today. This is an astonishing record. Probably never again will another country have so great an influence on our schools. The United States has itself become the greatest locus for experiments in education. From the Spanish American War of 1898 dates the rapid decline of

German influence on American life and culture. In addition to the fact that the American universities after 1900 took care of the great majority of American research students, the people of the United States resented the militaristic attitude of Germany at that time. After World War I more American students studied in France and England than in Germany.

Other Influences

Although England, France, and Germany contributed most substantially to the development of American culture and education in our formative years, other foreign influences have played an increasingly important part. Irish influence has been felt ever since our government was founded but became pronounced after the great Irish immigration commencing in the mid-eighteen-forties. The Irish are devout Roman Catholics and throughout the nineteenth century formed the great bulk of the adherents of the Roman Catholic Church in the United States. The priesthood and hierarchy were recruited chiefly from their ranks and they have exerted an influence upon American life out of all proportion to their numbers. They were very patriotic Americans and successfully opposed the movement toward segregation of foreign Catholic groups under imported national priests holding religious services in foreign tongues. It is a question, however, whether they did not encourage a divisive influence in our social life by their insistence upon attendance of Catholic children at parochial schools only. The public school has been throughout our history the chief amalgam in our national life. Though the Irish influence on the Catholic Church has remained predominant, it has been shared during the twentieth century by Italians, Poles, Czechs, and Germans chiefly as the result of the enlarging recruitment of the clergy from their ranks.

Another significant force in American cultural life has been the Mediterranean influence stemming from Italy and Spain. In its early days this influence was not a personal factor resulting from the migration of people from those countries to the United States. It was a deep-streamed cultural force transmitted from Italy into our literature by such leading American writers as Hawthorne and Crawford, and through the medium of Italian sculpture by Story and Powers. Of greater importance in our early history was the influence exerted by Spanish culture on the part of a succession of eminent American writers: Irving, Prescott, Motley, Bryant, Longfellow, and Lowell. Moreover, the Spanish influence was much reinforced by Latin American influence coming via our Southwest, which had a great effect upon American art conceptions by adding what was indigenous in New World art.

Indeed, foreign influences have come into the United States from almost all regions since the turn of the century. The plays of Ibsen startled Americans into new ways of thinking about human relations. The writings of Proust and the French symbolists made a deep impression upon our young writers in the decades after 1910 and influenced our new school of novelists. The power of keen analysis which characterizes the Jewish mind was applied with devastating effect to outworn beliefs and institutions in the fields of politics and economics in the years following the heavy Jewish immigration of 1890. The Russian Revolution resulted in a re-evaluation of our concept of "the general welfare", a loss of faith in *laissez-faire,* and a more responsive attitude toward state regulation and control. The increased power and importance of the United States in international affairs after World War I stimulated propaganda from other countries that were anxious to influence American thinking. This was at first of a "cultural" character such as that conducted by the Alliance Française or the English Speaking Union, but it was later devoted to a blatant attempt at influencing our immigrant groups politically by Italian Fascists and German Nazis.

If the transformation of the individual into what he finally becomes is primarily the result of the forces of environment upon him, it can readily be understood why the process in the United States has been one not simply of education but of re-education. In almost every other country it has been expected that the individual would pass his life in the social class into which he is born. In the great majority of cases he has, and his education—when any was provided—was intended to realize that objective. Not so in the United States.

When in the beginning of our national career John Adams said that the government should be in the control of "the rich, the well born and the able" he forgot that many thousands of the people who arrived on our shores between the settlement at Jamestown in 1607 and the Declaration of Independence almost 170 years later were indentured servants— poor, illiterate and not well born. They spent years working to pay off the price of their indenture. But they worked in a different atmosphere and within a different environment. An untouched empire of land in which they might share lay before them. Their future depended upon themselves, not upon a master. They went into the wilderness, carved out their own homesteads, built schools and churches and organized local governments. They were poor but free and on their way to security. They were independent and equal because they brought no privileges of birth and wealth with them. The indentured servants became re-educated by the changed environment. Throughout the nineteenth century each generation of their descendants in our western expansion passed through a similar experience. That experience has made of them a practical, hard-headed race, devoid of many of the amenities and refinements of life, but generally upright and God-fearing and generous to a fault.

That generosity prompted the United States to welcome the 36,000,000 immigrants who came to our shores between the founding of our government in 1789 and the Immigration law of 1924. They came inspired with the hope that they might lead a happier life than they had in the old country. They came where peace reigned and the arts of peace flourished, where militarism was unknown, where caste did not exist, where national hatreds were forgotten, where everyone hoped to give his children a better chance in life than he had enjoyed. Generally speaking, they came as poor, anxious, distressed immigrants; the new environment transformed them into energetic citizens, standing on their own feet, looking the world in the face, bowing down to no man. Their reeducation had been completed.

Immigration and the resulting foreign influences generally made for a freer life in the United States, a greater willingness to tolerate individual differences, a more widely spread enjoyment of leisure. But they necessarily had a disintegrating influence upon the old American ideals of life that prevailed in the last decade of the nineteenth century. The result is that American civilization is characterized by rapid change. Today it is a dynamic force which has expanded from inner pressure and made its influence felt throughout the world. American automobiles, American movies and American jazz penetrate to the most remote corners of the earth. No one would maintain that they give a true view of American life. That they unfavorably impress the foreign mind with American standards of life is unquestionable. Were they the only influence by means of which the rest of the world could judge America, the judgment would probably be as harsh as it would be inaccurate. Foreigners sometimes assert that American ideas are now conquering the world. This is a questionable generalization, but while American victories in the domain of material things have been dramatic, no less real have been American contributions to the life of the spirit.

CHAPTER IV

BRITAIN—BULWARK OF FREEDOM

British Ignorance of the United States

'PROFESSOR MURRAY," I said to Gilbert Murray upon my visit to England in July 1919, shortly after the signing of the Versailles Treaty, "I have been visiting your institutions of higher education and I am amazed to find not a single course on American history in any of them." "My dear Dr. Duggan," he answered, "had you carried your investigation farther, you would probably have discovered that we have no courses on the history and institutions of our own Dominions."

As far as courses relating to United States history are concerned, there was only slight change between 1919 and 1941, when the United States and Britain became belligerent allies in World War II. There is more news about the United States in British newspapers today and the American movies have been exercising an influence, such as it is. But there has been little change in the amount of attention to American history in educational institutions. There is now the Harmsworth professorship of American history at Oxford and the Eastman professorship; the one filled in 1922–1925 by Professor Morison and the other in 1933–1934 by Professor Frankfurter, both of Harvard. The Eastman professorship was filled in 1930–1931 by Professor Wesley Mitchell, and in 1939–1940 by Professor Joseph Chamberlain, both of Columbia. All these scholars made a strong impression upon teachers and students. The Commonwealth Fund established a professorship of American history at the University of London. The Woodrow Wilson professorship of international relations at the University of Wales is also a help. When conducting courses in the political and social sciences today, moreover, British professors make more frequent references to American experience. But the comparatively small progress made in the matter has led some Americans to believe that the former British attitude of treating us as colonials still exists despite the experience of World War I.

This is only partly a mistake. The United States certainly did not win World War I, alone, as some bombastic Americans sometimes assert, but it is probably accurate to say that except for our aid the Allies would not have won it. If that is true, many Americans consider it anomalous that twenty-five years should have passed and Britain still remain ignorant of our country and its history. The British have always been far more ignorant of us than we are of them. In practically all our high schools the history of Great Britain is given either in a special course or as part of the history of Europe. This is because of our historical association with Great Britain. We must know something about the source of many of our institutions and ways of life. The British of necessity have studied the historical relationships with their immediate neighbors who have been at times their enemies; but recent events have proved that their security depends more on the United States than on any other country. It was knowledge of this fact which last year led the British Board of Education at long last to promote the study of American history and institutions amongst all elementary and secondary school teachers and to introduce in the schools short courses on American history and current problems. Another reason for delay in the study of American affairs is that British education is much restricted in its liberty of action by its adhesion to examinations as a test of educational progress. This restriction does not make it easy to add courses in an entirely new field like American history. The situation up to the present, however, has been primarily determined by the forces of geography and history, and it is worth while to consider for a moment their interaction.

During the entire seventeenth century, the attention of Englishmen was taken up with the struggle for supremacy between King and Parliament. That struggle had hardly ended in 1688 in the supremacy of Parliament before the Second Hundred Years' War broke out between Great Britain and France. During those two centuries the American colonies were of necessity left largely to themselves. They learned to control their own internal affairs and to tax themselves for objectives which they themselves decided upon. When the great struggle between France and England ended in the defeat of France in 1763, the British government insisted that the colonies ought to bear a share of the cost of the war that relieved them of the French menace in Canada and it began to impose taxes upon the colonies. The British government was ignorant of the political evolution that had taken place in the American colonies in the two preceding centuries. It did not realize that the colonies had grown to manhood or it would not have attempted to *impose* taxes upon them. It would have appealed to the colonists' sense of fairness and would only have asked that they share the burden of debt. Admittedly that would have not been in accordance with the practice of the time in the relations between colonies and mother countries, but far-seeing statesmen like the elder Pitt, Edmund Burke, and Charles James Fox were aware of its importance. The controversy precipitated the Revolution and resulted in the independence of the United States. That is one of the greatest events in our history, but the Revolution became in the course of time an almost forgotten incident for the British. H. G. Wells in his *Outline of*

History neglects it in typically British fashion. However, they eventually learned from the experience the wisdom of better treatment for their remaining colonies.

The wars of independence of the English and Spanish colonies in America had one very dissimilar result. The Spanish colonies turned their backs upon the mother country and thereafter had few relationships with her. As already mentioned, the English colonies at once resumed all relationships with the mother country save that of political dependence and they remained spiritually colonies of Great Britain almost throughout the nineteenth century. Very few Britons visited our country and some of them returned home to spread contempt for what they had seen and heard. It was as late as 1869 that Lowell wrote "On a Certain Condescension in Foreigners", and his shafts were aimed chiefly at Englishmen. The British remained unaware that the experience of "The Winning of the West" and the coming of millions of non-British peoples with different ideas of life effected a subtle spiritual revolution in the United States, resulting in a new civilization founded upon the British yet different from it. The turn of the century brought to the attention of the most thoughtful British the new American literature and art and philosophy that gradually had been developed, but it was not until after World War I that knowledge of its significant character became general even among the intellectual classes.

English Education

In Disraeli's novel *Sybil* he explains the existence of "two nations" within the general body of the English people: the "respectable classes" and the "laboring poor". That distinction remained practically true throughout the nineteenth century and the system of education that prevailed in England during that century also partly explains the situation that existed there in 1919. The egalitarian philosophy of life that was held in the United States after the time of Andrew Jackson placed emphasis primarily upon the elementary school in order that the foundation for equal opportunity for all should be realized. An egalitarian philosophy had no place in Great Britain. Until the passage of the Forster Education Act of 1870, there was no publicly-supported elementary school system as we understand it. A free secondary school system waited for its establishment until 1902. The Provincial universities are almost all either late nineteenth or twentieth century products. The result was that university education was heavily concentrated in Oxford and Cambridge, whose students came largely from the "Public Schools", which in fact are aristocratic private schools. The Fisher Act of 1918 was a milestone in British education in the improvement of the elementary school system. The Hadow Report of 1926 and the Spens Report of 1938 made clear that British educators were determined to secure real equality of opportunity at the secondary school level. The Reports also indicated the existence of a strong popular movement in the direction of a national system of democratic education in which the Public Schools must find their place. That place as yet has not been established.

The aim of the education at the Public Schools and the two old universities was to make an "English gentleman". The classics and mathematics provided the chief intellectual pabulum but scholarship was not the primary goal. Sports, teaching cooperation and bringing out leadership all played a most important role. English education is largely responsible for the fact that the Englishman is essentially a man of will rather than a man of intellect, thoroughly practical and not speculative. That is what is meant by the saying that the Englishman "muddles through". He wants to see clearly the next step and how to attain it, not the theoretical final goal.

The British Empire was not built up as the result of careful thinking and planning. For a large part of the nineteenth century, the Dominions were regarded by many Englishmen with considerable indifference and by some as a positive nuisance. It was only toward the end of the nineteenth century —when Joseph Chamberlain, Cecil Rhodes, Rudyard Kipling and their associates expounded the philosophy of imperialism—that the conviction grew among some imperialists in England that the British Empire is the nearest approach to the Kingdom of God that exists upon this mundane sphere.

Oxford and Cambridge

It has always been a delight for me to visit Oxford and Cambridge, to observe the "backs" along the Cam behind the venerable college buildings which make up the University of Cambridge, and the quiet within the quadrangles of the Oxford Colleges. I particularly recall my first experience with "High Table" at Oxford. The dons sat at a table at one end of the dining room, elevated above the student tables. Grace was offered in Latin so rapidly as to be entirely unintelligible to me. It did not seem to inspire the students with holy reflections, and I understand that if the grace is too prolonged the students rattle their forks as a hint to bring it to an end. After dinner, several of the dons adjourned to one of their rooms and there ensued over the port a most stimulating conversation upon a variety of subjects. Some of those men were very much alive to the political and economic problems that confronted the post-war world, and I came away convinced that if it had ever been true in past times that Oxford was "the home of lost causes", it was no longer a fact. One had only to attend the forthright debates of the students at the Oxford Union on the most controversial problems of the day, domestic and international, to realize that he was in an unusually stimulating environment where he would hear many constructive suggestions. Incidentally, the so-called "Oxford Oath" of the early 1930's, urging students to refuse to support "King and country" in case of war, was a passing phenomenon. Nearly all the students who took the oath in those days are now enrolled in the fighting forces.

During a later visit, in 1934, I was invited to occupy the rooms of a don who was then away from college to carry on some research in Egypt. By that time some of the winter hardships of residence formerly existing in an Oxford college had been overcome. It is true that one had to get into a bathrobe, go down stairs and across the quadrangle to a basement in another building in order to take his shower, but he no longer took a sponge bath in his room in a tin tub. Each student had his servitor or "scout" who made a fire and brought breakfast. It is a long established custom to invite fellow students to breakfast and to bear the expense for parties of other kinds. These expenses made the cost of a typical education at Oxford or Cambridge beyond the means of many who therefore lose some of the fine social aspects of education at one of the older universities. The entire scholastic year at Oxford and Cambridge covered only twenty-four weeks, divided into three terms. In the intervals between terms students usually left the universities with their books, tramped or bicycled about Great Britain or a foreign country and had time for real study and reflection, and professors had time for research. It is easily understandable why some of the older men look back to the early days with nostalgia.

My visit to Cambridge in 1919 impressed upon me the strong spirit of independence found in each individual college, of which there were eighteen making up the University. Each college is headed by a Master (though King's has a Provost and Queens' a President) and all are under the general direction of a Vice Chancellor of the University, the Chancellor being nearly always a distinguished statesman. Sir Arthur Shipley, with whom I became acquainted when he visited the United States during World War I, was Vice Chancellor in 1919 and was gracious enough to invite me to spend a week with him. Sir Arthur was a fine old gentleman with delightful peccadillos. He led me to my bedroom the first night of my visit and proudly pointed to a four poster so high that I thought I would have to stand upon a chair to climb into it, and told me that Henry VII had once reposed there. I slept soundly, untroubled by Henry's ghost. I asked Sir Arthur whether it would be possible for him to suggest to the Masters of the various colleges the wisdom of entering into co-operative relations with some of our great universities. "My dear Dr. Duggan," he answered, "were I to do that you could rely upon its not being done. They would undoubtedly regard it as an interference." Perhaps he exaggerated somewhat for I afterward found several of the Masters happily disposed to the idea, but it gave me an inkling of the attitude of the individual college toward any central control. While at Cambridge I made the acquaintance of some fine scholars such as J. Holland Rose and Ernest Barker, as I did at Oxford. At the latter I came to know such eminent men as Lionel Curtis and Sir William Craigie. My repeated visits in later years to both universities were always among my chief pleasures.

The two old universities were left in a parlous state economically by World War I. The age-long endowments could no longer support them. The government followed the usual custom when confronted by a serious problem. It appointed a Royal Commission to consider the whole question of the support of higher education. The Commission reported in favor of making annual grants to all universities including the Provincial universities. Oxford and Cambridge at first viewed with hesitancy this system of subsidy as possibly forecasting an attempt at government control, which they had resisted for centuries. They were assured, however, that the government would not interfere with their independence or administration in any way, and that assurance has been faithfully observed. It is an attitude that some of our state governments, especially in the South, might imitate to the welfare of higher education in the United States.

Another point of comparison between higher education in Britain and the United States may be found in the splendid summer sessions maintained at Oxford and Cambridge. The summer schools in American universities are attended chiefly by teachers in our elementary and secondary schools who are primarily motivated by a desire to secure increases in salary or advancement in grade. The summer schools are also attended by students who wish to reduce the four-year period required to obtain a bachelor's degree and by other students who have flunked some course and must make up the lost "credits". There is no material interest served by attendance at a summer session at Oxford or Cambridge. The courses are of a purely cultural character and usually have to do with some aspect of British civilization. There might be a course on "The Elizabethan Drama", "The Lake School of Poetry" or "The Influence of the Industrial Revolution". After World War I, an increasing number of Americans who wanted no "credit" attended summer sessions at Oxford and Cambridge to such an extent that in 1937 they numbered at Oxford two hundred, half of all in attendance. This inspired the authorities at Cambridge in the following year to organize a summer session on the American plan, particularly for Americans. It was given up in 1939 because of the imminence of the war.

Rhodes Scholars

To an American one of the most interesting features of Oxford is the presence of the Rhodes Scholars. Their presence is due to the vision of Cecil Rhodes, the South African magnate who provided a sufficient endowment to enable two scholars from each of the American states and the British Dominions to spend the three-year period of study at Oxford. The aim in the education of the Rhodes Scholar was the same as that in the education of the young Englishman. Rhodes required each of his Scholars to be chosen from among those who exhibit moral character, leadership, and interest in their fellows, because "those latter attributes will be likely in after-life to guide him to esteem the performance of public duties as his highest aim." The Rhodes Scholars were distributed among the various colleges of the University. When the plan was first put into operation in 1904, the Scholars were selected by competitive examination from among juniors and seniors in American colleges. This method was not a success educationally or socially. Some of the students did not measure up to the scholastic standards of Oxford and some others came from a simpler, a less sophisticated, less sensitive way of life which made adjustment slow and hence retarded educational progress. The plan was fortunate in having Philip Kerr, who later became the Marquess of Lothian, as Secretary of the Rhodes Trust, and President Frank Aydelotte of Swarthmore as the American Secretary. They worked in complete harmony. As the result of twenty-five years of experience the plan was somewhat reorganized. The United States was divided into eight districts and four students were selected from each district. This permitted a choice from a larger number of candidates in a district. The reform resulted in a much better supply of Scholars and a happier relationship between the English and American students. In 1926 Rhodes House was built at Oxford as the headquarters of the Scholars. There the American students from the different states could meet one another as well as the English students who attended the various functions that were held at the House.

The objective of Cecil Rhodes, namely, the development of a better understanding between the American and British peoples, has unquestionably been furthered by the establishment of the Rhodes Scholarships. Many of the Scholars have occupied positions of some importance upon their return to the United States, especially in the field of higher education. Their influence enabled them to further the cause from which they themselves benefited. This fact became so obvious that the Commonwealth Fund, with an endowment provided by Edward Harkness, an American millionaire, established in 1925 the Commonwealth Fellowships for English students. By 1931 there were seventy-three Fellows studying in the research institutions and universities of the United States with apparently as great success as in the case of the Rhodes Trust.

The American University Union

Another organization that has had a great influence in developing good relations between Britain and the United States is the American University Union, the representative of the Institute of International Education in France and Great Britain. The Union was founded during World War I by Dr. Anson Phelps Stokes and Professor George Nettleton of Yale University to serve the needs of our college graduates in the American armies fighting in France. Because many of our troops passed through England on their way to France, an office of the Union was also established in London. When the war was over the Union decided to maintain the offices in London and Paris for peacetime purposes. It would be hard to overemphasize the admirable work performed by the Union as a liaison between the institutions of higher education of Great Britain and the United States. Research scholars and students from the United States were at once connected with the right institutions and organizations to enable them to undertake their special studies. They also had rooming and boarding houses recommended to them, places within the range of all incomes. British scholars and students going to the United States went armed with information and advice that usually proved invaluable to them after their arrival. The Director of the Union represented American higher education at all kinds of conferences of an educational and cultural character. The Union in the course of time came to be regarded as an American educational embassy to which our own diplomatic embassy and British government officials constantly turned for counsel in cultural affairs of an Anglo-American nature. In this work, Professor Dixon Ryan Fox, now President of Union College, who was Director in 1928–1929, and Mr. Willard Connely, who has been Director since, rendered outstanding service through their repeated visits to the institutions of higher education in Great Britain and through their splendid addresses at educational gatherings. During their administrations the American University Union became one of the principal agencies in developing understanding between the intellectual classes of Britain and the United States.

Provincial Universities

During my frequent visits to Europe in the period 1919–1939, I became much impressed by the excellent work carried on in the Provincial universities of England. These were nearly always established in municipalities and supported primarily by the municipal governments, though several received large—in some cases, princely—gifts from English millionaires. One objective of the Provincial universities is to serve the needs of their immediate environment, in addition to provid-

ing general academic education. Intensive research is undertaken in all aspects of the tobacco business at the University
of Bristol, Bristol being the chief center of that trade; in low
carbonization coal experiments at Sheffield; in oceanography
at Liverpool; in brewing at Birmingham, and in cotton at
Manchester. Most of the students in these and other Provincial universities come from what in England is called the
middle class. These institutions are progressive in spirit and
purpose, grant degrees equally to men and women, are well
adjusted to modern needs and are closely articulated with the
municipal public schools.

The University of London was established in 1836 upon a
foundation of two institutions, King's College under Anglican control, and University College under Dissenter control.
But in the course of time the University of London has grown
by accretion until today it includes some thirty-six institutions. Among them is the remarkable London School of Economics, for so many years under the supervision of its scholarly Director, Sir William Beveridge, now the Master of
University College, Oxford. The School has had a great career
and in its faculty have been numbered some of the most eminent British scholars in the social sciences. There is nothing
comparable to it anywhere else, though the New School for
Social Research in New York City may equal or surpass it as
the result of the addition to its staff of many refugee scholars
since the rise of Nazism and Fascism in Europe.

The Provincial universities have not the prestige of Oxford and Cambridge, and probably no professor at any of
them would refuse a call to Oxford or Cambridge any more
than a professor at a French Provincial university would refuse a call to Paris. The story is told of one *grande dame* to
whom mention was made by an American visitor of his indebtedness to an English scholar for assistance in research.
"Indeed," said the lady, "was he an Oxford or a Cambridge

man?" "Neither," answered the American, "he taught at Birmingham." "Is there a university at Birmingham?" inquired the lady.

The English Social System

England's social system is the result to a great extent of its organization of education, though history and tradition naturally play a large part. The social system is based upon class distinctions which exist to an extent unknown to the average American. The English aristocracy, however, has differed from the aristocracies of the Continent in having a remarkable assimilative power, so that even when a breach was made in 1832 in its monopoly of political power and even though that breach was widened by successive extensions of the suffrage, the influence of the aristocracy was not greatly lessened. It was saved by the absorption of the leaders of the new elements into its own ranks. A successful financier, industrialist or brewer might look forward to rounding out his career by elevation to the peerage. The result has been that though classes exist in England, the rigid caste system of a country like Germany has not prevailed. However liberal or even radical a new peer might have been as a Commoner, it was almost impossible to resist the seductive influences of old families and great houses. The new peer gradually became a conservative, a staunch upholder of throne and altar, and—if he had been a Dissenter—a member of the Anglican Church. If he did not become a conservative, his children usually did. With his wealth he could marry them into the old families, some of which were always impoverished. This system has resulted in a respect for aristocracy and a worship of titles that permeates almost every class of English society even today.

I experienced several times the charm of a week-end visit to one of the great estates. Before Sir Esme Howard retired

as British Ambassador to the United States in 1930 and just
previous to one of my visits on the other side of the Atlantic,
he gave me a letter of introduction to one of his relatives,
Vernon Watney. It is upon such an occasion that one admires
the quiet efficiency of the English servant who looks after
your clothes, your movements and yourself generally, with
no apparent direction from anyone. The form of breakfast-
ing, so different from our own, wherein each one takes from
a sideboard such food as he desires and then seats himself
with others at the table, was novel and interesting. Mr. Watney had invited a group of friends for the week-end and the
discussion around the fireplace on Saturday evening concerned
the future of the great estates in England. Mr. Watney stated
his belief that upon his death there might be enough fortune
left after the payment of the death duties, for his son to carry
on the estate, but he did not believe it would be possible for
his son's son to do so. I could understand the accuracy of the
statement when I accompanied the son the next afternoon on
a tour of the estate, Cornbury Park, which was in the neighborhood of Oxford. Though we tramped about it the whole
afternoon we did not cover it by any means. Information from
the taxgatherer in Great Britain in 1943 is to the effect that
there are only eighty persons in the whole country that now enjoy an income of more than $25,000. There are as many as
that on Park Avenue in New York City. It is probable, therefore, that the large part of the land still owned by persons
who hold five thousand acres or more apiece will suffer much
diminution after this war.

When Philip Kerr succeeded his cousin as Marquess of
Lothian he was compelled to sell some of his library, art
treasures, and other possessions to secure enough money to
carry on the estate. It is a question, however, how typical his
case was. His branch of the family never had much money
anyhow and he probably grew up never dreaming that he

would fall into a peerage. During one of my talks with him he told me that the estate had a large body of servitors most of whom had spent their lives upon it and who would have to be provided for, in some cases for the rest of their lives. Wealth in England carries with it a sense of obligation to individuals superior to that which exists in the United States, but probably less to society in general than in this country. Lord Lothian made an offer to the government to make over the estate as a public museum provided he might simply live in the house. The government rejected the offer. It did not want his estate; it wanted his taxes.

The cost of social legislation, when added to the interest on the enormous debt accumulated during World War I, caused a rise in taxation the like of which no other country had ever borne. It fell with particular severity upon the land, and some old families were compelled to sell estates that had been in their hands for centuries. The loss of their sons during the war and of their lands after it was a severe blow to England's ruling classes.

It was not only the landed interests that had to make a new orientation. The loss of markets and the burden of unemployment awakened the capitalists to the need of much reorganization in industry. Reliance upon old-fashioned methods and equipment that had sufficed in pre-war days meant failure in the face of the fierce competition of the post-war period. It even meant a reconsideration of the economic philosophy upon which England's industrial greatness had been built, namely, free trade. But it meant above all a demand for new men with broader outlook and more specialized knowledge. The Provincial universities which had always emphasized science and specialization assumed new importance and even Oxford and Cambridge undertook a revaluation of studies. Slowly but surely these old universities were being modified. Free scholarships for graduates of the new publicly-supported secondary schools have diluted the aristocratic character of the student personnel. During my last visit to Oxford in 1938, I was informed that more than one half of the student body were there on fellowships or stipends of various kinds. Many of the stipends, however, are small. Some of them are offered by municipalities as prizes for success in examinations like the $100 a year scholarships offered in New York State for success in the Regents examinations. Nevertheless, the change taking place at Oxford was obvious. Lionel Curtis introduced me to two brilliant students, one the son of a Welsh miner and the other the son of a London workingman. This was at All Souls, where the student body is wholly of a graduate character.

The British Labor Party

The changes described above have been coincident with the increase in power and influence of the British Labor Party. The growth of the Labor Party has been phenomenal. In 1906 it cast some 323,000 votes and secured 29 seats in the House of Commons. In 1929 it cast 8,383,000 votes and secured 288 seats. The gains of the Labor Party were almost wholly at the expense of the Liberal Party, which virtually passed out of existence. The Labor Party became "His Majesty's Loyal Opposition", a phrase which indicates that the opposition is a regular part of the constitutional machinery of Great Britain. The element of greatest influence in the composition of the Labor Party is the trade-unions. Their leaders are the men who determine its policies. They have come up from the ranks and are not intellectuals like the leaders of labor parties on the Continent. As with Englishmen generally, they are cautious, more concerned with a practical solution of a problem confronting them than with one in conformity with doctrinaire principles.

The reasons for the Labor Party's remarkable growth, from a narrowly trade-unionist party to one which after World War I appealed for support to all who "live by working" as against those who "live by owning", were characteristically British. The Party appealed to the moderates in the nation because though adopting a socialist platform it was opposed to class war and in favor of changes by parliamentary means and progressive stages and it wholly repudiated Communism. Moreover, it accepted the monarchy behind which it considered that democracy could function as well as in a republic. The laboring people of Britain were everywhere made to feel that they had a stake in the welfare of their country and had a right to have their opinion on policies heard. The loyalty that this attitude engendered was universal. I saw an impressive demonstration of this loyalty one day when I was about to take a train to one of the suburbs of London. I noticed a slightly bigger crowd than usual about the station, many of whom were workers. I inquired the reason of a nearby person. He answered, "The King is going to take a train." I waited and the auto of King George V passed into the station, preceded by a single auto filled with relatives or friends, amid the smiles of the people who all raised their hats. It was apparently generally known that he was coming, yet there was no soldiery to guard him. Nor was there any fuss about his departure. It was an evidence not merely of loyalty but of affection. To me it was a demonstrated justification of British faith in the people.

The existence of the Labor Party has had a great influence upon the individual laborer. In 1898, I once stood outside of a big factory in Glasgow and watched the workmen as they filed out. It was a sad sight. They looked undersized, undernourished, and ignorant. The work of the Labor Party in the fields of health, social service and particularly education, which the leaders regarded as the way to social emancipation and freedom, has immensely improved the morale of the worker and made him a very different person from the abject creature that I saw at Glasgow forty-five years ago. Successive British governments deserve some of the credit for this transformation in not only allowing but even providing opportunity for the Laborites to attain their objectives. This judgment has been substantiated through talks with British leaders representing all shades of political belief. Most of my friendships in Britain have been with Liberals like Sir William Beveridge, Sir Frederick Whyte, Gilbert Murray, and his son-in-law, Arnold Toynbee, Professor William G. S. Adams, and Professor C. K. Webster. But I have received much information concerning conditions from contact with fine Conservatives like Lionel Curtis, and by delightful correspondence with others like Lord Eustace Percy. I have also learned a great deal as the result of friendships with Laborites such as Sir Norman Angell, Professor Evan F. M. Durbin, and farther to the left, Harold Laski.

Some of the credit for the progress of the Labor Party belongs to the fair and honest attitude of the British press. However much Labor policies might be denounced in the "leaders", i.e. the editorials, the news columns usually give honest information as to what takes place. The British press is free, uncensored, unpurchasable, and under comparatively little indirect influence by the government. All sides of a question are expressed in the newspapers from Tory reaction provided by the *Morning Post* (recently absorbed by the Conservative *Daily Telegraph*) through the Liberal *News Chronicle,* to the Laborite *Daily Herald*. And influential newspapers are not confined to London. The Liberal *Manchester Guardian* probably wields a greater influence upon independent thinking than does the mildly Conservative London *Times*. All parts of England have honest newspapers to voice their needs and desires such as the *Birmingham Post*, the Edinburgh *Scotsman*, and the *Glasgow Herald*.

Since World War I, events in Great Britain have been moving in the direction of the goal maintained by the Labor Party, namely, increased governmental regulation and control. The Britain of the future is having its outlines defined during the present war and this tendency is accentuated. If the war is continued much longer there will be few even moderately rich people left. This will mean increased leveling of class distinctions. The Foreign Service has been reconstructed since the war began by the merging of the diplomatic and consular services, and, at least theoretically, will be open to all irrespective of birth or wealth by making grants for study and travel to suitable candidates without private means. The Public Schools will probably have difficulty in maintaining themselves, and if they receive government grants they must necessarily be modified to admit talented young people regardless of their parents' means. The need for maintaining the health of the troops and of the workers in munition factories in order to secure victory in the war has resulted in an aroused attention to diet, which has influenced considerably the administration of the common schools. The removal of factories from congested cities to rural areas, with the accompanying housing problems, has made obvious the need of changes to provide local governments with adequate powers to meet the new situation. An aroused public conscience has introduced far-reaching reforms in the social services maintained by the government. Large-scale planning has become the order of the day during the war and may bring about a considerable alteration of the social and economic system. The Beveridge Report's insistence upon the necessity for legislation to secure freedom from want is really the latest step in the long continuous movement for the amelioration of the condition of Disraeli's "second nation."

From these changes it is hoped a finer Britain will emerge. But the British are an essentially conservative people, and admitting that the spirit of reform is much stronger during this war than during the last, one must not forget the failure to realize after 1919 many of the changes hoped for during World War I. The British Labor Party published toward the close of World War I what was probably the finest program organized for the peace conference, but it was ignored by the British delegation at Versailles. It was often stated that the landed gentry would be "done for" as the result of the war, but it survived. Though a good deal of resentment was aroused against the Public Schools during the war the strong ones still flourish. Some of the Public Schools were given government grants and had to accept elementary school pupils up to 25 per cent. Class-conscious parents simply withdrew their children and sent them to the schools which had declined such grants. Britain was *the* nineteenth century country, and it is questionable whether it will readily accept twentieth century ideas that will be a hindrance—from an Empire point of view—to its power, its prestige, and its world position. Mr. Churchill has already stated—and wisely—that he did not intend to preside at the liquidation of the British Empire at the close of the war and Colonel Oliver Stanley, Secretary of State for Colonies, recently informed the world that Britain had no intention of turning over her colonies to the supervision of an international commission. It must not be overlooked that the representatives of Britain at the peace conference will be products of the Public Schools.

Some General Impressions

In my drives in Britain I was always impressed with the small size of the country and its congested character compared with the United States. The United Kingdom and Ireland together could easily fit into half of Texas and there would be much space left over. Great Britain has 46,000,000 people and Texas somewhat more than 6,000,000. There is considerable unoccupied land in Great Britain to be found in the great estates, but one cannot drive far from one town in England or Southern Scotland without soon coming upon another. There are no large areas such as those in our great West where one might drive for hours hardly meeting anyone else. This is primarily the result of the introduction of the auto, for in 1898 I tramped with a friend in the Lake District all the way from Derwentwater to Wastdale Water, meeting but a few people. When I visited the Lake District in the summer of 1936, the experience was not a particularly happy one. On a great holiday, like a Bank holiday, the English roads are crowded with buses and touring is not much of a pleasure. One can hardly fail to be struck, however, by the law-abiding character of the English people. This is not only true in great matters such as the General Strike of 1926 when not a shot was fired, but in the small affairs of daily life as well. There is much less parking of cars in forbidden places and littering of parks with refuse by picnickers than in the United States. Forty years ago I considered a picnic by the average English workman's family a pretty sad affair compared with one in Central or Southern Europe, but they have become much more joyous in recent years. They seldom, I believe, degenerate into the boisterous and sometimes destructive character of some picnics in our own country.

One characteristic of the British people that impresses a foreigner is the part religion plays in their lives. The British are a conservative people and they take their religion seriously. This is true not only of the conservative classes but of the masses of the people. The British Labor Party has a socialistic program but it differs from continental socialist parties in that its members are predominantly sincere adherents of some church. Until comparatively recent times the Anglican Church was largely formal in its religious practices, but it now takes a very active interest in social problems. With the passage of time the Established Church became increasingly aware of the great loss it sustained in the rapid development of the Wesleyan Movement in the late eighteenth century, due to the lack of a vital spiritual attitude in its practices. The Dissenting churches carry on vigorously and I have attended services in their churches with crowded congregations. It is largely due to the seriousness of the Dissenters that Sunday in a British city or town is usually a pretty dismal day. There is little to do but to go to church and take the air, though the London Sunday newspapers have in recent years become fairly widely distributed. The movies, however, are rapidly causing a change in this respect. The Roman Catholic Church has a small minority of the British people but Catholics are numerous in Liverpool and Glasgow as the result of Irish immigration to those cities. The Catholic Church is influential among the upper classes and is strong in the diplomatic service.

I made an effort during my visits to find out as far as possible what were the faults Englishmen of different social grades discover in our people. English shopkeepers and hotel owners were glad to welcome the hordes of American tourists that invade England every summer. But they do not make up the majority of England's population. It could not be expected that the large number of Americans, who make their one visit to England and want to see everything they possibly can in that one visit, should not give offense to a great many Englishmen. It is apparently human nature to be more enduringly impressed by a few experiences of an unpleasant character than by a large number of the opposite kind. The quiet behavior of the great majority remains unrecorded—in memory and in writing. American tourists were often regarded as loud and pushing and vulgar. The *arrivistes* annoy with their condescending attitude and their evident belief that money commands everything. Among intellectually minded Englishmen our penchant for lecturing the rest of the world on its shortcomings caused amusement and sometimes resentment. Nearly all considered our attitude on the debt question as unfair. They weighed their expenditure of blood against our expenditure of money. With almost all classes there was a good deal of dislike at the embarrassing familiarity of some Americans which often amounted to an intrusion on privacy. By way of contrast, Englishmen are regarded by Americans in general as stiff and reserved and superior in manner, and the Oxford accent is anathema in the United States. With increasing contact between Britons and Americans there has unquestionably developed a greater tolerance for the peculiarities of each and a willingness to learn from each other. Both peoples are foremost among the nations of the world in their love of sport; the Americans with a greater buoyancy of spirit, the English with a love of sport *per se*. There is a kinship in smaller but equally significant things, such as dress and the resort to colloquialism and slang for the trenchant expression of ideas.

British Foreign Policy

Beginning with the Tudors, the foreign policy of Great Britain has been based upon the principle of the Balance of Power. There have always been two potential enemies of Great Britain in Europe, one having the greater strength and therefore more to be feared. The British policy has always been to back the weaker even to the point of war, if necessary. Down to the Munich Conference of 1938 this policy has been consistently followed. There it was not followed. At the time of Munich, English public opinion believed that the two potential enemies of democratic Britain were Communist Russia and Nazi Germany. Of these two, Russia was regarded as the weaker. If tradition and precedent had been followed, Great Britain would have backed Russia as against Germany. It did not. It backed Germany and thereby enormously increased Germany's prestige and strength. This reversal of policy on the part of the greatest Power in the world really makes Munich a turning point in human affairs. What is the explanation?

The Russian Revolution of 1917 was regarded unfavorably by the mass of Englishmen, and with intense antagonism by the ruling classes. At the end of World War I the Coalition Government did all it could to destroy the Soviet system through military intervention. The English ruling classes have since watched the growth of Russia in economic and political strength with increasing dislike and fear. Politically they have regarded it as a potential enemy state; economically, as a destroyer of the capitalist system of which Great Britain is the greatest exponent; spiritually, as the assassin of Western culture because of its determination to destroy what they regard as the foundation of culture, namely, religion. This antagonism was strengthened among all Englishmen by the horrible treatment accorded to aristocrats, bourgeoisie, kulaks, and some intellectuals. Hence when Fascism arose in Germany and, taking its cue from Russia, also ruled by terror and brutality, English society was divided by its fears into opponents of Russia and of Germany. The ruling classes continued to fear Russia more. But necessity controls in international affairs as in most things. When Hitler attacked Russia in June 1941, Britain, though controlled chiefly by the Tory Party, gladly welcomed the Soviets as an ally. Since then, the agreement has become more complete and extends to cooperation in international affairs in the post-war period. If this cooperation is realized it augurs well for a durable peace in Europe.

Britain's Place in the Post-War World

What Britain's position will be in the post-war international world will depend upon the nature of the victory. But it is obvious that it cannot be what it has been up to the present time. Until World War I the British navy did "rule the waves" primarily to protect British commerce, but incidentally it maintained peace in far-removed corners of the earth. Britain until then was dominant but with a benign dominance that interfered little with the affairs of other nations. She lost that dominant position in World War I, a position since taken by the United States. Some publicists believe that even the burden of empire may be too great for Britain to carry after this war.

The three most important elements in the recent foreign policy of Britain are these: 1) Britain is geographically part of Europe and cannot be isolated from the solution of Europe's problems. 2) The maintenance of the British Commonwealth of Nations is essential to the existence of Britain as a Great Power, but the Dominions will unquestionably in the future pay greater regard to their own interests, especially their security, and may orient themselves more in the direction of the United States. This would be true especially of Canada. And it is a question how much longer India can be held in the equivocal position of today and denied a greater degree of independence. 3) British foreign policy must be so conducted as to maintain friendly and harmonious relations with the United States. Assuming victory for the Allies, there will be in post-war Europe three first-class Powers: Great Britain, Germany, and Russia. If the new World Order of the

Allies as outlined in the last chapter of this book should include a European federation, Britain—with the continued support of the British Commonwealth of Nations and the moral support of the United States—should have an almost decisive influence in European affairs. And its importance in a world federation of regional federations would be very great. Though Britain will no longer occupy the dominant position of the past, it will exercise a strong influence on the future of mankind.

My own admiration for the British people during this war has been profound—especially when, after Dunquerque, they stood absolutely alone in a sea of gloom, apparently without a friend in Europe. But they were sustained by the remarkable leadership of Winston Churchill who assured them of eventual victory but only at the cost of much "blood, sweat, and tears". British civilization has its faults like all civilizations, but without forgetting the faults I prefer to admire the multitude of fine elements in that civilization. On Sunday, October 21, 1928, *The New York Times* published a *jeu d'esprit* called "Good-bye, England", which I wrote as an answer to the "Farewell to America" written by that splendid journalist of the *Daily Chronicle,* Henry W. Nevinson, when he was departing from our shores in March, 1922. The lapse of fifteen years has resulted in a few statements being outmoded. The "pub" and the snob exercise relatively less influence, but by and large the sentiments expressed are those I hold today, only with increased conviction.

GOOD-BYE, ENGLAND
October 21, 1928

The great liner weighs anchor, casts off her hawsers and noses toward America. Down Southampton Water, past fertile fields and lovely villages, through the Solent and around the Needles into the Channel she steams. My happy stay in Britain is ended.

Hospitable welcome, motor trips across park-like landscapes, generous exchange of opinions, sincere adieux are over. Good-bye, England. I'm going home!

Good-bye to the divorce between spelling and speech; good-bye to Cirencester, called Sisister; to Daventry, known as Daintry; to Brightlingsea, named Bricksley. Good-bye to rolling plains and gentle valleys that support sheep rather than men. Good-bye to attractive hamlets with streets of thatched houses in which live kindly people; to curving roads trimmed with fine hedges and dotted with Baby Austins, motorcycles and charabancs. Good-bye to the drab factory towns with their streets of monotonous houses guiltless of sanitation; to third-class compartments devoid of air or conversation, drear as the fog outside. Good-bye to newspapers whose front pages carry nothing but advertisements, but whose editorial sheets command admiration.

Good-bye to London, city of a thousand years and many more memories, where avenues are almost unknown, but where instead are found Tottenham Court Road, Oxford Circus and Cheyne Walk; city of narrow and historic streets and many parks, of stately, yet comfortable clubs, of the Underground, clean and bright, where one pays for a seat and gets it.

I'm going home! Home to a land where spelling has at least a tenuous connection with sound; where Prairie du Chien is Prairie doo Sheen, Joliet is Joliette, Vincennes is Vincenz; to a land of magnificent distances, with every variety of landscape; across which one can travel by rail for almost a week without meeting a customs officer; to a land covered with towns that differ only in name; towns connected by great cement ribbons garnished by "hot-dog" stands and enormous billboards.

I'm going home to New York, true Mandate of Israel, city of wonderful site, of beautiful architecture, of strenuous life, with its subway in which seats are paid for but not secured, in which a myriad faces suggest the melting pot and words and actions sometimes remind one that the cave man is not extinct.

* * *

Good-bye to heavy breakfasts—porridge, kippers, bacon and eggs, strong tea * and cold toast; to dinners of meat and pudding,

* At some places there is offered to the unwary foreigner, a dark, muddy, bitter drink alleged to be coffee.

with no fruit and a choice of three vegetables—two of which are cabbage; dinners at which no one drinks water because all "prefer Bass". Good-bye to cold houses and miniature hearths which heat by suggestion, and where chilled energy is thawed by afternoon tea. Good-bye to the pubs where drunken men and sodden women squander more wealth than would support the dole. Good-bye, England! Land of political liberty and social snobbery, land of tradition and caste where each class apes the class above and only the Dukes live free.

I'm going home! Home to the land of bright sunshine and extreme temperatures, made bearable by houses with steam heat and Frigidaires; to the land where health is a religion and diet a science, to breakfasts of California fruits, cereals, strong coffee and hot toast made by electric percolators and toasters hooked up on the table. I'm going home where the saloon has been abolished and where bootleggers from Eastern and Southern Europe accumulate fortunes by selling in dialect English forbidden rum to law-breaking natives; to a land where "class" is anathema and where the variant from the general run is a freak; where love of liberty has been displaced by the craze for equality. I'm going home to the Women's Clubs, to forums and Chautauquas, where all sides of a question are discussed and the question itself remains unanswered.

*   *   *

Good-bye, Oxford and Cambridge, seats of traditional learning and teaching! Good-bye to venerable colleges, wonderful courts and beautiful "backs"; to comfortless quarters and attendant "scouts" to "high-table" where soup is preceded by an unintelligible prayer and meat is followed by adjournment with napkin to another room for dessert and wine and coffee and delightful conversation. Good-bye to the rational curriculum which provides for concentration in studies and intercourse with teachers and a final examination in the entire field of study. Good-bye to students who scorn to be passmen and to modest dons who fear to dogmatize in their own subjects and profess complete ignorance in all others. Good-bye to Isis and Cam, to cricket and delightful days in punts, to sport for the sake of sport and the fun one gets out of it.

I'm going home! Home to colleges with comfortable dormi-

tories arranged into delightful suites, with lounging rooms for
girl students who smoke; colleges with wonderful gymnasiums,
hygienic showers and inviting pools; true models of efficient administration and quantity production. Where sport is a spectacle
and a combat applauded by 100,000 gathered in a stadium that
dwarfs the Roman Colosseum, applauded not spontaneously, for
applause, like everything pertaining to sport, is "organized", and
one claps and shouts at the signal of a cheer leader. I'm going
home! Home where professors pontificate in all subjects and
where the extra-curricular activities form the main interest of
student life; where degrees are obtained by accumulating "credits"
attached to subjects diffused over unrelated fields and elected
by students who regard the passing mark as that of a gentleman,
and who recover from "conditions" by securing additional
"credits" at summer sessions—at $10 each.

*   *   *

Good-bye, England, land of grinding taxes and falling wages
and disappearing estates: good-bye to political parties which
stand for definite principles and to political meetings, where
orators dare not talk humbug but are heckled into honest admissions. Good-bye to the tolerance of views that one meets in
private homes; good-bye to Hyde Park, where throne and altar
are attacked and communism preached and yet no one is afraid.
Good-bye, brave men and women who face a dark future with
strong hearts and firm wills and who do not whine!

I'm going home! Home to a land that would have delighted
Joshua's spies, whose infinite resources could supply its men and
women according to their deserts and in conformity with their
needs. I'm going home, where the difference between Democrats
and Republicans is so tenuous that half the voters do not think
it worth while to vote; where mediocrity flourishes under the
aegis of 100 per cent Americanism, where teachers must exalt
the untarnished virtue and infallible judgment of the Fathers,
and where the mild critic of ancient abuses and outgrown institutions is denounced as Bolshevik. I'm going home to Chicago to
be protected by the blacklists of the Key Men of America and the
Daughters of the American Revolution; protected, not against
gangsters and gunmen, but against "dangerous thoughts".

*   *   *

Good-bye, England, land of beautiful cathedrals, old-fashioned faiths and steady worshippers; land of queer people, burdened by the hardest problems of twentieth century materialist civilization, yet discussing the metaphysics of the Prayer Book with sixteenth century religious fervor. Good-bye to religious toleration and individual freedom. Thanks, England, for the spiritual heritage you bequeathed us, requited by the affection of our best.

I'm going home! Home to the land where sects are as the sands of the seashore and no belief is too queer to become a cult; to the land of sumptuary laws, where your neighbor is your moral censor and may denounce the vice you have possibly acquired of smoking a cigarette every other Wednesday night; I'm going to Boston, original site of the Puritan Commonwealth, where now a Cardinal decides what shall be read; and to Tennessee, native heath of the Fundamentalist, where the Klan determines what shall be taught. I'm going home to the land I love, where, despite luxury and plutocracy, plain men and women are struggling in the spirit of Jefferson and Lincoln to maintain a democracy, not yet with success but not without hope; a democracy wherein opportunity will be given to capacity to assume the place in society which its merits justify.

CHAPTER V

FRANCE—THE CRISIS OF A GREAT CIVILIZATION

IN THE late summer of 1938 I made my last visit to France previous to the outbreak of the present war. I was engaged in writing some reports and settled with my daughter and her husband at a small hotel on beautiful little Lake Aiguebelette in Savoie. We were the only foreigners there, the other thirty guests being bourgeois Frenchmen. They were all engaged in business of some kind, except for a colonel from Algiers and his wife and son, with whom we became well acquainted. Hitler was dictator in Germany and the propaganda for Anschluss with Austria was in full swing. The immediate future in Europe was one of the topics of general conversation at the little hotel. I was not surprised that my fellow guests usually gave a negative answer to my inquiry as to whether they believed France would act to prevent Anschluss with Austria. But when they similarly replied in the negative to my question whether France would act were Germany to attack Czechoslovakia, I was amazed considering what that might mean for the growth of German power and prestige. "But you have a treaty of alliance with Czechoslovakia which obligates you to go to her defense," I said to one of my neighbors. "Circumstances alter alliances," he answered and proceeded to explain what I later discovered to be a quite general attitude. I was greatly shocked at this contemplated betrayal of an ally—an attitude wholly foreign to French char-

cter—and determined to seek an explanation. I found that
o understand it I would have to go back to the Revolution
of 1789.

The Principles of the Revolution

The French Revolution marked the triumph of the bourgeoisie in French life. They have been in control ever since,
and they intend to remain in control if they can. France was
until yesterday the most bourgeois of the great civilized coun-
ries, and an appraisal of her virtues and weaknesses means
an evaluation of almost a century and a half of dominance by
the bourgeoisie. The Revolution of 1789 had a wholly different effect upon French society from that which the English
Revolution of 1688 had upon English society. It definitely
divided French society into two antagonistic and almost irreconcilable groups. The first consisted of those whose position
had been reduced socially and materially by the Revolution,
the nobility, the aristocracy, and the clergy, whose privileges
had been abolished and whose estates had been sequestrated.
These classes never accepted the Revolution and its logical
consequences. They and their adherents have since always
supported the conservative political parties. The second group
was made up of those who profited by the Revolution: the
middle class which was freed from many absurd restrictions
upon individual initiative to undertake the development of
commerce and industry; the worker who learned very slowly
the need of collective effort for his own welfare, and the
peasant who became a small landed proprietor and who cultivated his farm himself with the aid of his family. There was
really a third group, small but of much importance, the intellectuals devoted to the Declaration of the Rights of Man.

These classes not only accepted the Revolution and its
principles but became its guardians. The chief crises in
French politics down to World War I were due to a belief on

the part of the second general group that the principles of the Revolution were in danger and must be safeguarded. A long period elapsed between the Revolution and the Franco Prussian War of 1870, during which it was questionable whether the conservative forces would not win out, but the failure of the attempt of the second President of the Republic after that war, Marshal MacMahon, to restore the monarchy gave the Republic a strong start. It maintained itself and whenever its security was endangered parties coalesced for its defense as in the case of the republican *bloc* in the Dreyfus affair and the Union Sacrée at the outbreak of World War I. By the time that war took place, the principles of the Revolution had been adopted. *Liberté* had been won for the individual, liberty of thought and expression. *Egalité* of rights for all men had been secured. And *fraternité,* at least in the conception of brotherhood in a glorious nation, nationalism *par excellence,* had become practically universal. But to the believers in the principles of the Revolution, the Revolution was incarnated in the Republic. Had France suffered defeat in World War I, in all probability not only would the Republic have disappeared but loyalty to the principles of the Revolution would have been greatly diminished. Twenty years later both events took place. A description of the experiences I had during the five visits I made to France within those twenty years may throw some light upon the steady moral deterioration that took place there, ending in the débâcle of 1940.

French Leadership in Culture

After World War I, Security became an obsession with the French. It dominated all aspects of French life: political, economic, social and cultural. In 1918 France emerged successfully from a terrible trial. Allowing for the aid of their allies, the French believed that their success in the war was due to the strength of their institutions built up during the previous century and a half, which were to a great extent products of their system of education and culture. Before World War I, there was one school for the children of the peasant and worker, the *école primaire*, and another for the children of the bourgeois, the lycée. In the former, which was free, the child began his school career at six or seven and finished it at thirteen or fourteen, when he went to work on the farm or in the factory. In the latter he began at the same age and finished at eighteen or nineteen. The fee charged in the lycée was small, but it was sufficient to be a real obstacle to the entrance of the child of the worker, though a liberal system of scholarships enabled a gifted child to enter. As entrance to all the professions and the higher civil service required the *baccalauréat* of the lycée, it is easy to see that the controlling positions of society were filled chiefly by the bourgeoisie. The bourgeoisie intended to continue to fill them, if possible.

Shortly before World War I a movement had started for the establishment of a school in which the children of all classes should study together—the *école unique*, the common school. It made little headway. Lack of financial resources was undoubtedly one of the causes for the failure of the state to establish to a greater extent the *école unique*. Many of the lycée professors were also unfavorably disposed because of a genuine fear that the change might result in a lowering of intellectual standards. The antagonism of conservative people, however, was the chief influence in the failure of the movement. They did not intend to share the control of society with the lower classes. But the new spirit introduced into French life by the idealistic pronouncements made by Allied statesmen and the need to safeguard all national resources, human as well as material, in the face of international

peril could not be withstood. Socialists and extreme radical
made the *école unique* part of their political program. A law
was passed providing for the gradual elimination of all fee
in the lycée so that in 1936 it became wholly free. When
discussed this movement with conservative people they com
plained that it endangered the existence of the intellectua
élite—the great pride of France. They regarded with anxiety
the relative decline in the influence of the old studies and in
the number of students pursuing them. Mathematics, science
and modern languages were slowly but surely supplanting the
Latin, Greek, and philosophy which formed the staple of the
traditional culture. The real cause of opposition to these
changes was that in them the conservatives saw the destruc
tion of a bulwark against the rise of the lower classes. *Egalité*
did not mean real equality of opportunity in the new law.

Nature of French Culture

During the past two centuries France has been one of the
greatest contributors of new ideas in politics, literature, art,
and other fields of human thought—ideas which have sometimes had revolutionary effects. Nevertheless, her culture has
been founded upon the classical tradition, the heritage of
Greece and Rome, so greatly strengthened by the Revolution
and Napoleon. However radical an intellectual might be in
his political, social, or religious views, he was usually, like
Anatole France, an enthusiastic adherent of the classical
training. It is difficult for other people to understand the devotion of the French to their own culture. The most outstanding men of the radical parties in France have been men
of as high cultural attainments as were those of the more conservative parties. Monsieur Herriot was a professor of French
literature and historian of French letters. Monsieur Painlevé
is a great mathematician. The most leftist of all, Monsieur

Blum, is a man of letters and a book lover. Not nearly so many of the leaders of socialism in France have been workers as has been the case in Great Britain. The contributions of the scientists have been chiefly in the domain of pure science, like mathematics, rather than in the mechanical sciences, like engineering. Partly because of their economic system of small industries the French have not been so active as other peoples in the application of the results of their scientists' speculations, although, of course, there have been notable exceptions as in the case of Pasteur.

France reached a position of stabilization and contentment at the close of World War I. Whether she would continue to contribute new and revolutionary ideas to humanity was a question. In the field of politics and social organization the French bourgeoisie became very cautious and little progress was made. In the field of ideas proper, philosophical, literary, artistic, Frenchmen were still bold, destructively so, conservatives maintained. But there could be hardly any doubt of the desire of all Frenchmen to maintain leadership in the domain of culture. Paris was in process of resuming the place of leadership in the field of education and culture that it maintained during the later Middle Ages. In 1935 its university had almost half of the students of all the French universities, and almost one-quarter of its students were foreigners. After the war the beautiful Cité Universitaire was established on the outskirts of the city. In it there have been erected eighteen dormitories of which fifteen were built by nations other than France, to house their students in association with French students. Nearly all these buildings are of fine architecture and the central building, provided by Mr. Rockefeller, has under its roof a commons, reading room, lounging room, library, theatre, gymnasium and swimming pool. It was a splendid addition and rendered a great service to the students, French and foreign.

French Feeling of Cultural Superiority

We usually think of the English as supremely indifferent to what other people think of their civilization but that is as nothing compared to the complacency with which the French regard the superiority of their culture. I repeatedly met evidence of this attitude. The American University Union, whose origin was described in the previous chapter and which was the representative of the Institute of International Education in France, was always my headquarters when visiting Paris. The Director of the Union, Dr. Horatio S. Krans, during his twenty years of service had done more to develop real understanding between the French and the American people than any individual American I know. He was, indeed, an unofficial ambassador of culture and had become an institution in Paris so well known was he to all official and cultural France. Whenever I visited the city Dr. Krans arranged a luncheon in my honor in cooperation with the Rector of the University and the Minister of Public Instruction.

On one of these occasions, after some of the usual complimentary remarks about French and American civilization, the toastmaster said, "Now, Dr. Duggan, is there not some aspect of your culture from which we may learn?" I was not aware at that time that no Frenchman would expect an answer in the affirmative. After a moment's hesitation I replied, "Yes, we have so much to learn from other peoples that I hesitate to mention it but in the domain of library economy I think we Americans have made the greatest progress." Attention around the table immediately became acute. I described the remarkable efficiency of our methods of cataloguing and distributing books and informing the public of new additions. I grew quite eloquent in explaining how no town and even few villages were without a public library to whose shelves people had access. When I finished the toastmaster said, "Ah, yes, I am confident that in your civilization what you describe is true and necessary. But you see in France every family has its own library and the children are brought up in the traditions of our literature. We are not so dependent as you upon public libraries." Of course, what he said was nonsense. It applied only to the *haute bourgeoisie* and not to the *petite bourgeoisie* nor to the workers. There are some libraries in French towns but the librarian usually regards the library as his own personal perquisite and sometimes looks askance at the entrance of a prospective borrower.

The French are the greatest exponents of cultural imperialism. Almost everywhere I have visited, whether in China, Brazil, Czechoslovakia or elsewhere I found *Instituts Français* and the *Alliance Française* propagating French culture. Distinguished professors from the Sorbonne especially in literature, philosophy, and history, gave lectures at the *Instituts,* which were usually attended by the élite of the community. This propaganda was not carried on in the offensive manner sometimes shown by German professors of deriding the culture of another country. The belief of the French in the superiority of their culture rendered that wholly unnecessary.

French and American Cultural Cooperation

That belief did not affect their hearty cooperation with the Institute of International Education in developing cultural ties between France and the United States. I have described at length in Chapter II the *modus operandi* of the exchange of students and teachers between the two countries. There were many other ways in which this cooperation was carried on. In 1922 the French *Office National des Universités et Ecoles Françaises,* the organization with which the Institute collaborated, offered to provide ten—later increased to twenty —*postes d'assistant* at boys' lycées in France to American men, preferably teachers. These were not fellowships but they partook of some of the aspects of fellowships. The holders of the *postes* were to be college graduates who had some knowledge of French. They were asked to give two hours each day to the teaching of oral English. They were to receive no salary but were provided with board and lodging in lycées, usually in towns near universities so that the holders might pursue courses while engaged in teaching. The *postes* were held in high esteem by young American college graduates as providing unusual opportunities to obtain a fluent command of spoken French, and to secure a knowledge of the French people, their customs and institutions. They also imparted a more correct impression of American civilization and culture than that previously held by the French students. The *Office National* provided twice as many *postes* to Englishmen as to Americans, for the French frankly admitted that they preferred the English speech of England to that of the United States.

Of even greater importance was the institution known as the "Junior Year Abroad". The University of Delaware requested the cooperation of the Institute of International Education in organizing in France a program of studies which Delaware could accept in lieu of the regular work of the junior year. The students selected were men and women of excellent scholastic standing, especially proficient in French, and of a temperament which gave promise of quick adaptability to a strange environment. They went directly after the close of the college term in June to the University of Nancy where for three months they participated in an intensive course in French designed to give an ability to understand spoken French so that they might attend lectures and to speak French so that they might discuss in class. In October they moved to Paris and matriculated at the Sorbonne. Here they pursued a carefully organized program of studies known as the *Cours de Civilisation Française* which was designed to give the foreign student an adequate knowledge of French civilization and culture. At Nancy and Paris each student lived in a carefully selected French family usually as the only foreign member of the family. He pursued his studies under the immediate daily supervision of an American professor. In addition to their daily studies the students attended the best operas and plays, visited under competent guides the museums, libraries, and churches, and made week-end trips to places of interest outside Paris.

The Junior Year Abroad was an immediate success. The students, the French educational authorities and the faculty of the University of Delaware were enthusiastic about the results. In 1923, nine students were enrolled in the Delaware group studying at Paris. Ten years later the number had increased to ninety. In subsequent years the University of Delaware accepted among its groups students from other institutions. and one hundred and twenty colleges were eventually included. In 1925 Smith College established for its own students a Junior Year Abroad which became equally popular. In that year about thirty-two attended the preliminary courses at the University of Grenoble and later the *Cours de Civilisation Française* at the Sorbonne. By 1932 the number of students in the Smith College group had risen to 49. The success of the Junior Year Abroad in France inspired the German educational authorities in 1931 to establish a similar program at Munich, although it had by no means the success of the French experiment because it was animated more by propagandist than by cultural motives.

French Education as an Intellectual Discipline

World War I struck a hard blow at the bourgeoisie. The *rentiers,* the people living on dividends, the professional classes, and the teachers in lycées and universities, found their incomes cruelly reduced. Many of the bourgeoisie could no longer support their children through the secondary schools and universities. Their sons and daughters were turning to trade and industry. Yet it was those very sons and daughters who were the heirs of the so highly prized cultural heritage. Before World War I the great majority of the advanced students in French universities were full-time students and remained so until they "conquered" all their diplomas. Since then a large proportion have had to work their way by taking such odd jobs as they could get. This situation constituted a real danger for the future of higher studies in France. Adding to this an increased economic pressure, higher standards of living or an ambition to live more comfortably than in the past, the result might well be a decrease in the number of men who give themselves entirely to disinterested studies. The increase in the number of scholarships made by the government was no effective remedy. It could not encourage the maintenance of the genuine culture which springs from society itself. This was really one of the biggest problems which confronted the French. The change in the situation caused considerable change in their outlook upon life. It embittered many of the sons and daughters of the bourgeoisie. To be compelled by necessity to fall into the ranks of the *ouvriers,* the workers, was regarded as a personal tragedy.

The effect of World War I in intensifying the competition for the prize positions in the professional, administrative, and social life of France was profound and had a great influence upon education in the lycée and university. As France is a stabilized country with a stationary population, the prize positions are not numerous and increase but little. The competition for them can be described best by the term fierce; hence no time in the period of preparation—in the lycée and university—can be lost. The French lycée is a place of work, even of grind. There are no extra-curricular activities, no dramatics, debating societies, musical clubs or magazines, which form so large a part of the life of the American college. Students work from early morning to late afternoon at their studies and then are given much work to prepare for the next day. To engage in any activity other than study is to endanger one's standing in the examination at the end of the course and possibly one's position in life.

The lycée is, therefore, a place of intellectual discipline *par excellence*. Little attention is given to physical training. Young men secure this during their period of military service, though since World War I sports have assumed an increasing importance. Moral education has a place in the curriculum, but it is nevertheless considered primarily a matter for the home. As in the United States, the French educational system permits of no religious exercise in the schools. Hence the conservatives in France like some in the United States regard the public schools as "godless". The splendidly trained teachers in the lycée give excellent instruction in the comparatively narrow curriculum, into which no "fads and frills" have a chance of entrance, as have also no such innovations in school administration as student self-government and parent-teacher associations. Mature and experienced professors who have graduated from the lycée, concentrated on their specialty in the university and taught at first under supervision, are supposed to know how to administer education. It is easy to understand why the graduate of a French lycée has a disciplined mind and a knowledge that is thorough and accurate. One has only to listen to an *"explication de texte"* to become convinced of this. This minute, detailed, intensive study and mastery of a few masterpieces or parts of masterpieces of French literature constitutes a lesson in criticism which gives students a kind of critical method applicable to all literary works. It enables the French lycée student to distinguish the first-rate from the mediocre and the third-rate, and this discerning judgment is in itself an element of culture.

I once suggested to a French educator that this proficiency might be bought at too great a price, that I saw very little attention given to the health of pupils in the schools and that practically no physical exercise was provided as a relief from mental strain. He answered, "Dr. Duggan, have you ever known of soldiers who fought as ours did at Verdun?" It was no proper answer. It did not explain the many whose health was affected by the strain and who failed to fight at Verdun or anywhere else because they did not measure up to the physical standards of the army, which were certainly low enough. My suggestion was prompted by the experience of a friend who went over with our army in 1918 as a bacteriologist. He placed his son of eleven or twelve in a lycée. One afternoon the boy was stricken by a bad toothache and had to have the tooth extracted in the evening. The next morning his mother accompanied him to the lycée and explained the circumstances to the Directeur. "When was his tooth drawn out?" asked the Directeur. "At dinner time," answered the mother. "Why didn't he do his home work then?" demanded the Directeur.

It is worth while to digress sufficiently long to contrast the educational situation in our own land with that in France. We are a young country with immense natural resources and room for more people. Our population actually increased in the decade 1920–1930 by 14,000,000. In other words, we had to provide all kinds of services not only for the population of a decade before, as did France, but for the great increase also. Moreover, during that decade, in addition to the remarkable expansion of industry generally there was the astonishing growth in our comparatively new industries, the automobile, cinema, radio, and aeroplane. These required initiative, self-reliance, creativeness, and pluck, qualities that were often as well developed by the extra-curricular activities as by the regular studies of the college. Then why be a "grind" and devote oneself to things purely of the intellect? Up to 1929, it was a poor American college graduate who could not get a job fairly early after leaving college. This was not true of the European graduate. Since 1929 the favorable condition no longer has existed to the same extent in the United States, and the possibility of the development of an intellectual proletariat now confronts us. One good educational result of the depression has been the greatly increased serious attention of our students to their intellectual as contrasted with their extra-curricular activities.

The French Family

The legal requirement introduced at the time of the Revolution that property be divided equally among a man's children resulted in the peasant's restricting the size of his family so as to secure to a few children a proper livelihood on the farms of reduced size. In this the peasant imitated the bourgeois who, in addition, demanded an easier life. The result is that from being one of the most populous countries of Europe at the time of the Revolution, relatively speaking, France is now one of the least populous. The *fonctionnaires* employed by the centralized state grew to a veritable army, making the French government one of the most overstaffed in Europe. The great majority of these *fonctionnaires* received very small salaries, but they had permanent jobs and each was entitled to a pension at the close of his official career. Their security was assured. Security was the touchstone in business life also. A young Frenchman inheriting a business would bring disgrace not only on himself but on his family were he to fail in his business and not to conserve it at least as he inherited it. Hence caution marked his activities and he grew rich slowly. Contrast this attitude with that of the young American in business, who is ever ready to take a chance. If he fails, there is no disgrace incurred, nor is he usually discouraged. He simply tries again in the same business or in another, in the same place or elsewhere.

Security plays a far greater rôle in family life in France than in Anglo-Saxon countries. Though a more lenient attitude toward masculine defections probably prevailed than among Anglo-Saxon peoples, the belief that existed quite generally among the ill-informed before World War I as to the moral laxity of the French was very inaccurate. The foreigner has usually made the mistake of regarding the boulevard life of Paris as typical of France. As a matter of fact, in no other country is the family so strong and carefully guarded an institution. The reason why the foreigner has known so little about it was because he has so seldom been admitted into it. In the family, tradition has a large place. The respect for parents is unquestioned, and control is still in their hands. Chaperonage for daughters was always more pronounced than with us though it is now in process of rapid disappearance. Security for daughters in marriage is still usually assured as the result of long and direct negotiations between both sets of parents. My own experience with French families taught me that their family life was very enjoyable, more formal than ours and perhaps with less intimacy between parents and children but nevertheless a very closely knit unit.

It was inevitable that when daughters of the common people entered the munition and other factories during World War I, family life would be much influenced. The relation of the sexes toward each other became much freer than ever before, particularly among the middle classes. Moreover, France had two million more women than men, and as marriage was out of the question for many women, they demanded the right, even before that war, to enter vocations hitherto reserved for men. They are now found in all the professions. This insistence compelled the state to provide greater opportunities for women's education. There have been lycées for girls since 1882, and French universities had women students before World War I. Since then girls have also been admitted occasionally to boys' lycées. All this makes for a distinct break in the traditional place of women in French life, in which they have been the center of the family but not an active force outside of it.

Individualism in French Life

The chief moral influence of the Revolution was an extreme emphasis upon individualism. This has been manifest in the domain of industry also. The French employers almost to this day have remained small industrialists, not inclined to merge into large corporations. French objects of export, mainly articles of luxury, are largely the results of individual workers' efforts, not of machines. Conservatives were united against the introduction of American methods of mass production in industry as destructive of the true spirit of French life. But after World War I it became a question how much longer France could hold out against greater general concentration into larger corporations. In addition to her Briey iron resources France acquired more by the transfer of Lorraine to her at the close of the war. She was also given the use of the coal mines of the Saar until 1935, while her own coal mines of the Nord were being rehabilitated from the damage inflicted by the Germans. These improved conditions suggested a change of policy. The change took place, but with characteristic French conservatism—with the consequence that French industry was unable to meet the necessary demands upon it when the present war broke out.

Individualism was also characteristic of the other factor in the industrial process, the worker. The Law of Coalitions of 1791 was passed in the interest of individualism. It abolished guilds and corporations, and established freedom of contract for individuals only. Trade unions among workers as well as combinations among employers were made illegal, but as time passed employers were easily able to evade the law. The law was not repealed till 1884 and in the meantime the worker had become a thorough individualist. Throughout the nineteenth century he suffered from low wages because to a great extent he was unwilling to be submerged in a labor union. Trade unions were, however, rapidly expanded and federated into the C.G.T. (*Confédération Générale du Travail*) in 1895. During all these years and down almost to the opening of World War I, Communists formed only a minority of the workers, though as everywhere a noisy minority.

France has been basically strong because of the stabilization of her national economy. Her population is fairly evenly divided between agriculture and industry. While the Bolshevik politicians in Russia were building a new social system in that country in favor of the proletarian worker and on the back of the peasant, the French politician has been in mortal terror of the peasant and feared to place upon him even his just share of the burden of the state. Because of the distribution of the land into small farms and the love of the farmer for his fields, most Frenchmen took the "Communist peril" lightly before World War I. Moreover, this attitude was justified not only by the existence of the landowning peasantry, but also by the fact that there was little concentration of wealth in a few hands, no real plutocracy. Nevertheless, many Frenchmen professed to be alarmed at the appearance of Communism as a menace to national tradition, national solidarity, and national security.

The French Political System

Britons and Americans familiar only with the two-party system and unfamiliar with French political life have always expressed amazement at the possibility of carrying on government with the multiplicity of parties which characterized France. Political parties were really only groups held together by very tenuous ties. It was often hard to tell to what group a deputy belonged, he changed so often. He became irresponsible and one of his chief functions, somewhat like a Congressman in the United States, was to secure benefits for his constituency, especially jobs for his constituents. The consequence of the "group system" was that the ministry governing the country at a given time was the result of bargaining among these groups. If one group did not like what the ministry did, it withdrew its support. The ministry then no longer commanded a majority in the Chamber of Deputies and had to resign. The explanation for the existence of this unstable system was historical. Napoleon I overturned the First Republic; Napoleon III, the Second Republic; and President MacMahon tried to overturn the Third. Hence the fear on the part of millions of Frenchmen of strengthening the executive power. All the political powers of government up to the recent débâcle were in the hands of the elected parliament. The President had been reduced to a figurehead. It became a political commonplace to say that in England the King reigned but did not rule; in the United States the President ruled but did not reign; in France the President neither reigned nor ruled.

Since the Treaty of Westphalia in 1648 France has had a wonderful history. During a large part of that time she has been the predominant power in Europe. The glory of her arms, the prestige of her diplomacy, and her historic rôle in world affairs have been very dear to her citizens. France would never voluntarily accept a position of permanent inferiority to any other European nation like Germany, no matter what the facts of population and birth rate might indicate. After the close of World War I she resorted to various devices to combat the German peril, but each of them was futile owing to the growing European disbelief in collective security. The building of the Maginot Line was the final supreme effort of the French to maintain security independently. But with the passage of the years security for France began to look more and more dubious as much because of internal decay as because of foreign peril.

The success of the Popular Front in the general election of 1936 marks the turning point of the French conservatives away from real support of the Republic. They did not hesitate now to cooperate with their old enemies, monarchists and clericals, who had never been willing to accept the principles of the Revolution. And at the other end of the social scale, the workers were determined to maintain the advantages they had gained and extend them by every means at their disposal. This attitude is entirely understandable, but it was taken regardless of foreign competition in industry or even of national defense. The sit-down strike and sabotage were used in munition factories working for the government. A large minority of the workers had become Communists and their leaders were more interested in the security of the Russian system than of the French. This attitude was taken with the knowledge of the ruthless suppression of all labor unions by Hitler in Germany.

The times were full of menace for French civilization. By the agreement of most of the political parties in 1934, Monsieur Doumergue, a former President of the Republic, was called at seventy-two from his retirement to form a ministry of truce. Under the French political system the Premier had no right to dissolve Parliament and demand a general election, that is, to appeal to the country unless he had the consent of the Senate. M. Doumergue demanded three reforms: 1) the Constitution be amended so that the President would have power to dissolve the Chamber of Deputies without the consent of the Senate; 2) the Chamber of Deputies retain its right to strike out items in the budget presented by the ministry but lose its right to add items; and 3) he hinted that the Premier or Ministry should have the right to dismiss from the civil service any civil servant who goes on strike and thereby endangers the efficiency or possibly even the existence of the administration of government. But M. Doumergue, who was being increasingly accused of Rightist tendencies, was compelled to resign on a budget technicality. Everyone knew that his defeat was really due to his demand for the reforms which he insisted could alone save France from dissolution.

The French people now became utterly wearied of party programs and would gladly have turned from the miserable stupidity and incompetence of the politicians to a real leader. But there was none. The German people had had a similar experience a few years previously and the majority turned to Hitler for relief. About the same time the American people gladly accepted the personal leadership of Franklin Roosevelt because of the bankruptcy of the programs of the Republican and Democratic parties. And some years later, in the desperation born of war and defeat, the British people rejected the palsied ineptitude of the Conservative party to accept the brilliant leadership of Winston Churchill. Each of these leaders was able to count on the support of many younger, able assistants in responsible administrative posts. In France during the 1920's and 1930's, however, the development of potential leaders from the strong middle classes had been stifled by the confusion of educational ideals, the restricted curriculum of the French lycée which failed to prepare for leadership in practical affairs, and the increasing inability of the bourgeoisie to pay for secondary schooling and university training. The French had no system of adult education and therefore the masses of the people were not sufficiently well informed to insist upon a strong purposeful government in the developing crisis.

In this crisis the French press was worthless. French newspapers provide their readers with excellent articles on literary, artistic, and philosophical topics, but unlike British and American newspapers they give little information about events taking place in foreign countries. The newspapers of Great Britain and the United States do not differ from those of France in representing various interests but they differ greatly in making some attempt to present the views of the opposite side. In recent years the opposite side in the French press was usually the object of bitter and unjustified diatribes. The press was not an educative influence on the French people in political, economic, and social matters, especially when these matters were of a controversial nature. Paris, moreover, has always had a reptile press which was purchasable and which even before June 1940 became the creature of Germany.

The scene in France was like that of a Greek tragedy, the inevitable approach of impending doom. The French people entered the present war in a spirit of discouragement, with ignorant military leaders, and incompetent civilian administrators. The war was lost before it began. The débâcle came swiftly.

The Vichy Interlude

Immediately following the armistice a new government was established at Vichy with Marshal Pétain as Chief of State. The Constitution of the Republic was abrogated by the Naional Assembly and a Constitutional Law adopted giving all power to the Marshal. For the old motto of the French state, "Liberté, Egalité, Fraternité" was substituted, "Travail, Famille, Patrie", indicating the replacement of individualism by paternalism. The Marshal, in whom the French people at first placed great confidence as the one who would lead them out of their chaos, regarded himself as in loco parentis and as such justified in ruling by authority and discipline. He was a known and pronounced Rightist who surrounded himself with men of his own views. In a short time the majority of officeholders having opinions not in conformity with those of the Marshal were removed and the administration of government, central and local, was placed in the hands of his adherents.

The Marshal understood the importance of using the school as the instrument to realize his views, and he personally assisted in drawing up reforms of a reactionary nature. The elective element in educational organization was abolished and teachers' unions prohibited. Religion was made a compulsory subject in the schools and Catholic schools received state support. Manual training was emphasized in the elementary school, a good thing in itself, but so implemented as to emphasize the division between those who work with their hands and those who work with their heads. The old classical curriculum of the lycée was restored in full vigor and the modern subjects limited in scope. The fees abolished by the Republic in 1936 were restored and, as in the universities, Jewish teachers were removed.

These "reforms" practically restored the conditions that existed in education when the Republic was founded after the Franco-Prussian War. The chief effect of the "reforms" was to accentuate the unfortunate divisions that already existed among the French people. The press, because of its very unfair and dishonest partisanship, was an obstacle to the de-

velopment of a public opinion that would rally the people
around a leader determined to work solely for the welfare
of the Republic rather than for any class within it. In other
words the institutions of the country which are of primary
educational influence functioned badly and the really noble
ideals underlying French civilization lost their grip upon the
people. Similar conditions in any other country can be ex
pected to bring about equally tragic results.

The Future

Can France survive this greatest defeat in her history and
resume her place as a first class power? She has done so after
major defeats in the past, in 1815 and in 1870. But in 1815
her population was greater than that of Germany and in 1870
it was the equal of Germany's. France was bled white in
World War I. Since then she has continued to practice birth
control, something to be applauded for Japan but deplored
for France. Today she has fewer people than when World
War I began. It is a question whether she has the manhood
necessary to maintain the status of a first class power. Great
Britain with a population not much greater can probably
still rely upon the Dominions inhabited by her own sons.
But for France the question is whether, in the face of such a
defeat, she can maintain prestige in colonies populated by
peoples who admire military power.

Moreover, France suffered tremendous losses of wealth in
World War I. At the close of the present war she will be
greatly impoverished. The Germans have taken everything
they could seize and as the result of devious methods of eco
nomic penetration they have a stranglehold on the economic
life of France. Today the status of a first class power neces
sitates immense resources. France was partially dependent
upon her colonies for those resources. Will she be able to

exploit them in the future as she did in the past? Material resources, however, are not the first consideration in a possible French renascence. That will be a matter of morale. At the present moment there is no such thing. The French in the homeland are dazed, confused, discouraged, characterized by an almost complete lassitude. In 1871 there was not only the desire but the determination to recover the former French position in European affairs. That was also true at the close of World War I. But in 1871 the French had Thiers and Gambetta, and in 1918 Clemenceau and Poincaré. Will a leader emerge to unite and inspire France today?

CHAPTER VI

GERMANY—HUMANISM VERSUS BARBARISM

In 1935 I visited the University of Leipzig, among other institutions, and was entertained at dinner by Professor X,* who had brought together a number of friends among the teachers of the University. After dinner he said, "Dr. Duggan, we frankly do not understand the resentment of other nations at our announced policy of rearmament. Admittedly it is a unilateral denunciation of the Treaty of Versailles but Germany cannot be accused of having commenced the process of violating treaties. That began with the repudiation of Czarist debts by Soviet Russia, now the bitterest critic of Germany. Poland's seizure of Lithuania's city of Vilna was a simple case of *force majeure,* overlooked by the Allies and the League of Nations. The evident intention of the European governments not to pay their war debt to the United States is hardly an evidence of a high regard for the sanctity of commitments. The action of Japan in Manchuria was a flagrant violation of several treaties. None of these states is a friend to Germany. Is it because we are friendless that we are condemned?" These fine men did not seem impressed by the probable evil consequences of the Nazi propaganda already in full swing in the schools and universities. The rest of the evening was spent chiefly in a discussion of the reasons for the position maintained in international affairs by Germany

* For obvious reasons I shall not give the names of living friends in Germany but only of Nazi officials, refugees, and those who are dead.

at the time and the inability of Germans to understand the dislike of them by other peoples. It was a most interesting analysis of the historical background and is worth repeating here.

Germany was almost destroyed in the religious wars following the Reformation. She lost almost half her population and had imposed upon her by the diplomacy of Richelieu a condition of impotence that lasted for two centuries. Richelieu inaugurated the French policy of keeping Germany divided into a large number of weak states faced by a strong and united France. From that time down almost to Bismarck no one referred to Germany but to "the Germanies". Germany became to a great extent the battleground of Europe. Louis XIV and Napoleon fought most of the battles on German soil. Russian, Austrian, and Swedish armies traversed German territory. When the French Revolutionary armies marched over Europe calling upon peoples to cast off allegiance to kings and give their loyalty to the nation, it was natural that the Germans would want to see their many states transformed into a united nation. Bismarck was admired by Germans because he was the architect of United Germany. Professor X considered that all these statements made by him were justified.

I did not fail to point out that while it was true that French armies fought their battles largely upon German soil, the Prussian armies of Frederick the Great also fought theirs on foreign soil; that while France conspired to keep Germany disunited, the same Frederick was the leader in the total destruction of another nation, Poland; that while Germans owe a debt of gratitude to Bismarck for the unification of their country, they must perforce admit that in accomplishing it, like Frederick the Great, he showed a ruthless disregard of the rights of peoples in his treatment of such states as Denmark and Hanover, and used some very shady methods such as the doctoring of the Ems telegram; and that though up to the time of my visit they were guiltless of violating engagements since the close of World War I, it was the Germans who inaugurated in recent times the whole bad practice by their sudden attack upon helpless Belgium in 1914 in violation of the treaty to protect Belgian independence, and afterward referred to that treaty as "a scrap of paper". My friends were fine men and admitted the truth of these statements but they did not have much difficulty in pointing out that other states had also been guilty of similar practices. They were particularly insistent that the Allied Powers promised at Versailles a program of disarmament for themselves and that this was not carried out, leaving Germany the only great power to be disarmed.

In Retrospect

The establishment of the German Empire in 1870 was welcomed by liberals generally. Germany was then populated by an intelligent and industrious people. Her universities were the rendezvous of students from other European countries and from the United States. Her attractive culture was tinged with an element of romanticism that appealed to the liberalism prevailing in the West at that time. Germany in the mid-nineteenth century was essentially the land of the poet and the thinker. But the Germany of 1870 was based primarily upon an agricultural economy that could not support her rapidly growing population. Tens of thousands of the most virile people emigrated annually. They were saved for the Fatherland by the industrialization which had begun in the decade 1850–1860 but which was much enhanced by the increased vitality that accompanied unification.

Industrialization meant competing with Great Britain which for a half century had been building a magnificent

plant and a technique of financial, commercial and industrial administration that came only with long experience. It
meant competing with the United States whose apparently
inexhaustible resources enabled her to carry on regardless of
waste and extravagance. Germany did not have these advantages and deliberately determined to rationalize her national
life. She developed scientific education on a remarkable scale.
She applied science to all forms of industry, studied the methods of business administration of her competitors and improved upon them, sent her agents to all quarters of the earth
to learn the psychology of other peoples so as to provide for
their needs. In a generation she had forged ahead to a position in the world of industry second only to that of Great
Britain and even menacing British primacy. But industrialization brought in its train additional conflicts of classes. As
in England it arrayed the agrarian and industrial interests
against each other and the workers against the capitalists.

Some Characteristics of Germans

It is fashionable among some writers in Allied countries
today to maintain that ruthlessness and brutality have been
characteristic of the Germans throughout their history to a
greater extent than is true of other peoples. These writers
emphasize the influence of the legends of Valhalla, afterwards
incorporated in the Nibelungen operas of Richard Wagner.
They point to the extermination of Slavs during the Middle
Ages by the Teutonic knights and the butcheries that took
place in the conduct of the opposing armies in the religious
wars of the sixteenth and seventeenth centuries. And they
point to the deceits practiced by the Germans during the Bis-
marckian period and since. They forget, it seems to me, that
Wagner also composed *Parsifal, Lohengrin,* and *Tannhäuser,*
which present a different attitude toward life than does his

Nibelungen cycle. Chivalry existed in Germany throughout the Middle Ages as it did everywhere in Western Europe. The religious wars in Germany were certainly characterized by fanaticism and cruelty but no more so than the wars between Catholics and Moors in Spain. Coming nearer to our own heritage, students of history will not forget the inhuman treatment of Catholics in Ireland, including clergy and civilians, by Cromwell's soldiery. Die Aufklärung, the period of Goethe, Schiller, Heine, and Lessing, and the first half of the nineteenth century saw the growth of a spirit of a fine humanism and liberalism particularly in Western and Southern Germany.

Cruelty and brutality were the characteristics rather of Prussian militarism than of all Germans, and the ruthless disregard of human rights and international obligations became a part of German military policy as the national forces were solidified under Prussian leadership. The deceit and violence practiced by Frederick the Great became the tradition inherited by Bismarck, who incorporated it into his policy of "Blut und Eisen." The long reign of Wilhelm II was characterized by repeated alarums caused by his speeches and posturings but not by cruelty and brutality. Those are the recent contributions of Nazis to German life.

The remarkable development of Germany after 1870 had been made under a constitution by which the King of Prussia was German Emperor, and Prussia had the determining voice in the government of the Empire. In Prussia in turn it was the Junker agrarian nobility that had the deciding influence. They officered the army and navy and filled the chief positions in the diplomatic and civil service. The civil service which was organized in both the imperial and state governments was founded upon merit. It was bureaucratic but astonishingly efficient. An official was devoted to his work, proud of his position and of the honor attached to it. Every official had his place in the hierarchy and looked up with respect to those above him. This stratified bureaucracy was an instrument of the Junker aristocracy and the industrialists in controlling Prussia through a complicated system of preferential suffrage. But it formed a bulwark against the control of society by a reckless plutocracy such as that which controlled some other industrial societies. There was no country in the world before World War I where the government so watchfully safeguarded the welfare of all classes of the population as did Germany. She was visited by experts from the most advanced countries to study her system of social legislation and municipal administration. But this remarkable progress was made at the expense of the political experience of her people. They did not govern, they were governed. At the outbreak of World War I from the standpoint of popular self-government Germany was little more than a political kindergarten.

The German Educational System

The aristocratic control of society, moreover, was maintained by means of an efficiently organized educational system. Beginning with the reforms of Frederick the Great, German education had spread to all classes and made Germany one of the most literate countries of the world. But education was organized into two parallel systems, one for the masses, the other for the classes. The Volksschule provided an excellent elementary education for the children of the workers. In its control clerical influence played a large part. It extended from the sixth to the fourteenth year, after which the children went to work and pursued their studies in the Continuation School to increase their efficiency in their vocation. The Gymnasium and Oberrealschule, which were pay schools, provided an education for children of the classes extending from the ninth to the eighteenth year. Immediately upon entrance a student began the study of the classics or modern languages and higher mathematics. As none of these subjects was studied in the Volksschule, even if a child of the workers could afford the small tuition fee upon graduation from the Volksschule, he would have been unable to transfer to the Gymnasium. There were, however, a considerable number of stipends to enable the sons of workingmen who showed real promise to transfer from the Volksschule to the Gymnasium, at the age of nine. As graduation from the Gymnasium or Oberrealschule was a qualification for admission to the university, to all the learned professions and to the higher positions in the civil service, it is obvious to what an extent the aristocracy and plutocracy controlled German life in 1914. Yet despite the worship of titles and the snobbishness that existed in so-called "society", nowhere were the artist and the academic and literary man more highly honored than in Germany.

The Revolution of 1918 delivered a staggering blow to this imposing political and social edifice. The Republican tradition had little strength in Germany and some of the forces that rallied to its support did so for other reasons than belief in its efficiency; for example, members of the Catholic Center Party felt that they would have much greater influence under a free Republic than under the Empire dominated by the Protestant Hohenzollern dynasty. By the Treaty of Versailles, the German navy was destroyed and the army reduced to a police force. The result was that the military caste, deprived of its position, lost greatly in political influence and became an irreconcilable element in the new Republic. The generals were replaced by the rich industrialists who after 1919 wielded a much greater influence than under the imperial regime. The industrialists were opposed by the workers who lost the docility that characterized them during the imperial regime and were determined to retain the gains made by the Revolution. The agrarians, who as in most countries prospered during the war and suffered great reverses after the war, insisted that their interests were being sacrificed to those of the industrial classes and demanded relief in the form of subsidies.

The Weimar Constitution provided for the establishment of the Grundschule which all German children were to attend for the first four years of their school life, and which was intended to be not only a common school but a nonsectarian school. It aimed at greater equality in the social life of the nation as did the abolition of all titles and privileges of birth and wealth. But it is easier to provide for a new edifice than to construct one. The Grundschule met with the opposition of conservative teachers and had little enthusiastic support from Republicans. It disappeared shortly after the advent of the Nazis.

Our American-German Cultural Relations

Under the Republic I was always a welcome guest in Germany, because five years after the signing of the Treaty of Versailles the American German Student Exchange was established, largely as the result of the vision and enthusiasm of Dr. Carl Friedrich, now Professor of Government at Harvard University. I had always advocated doing everything possible to heal rapidly the wounds left by the war and gladly cooperated with Dr. Friedrich, whose headquarters were at the Institute of International Education. When he was invited to teach at Harvard in 1927, the Institute took over the administration of the Exchange. The Institute became the sole representative of the Deutscher Akademischer Austauschdienst in the United States, and the Austauschdienst became the sole representative of the Institute in Germany for the exchange of students. In order to avoid confusion and duplication of work, it was agreed that the Institute would consider no request from Germany for a fellowship unless it came through the Austauschdienst and that the Austauschdienst would consider no request from the United States unless it came through the Institute.

During the period of the Republic the relations between the two organizations were most happy. Dr. Adolf Morsbach, the Director of the Austauschdienst, who was a very patriotic and efficient German, visited this country several times and became so thoroughly acquainted with our system of higher education that he did a great deal in a few years to help make the American German Student Exchange the largest of any under the auspices of the Institute. He was later put into a concentration camp by the Nazis, at the time of the Roehm affair in 1934, and died soon after. During his tenure of office there was developed a modification of the exchange with Germany, and afterwards with other nations, called the Work Student Movement. This was initiated and successfully administered by Dr. Reinhold Schairer.

The Work Student Movement

Under the Work Student Movement graduates of universities in Germany were permitted to enter the United States on non-quota visas, not to study in the institutions of higher learning but to secure employment in our industrial plants. These work students, as they were called, were carefully selected because it was expected that they would occupy executive and managerial positions in industrial plants at home. They wished to study American efficiency methods in industrial management and also the relations between the workers and the managers, which are on a happier footing in this country than in most parts of Europe. Although the majority were graduates of engineering faculties and wanted to enter our great industrial plants, there were some who went on farms that were scientifically worked and some who entered financial and commercial establishments. The plan was adopted with the agreement of the American Federation of Labor upon the condition that it be restricted in numbers and carefully supervised. In 1928 there were about one hundred and fifty work students, chiefly from Germany. The opportunity to come to the United States for this purpose was highly prized by the foreign students and there were always many more applications for the privilege than could be granted.

The advantages to the foreign work student were obvious. He was enabled to study our system of industrial management while actually earning his living in association with our own workers. He learned to know that important element of our social whole, the workers, often neglected in the observations of the university student. He usually returned to his own country with a valuable equipment of knowledge and skill which were real assets in his future career. Earnest endeavor was also made to acquaint the work student with the manifold activities of a cultural nature in the United States. Various national agencies appointed representatives on a central committee under the chairmanship of the Director of the Institute of International Education to meet from time to time for the purpose of exchanging experiences and discussing the problems of the work student movement. Unfortunately, with the deepening of the economic depression in the early 1930's, our Bureau of Immigration requested that the movement be given up. With millions of unemployed in our own country every job was needed for a citizen.

In the summer of 1929 a conference of returned German

work students and industrialists who had helped to finance the activity was held at Dresden. The students took a militant attitude toward work conditions in German factories. They described the happier personal relations that existed between workers and bosses in the factories of the United States. They mentioned that when a foreman or superintendent entered the factory, he had a "good-morning" for the workmen whereas in Germany he walked stiffly to his office without a word to them. The students also pointed out that whereas industrialists in Germany were frightened at socialism, there was no socialism in the United States because workers there knew of the many instances of members of their class who had become industrialists themselves. Whether these and other statements of the students had any effect in developing more human relations between workers and bosses in German factories I had no way of knowing. But they certainly impressed the industrialists who attended the conference.

In the meantime a group of fine-spirited Americans, most of them of German ancestry, established in 1930 in the United States the Carl Schurz Memorial Foundation, whose sole object was to foster cultural relations between Germany and the United States. Its officers included some of the most distinguished figures in our national life. The Foundation had a splendid program of activities and was fortunately provided with funds almost adequate to realize the program. It sent specially selected groups to study conditions in Germany which were relevant to their own work and in which Germany had attained admitted excellence, such as forestry and municipal administration. It brought exhibits of modern German art, bookmaking and handicrafts from Germany and sent them around to our schools and colleges. It also contributed generously to the American German Student Exchange of the Institute of International Education, whose

Director was one of its founders and became one of its trustees. In Germany a similar organization with the same general objectives was founded, namely, the Carl Schurz Vereinigung.

Nazi Propaganda

It is frequently stated that the Germans have been very unsuccessful in understanding the psychology of other peoples. This has been particularly true of the Nazis. Neither Hitler nor Goebbels had been abroad nor was aware of what the probable attitude of foreigners would be toward the kind of speeches and actions that had won success for the Nazis in Germany. This was even more true of the group of secondary leaders of the Nazis. Their attention had been concentrated upon winning control of Germany. Moreover, they did not care about foreign opinion. Almost immediately after Hitler became Chancellor there was established the *Aussenpolitischesamt,* i.e., the foreign department of the National Socialist Party under the supervision of Herr Rosenberg, who acted without any reference to the Foreign Office. The Foreign Office was often in complete ignorance of the activities of the *Aussenpolitischesamt,* to nearly all of which it was opposed. But in the early days of success and elation, and of control by inexperienced youth, the Foreign Office was ignored. The result was that throughout Europe, Nazi propaganda had aroused alarm and fear. The movement was not long in crossing the Atlantic and penetrating the American republics, especially the United States. It was natural that an organization like the Institute of International Education, devoted to international cultural activities, would soon become affected by this propaganda. It was when the activity was undertaken here that I became convinced of the apparent inability of the Germans to comprehend the psychology of foreign peoples.

I have mentioned that the exchange student plan met with

an enthusiastic reception abroad as well as in our own country. It was carried on smoothly and efficiently, and nowhere more so than with Germany, which was still smarting from dislike and prejudice in 1924 when the American German Student Exchange was begun. Moreover, no foreign students were so popular in our colleges as the Germans, who were attractive young men and women as well as good scholars. This situation, however, gradually changed under the Hitler regime, because many Americans began to regard German exchange students as Nazi propagandists. When a good Jewish friend, Judge Julian Mack, discussed this possibility with me I determined to gather first-hand information so as not to be influenced by individual opinions. I wrote, therefore, in 1938 to the presidents of the institutions that were most accustomed to select German students, inquiring whether they or the professors who were chiefly responsible for the orientation of foreign students would let me know whether they were aware of German exchange students engaging in propaganda. Of the sixty replies, forty-nine said they knew of no such propaganda, five thought there was some suspicion of it and the other six did not think their experience justified either a negative or affirmative answer.

I believe that the curiosity of German students about American conditions helped spread the opinion that these young men and women were engaged in propaganda. They asked more questions than other foreign students about our policies and problems, about the New Deal, the Supreme Court controversy and other issues. Our own students in Germany were at the same time asking their German fellow students about the objectives of the Nazis in many fields. No one but myself was aware that some of the German students had visited me at the close of their term to ask whether there was no way of staying in the United States. Such action would be in violation of the agreement that all exchange students return to their own country when their scholarship tenure ended. I was, I think, in better position than anyone else to realize the great influence American free life was having upon German students, as upon all foreign students.

Propaganda Run Amok

I spent some time in Germany in the summer of 1938 and as was my custom I had several interviews with the authorities of the Austauschdienst in Berlin. The Austauschdienst had sent Dr. Georg Rettig to the United States the previous year to report on the situation in higher education here. The Institute facilitated his investigation by providing him with letters of introduction to our college and university authorities. When I visited the Austauschdienst in 1938, I became acquainted with the real purpose and the results of Dr. Rettig's visits to our institutions.

Dr. Burmeister, who was then the Director of the Austauschdienst, informed me that it had been decided to open a German University Service in New York under the administration of Dr. Rettig. He was very emphatic in insisting that the project would not affect the relations between the Austauschdienst and the Institute of International Education in any way, that the Institute would remain the representative of the Austauschdienst in the United States and would continue in charge of the student exchange. He assured me that the new bureau would concern itself only with the physical and moral welfare of the German exchange students and give them advice upon personal problems. I answered, "If the other exchanges like those with France and Italy find entirely satisfactory the guidance and assistance the Institute renders their students, why is the German exchange not satisfied? As a consequence of your action the other large exchanges also will unquestionably want to establish university bureaux in the United States and that will endanger the success of the whole exchange movement. I want to tell you frankly that there is a growing dislike in the United States of the Nazi movement. The projected bureau will unquestionably be regarded as a matter of propaganda pure and simple."

My advice was not taken and in the fall of 1938 the German University Service was established. In the months following Dr. Rettig's arrival he visited a large number of colleges and universities and suggested to their administrative authorities that he would be glad to place exchange students in them, outside the regular exchange conducted by the Institute. This was in violation of the agreement between the Institute and the Akademische Austauschdienst at Berlin to centralize exchanges in each country in order to avoid duplication and confusion.

I was not surprised, therefore, when one morning in January 1939 Dean Schenk of Bryn Mawr College walked into the office with a message from President Marion Park. The Dean was obviously much upset. She informed me that their German exchange student, a fine young scholar, had become much disturbed upon receipt of a letter sent by Dr. Rettig to all the German exchange students. The part of the letter which gave most offense follows:

The Zweigstelle can be successful in its work only if individual exchange students supply it continually with short pertinent reports. Reports on the guest university are wanted from the academic as well as the political points of view. Generally speaking, there are three questions to be answered:

   (a) Which faculties come into question for a German student?
   (b) What is the attitude of the individual members of the faculty, of the head of the institution and of the student body toward the exchange and Germany?
   (c) What political and financial influences stand behind the university and influence its attitude?

Furthermore, reports are to be sent on congresses at the university in question or in the corresponding university cities. University and college papers are to be followed, and I ask you to send me all clippings from these papers which concern the academic and political relations of Germany to the U.S.A., of South America and of the Far East (Japan and China) to the U.S.A.

Heil Hitler!

Rettig

Dr. Rettig's letter to the German exchange students was unquestionably an attempt at espionage. I suggested to Dean Schenk that the College leave the matter in my hands and not publicize it. The following day I went to the State Department and showed the letter to Sumner Welles, with whom I was well acquainted as the result of cooperating with the Department in cultural matters of an international nature. Mr. Welles stated that he thought my view of the matter was correct and asked me to leave it in the hands of the State Department. I do not know what action the State Department took but in less than a month the German University Service was shut up and Dr. Rettig was on his way home.

Rettig's activities which had aroused increasing resentment in college and university circles resulted in the following resolution's being adopted by the Board of Trustees of the Association of American Colleges at its annual meeting in 1939, which was held before his action in the espionage matter mentioned above:

The Board recommends that the Association re-affirm its confidence in the Institute of International Education and that it put itself on record as being in favor of continuing student exchanges with Germany exclusively through the Institute of International Education.

A Friend in Need

It was fortunate that Dr. Schacht's visit to the United States which is described on page 62 preceded mine to Germany in the summer of 1934. Schacht wished to have it believed in the United States not only that he was not a member of the Nazi party but that he deplored its extreme actions. He invited me to lunch after my arrival—partly, no doubt, as a return for my assistance during his visit to our country but also, I think, in the belief that I might have some influence upon the thinking of persons in university circles. There were present about a dozen others from among banking and financial groups, who questioned me about American antagonism to German autarchy. I did not know at the time how valuable the renewal of our acquaintance would be to me. When I left the United States to go to Russia my letter of credit was made out solely in my name. I simply paid the bills of my daughter, who joined me in England, by drawing the necessary amounts. There had been no difficulty in England, France or Switzerland before my visit to Germany. The Nazis have always boasted of their efficiency, but I found myself in trouble because some of their banking regulations contradicted others.

When my visit to Berlin drew to a close I secured from the hotel the bills for my daughter and myself and went to the bank to draw the amount necessary to pay them. The bank official refused to permit me to draw any money to pay my daughter's bill, because a regulation provided that amounts could be drawn on a letter of credit only for the persons in whose name the letter of credit was made out. I explained that I was about to leave Germany and must of necessity pay both bills. He was polite but adamant. I returned to the hotel and explained the situation. The official there was equally polite but informed me that we could not leave until the bills were paid. I went back to the bank and again received a firm refusal to allow me to draw the necessary funds. I asked to see the chief official of the bank who was equally polite but who also refused to accede to my request. Then I thought of Schacht. I said to the official, "I am a friend of Dr. Schacht. Will you please call him up and explain the circumstances." He was quite flabbergasted by my statement but promised to fulfill the request. In a few minutes he returned to say that Dr. Schacht had ordered that I be allowed to draw whatever I wanted. I am still wondering what I would have done save for his mediation.

Nature of the Nazi Party

The National Socialist Party was above all nationalist. From the beginning Hitler repeatedly denounced the *Diktat* of Versailles. It can be readily understood how his repeated enumeration of the terms would arouse the passionate resentment of the patriotic youth. I listened one night in the early days of his triumph to the screaming of these terms by Hitler in the Berlin *Sportpalast* accompanied by the enthusiastic Heils of Berlin's youth and middle-aged. There was no one then left in Germany who would dare enumerate the far more outrageous terms imposed by Germany upon Russia in the Treaty of Brest-Litovsk in March 1918 or to suggest the probable nature of the peace Germany would have imposed upon the Allies had she won the war.

The Nazi party was also Socialist. The possessing classes had been almost ruined by the inflation. The lower middle class, largely jobless and hopeless, rallied to Hitler's support in the belief that his proposed economic reforms to bring industry, agriculture, and life generally under state control would provide it with a future. The periods of depression which followed World War I created a scholarly proletariat in Germany that provided a reservoir of restless young intellectuals from which Hitler drew his most aggressive followers. Intellectual man made way for barbarian man. The Socialists and Catholics, the chief supporters of the Weimar

Republic, were frightened by the amazing growth of their enemies, the Communists. The timid, scared by the violence of the fighting in the streets between Communist and Nazi mobs, joined the Nazi movement in the sedulously propagated belief that the only alternative was chaos. The industrialists and financiers endowed the Nazi movement in the belief that if it succeeded, Hitler would become their creature. It was a case of both ends against the middle. The influential classes that had never rallied to the Republic but only tolerated it joined forces with revolutionists to overthrow the sole support of democracy, the Republic. Hitler succeeded and out went both liberals and socialists from all positions in national, state, and local administration.

The Persecution of the Jews

In a revolutionary period there is always the attempt on the part of the leaders of the revolution to find a scapegoat upon whom the blame for the evils of the day may be placed. Hitler made the Jews the scapegoat in Germany. There had always existed some anti-Semitism in Germany and the Nazis built upon it to spread a hatred of Jews generally. The persecution resulted in regulations of ever-increasing ferocity and indecency. It became obvious that the Nazis were determined either to drive the Jews out of Germany or to exterminate them. The culmination of Nazi mass tyranny has been the deportation of urban Jews to unproductive parts of rural Poland where it would be almost impossible to survive.

The effect of the repetition of an evil action in sometimes finally causing a callous attitude toward it was made plain to me in my visits to Germany after the advent of Hitler. During my visit in 1934 some of my friends expressed as great disgust as I did toward the persecution of the Jews and showed active sympathy for their Jewish neighbors. Two years later the disgust was less pronounced in expression, and in 1938 I was made to feel that the subject was one which my friends did not want to discuss. Of course it had become dangerous to do so; and as by that time the censor prevented news of foreign disapproval from reaching the people, and as the official propaganda agencies continued to pour forth lies concerning the Jews, some of these friends may have been converted, but I doubt if many were. The fact that we are now at war with Germany does not affect my belief that the mass of the German people, like the mass of our own people, are essentially decent and humane.

The one center of open and determined opposition to all that the Nazis stood for was the American Embassy. The last time I visited my old friend, Ambassador Dodd, he was more outraged than ever. "Dr. Duggan," he said, "I hope that as you attend dinners and luncheons, you will express your opinions about conditions here as freely as you have to me." This was unwise counsel. Had I done as he suggested I would have learned nothing about the situation. Dr. Dodd was a noble gentleman but as a result of his attitude the American Embassy was to a great extent ostracized and had practically no influence with either the German government or the people. Mr. Messersmith, our consul general at Berlin, was as bitterly opposed to the regime as was Dr. Dodd and practically everybody knew it, but his attitude was accompanied by more official reserve.

At a conference held at Berlin in 1938, one young representative of the Foreign Office remarked across the table, "I hear, Dr. Duggan, that you have been imitating Dr. Goebbels." "Impossible," I answered. "How?" "You have recently established a propaganda office in your State Department, which you camouflage as a Division of Cultural Relations. I hear you are concentrating its activities on Latin America. Why?" I explained that whereas we had intimate cultural relations with European countries we had unwisely neglected to develop them with our nearest neighbors and that our intention was not propagandist but that it was to get our people better to understand and appreciate the civilization of the Latin American peoples and to get them to do the same with regard to our civilization. My explanation met with derisory smiles.

Nearly all the forces that had united behind Hitler learned to regret their allegiance. The industrialists and financiers who had expected to put Hitler into their pocket found the position reversed and were gradually compelled to put their businesses entirely at his disposal. They learned the unwisdom of financing violence. The labor unions were suppressed, their funds confiscated, and their leaders imprisoned. The unemployed had been organized into the Brown Shirts, Hitler's private army who were ready at any moment to engage in acts of violence against the Jews, liberals or persons suspected of enmity toward the regime. I was amazed at the amount of marching and countermarching in the streets of whatever city I visited. One day in Stuttgart I said in English to my daughter as we waited until the Brown Shirts passed in order to cross the street, "Certainly, the Brown Shirt is everywhere very much in evidence." A man who stood next to me and overheard me said, "What can you expect? They're well bought. That brown shirt is the only one they have, and, moreover, they get a good dinner every day." The basic reason for the consolidation of Hitler's power was the placement of even the minor leaders of the Brown Shirts in remunerative jobs.

The Decay of Spiritual Influences

Naturally, my chief interest was to discover the influence of the Nazi revolution upon the spiritual life of the nation.

It was deplorable. The Church, the university, the theatre, the press, the radio, all cultural agencies were *gleichgeschaltet,* i.e., coordinated. If the machine had become the God in Russia, the State was now the God in Germany. Of all the religious groups, the Jews of course suffered most, but they were not alone in their persecution. The Lutheran Church had always been influenced by the government in Germany but now the attempt was made to control it entirely. Many Lutheran clergymen were imprisoned or put in concentration camps. Church papers were wantonly suppressed, while the neo-pagan writers were given full liberty for their attacks. The Nazis also attempted to extend their control to the Catholic Church. But in the case of the Catholic Church, the Vatican had to be taken into account. A concordat was signed between the Vatican and the German government but was very seldom honored by the Nazis. The Catholic youth like the youth of the Protestant churches had to be transferred to the Hitler Jugend. Young Catholics in the Nazi youth organizations were compelled to engage in drills and other exercises at such times as to prevent their attendance at mass and other religious duties. They were obliged to hear constant insulting remarks directed against the sacred traditions of Christianity. The Christian Church could not fail to protest against the activities of Dr. Rosenberg, the philosopher of the Nazi revolution. He regarded the Church as an outmoded institution, teaching an effeminate way of life unworthy of Germans. It was to be supplanted by the neo-pagan Nazi state, which provided a manly philosophy of life that rejected the meekness of Jesus in favor apparently of the virility of Wotan.

Other agencies of culture had less stamina in withstanding the Nazi onslaught. The press was first put under control to do the bidding of the government in providing the "right" information to the people. Only such plays could be produced in the theatre or shown on the screen as conformed with the standards of morality and patriotism of the Nazis. All Jewish musicians and artists, and others of dubious loyalty, were forbidden to engage in their professions. This was equally true of litterateurs. The writers were forced into a literary academy from which all liberal-minded elements were arbitrarily excluded. Publishers were forbidden to bring out any work, no matter how scholarly, that might have an appeal to the mass of readers unless it incorporated Nazi philosophy. Although all the agencies of culture continued to function, the result was sterility. Many of the most creative figures in the arts fled from the country and made their contributions to the culture of other nations.

But it was in the field of education that the worst of the evil was felt. The schools gave increased attention to questions of health and diet and the building of a robust youth. Brawn, not brains, was what Hitler wanted for his army. Work camps had been established under the Republic and retained by the Nazis. In 1934 I visited seven work camps, two of which were for women. The members were a cross section of German society from aristocrat to proletarian, the idea being to transform all classes into a unified whole. Like everyone else in the Nazi regime, the members were under military discipline. Some cooked and served food and made beds, others went out to drain swamps, dig ditches and clear paths in forests. All came together at night to listen to music and readings and especially to lectures pouring contempt on democracy and indoctrinating the audiences with Nazi philosophy and its accomplishments. One should not fail to mention the summer holidays, with ocean voyages, provided for working men. Although the whole *Kraft durch Freude* movement had its origin under the Republic, it was expanded and exploited by Hitler.

New schools for the training of leaders were established

outside the regular school system and under the direct control of the Nazi party. They were characterized by an exaltation of physical fitness, a disdain of intellectualism and an emphasis upon race. They were intended to produce and did produce men devoid of weakness and humane considerations, fit instruments to supervise the worst of the Nazi policies such as mass deportation of undesirable elements in the population of subjugated countries.

The universities and Gymnasien were denuded of some of their most distinguished scholars simply because they were Jews or had been liberal in their teachings. The teachers in the sciences were least affected but all professors of history, philosophy, psychology, and economics had to make their lectures and publications conform with the views held by the Nazis in their fields of scholarship. Promotion in rank was in direct ratio to enthusiasm for the Nazi cause. Thus men of inferior quality were placed in chairs of great distinction. Bonfires were made of the books of the proscribed. Lectures and research were disturbed by the withdrawal of students to engage in political activities, to attend mass meetings and march in parades. It would be a mistake to suppose that no good work was accomplished in the German universities. In engineering, and technical work generally, the former high standards were maintained because the graduates of technical schools were needed for war purposes, but in medicine standards were unquestionably lowered. Most important, the *Lern- und Lehrfreiheit* of the university, hitherto the pride of German culture, had become a thing of the past.

One ought not forget, however, Nazi achievement in other fields. The country became covered with splendid motor roads, made unquestionably for strategic purpose, but opening up new areas for exploitation. Rivers were deepened, canals built and harbors improved. Berlin became to a considerable extent a transformed city as the result of the large building construction undertaken according to the standards of modern architecture. Rationalization made industry very efficient, usually at the expense of the worker, and Dr. Schacht with his economic missions in other countries developed a successful foreign trade.

The Germans accepted totalitarianism with comparative docility. This was true even among the intellectuals, induced by a sort of fixation of utter helplessness resulting from a powerful governmental censorship and from fanatical public excitement caused by constant and one-sided propaganda. The European nations at first regarded the Nazi upheaval with interest but comparative indifference. They had already endured eleven years of Mussolini's rantings and no great changes had taken place in the international sphere. The Nazi movement was more violent than the Fascist but it was expected that it would pass or, if it survived, would become like Fascism in Italy—more moderate with time. Moreover, in most countries Hitler was underrated. A man who at forty-five had been a failure in life, who had no educational background and little general experience, could not be expected to receive much attention. *Mein Kampf* was written while Hitler was doing time in prison for participating in the abortive *Putsch* of 1923, but it was not read till he became a national figure. Even then it was not realized that the book was really a blueprint of the future organization of Europe. Nor did the emphasis upon lying, deception, violence, and use of any means to attain the end do more at first than bring condemnation and disdain for such a leader.

But lying propaganda at home unrelieved by truthful information from abroad began to have effect. The German people gradually became convinced that a conspiracy had really been organized by the former Allies to keep Germany weak and prevent her from securing equality among the great powers of Europe. The series of diplomatic triumphs of the

Nazis beginning with the reoccupation of the Rhineland and including Anschluss with Austria, annexation of the Sudetenland and occupation of Czechoslovakia—all made without cost to Germany—unquestionably gave the majority of the German people increased confidence in the Nazi regime. The rapid succession of Nazi military victories after the war broke out in 1939, moreover, stimulated the belief among considerable numbers of Germans that they were a *Herrenvolk,* a superior people destined to govern. Politically the *Herrenvolk* hoped to organize a New World Order which would maintain peace and stability and in which they would be the administrators. Economically the New World Order would mean that the other peoples would restrict themselves to agricultural and mining occupations to provide the *Herrenvolk* with raw materials for conversion in German factories into manufactured goods, largely for sale to the inferior peoples. The New World Order was put into effect at once with utter ruthlessness among the conquered nations of Europe. They were systematically robbed of their possessions, and their soldiers who had been made prisoners of war were sent to work in whatever regions they would be most productive for the German war machine. The New World Order brought neither peace nor stability, only hatred and sabotage.

The outrages inflicted upon the subjugated nations have aroused hatreds that bode ill for the German people. On the day of the armistice it will be necessary for Allied troops swiftly to overrun all Germany, primarily to prevent the chaos that would otherwise probably follow the surrender of the German armies but also to let the German people understand through personal experience something of the bitterness they have aroused in other nations where their troops have taken over. The government immediately to be set up must of necessity be an Allied government, for it would be hopeless to decide at once to what German group that job should be given. Relief, rehabilitation, and re-education must follow, among which re-education is the most important and most difficult. If the fanatical attachment of the German youth to Nazi philosophy is not exorcised, there can be little hope for permanent peace in Europe. The Nazi terror must be extirpated and whatever government will be set up in Germany after its extinction must destroy the Junkerdom which has been the most continuous source of German militarism. That will take much time. But only then there may be some hope that the German people will graduate from the kindergarten stage of political development and undertake to govern themselves.

CHAPTER VII

RUSSIA—THE PASSING OF CAPITALIST CIVILIZATION

I FIRST entered Soviet territory by the back door, Manchuria. I bade "good-bye" to Dr. and Mrs. Grant, my hosts in Peking, one evening in early July of 1925 and left for the station to take my train across Siberia. One of the officials of the Ministry of Education was at the station to see me off, a courtesy the Chinese never fail to show and one which I deeply appreciated. The train arrived at Harbin the morning of the second day. As was my wont when traveling, I immediately began to make the necessary arrangements for my departure. To my horror I discovered that I had left my passport in a drawer at Dr. Grant's home. As the Trans-Siberian ran but once a week at that time, I resigned myself to at least a week's stay in Harbin. A young American at the local branch of the National City Bank where I presented my letter of credit gave me excellent advice as to accommodations and stores. A Russian who could speak English was working at the hotel at which I stopped and became my guide during my stay.

Harbin was then a city of two nationalities, Chinese and Russian. There were at least 75,000 White Russian refugees who formed the Russian city, living as best they could, many of them in direst poverty. Most of them had been members of the upper and middle classes and were not accustomed to fend for themselves. However, there were some physicians and engineers who managed fairly well, a few of the engineers being employed by the government of the Chinese war lord, Chang So-lin. I had to have a tooth attended to while in Harbin and the Russian dentist proved most expert. The dentist was a woman who had studied in the United States. I admired the Russians' willingness to do the most menial tasks in order merely to live, and I particularly admired their efforts to help one another and to maintain whatever they could of the old Russian way of life. They had organized a few of the finer activities of civilized life, and on the second evening of my stay I attended a concert given by a volunteer orchestra. It was an excellent concert. The saddest aspect of the situation was the unhappy fate of the women, most of them refined women. Their opportunities were few and seldom pleasant. Some had become mistresses of rich Chinese. Some had fallen even lower. The Chinese treated the Russian refugees with disdain, but the refugees were glad of any haven from the Bolshevik terror.

My passport arrived before the end of my week in Harbin, and I visited the splendid building that had formerly housed the imperial Russian administration in Manchuria and now served as the consulate of the Soviets. There must have been four hundred smelly peasants milling around on the ground floor without anyone in sight to give them information. The atmosphere was suffocating. Finally, I mounted a flight of stairs which I saw in one corner of the room and found the second floor divided into offices containing clerks. I went into several of these rooms saying in each case, "Do you speak English?" When the clerk looked blank, I inquired, "Können Sie Deutsch sprechen?" and when he still looked blank, I asked, "Pouvez-vous parler français?" That was the end of my linguistic accomplishments and I usually met with no response. Finally one man who spoke very poor German led me to a room where there was a young woman who did speak English.

I shall always be eternally grateful to that young woman.

She was kindly, intelligent, and efficient. She assisted me in filling out the many blanks which made up my application for permission to depart for Russia, and assured me she would try to push through the application so that I might leave on the train the following afternoon and not be detained another week. And she kept her word. When I returned the next morning she had arranged everything. Then I made a terrible blunder. I offered her—as delicately as I could—ten roubles. Her face flamed scarlet. "You miserable bourgeois," she exclaimed, "you think you can bribe poor people anywhere. But you will learn you can't bribe in our new society." I was never so apologetic in my life. I explained that I had just come from China where one could get almost nothing done without tipping. I begged her to excuse my ignorance of the "new society". All to no avail. She told me to get out. I did, and I made sure to get the train that afternoon. Incidentally, I discovered that any member of the "new society" working on the train would be far more willing to do a favor as the result of a tip than without one. However, I hasten to add that this young woman was but one of many sincere fanatics whom I met in Russia.

On the Trans-Siberian

Because of my illness at Peking I had been advised to stop off for a few days at a "rest house" on the railroad, halfway up Manchuria. It had been established by the imperial regime as a kind of sanitarium for officials of the South Manchurian Railroad. I arrived at the place fairly early in the morning and after breakfast followed the usual procedure of visiting the physician's office for directions. The physician told me to undress and sit in the sun for two hours, then to go to my room and lie down and he would send someone to give me a massage. To my amazement and embarrassment it was a

woman. She proceeded to her work in the most matter-of-
fact way and without any embarrassment. She was a Swede,
and spoke German and gave me a great deal of information
about the surrounding country. I found out afterward when
visiting hospitals in Moscow that the physicians did not cover
the middle part of the body when performing an operation.
Our physicians do, out of consideration, I assume, for the
feelings of our women nurses. But since a trained nurse must
study human anatomy before being licensed, the Russian
practice seemed to me the more rational. However, when I
mentioned this to physicians at home, they reacted very nega-
tively.

The rest house was not in a town or even a village. It was
isolated and perfect for its purposes. There were horses that
one could hire in order to roam about in the neighborhood.
"Roam" is the right word to use; for Manchuria then was
like our Far West in the mid-nineteenth century. One saw
plains in every direction as far as the eye could reach. In all
the country round about there was only one road, upon
which Chinese peasants from Shantung might be seen almost
daily moving north with all their household goods piled
on their little carts. The cart was nearly always pulled by a
tired horse and to the tail of the cart were tied whatever
cattle a peasant might possess. They were fleeing from the
civil wars and bandits in the homeland and seeking a haven
in which to start life anew. The Chang So-lin government
approved of their coming and they were rapidly filling up the
country. When the Japanese seized control of Manchuria six
years later, they had the government but the Chinese had the
land. At that time almost 30,000,000 of them were there.

When I took the train again at the rest house railroad
station I was fortunate enough to find on board Mr. Olin
Wannamaker, the representative of Lingnan University in
Canton. Both Mr. Wannamaker and I had been warned at

Harbin that the food on the train might not be all that could be desired, so we had brought with us considerable amounts of tinned food. As a matter of fact the meals on the train were quite good; and when the train arrived at each town most of the peasants from the surrounding country were gathered at the station to sell excellent bread, a good many varieties of cheese, boiled milk, fruits, and cooked vegetables. The prices were amazingly low because a large proportion of the passengers were peasants. We bought a delicious broiled chicken for twenty-five cents. Unlike Russia itself, the region along the Trans-Siberian suffered from no famine conditions, and we fared well throughout the journey.

Except for the gatherings at the stations the journey was pretty monotonous. There was little variety of scenery, the railroad running across tundra as extensive as our western plains and as hot and dusty as ours. I had an amusing but somewhat unfortunate experience on this part of our route. We reached Irkutsk one day about seven in the morning. It had been a hot night. I was thirsty and anxious to get a good drink of bottled water. Now the Russian word for water is "voda" and is easily confused with Vodka. When I entered the station I pointed to bottles on a shelf and said "voda". I hastily lifted the bottle to my mouth and took a long drink. I thought my throat was burned out for good for the bottle contained Vodka which is almost 50 per cent alcohol. A soldier seated near by roared with laughter at my sputtering and discomfiture. He became quite abashed when I returned good for evil by giving him the bottle, which he promptly started to empty and did empty in a remarkably short time.

We arrived at Moscow on scheduled time, doing as well—be it noted—as Mussolini's trains were then supposed to do. I do not know whether it was a unique performance of the Trans-Siberian to arrive on time or whether because of the importance of the Trans-Siberian it always arrived on time. I say this because the transportation system in Soviet Russia was in very bad condition not only in 1925 but nine years later when I visited Russia again. Derailments, breakdowns collisions with loss of life were quite frequent and usually resulted in a prison sentence for the engineer, who might have been wholly guiltless. Soviet justice always demanded that someone suffer in such a situation. To go upon a railroad journey in either year one simply placed himself in the hands of God and hoped for the best.

The Philosophy of the Communist State

It is impossible to follow intelligently events in Russia since the Bolshevik Revolution of 1917 without some understanding of the philosophy underlying the Communist state. I am dealing with this briefly in order to explain the reflections I drew from my experiences.

In August 1917, Lenin wrote *The State and Revolution,* descriptive of his concept of the Communist state. With Russian ideologists, Lenin is "always right". According to Lenin, the chief characteristic of the bourgeois, capitalist, democratic state is the existence of two great classes, the exploiting capitalists and the exploited proletariat. Lenin, like Marx, maintained that the state is the product of the class struggle; it is always the dictatorship of the ruling class and cannot be anything else. Since it is absurd to assume that the ruling class in the bourgeois state, the minority of capitalists, will ever voluntarily give up their control and privileges, their downfall can be brought about only by their forcible overthrow by the majority, the proletariat. The proletariat will then become the ruling class and the government will be the dictatorship of the proletariat, only, however, as a transition step to the Communist commonwealth of the future. Until that ommonwealth has been realized, the government will need he resolute leadership of a well-organized and disciplined evolutionary party, i.e., the Communist Party.

The state can exist only so long as there are classes. The inal aim of the proletarian revolution is the creation of a lassless society, and the first step in that direction is the detruction of the instrument of capitalist control, private proprty, and the nationalization of all means of production. It annot be expected that the transition from capitalism to Communism will be immediate. The proletariat, therefore, vill need a state but a state that will "be so organized that it nust begin at once to wither away". Lenin did not forecast vhen the state would "wither away", but merely asserted hat in a classless society the state, the instrument of coercion, vould have no *raison d'être*.

This is a very brief and, of course, inadequate description of Lenin's view of the state, a view accepted and maintained by Trotsky, Radek, Zinoviev, Bukharin and the other Fathers. The Fathers were idealists unwilling to make the compromises apparently demanded by the events of subsequent years. All of them save the exile, Trotsky, were "liquidated", while Trotsky was later murdered in Mexico.

Commissars, Workers, and the OGPU

I had hardly stepped off the train at Moscow when I made my first acquaintance with one dreadful condition which existed in Russia at that time, namely, the hundreds of thousands of homeless children wandering from place to place. Their parents had been killed in the civil wars between the Red and White Russians or they had been separated from them, in most instances never to see them again. "Bitte, geben Sie mir etwas zu essen" said a little boy to me in excellent German. I gave him some money for which he expressed great gratitude. He belonged to one of the German colonies that had been established in South Russia by Catherine II, about 1780, with the object of providing good farmers whom the Russian peasants might imitate. The Soviet government was making great efforts to collect the children into communities, for they were rapidly becoming wild. Eventually the government succeeded.

I was met at the station by Mr. Harvey Anderson and Mr. Ethan Colton of the American Y.M.C.A., its last two representatives in Russia. Mr. Anderson had been permitted to remain because he was employed by the government as a teacher of physical training. He was very popular as a football coach though he was not allowed to violate Communist principles by arranging matches between teams. These men advised me not to accept the government's invitation to stay at one of its hotels, because I should always be subjected to supervision and espionage. I gladly shared the expenses of their ménage, which contained another American, Alvin J. Miller, now Professor at Kent State University. The Russians who ran the ménage could neither speak nor understand any language but Russian, so we felt free to talk frankly about conditions. Mr. Colton left for home shortly after the close of my visit and Mr. Anderson was later expelled. The only other men with whom I talked freely were the correspondents of American newspapers, most of whom I greatly admired. I afterwards met Walter Duranty in New York. He appeared to have the greatest influence of any of the correspondents with the Soviet government, probably because of the nature of his despatches home—which often resembled bed-time stories. Some years later Mr. Duranty wrote a volume entitled *I Write as I Please*. That must have described his attitude *after* his Russian experience. Despite the generally friendly attitude of the Russian authorities to American correspondents, I doubt that any one of them wrote as he pleased while in Russia. Later I also met in Paris William Henry Chamberlin, the representative of the *Christian Science Monitor*. He appeared to me to be the most analytical of all the correspondents. This may have been partly due to his seven years of residence in Soviet Russia. The correspondent I admired most was Joseph Barnes, who later joined the staff of the *New York Herald Tribune*.

While in Russia I was taken upon several expeditions arranged by the government bureau in charge of cultural relations with foreign countries. For these expeditions the bureau always provided one of its few automobiles and a man who acted as guide and interpreter. At that time the guides were a pretty poor lot, looking as if they had recently arrived from the slums of big European or American cities. When I visited Russia again a decade later there had been a marked improvement in their appearance, intelligence, and subtlety in putting over their propaganda. However, on both occasions it was utterly impossible to make them believe any of the statements I made concerning the condition of workers in the United States.

I asked one of the most intelligent of the Soviet officials I met how true was the belief widely held in the United States that the Soviet regime was dominated by Jews. He laughed the idea to scorn. "Dr. Duggan," he said, "ours was a workingman's revolution. Even our leaders knew little about business, finance, and industry. But the Jews do and they also can speak foreign languages. Now many of the men who visit us from Western Europe and the United States are business men who hope to exploit us. They discuss business questions with our Jews who know how to meet them on their own ground. Then they return home and tell people that the Soviet Revolution was a Jewish affair. The Jews are not in control here and we should not hesitate to liquidate any of them if we found them engaging in wrong practices." I think this was a sound explanation. More than a million of the most able, intelligent and cultured Russians fled from their homeland at the time of the Revolution. The country was largely denuded of intelligence and ability. The Revolution abolished all race distinctions and the Jews, of whom Russia had several millions, received the first opportunity in Russian history to show their constructive capacity. Of the nine Commissars in office at the time three were Jews, a number out of all proportion to the size of the Jewish population.

Lunacharsky and Trotsky

The first Commissar I visited was Mr. Lunacharsky, Commissar of Education, a delightful and cultivated man who despite his culture had joined the Communist Party in the pre-war days. It was he who, when the White Russians were within twenty miles of Leningrad, had helped Trotsky put in underground places of safety the chief treasures of the Hermitage, Russia's great art museum. Mr. Lunacharsky said to me, "Dr. Duggan, I hope you will visit as many of the *Rabfaks* as your time will permit and report what you think we ought to do with them." The *Rabfaks* were the Workers' Colleges and I performed my task rather thoroughly in and around Moscow and then reported to him. "Well," he said, "what ought we to do with the *Rabfaks?*" "Shut them all up," I answered. He laughed and said, "Pretty drastic treatment! Why?" "Because," I answered, "the *Rabfaks* have no entrance examinations, no tests on the way through, and no final examinations. You say you are building a new social system. The *Rabfaks* are turning out men to help build it who are wholly incompetent for their jobs. They are drags on the whole movement." Lunacharsky laughed again. "Dr. Duggan," he said, "you have politics in your country and we have politics in ours. Our politics don't admit just now of shutting up he *Rabfaks*. But I shall emphasize what all foreign educators ay about discipline and examinations." In all probability the eports of the foreign educators would have had only slight ffect, but it was discovered, particularly after the introduc- ion of the Five Year Plan, that the technicians graduated rom these schools were almost worthless. Shortly afterwards he *Rabfaks* were emptied of their students and the reforms hat had been suggested were introduced. When I revisited Russia in 1934 I found the *Rabfaks* doing a good educational ob.

Trotsky was the next Commissar with whom I had an inter- iew. I believe he was called "Commissar of Foreign Trade". He was unquestionably a strong, dynamic, and dominating personality. Mr. Lunacharsky had talked to me in French because he did not know English. I thought I could talk to Trotsky in English because he had lived for a time in New York City (in the Borough of the Bronx) but he preferred to alk in German. Among other duties he was in charge of ranting concessions to foreigners, and his talk with me had o do entirely with business relations between the United States and the Soviet Union. He insisted that the economies of the two countries were complementary, since the Soviet Union was a great farm and the United States a great factory, nd that the Soviets needed equipment for building rail- oads, dams, and factories which the United States could sup- ly. He said that Germany would do it if the United States did not, but he preferred the United States and hoped that ecognition by the United States would not be deferred much onger.

I think Trotsky was sincere in what he said. He whole- heartedly believed in the principles of the Russian Revolu- ion and hoped they might be successfully extended to all the world. He was not an opportunist like Stalin nor as much of realist. By the time of Lenin's death (1924) it was obvious

to Stalin and other practical-minded men in Moscow that
world revolution would have to be indefinitely postponed
Stalin upheld the banner of "communism in one country",
i.e. Russia, as a model for the rest of the world to imitate
Practically all the Old Bolshevik leaders sided with Trotsky
But as permanent secretary of the Communist Party Stalin
had secured control not only of the party but of the govern
ment, and gradually safeguarded his place as dictator. In 1937
he accused the Old Bolsheviks of being Fifth Columnists for
a foreign enemy, notably Germany. Most of them were con
demned to death and at the same time the army was purged
of doubtful adherents. This is usually the way with dictators
Hitler also was compelled to purge the Nazi party of many
of his old comrades only a year after his accession to power
in 1933.

One of the visits arranged by the bureau that had us in
charge was to Prince Yussopof's beautiful estate about fifty
miles from Moscow. Prince Yussopof was the nobleman who
with some friends invited Rasputin to dine at his palace in
Leningrad one night during the war. The friends rid Russia
of that sinister figure on that night. His death did not prevent
the Russian débâcle which came shortly afterward and for
which he was to such a great extent responsible. Yussopof's
estate had been turned into a rest house for teachers. It was
one of many that the Soviet government had established
throughout Russia for people of various vocations, chiefly
workers—an admirable policy. I was shown about the estate
by the party man in charge and was accompanied by a pro
fessor of history. The professor was one of the handsomest
men I saw in Europe, tall, heavily built, with a noble beard
I had just come from Japan and was describing the damage
done to the docks at Yokohama by the earthquake of 1923
In the midst of our walk a boy hurried up to the party man
to say that he was wanted on the telephone for a call from

Moscow. He had no time to provide a substitute and was hardly out of sight when the professor said in French, "The Japanese earthquake doesn't compare in its effects with the earthquake which occurred in this country in October, 1917." He then described to me the wretched life he lived, cut off from friends, compelled to teach an interpretation of history he did not believe in, and constantly subject to espionage and insult. I marveled at his willingness to speak so freely to me. I assume that he was so overwhelmed by despair that he simply had to talk as he did for relief. I have often wondered when the poor man was "liquidated", for by the time I returned to Russia practically all of his kind had disappeared.

An Educational Fiasco

The Soviet government invited me to visit the U.S.S.R. again in 1934 to discuss the possibility of organizing a summer session at the University of Moscow, the first ever to be held in a Russian university. The program was to be organized for American and English students and teachers, and modeled after American summer sessions. I gave a great deal of time in the winter of 1933–1934 to discussing the project with several American educators and with two representatives of the Soviet Society for Cultural Relations with Foreign Countries who had been sent from Russia to the United States for that purpose. The result was a really fine program of courses designed to afford an understanding of the most important changes that had taken place in Russia since the Revolution, in education, literature, art, and social reform. The courses were to be given in English by Russian professors. Any intelligent foreigner attending them would naturally realize that they would not provide an objective exposition of the subjects considered, but would be heavily weighted in favor of the Communist point of view. Two hundred

American and thirty English teachers and students registered for the courses. I went to Russia accompanied by my daughter some three months before the opening day in order to make sure that proper provision had been made to meet such eventualities as American experience indicated might arise. I left Leningrad early in June satisfied that the arrangements for the summer session were adequate and sufficiently well organized.

My daughter and I returned from Russia to England by way of Helsingfors, as the capital of Finland was then known. I encountered the same evidences of distrust and fear that I had observed when entering Russia by way of Poland. The Russian side of the border was lined with barbed wire and guarded by Russian soldiers, and we all had to alight and have our baggage searched to make sure that we were not taking out any forbidden things. A short distance farther on, a similar barbed wire line, guarded by Finnish soldiers, confronted us and again our baggage was searched, this time primarily to prevent the introduction of Communist literature. It is difficult to describe the change in conditions and atmosphere that one experienced in Finland—the cleanliness, the good food, the obviously greater contentment of the people, and the freedom of expression and movement. We remained in Helsingfors only a day and a night but it was a delightful visit. An attractive young man whom I did not know, but who was connected with the steamship line to England, invited us to spend the morning going about the bay in his motor boat, visiting the different islands and stopping at one of them for lunch. In the afternoon we roamed about the really charming little city and left it with regret at the shortness of our stay. The Finns won our hearty admiration, which was greatly increased a few years later by the magnificent fight they made at the time of the outrageous Russian invasion. Nevertheless they are now an ally of our enemies and I see no valid reason why we should not follow the example of Britain and declare them an enemy.

Shortly after my arrival in London I was invited to make an address on my Russian experience at the regular monthly meeting of the Royal Institute of International Affairs. One of the officials of the British Broadcasting Corporation who happened to be present asked me whether I would condense my address into a twenty-minute broadcast. On the day after I delivered the broadcast I received an invitation to lunch from Sidney Webb and his wife, and my good friend Sir William Beveridge, then Director of the London School of Economics, drove me down to their place in the country. The Webbs were at that time the best known supporters in Great Britain of the Soviet regime in Russia. They had invited me to lunch in order to discuss my broadcast, with which they found a great deal of fault. They were a remarkable pair, simple, unaffected and sincere, and I enjoyed my visit. But I have seldom met people who were so naïvely impervious to reasonable argument on the Russian experiment.

As the result of my broadcast on Russia, I also received an invitation from Lady Astor to lunch with some of the people who had accompanied her to Russia several years before. George Bernard Shaw was there as was Lord Lothian, with whom I had long been acquainted. Malcolm Muggeridge, then a chief exponent in England of the Communist peril, was another. I was delighted to meet again young William Astor, with whom I had collaborated a few years previously at the meeting of the Institute of Pacific Relations at Honolulu. But I was particularly glad to meet Mr. Ivan Maisky who was then and has since remained the Russian Ambassador to Great Britain. There was considerable good-natured chaff around the table concerning the exaggerated claims of the new Utopia in Russia.

My reason for being glad to meet Mr. Maisky was the bad

news I had received that morning about the Moscow summer session. It appeared that when the American and British teachers and students landed at Leningrad they were met by the two Soviet scholars who had collaborated with me in New York and were told by them that there would be no summer session. They vouchsafed no reason, but offered to arrange tours about Russia in lieu of the courses. Immediately after the lunch at Lady Astor's I inquired of Mr. Maisky whether he knew the reason for the cancellation of the summer session. He did not, but promised to cable to Moscow at once. However, he received no answer. When I finally reached home I inquired of Mr. Troyanovsky, the Russian Ambassador to the United States, but he could supply no information. Then I wrote directly to the authorities in Moscow and received no acknowledgment of the receipt of my letter. The whole incident was an outrage on the part of the Russian authorities.

Some Comparisons between 1925 and 1934

Despite my keen disappointment over the outcome of our work for the summer session, I greatly valued my second visit to the Soviet Union because it enabled me to appraise some results of the Soviet experiment. As I walked the streets of Moscow and Leningrad the second time I was struck by the atmosphere of intense activity which prevailed. Building was going on everywhere—building of factories, workmen's houses, the new underground in Moscow and similar important enterprises. Whereas in 1925 Moscow and Leningrad had been largely paved with cobblestones, in 1934 they were to a great extent asphalted. The number of workmen's houses that had been built was astonishing, and they were superior to the old ones. But as Moscow had less than two million people at the time of the Revolution and by the mid-1930's had nearly four million, the congestion was very great. A person with a room to himself and a family with two rooms were lucky. Privacy is not a privilege highly regarded by Communists and was then almost impossible of attainment in the great cities of Russia.

Whatever may be thought of the machine age in the West, the machine was the god of Russia in 1934. The number of factories that had arisen since 1925 was very large, and they seemed to be provided with the latest machinery. Attached to most factories were technical schools for the training of factory workers and also crèches in which mothers placed their infants while at work. The machine was the instrument by means of which the Communists hoped to realize one of their objectives, namely, to make Russia as nearly as possible a self-sufficient state. They borrowed from the bourgeois countries not only the most recent types of all kinds of machinery but also practices in factory organization, such as piece-work, overtime, and bonuses for unusual accomplishment, all of which they had scorned a decade before. Attempts at running factories by councils had been given up. The Soviet government was in a hurry and only results counted. What has been accomplished since the Revolution in the rebuilding of Russian industry is little less than marvelous. In all industries the level of before World War I has been surpassed quantitatively. The best opinion seems to indicate, however, that it has fallen short qualitatively, that at least the consumers' goods produced are of lower standard. The amazing achievement of the Russian armies in World War II has revealed that in both quantity and quality Russia's new capital industries are probably unsurpassed.

The average wage was small, barely sufficient to support the workers upon the low standard of living to which they were accustomed; but the more intelligent and able received higher wages and could live better. What I have said about wages was also true of hours of work. The work-day was legally seven hours, and the week five days. But both these limitations were ignored when time was pressing. Sometimes I came across cases where men, and women also, had worked very long hours.

Then there were the *Subotniks*. Subotnik means literally Saturday, but the technical meaning is voluntary labor on the rest-day, the sixth day. All good comrades were supposed to devote part of their free day to voluntary work. In the case of the enthusiastic young Communist this was a fact, and it was really an inspiring sight to see groups of them marching in the pouring rain to some factory or public work singing lustily. But human nature in Russia is like human nature everywhere. Most comrades would have been only too glad to enjoy their rest-day undisturbed, and it was true that many performed their *Subotniks* largely because of social coercion. It did not look well to refuse to give *some* time, and it was not good policy to have the reputation of doubtful loyalty or enthusiasm. When I was in Moscow in 1934 it was estimated that one hundred thousand people were engaged in *Subotniks*. I watched them one day working on the new underground. I did not think it very productive labor. They were chiefly young people and apparently looked upon it as a kind of lark. I was told by unbiased non-Communists, however, that in time of stress very hard work was done. Certainly the new subway is a striking monument to Soviet initiative.

Soviet Russia is not a paradise for the workingman. He probably lives very little better than in 1913. Nevertheless, the great mass of workers are strong adherents of the present regime. Why? First, because they are not permitted to know that workers in other countries are any better off. Second, because of the benefits received in the way of educational and recreational opportunities, sickness and unemployment insurance. Third, and most important, because the Russian worker for the first time in his history is treated as a person and not despised. He is no longer harried by the police. He is not only permitted to participate in the administration of government, but he is a privileged member of the government.

It should be understood that Russia cannot be measured according to Western standards: not materially, because its standard of living in almost every respect is low compared with ours; not spiritually, because Russia has been shot through with the Asiatic attitude toward life, in which there has been a mixture of fatalism and mysticism, in which life has been held comparatively cheap, in which amazing hardship has been borne with little complaint, hardship that would have caused revolt in the West. Particularly is it true that the value of the person as an individual is simply not recognized in Russia. Everyone is a social, not an individual, creature, and his life is determined by the dictates of the state.

In the great Cathedral of St. Isaac in Leningrad, which is an anti-religious museum, there is a striking poster depicting the mass of the people, the peasants, supporting upon their bended backs the bourgeoisie, above whom are the aristocracy, and above them the Czar. That picture, so far as the peasants are concerned, is still true to the facts. It is upon the peasantry that the weight of the new regime falls. They support the proletariat and the bureaucracy, and in hard times they suffer most. In the winter of 1932–1933 famine prevailed in the Ukraine and the Kuban. The starving peasants flocked to the cities, but the passport system was introduced for residents of the cities and the peasants were ordered to go home and till the soil, little if any help being extended to them because of the anger of the government at the results of their partial sabotage. Of course the people in the cities suffered also, the déclassés, i.e. the bourgeoisie, most. However, I was always irritated in the years following Mussolini's March on Rome when attending social functions at home, to hear violent denunciations of Bolshevism, coupled with admiration for the accomplishments of Fascism. The ideas were expressed, of course, by the socially elect who were afraid of losing their property in some way as the result of the increasing demands and influence of the workers. Certainly Mussolini's objective had little or nothing in common with the American social ideal of which these people were supposed to be adherents. My irritation at these people was always equalled, however, by disdain for the sentimentalists who accepted as truth Bolshevik propaganda describing Communist Russia as a heaven for workers and peasants.

Under the first Five Year Plan the farms had been collectivized, and farming organized as a large-scale industry with the use of machinery. But only in 1934 did the total crop equal that of 1913. Collectivization had not measured up to the expectations of the Communists. The *Kolkholz* (collective farm) I visited was admirably organized and administered. The people seemed well fed and fairly well housed. The two schools were filled with bright children, and a goodly number of cattle were in evidence. The peasants in that Collective were apparently content with their situation. But it must not be forgotten that as a guest of the government I was naturally brought to one of the most successful Collectives.

In the dictatorship of the proletariat, aristocrats, bourgeoisie, clergymen and anyone else profiting by the labor of others were disfranchised and had no political rights. This restriction was removed by the Constitution of 1936, but the new regime is essentially a government of workers and peasants administered by Communists. The Soviet government and the Communist party are one and the same thing, however much the government may attempt to disguise the fact. About three million Communists are today (1943) governing one hundred and seventy million non-Communists in Soviet Russia. Inside the party itself iron discipline prevails and no dissent of any kind from the decisions of the Party Congress is permitted. Within the never-to-be-forgotten limitation that no criticism of the Communist regime itself is permitted, great freedom of criticism of local government, industrial conditions, and bureaucratic inefficiency is permitted to workers and peasants. This is the "democracy" about which the admirers of the Soviet system in foreign countries grow lyrical. But similar criticism from former bourgeoisie or aristocrats would be considered counterrevolutionary and would mean prison, Siberia, or death. As a matter of fact members of those classes avoid talking to a foreigner even when he has letters of introduction, for the espionage system is as ubiquitous as under the autocracy and far more efficient.

On one occasion in 1925, I had been invited to Sunday supper at a bourgeois home in an apartment house. I was admitted by a man who acted as concierge. He had owned the house under the old regime, but now was only permitted to have a small apartment in return for his service as janitor. The bourgeois whom I was visiting lived with his mother in their small apartment. He had no job and they were dependent upon the money they received from abroad as the result of the sale of jewelry that had been smuggled out by friends. What they would do when that resource was exhausted they did not know. While we were talking I heard a man with a magnificent voice singing in the court below and threw down a coin. Immediately my host and his mother showed that they were greatly disturbed. They said someone would surely report to the authorities out of which window the coin had been thrown to the singer, a former army officer who could get no work. "But," I said, "the man will starve if no one helps him." "Yes," my host answered, "but the help must be given surreptitiously. It is expected, and intended, that all bourgeoisie shall starve." Whether that is what actually happened to my host and his mother I do not know. In 1934 I could find no trace of them. However, many things other than starving might have happened in the interval of nine years. Nevertheless, I had unconsciously done an imprudent thing.

In 1934 William Bullitt was our Ambassador to Russia, the first American Ambassador since the overthrow of the Czarist regime in 1917. I knew him slightly at home and paid a courtesy call upon my arrival in Moscow. Certain acquaintances in England had asked me to give some helpful things to friends of theirs in Moscow upon my arrival there. When I mentioned the fact to Mr. Bullitt he urged me not to do it. "As soon as you left," he said, "those people would be visited by an agent of the OGPU, to discover why they had been called on by a foreigner. It would probably get them into trouble."

Though more stores were open than during my first visit, and though they were much better stocked, the Russians still presented a pretty drab appearance from the standpoint of dress. Practically no Russian man or woman wore a hat. Men wore caps; women, berets. To be well dressed meant that one was a foreigner. In 1925 it was *comme il faut* to disdain to be well dressed. The sincere Communist looked upon good dress as bourgeois and most of the rest of the people had none to put on. But in 1934 even Communists aspired to bourgeois dress. At the opera house and theatre, filled almost exclusively with proletarians, silk stockings of inferior quality, an incongruous array of colored shawls and shirtwaists, and necklaces of great variety gave evidence that the extra money made by piece-work and overtime was used by many women for personal adornment. Human nature will always conquer ideology. I was much interested in watching the way the women stared at my daughter's clothes when we attended the theatre or opera though she had intentionally worn very modest apparel. Because of her silk stockings and good shoes they regarded her legs with particular interest when we walked in the foyer while they munched their apples or bread. Even many of the Russian men tried to make a better appearance in dress. However, I made the great mistake on the night of my arrival in Moscow of attending a dinner given in my honor in a dinner coat. It was the only time I used it!

Education and Culture

It is hardly possible to overestimate the spiritual transformation that has taken place in Russia since the Revolution. The old culture in practically every aspect was scrapped and a deliberate effort made to produce a new human creature. Nowhere did the Communists lose sight of their prime objective or the determination to realize it at any cost—a classless society in which there will be no exploitation of men.

It is unnecessary to speak at length about the accomplishments of the Soviets in spreading education among all ages from infancy to adulthood and about their use of the most modern devices, like the radio and the cinema, for educational purposes. When World War I broke out in 1914 illiteracy in Russia amounted to 70 per cent; in 1939 it was 18.8 per cent. In 1914 there were about 8 million pupils in Russian elementary and secondary schools; according to the census of 1939 there were almost 32 million. At the start of World War I there were slightly more than 100,000 in institutions of higher education; by World War II, in the neighborhood of 600,000. In 1939 almost 90 per cent of the population with a secondary education and 70 per cent with a higher education were under 40 years of age. This means that they had received their education and their ideals of life under the Soviet regime. But it is worthy of mention that between 1925 and 1934 ill-considered experiments in elementary education were discarded. The Dalton Plan and the Project Methods went the way of the Dewey system and of other systems, and the Russians stabilized their elementary education according to their own ideas. All children were taught the same things: boys like girls were taught sewing and girls like boys manual training. The teacher regained his authority and, except for a greater freedom from discipline, a visitor to a Russian school would see little difference in methods from those of the West. Pedagogy made great strides both in materials and methodology. I visited an Institute of Children's Books which was quite entrancing. The books were well printed and attractively illustrated, and in content and structure seemed based upon sound principles of child psychology. The intelligent teacher in charge was showing lantern slides of places in foreign countries to an excited group of children. When his talk was finished he lent them books dealing with the places described.

I have already stated that the machine is the god of the Soviets. This is reflected in their educational system. From beginning to end, but particularly in secondary and higher education, applied science and technical subjects almost monopolize attention. The humanistic subjects occupy a very inferior place. During my last visit to the U.S.S.R. I asked a young woman student of engineering who spoke English to let me see her program of work for the current semester. There were 160 hours each of mathematics, physics, chemistry, and mechanics, 120 hours of "philosophy", and 40 of foreign language. When I asked her whether she was studying the philosophy of Plato and Aristotle or Descartes and Leibnitz, she answered, "None of that nonsense, I am studying Leninism." The girl was thin and obviously was working too hard. She was an enthusiastic Communist and in addition to her studies performed her *Subotniks* faithfully. When I asked her whether she studied history or literature, she told me that she took them as voluntary subjects at night—when she was too tired to appreciate them. Education, of course, was free and at that time students received stipends from the government in addition to board and lodging in dormitories. But many also had outside work, for family or other reasons, and these students were obviously overworked, as are most such students in the West. A recent government decree provides that hereafter only elementary education will be free—another indication of the move away from the "classless society", despite adherence to ideology.

The Russian university in our sense of the word disappeared in the Revolution. The First Moscow University consisted of a group of *Instituts,* chiefly of a scientific and technical character. Not all Institutes were part of or affiliated with the University; for example, the Institute of Law was not. Some of these Institutes were doing remarkable work. Probably nowhere in the world were more fruitful studies being made in anthropology than under the Institute of Anthropology in the distant parts of the U.S.S.R. In other branches of science valuable discoveries were made with the most inadequate equipment of books and apparatus. Everybody in the academic world is familiar with the fine work done by Pavlov in the Institute of Psychology in Leningrad. In 1934 I had the good fortune to have a talk with that remarkable old scholar of eighty-five, who was still to be found daily at the Institute supervising the work of a group of chosen disciples. In public health great progress had been made and the sanatoria, particularly in the South, were among the finest in the world.

But I doubt whether the physicians graduated from Soviet Institutes were as well trained as those of the West. In fact, despite the excellent work done in several of the fields of science and the undoubted scholarship of some of the professors, I do not believe that higher education even in science could be compared in the mid-1930's with that of the West. But when I mentioned these views to groups of students they expressed the greatest incredulity. Of course in the social sciences and humanistic branches—history, economics, politics, sociology, and philosophy—a research student going to Russia would quickly discover how the material of these subjects can be pressed into the service of Marxian dialectics. Nevertheless, I believe that whatever our political relations with Russia are to be, our educational relations should be the same as with other countries. Intellectually Russia is partly in darkness due to the ignorance resulting from isolation. News of the outside world is colored to suit the views of the government. I am convinced that the restoration of Russia to more reasonable views of Western attitudes toward human affairs will be greatly facilitated by the visits of our teachers and students to her institutions and of her teachers and students to our institutions. I do not think it would be unduly difficult to prevent efforts at propaganda. It is along lines such as these that cooperation between Russia and the West must be made, for to the observer who has information from those unfriendly to the Soviets as well as from those in government circles, there seems to be no prospect of an early change in the present regime.

The school is the chief instrument of the Communists for the perpetuation of their regime. From the kindergarten to the university, incessant propaganda is carried on in the principles of Communism and in instilling atheism and hatred of the capitalist regime and all it stands for. Every subject of study is interpreted from the Communist standpoint and any other point of view is presented not for purposes of scientific investigation and comparison but of ridicule. Should any teacher of history, politics, economics, sociology or philosophy attempt to interpret his subject from any other than a Communist standpoint, he would lose his place at once. There can be hardly any doubt that in this campaign the Communists are meeting with a large degree of success with the rising generation. This is partly due to the psychological law of repetition. It is even more due to the character of the school and university population. There are not enough seats for all applicants for admission, especially to the universities; hence preference is given first to children of the proletariat, then of the peasants, then of other people, and few of the last can be admitted. Not the least hard of the many discriminations suffered by the remnants of the aristocracy and bourgeoisie is the knowledge that their children are growing up with only so much of the heritage of culture as they themselves can impart. The most tragic people in Russia are the intellectuals who suffered persecution and exile under the Czarist regime for the sake of liberty of thought and its expression and who find themselves today the chief suspects under the present regime.

Religion in the Soviet System

In no field of culture has the early Soviet attitude changed more than in religion. That change was not due to any lessening in antagonism toward theistic religion, but to the lessened fear of the Church. The Church had been regarded as the greatest bulwark of the old regime and was to be harried out of existence. The results of ten years of persecution were evident during my visit in 1934. Moscow was formerly known as the city of forty times forty churches—undoubtedly an exaggeration. In 1934 there were but one hundred and forty-six left and fifty of these had been turned into museums and headquarters for Komsomols (Young Communists). But the flaring sign that I saw in Red Square in 1925, "Religion is the opiate of the people", had disappeared. The Anti-Religious Museum, instead of being the source of merely ridiculous propaganda, had been turned into a place for scientific study of the evolution of religion.

To what extent religion has disappeared from the lives of the mass of the people is a question that only time can answer. Every instrument of propaganda has been employed to discredit it and to ridicule the priest and the nun. In the Collective which I visited a young peasant showed me with pride his house which was unusually clean and attractive. In the corner of the main room were a number of ikons. "These are for my mother," he said, "I have no use for them." I attended a service one Sunday in a village church and was quite surprised to find it about half full. It was evidently baptism day and, though the majority of the congregation was composed of old and middle-aged people, there were some fifteen mothers who had brought their infants to be baptized. This showed that religion was not wholly dead, for it took courage to oppose the prevailing attitude. Neither was superstition dead, as was made evident by the kissing of the ikons that took place in the church after the service. This mixed attitude was well illustrated when one visited Lenin's tomb. There the peasants from the country would move respectfully around the rail separating the body of Lenin from the rest of the red chamber inside the tomb and then, upon leaving the tomb, would cross the Square to enter very reverently the most sacred religious shrine in all Russia, the "Iverskaya". Since 1934, improvements in the Red Square have necessitated demolition of the shrine.

When the Czarist police state fell in 1917, religion was almost extirpated. Its sanction of morality likewise disappeared and the early years of the Soviet regime were characterized by much licentiousness. Faced by intervention, civil war, and famine, the Soviet leaders, none of whom approved of the prevailing license, had little time to devote to moral problems. It was the existing immorality that permitted the myth of the nationalization of women to be accepted in the West, and with it the belief that the Soviets wished to destroy the family. With greater stabilization came a sterner attitude toward immorality. I found the Soviet leaders were Puritans. They frowned upon drunkenness, debauchery, and graft as great obstacles to the realization of their objectives. As in America, they introduced Prohibition, but they soon repealed the law because of the need for revenue. I saw but two drunken men during my second visit.

Divorce had been made easy. I visited the marriage and divorce bureau to see how it worked. It was merely a matter of filling out forms, whether one wanted to be married or divorced. Probably the facility of divorce, as well as the condemnation of sexual license, may account for the diminution of the latter. In the case of divorce the father of children must, according to law, give a certain percentage of his wages to their support. But Russia has been to a considerable extent a land of migrants, and an inefficient administration sometimes had difficulty in following the changes of residence of divorced men. As far as my personal observation enabled me to judge, there was very little danger of the disappearance of the family as an institution. Family life appeared to be about the same as in the past. The peasant did not beat his wife as much as formerly, partly because he did not get drunk so often but chiefly because the law emancipated woman from the status of little more than a beast of burden and placed her upon an equality with men in every relationship of life. Children, moreover, were much freer in their attitude toward parents. But the family picnics that one saw along riverbanks and lakesides seemed to indicate about the same solidarity as in the West.

Place of the Arts in Soviet Life

In the arts also the Soviets have gradually receded from their early extremism. The traditions of excellence of the old regime again govern the stage. There is no theatre, opera, or ballet in the West to compare in excellence and magnificence with the Russian. Even the most insignificant parts in a drama are played by real artists. The staging, the equipment, the lighting are wonderful. And this was even true in 1934 whether one attended the Moscow Art Theatre, where the older dramatic tradition held and where the seventy-year-old Stanislavsky still reigned, or the more modern and simple Kamerny Theatre supervised by Tairov. Nothing could have been more stimulating than the two Children's Theatres that I attended, at one of which I saw a splendid performance of "Tom Sawyer". In the early years after the Revolution most of the plays were purely Communistic propaganda, excellently staged and performed, but made to order. That could not last forever. The best of the propaganda plays, like "Red Bread" and "Fear", continued to be performed for a decade or more, and that they still had their effect was evident by the thunderous applause that always greeted the success of the Communist hero; but there had been a steady drift toward other subjects for plays, and toward the older dramas like the "Cherry Orchard", which was performed during my second visit. The rapt attention given by the proletarian audiences not only at the theatre but at such operas as "Prince Igor" and "Lohengrin", would put to shame audiences in the West. The people forgot their troubles.

What has been said about revitalizing the drama is equally true of the novel and the poem. In the 1920's Rapp, the official organization whose approval was needed in order to secure a hearing for a new book, was practically in absolute control. The result was an output of novels which became so stereotyped that no one read them. In 1932 Rapp was disbanded and a literature of greater verisimilitude came into being.

In one field of spiritual life, namely, intellectual freedom, the Soviets have not changed their position. Despite the new Constitution of 1936 restrictions are still enforced against freedom of speech, of the press, of assembly, of teaching, if criticism of Communism or of the Soviet regime is undertaken. That is regarded as counterrevolutionary. Whereas ten years' imprisonment is the maximum penalty for any other crime, including murder, death is the penalty for counterrevolution. Hence it seldom raised its head.

I had felt for some time during my second visit that I was free from one form of government repression, namely, espionage; and then an incident happened which caused me to doubt. I felt very tired one afternoon and quietly slipped out of the hotel and walked to the park under the shadow of the Kremlin, where I enjoyed watching the children play. When my daughter later came down stairs to go out, the manager asked pleasantly, "Isn't your father going out with you today?" "He is out," answered my daughter. "He is out, where has he gone?" said the manager obviously disturbed. "I don't know," answered my daughter. "But he may get lost, or something might happen to him." Obviously, the hotel people were quite concerned, and they appeared much relieved upon my return. My daughter and I had been accustomed to going out together and it was an easy matter to keep tab on us if that was what was wanted. But it was the first time I was made aware that my movements were watched.

A very different experience brought me again into touch with government espionage, this time of an undoubted character. I had learned soon after my arrival in Moscow that the ablest foreign representative there was the German Ambassador, Baron von der Schulenburg. I had received in Germany letters of introduction to various people in Moscow, some one of whom must have spoken about me to the Ambassador, for my daughter and I soon after our arrival received an invitation to lunch at the Embassy. It must be remembered that the time was about fifteen months after Hitler had become Chancellor, as the result chiefly of his anti-Communist campaign. After we entered the drawing room and had been greeted by the Ambassador, he said, "Come over here to the window. Do you see that man in the window of the house opposite? Either he or someone else is always stationed there to report who visits this Embassy."

The result of the censorship which prevailed in Russia was that the mass of people and even the intelligentsia were ignorant of the true meaning of what was taking place outside of their own country. They were kept fairly well informed by the press, but the facts were presented in such a way that they focused on one conclusion—the superiority of the Communist regime. This led to a real and widely spread belief in Russian superiority. While in Leningrad I gave a lecture in the Hall of Science to those who could understand English. It was entitled, "The Psychology of the American". I began my lecture by saying, "We Americans have unquestionably been boasters. We have told other peoples of our great achievements and assured them that to improve their condition they had only to imitate us. Then came the economic depression of 1929. We learned the virtue of humility and bequeathed all our boastfulness to you Russians." They laughed heartily and applauded. After all, it was a well educated audience and though they too were pretty well doped with propaganda, they surmised that a good deal of it was mere braggadocio.

History Repeats Itself

My observations and experiences in Russia during 1934 convinced me that once more history was repeating itself. In 1917 we witnessed a tremendous upheaval in human affairs in which old traditions, old values, old attitudes toward life were all thrown into the discard. Only seventeen years had passed and already some of the fundamentals according to which men must live in order to survive, together with some of the evils resulting from the weaknesses of human nature, were slowly regaining recognition. In industry, in education, in administration, in diplomacy, discarded practices were being resumed. Many evils had been extirpated, and certainly many benefits destroyed. Communist Russia was slowly receding from extremism. But Russia will never again be anything like what it was before the Revolution. Neither will the capitalist West, for Russia has given an impetus to state control that is being felt in every corner of the globe.

I do not want to give the idea that the Russian Communists had by 1934 relinquished their objectives. Where they yielded it was from necessity, not desire. If the world revolution had a minor place in their program it was not only because they found it did not pay, but also because they had convinced themselves that as capitalist society was in process of decay, they had but to wait for the realization of their objective. By 1934 they were firmly entrenched in power. The party numbered less than three million, and though undoubtedly some self-seekers were found in it, the party-worker's enthusiasm, determination, and ruthlessness were maintained by the difficulty experienced in becoming a member, by the strict discipline enforced, and by the periodic purgings that took place to get rid of slackers. Not only the men at the top, but the leaders below in the ranks were sincere and devoted. They were all overworked. They were all trying to do too much in too short a time. The result was a great deal of inefficiency in administration. Promises were not kept, commitments were not honored, delays were interminable. But I believe these faults were due not to insincerity in promising, but to attempting more than was humanly possible.

Moreover, they still had the faith of religious fanatics. I discussed their ideals with some of their intellectual leaders, pointing out that other great idealistic movements such as Christianity, the Reformation, and the French Revolution were of necessity seriously modified with the passage of time. Their answer was that those movements never got down to fundamentals, that their leaders, unacquainted with the philosophy of economic determinism, were unaware that the profit motive was at the bottom of practically all human evils. I discussed especially their belief that they were transforming human nature. I pointed to the illicit trading and speculation which were quite general in Russia, and they answered that seventeen years were a very short time to eradicate such entrenched evils. I asked whether they expected such human traits as ambition and pride and envy and hate to disappear, and they answered in the negative, but insisted that they could be directed to better purposes. I asked whether they did not believe that, generally speaking, those endowed with superior talents would eventually gain control. They answered that we in the West confused individualism, which they despised, with individuality, which they approved. As an instance, they pointed to the fact that as soon as they discover superior musical or artistic talent in a child they withdraw him from ordinary education to receive special training. Nevertheless, it seemed to me that a new governing class was already in process of development. The technician and bureaucrat of high rank, because of the compelling need for their services, form the new aristocracy who receive higher wages, better housing and other privileges. Lip service to Lenin's ideal is still the order of the day, but Leninism is more honored in the breach than in the observance.

The contradiction between theory and practice is too flagrant to be ignored even among Russians doped with propaganda. Stalin, who now is the one "always right", has explained the discrepancy. It is due, he maintains, to the capitalistic environment of Russia and to the activities of foreign spies and saboteurs. However, Stalin insists that the first stage in the history of the Soviet Union, namely, the liquidation of the exploiting classes, is over and that the Soviet Union can now proudly march forward to the realization of the principle of integral Communism: "From each according to his abilities, to each according to his needs." Can it be done? Already the principle is interpreted, "From each according to his abilities, to each according to his work," i.e., his accomplishment. Communism has accomplished some great things, but the answer to the question will probably be determined by the issue of the war and conditions which prevail at its close.

The Soviets and Other Nations

I have stated that the Soviets were in a hurry to realize their objectives. This perennial haste had a profound effect upon their foreign policy. As already mentioned, it was resolved to begin in 1928 an intensive scheme of industrialization under the Five Year Plan. For its success peace with the outside world was essential. Japan was an ever-present potential enemy, but nevertheless, the Soviets wished to avoid war with Japan if possible. They knew they were not ready. Part of the Trans-Siberian Railroad still had not been doubletracked, and the munitions plants in Siberia were by no means complete.

Until the rise of Hitler, Russia was the strongest European advocate of disarmament and of the release of the defeated nations from the restrictions of the Versailles Treaty. From the date of the Rapallo Treaty with Germany in 1922 she regarded Germany as her one friend among the great powers and was loud in her denunciation of the imperialistic victors of Versailles. Hitler's success in a campaign directed against the Communist peril changed all that. Hence occurred the complete reorientation in 1934 of Soviet foreign policy toward cooperation with France and her allies of the Little Entente, whom Russia had regarded as her worst enemies a decade before. The Soviet leaders were realists. To them disarmament now meant German rearmament, and a rearmed Germany the Soviets then considered as great a menace to them as to France. In the case of war with Japan a French alliance would in all probability immobilize an enemy in the West. In 1917, the Soviets announced that they had broken completely with the diplomacy of the past. In 1934, they were leaders in that same diplomacy.

Russia under the Czarist regime was a great land mass with but inadequate outlets to the sea. Russian foreign policy had for one of its main objectives securing more seacoast, especially on warm waters. As a result of the first World War and the Communist Revolution, Russia lost immense territories through the erection of Poland, Finland, Latvia, Estonia, and Lithuania as independent states. Later Bessarabia was taken by Rumania. All these territories had seacoasts and Russia became more landlocked than ever. The Soviets were never reconciled to their territorial sacrifice and waited for a favorable opportunity to recoup their loss. The opportunity arrived when it became increasingly evident that the relations between Germany and the Western Powers, France and Great Britain, would end in conflict. Both sides started to bid for Russian support. The Anglo-French negotiations were carried on with obvious distrust of Russia and with considerable reluctance. The fact is that the conservatives of England and France would have been glad at that time to divert Hitler into a conflict with Russia and thereby become rid of both the Nazi and Communist menaces. Germany had no more faith in Russia than did England and France, but was actuated solely by the needs of the moment and offered greater and more immediate gains. With German acquiescence the Soviets coerced Latvia, Estonia, and Lithuania into union with the U.S.S.R. When Germany attacked Poland in the summer of 1939, the Soviet Union in the manner of Catherine II united with Germany in its partition. Then in true imperialist fashion it demanded the cession of strategic parts of Finland and when the demand was refused began war upon that country. It was a far cry from the ideals of 1917.

The agreement Hitler made with Stalin was not of long duration. Stalin probably entered into it to enable Russia to complete the rearmament which he believed might be necessary to fight whichever side would be victorious. Hitler had entered into it so as to be relieved of that nightmare of the German General Staff, a war on two fronts. Secured on his rear, Hitler smashed his way through western Europe, failing only to conquer Britain. The loot he secured was enormous, but he needed many additional raw materials and minerals, especially oil. He fixed his eyes upon Syria, the terminus of the Mosul oil fields in Turkey, but the British forestalled him by occupying Syria. It was essential that he secure, somehow, the necessary additional quantities of oil and raw materials. In *Mein Kampf* he had already stated that these could be obtained in the Caucasus and the Ukraine.

On June 22, 1941 Hitler treacherously attacked his "friend" Stalin without warning. Stalin immediately became the ally of Great Britain whom he had sold out to Germany less than two years before, a sell-out which had resulted in so much ruin in the West. The Russian soldiers showed unusual bravery and the Russian commanders remarkable ability. It is true that in a few months the German armies had smashed their way to Leningrad, Moscow, and later Stalingrad, but they captured none. Nor did they realize their boast to destroy the Russian armies. As Czar Nicholas I said in the Crimean War, they had immense difficulty in fighting Général Janvier and Général Février.

The Russian campaign was a godsend to Great Britain and its new ally, the United States. They are furnishing aid to Russia to the limit of their capacity in their own interest and in that of the world generally, and in the meantime are preparing for the final showdown with Hitler. In this they should receive the enthusiastic support of all lovers of individual freedom and national independence. Many ultra-conservative Americans, however, have insisted that while we must aid Russia to win the war we must be on our guard against her at the peace table. No war was ever won by an alliance founded on distrust.

If harmony and unity are maintained among the chief members of the United Nations until victory has been won, all of them will want to meet the desires of their fellows to as great an extent as possible in the ensuing peace which, as is usually the case after a great war, will be a compromise peace. It is to be hoped that Russia will be willing to implement the second of the Four Freedoms, freedom of worship, which Great Britain and the United States have so much at heart. She has not only given evidence of a real desire to do that but, of even greater importance, she announced, on May 22, 1943, the abolition of the Comintern, the organization devoted to the spread of the world revolution within other countries. As the fear of the Bolshevisation of their countries was the chief reason for support of the Nazis by people in other nations, the abolition of the Comintern was a great force in strengthening unity among the United Nations. At the same time, one of the principles of the Atlantic Charter, to which the United States is committed, provides that each nation shall have the right freely to decide upon its own form of government. It is to be assumed that the United States sincerely believes in that principle and expects to see it realized at the peace table. For Americans now to doubt Russian sincerity or for Russians now to doubt American sincerity is to endanger the survival of freedom in all its forms.

CHAPTER VIII

ITALY—FASCISM, A PSEUDO-RENAISSANCE

Fiume o Morte

"DR. DUGGAN, why do you want to go to Fiume? Conditions are very chaotic there and it might be dangerous. Moreover, even if I gave you a permit the commander at Trieste might find it unwise for you to go." This was the answer Count Carlo Sforza, Italian Under Secretary of State for Foreign Affairs, gave in August 1919 to my request to be permitted to see for myself what was taking place in Fiume. I left Paris much too late to see the great demonstration in Rome which was the answer to President Wilson's attempt to appeal to the Italian people over the head of the Italian government on the Fiume question. Count Sforza, who was one of the finest gentlemen and ablest statesmen I met in Europe, finally relented and gave me the permit and the commander at Trieste honored it. I shall never forget the wild ride in an army camion over the mountains of Istria. There were but two passengers, an Italian army officer and myself. The driver went at such breakneck speed around dangerous corners that the officer had to order him to go more slowly. Once we reached the seaside resort, Abbazia, the ride along the beautiful coast was delightful. We arrived at Fiume just before dinner and I at once became the target of propaganda.

At dinner I sat opposite a charming old gentleman who regaled me with an earnest statement of the lack of culture

of the Yugoslavs and the primitive nature of their civilization. "I am amazed that your President, a university professor, should want to place this city in the control of such a
crude and ignorant people." This was the general attitude
of the Italians in Fiume who formed the upper class as well
as the majority of the population. The city was under the
administration of the Inter-Allied Council, awaiting a settlement. That night I wandered about the streets and read flam-
ing electric signs such as "Italia o Morte", which indicated
the determination of the Italians that the city was to be
theirs. There was an atmosphere of restlessness and tension
among the population which boded ill for whatever settlement might be reached. I spent the whole next day talking
to and questioning people in different parts of the lovely little city in the hope that I might arrive at some idea of a fair
solution. The city had been built up at enormous expense
as the one port of the Hungarian part of the Austro-Hungarian monarchy and a splendid commerce had been developed. The Yugoslavs regarded it as the only outlet for their
great hinterland and feared that the Italians would discriminate against it in favor of Trieste as a port, a suspicion which
was later to prove true. I crossed the bridge over the little
stream which separated Fiume from its Yugoslav suburb,
Sushak, and watched the peasants bringing their produce to
Fiume. Although Fiume could not live without the imports,
the Yugoslavian peasants had to pay the tariff on their produce before they were allowed to enter the city.

It was most fortunate that I stayed in Fiume but a few days,
because before a week had elapsed d'Annunzio settled the
question by seizing the city for Italy on September 12, 1919,
and no one was permitted to leave it for some time. As I
passed through the cities of Northern Italy upon my return
to France I found prevailing the same spirit of restlessness
and tension that existed in Fiume and a feeling of forebod-

ing as to the future. For an adequate understanding of this attitude a brief glance at the recent historical background is necessary.

The Risorgimento *and After*

The political unification of Italy which was consummated in 1870 was the work of liberals, among whom were found the most enlightened aristocrats and bourgeois. They were nearly all of Northern and Central Italy; but the great mass of the peasants had been indifferent. South of Rome the majority were probably ignorant of what had taken place. The succeeding task of developing spiritual unification was herculean. The people of the different parts of Italy were separated from one another not only geographically, but linguistically. They often had difficulty in understanding one another's dialects. The general use of the Italian language of today is the result not only of the spread of schools but of the transfer of army recruits from one part of Italy to do service in another. The consummation of unification left much bitterness in its train, particularly in the relations between Church and State, and the Roman question with its "Prisoner of the Vatican" remained an open sore in the body politic down to the advent of Mussolini.

The country was very poor, without any of the natural resources of coal and iron which would enable it to participate in the great industrial development that characterized northern Europe in the last decades of the nineteenth century. The international situation was not the happiest. The Austro-Hungarian monarchy on the northeast was an enemy, and France on the northwest was unfriendly. Italian unification was too much the result of foreign assistance and too little of Italian effort. This fact impressed itself upon the Italians themselves and after the enthusiasm over unification had been spent, Italy resigned itself to the more urgent task of building the economic and financial life of the nation.

This disillusionment had developed a spirit of pessimism among the intellectuals. Italy's spiritual contributions to humanity had been largely idealistic, in the field of literary and aesthetic criticism, of philosophy and ethics. But gradually an arid, sterile positivism characterized her scholars who regarded Herbert Spencer as a prophet. A soulless materialism developed among the middle classes. The parliamentary regime which had been introduced in 1860 resulted in a breakup into numerous political parties often animated by selfish personal and group interests. In the competition among them for support, the suffrage was extended to larger and larger groups of illiterate and politically inexperienced people. The result was that local politics was almost everywhere characterized by boss rule in its worst form, and national politics by inefficiency, incompetence and considerable corruption. The pessimism of patriots was increased in 1896 by defeat in the war with the "despised" Abyssinians and by the resulting loss of prestige in Europe. The opening of the twentieth century saw Italy pervaded by a spirit of intense dissatisfaction in spite of the fact that its economic condition had greatly improved.

At the same time the Italian national spirit had been roused again by the remarkable work of Benedetto Croce, and to a considerable extent of his disciple, Giovanni Gentile, with whom Croce later broke off all relations. These two philosophers diverted attention from foreign spiritual influences, directed it to the great contributions of Italy in the field of literature, art and philosophy, and succeeded with the younger scholars in substituting for the materialistic philosophy of life then general among intellectuals an idealistic philosophy in consonance with the Italian spirit. When World War I broke out a new vital spirit already inspired the young scholars and intellectuals who were demanding a revived Italy. With time they might have succeeded in inspiring their countrymen generally, but at the moment they were politically a minority.

Italy went into World War I in May 1915 with her people divided in sentiment. They suffered great hardships during the conflict and were completely disillusioned at its outcome. They believed the other Allies had seized the major prizes and left them with gains wholly incommensurate with their sacrifices. The disbanding of the armies increased the unemployment which was already so pronounced. The years 1919 and 1920 were years of enforced idleness and hunger. A general revulsion against the war policy, and everybody that favored the war, took place. An army officer's uniform was a signal for insult, not acclaim. Strikes and lockouts spread in all the industrial centers. The farm laborers demanded not only an increased share in the crops but a division of the big estates. Finally, in Piedmont and Lombardy the workers seized the factories, which they worked themselves, and in some instances ran up the red flag. But when the stock of materials on hand was exhausted and they could receive no credit from the banks, they marched out, the factories reverted to their owners, and normal conditions soon followed.

The Fascist Revolution

During this chaotic period the Fascist group formed a small and unimportant party. At the last free election in 1921, they elected only thirty-five out of five hundred and thirty-five members of parliament. The Italians, unlike the Germans, never voted for Fascism. It was really when the Communist movement had already failed that the Fascists came to the front. Moreover, there was an open opposition to Mussolini for three years after he came to power in 1922. The Italian people are guiltless of the crimes of the Fascist regime. Some of the original Fascists were idealists, rather proletarian in their sympathies, but the majority were selfish opportunists determined to seize upon the prevailing chaos as the chance to realize their ambitions. After the seizure of the factories by the workers, they were joined by super-patriotic students, young ex-soldiers, officials and capitalists, and moved farther and farther to the right. The utter breakdown of the government during the previous years of anarchy, the incapacity of the old politicians to meet the situation, their bickering and petty trading in the face of social chaos persuaded many that the only hope for the permanent return of law and order was in supporting the Fascists. Their strength grew with the passing months until finally as the result of the March on Rome in October 1922 the Fascists, in violation of the "Statuto" or constitution, took over the government of Italy and the control of society.

The Fascist hymn is entitled "Giovanezza, Giovanezza"—Youth, Youth. The youth of Italy particularly had been inspired by the revived idealistic philosophy of Croce, emphasizing the Italian spirit; they had become intensely patriotic as the result of the war and its subsequent disappointments; they were outraged at the impotence of the democratic parliamentary regime to function in the face of national danger and humiliation. They turned readily to a different conception of society which promised more for Italy. The Fascists were originally composed of so many diverse and even irreconcilable elements that a philosophy of the movement only gradually evolved, largely as the result of frequent purges. Their conception of society, as in all totalitarian countries, is absolutely at odds with that of the liberal state. With them the state is the one stable element in a changing world. It is an end in itself, and the loyalty and obedience of the individual to the state is unquestioned. In return every individual, according to Fascism, enjoys the protection of the state. His voice is supposed to be heard in its policies though it is in reality only a "yes" voice. Fascists maintain, however, that the individual cannot express himself through representation based on geographical divisions because of their many conflicting interests. Representation is to be vocational and equally divided between employers and workers. The strikes and lockouts which had characterized the former regime had no place in the new one.

Since the Roman Catholic Church represents the historic faith of Italy, Fascism practically predicates the union of Church and State. This attitude culminated in the Lateran Treaty of February 11, 1929, which finally settled the Roman question. The Vatican had always maintained that the Catholic Church could not function as a universal institution if it were subordinated to any national state. The Lateran Treaty provided that Vatican City was to be an independent entity with the right to receive and send ambassadors and to have other practicable civil rights as a sovereign state. The Lateran Treaty introduced an anomaly within the Italian state, but it removed a long-standing bitterness which had been the cause of disunion among the Italian people. It was the one successful act of Mussolini's diplomacy.

Education under Fascism

Croce had taught that what is needed to create a new education is not a mere dissolvent of the old but a new force and a new purpose. Gentile found these in Fascism. Fascism, like every revolutionary movement, used education as the chief instrument to realize its objective. Its objective was an organic and totalitarian state, controlling the lives, wills and consciences of its people, a state which would emphasize not free social inquiry, opinion or action but its own authority.

Gentile was appointed Minister of Education with extraordinary powers in October 1922. He was a progressive reformer and at once gave a new direction to the Italian school system, reforming its aims and curricula without tampering needlessly with the organization that already existed. He abolished the non-sectarian school and based education upon the religious and aesthetic principles in life, contending that education must be religious because children need a foundation for moral life and it must be aesthetic in order to free the creative element in life and contribute to its spiritual enrichment. Had the Gentile reforms been realized the cause of progressive education in Italy would have been greatly advanced. He strongly advocated substituting new ways inspired by a new zeal and experimentation for the old formal instruction, rigid curriculum, bureaucratic administration, working for diplomas and other outmoded practices. But everything was to be done within the principles of the absolute state, the "Nuovo Stato". Unfortunately for Italy, Gentile, who was more interested in education than in politics, was followed in a very few years by a rapid succession of Ministers of Education who were ignorant of his aims and purposes and devoid of his enthusiasm. Gradually clerical control was extended from the elementary to the secondary school, and textbooks had to receive clerical approval. University rectors and deans were no longer elected by the faculties but appointed from Rome. No professor dared teach in opposition to the regime.

The early changes in education were but a part of the greater changes in government generally. Shirking and inefficiency in administration were swept away. Intensive programs in irrigation, road building, public health and sanitation were undertaken, even beyond the financial ability to support them. Recreational opportunities for the workers, sports, and competitive games were blue-printed and in some places introduced. The whole life of the people was suffused with pride in their country and of confidence in its future. The former inferiority complex of the Italians seemed to give way to a swashbuckling attitude toward the rest of the world. The Junker spirit had crossed the Alps and Deutsche Kultur gave place to Italianità.

The Fascist achievement in the beginning was valuable, but it was accompanied by an increasing loss of liberty. The narrowing of legislative activity finally resulted in absolute control vested in the Dictatorship. Local self-government was abolished and administration centralized at Rome. The press was muzzled and freedom of speech and of assembly disappeared. The regime was soon firmly in the saddle; but before a decade had passed, the murmurs of discontent were audible and came from practically all classes of society. Yet espionage and delation made men wary of expression. When two friends met in Italy at that time they criticized the regime; when three met, they sang Giovanezza.

Personal Experiences with the Fascist Regime

In 1928 I sailed to Naples via Gibraltar and was met by my good friend, Raffaelo Piccoli, Professor of Philosophy at the University of Naples. Professor Piccoli, who spoke English admirably, had been in the United States several years before and had been circuited by the Institute of International Education among our colleges to lecture on Italian civilization. He became an ardent admirer of American civilization and before his return home married Miss Blanche Goode, Professor of Music at Smith College, and at the time of my visit had three small sons. I had not been in Naples since 1898 and found it a transformed city. It was thoroughly clean, the cows were no longer driven to your door to be milked, and

the importunate beggars had become invisible. How much
of this reform was to be ascribed to Fascism is a question, but
the change was certainly considerable. While traveling in a
tram with Professor Piccoli, I happened to mention Mussolini's name. Professor Piccoli looked around and whispered,
"Don't mention his name. Everyone will at once listen. You
may be understood and what you say may be reported. Use
a circumlocution."

Professor Piccoli was not only a non-Fascist but he was
known as a liberal. Nevertheless, he was respected by the
Fascists. He took me one evening to visit Benedetto Croce
and regaled me on the way by describing the manner in
which Croce and his wife routed a band of violent Fascists
who had invaded their house on the night of October 26,
1926, in order to give castor oil to the philosopher. His wife
met them at the door of the bedroom and denounced them
so vehemently and wielded her broom so emphatically that
they had to be satisfied with the partial destruction of his invaluable library. Croce happened to be in a gracious mood
on the night of my visit and I enjoyed his comments on prev-
alent conditions of Italian culture. They were not at all favorable. He obviously liked Piccoli, as apparently did everyone
I met in Naples. As I left Naples for Rome and bade Professor Piccoli and his wife "Good-bye" he said, "Please, Dr.
Duggan, try to secure an invitation for me to an American
college, however modest the position and stipend may be. I
cannot stand it here any longer." I promised to do so and immediately upon my return to the United States I consulted
President Neilson, who also admired Piccoli, and he extended
an invitation to him to become Assistant Professor of the Italian language and literature at Smith College. Before the invitation arrived at Naples, Piccoli had accepted a call to become
a professor at Cambridge University in England. The family

settled there very happily but unfortunately Professor Piccoli died within three years.

My Interview with Mussolini

Rome in 1928 was also a very different city from the Rome of my visit ten years previous. Mussolini boasted that it was no longer a morgue in which to observe the dead monuments of the past. A spirit of energy and vitality appeared to dominate the place. Blackshirts were everywhere, sometimes rendering real service, sometimes making a nuisance of themselves by their officiousness in interfering with the ordinary affairs of ordinary citizens. By this time, most of the enemies of the regime were in exile. Two friends, Count Sforza and Professor Salvemeni, were doing yeoman service in our country by means of their lectures and writings in combatting the Fascist propaganda that was in full swing not only among Italian colonies in our large cities but among susceptible elements to be found in the salons of many conservative people of wealth and influence. In the United States at that time I sometimes heard it stated, "We need a Mussolini here."

I was not long in Rome before I was invited to dinner by Nelson Gay. Gay had lived in Rome almost his entire life and was the most influential American in the city. He was a real scholar in Italian culture and had what was probably the finest library of the *Risorgimento* in all Europe. He had invited the Minister of Education to meet me because of the latter's desire to have Italy become a participant in our student and professor exchange with foreign nations. I did arrange for the exchange with Italy a little later during my visit, with excellent results. But the reason the Minister was most anxious to meet me was to explain his desire to select an Italian university which might become a real center for American students in which, while studying in their special

field, they might become familiar with the language, literature, history and civilization of Italy. He had decided upon
Padua as the university and requested me to be the guest of
the university during a visit to Padua to discuss with the Rector and deans the means whereby the desired objective might
be realized. I personally believed that Florence would probably be a more desirable place to launch the project, but
since I had never been to Padua, I told him I would gladly
go there on my way out of Italy. He assured me that he would
telegraph ahead so that I might be met and proper arrangements be made for my visit.

Before the visit to Padua, Mussolini's teacher of English,
a lady with whom I had become acquainted, made an arrangement for an interview with him. Upon my arrival at
the Palazzo Chigi I found his anteroom crowded with officials
and visitors awaiting their turn to be heard. When the door
was finally opened for my entrance I found myself in the
celebrated long room across which one would have to walk.
Mussolini was seated at the end opposite the door and sur-
veyed the visitor as he approached. Our interview was in
French because at that time his English was very feeble. I
found him to be a man of apparent strength and power. He
was very gracious and after the usual courtesy of inquiring
whether my visit to Italy was a happy one, he began to talk
of the project of Padua about which the Minister of Education had evidently informed him. But not for long. A secretary came in with a note, Mussolini excused himself, the
doors were thrown open, thirty Bolognese lined up with
Mussolini in the center, a moving picture was taken, a photograph of Mussolini was handed to each of the Bolognese,
who departed rejoicing that they had personally spoken to
Il Duce. It was a great show, not unknown in other countries.
Noting the crowd of persons outside waiting for an audience,

I said a few words of adieux to Mussolini and took my departure.

To Padua and Out

I was unable to discover whether the trains in Italy were now on time, a fact much vaunted by the Fascists, because an American friend invited me to motor north through the hill towns, a trip which I enjoyed very much. I had always admired the sturdy Italian peasant folk whom I had found to be a kindly and tolerant people. Their attractive qualities had not been modified by Fascist propaganda. Many had put on a black shirt to camouflage their real sentiments. I stopped to visit a friend, Miss Edith May, several days at Florence. She was highly regarded by the Italians, Fascist and non-Fascist, because she maintained a fine, high class center for American young women of wealth and intelligence to which she invited distinguished European scholars and men of affairs to discuss problems of contemporary interest. Miss May personally was careful to keep her opinions to herself but her old mother had no such inhibitions and denounced Fascism in unmeasured terms. Their butler also told me of the beating up of his young son of seventeen by a Fascist gang because of his refusal to enroll as a Fascist.

On the day of my departure for Padua I was so busy that I was unable to take a train at an earlier time than one that arrived at Padua at 10 P.M. Alas, Fascist efficiency had fallen down! There was no one to greet me, and no one at the station who could speak English, French or German. I managed to make a taxi man understand that I wanted to go to a "buon albergo". As was my custom in a strange city, I watched intently the streets we passed through till we came to the hotel. It was a comfortable inn and after breakfast the next morning I started out about nine o'clock to go to the university. When I arrived I was told that the Rector would not be there until eleven. As it was evident that no one expected me, I decided to return to the hotel. But I suddenly realized that I knew neither its name nor its location! I had arrived quite late the night before and had not noticed the name and I had sallied forth in the morning without taking note of it. It was quite a perplexing situation, for my bag with all my belongings was in the hotel. At first I thought of visiting the police and asking them to call up the hotels but gave that up as asking too much. Finally, I went back to the station and hired a taxi, telling the driver to take me to a "buon albergo". As we drove along I again watched the streets even more intently than on the night before. Presently we came to a big building where I remembered that on the previous night we had turned the corner to the left. I ordered the taxi driver to do so and we did not go far before I recognized the hotel.

When I returned to the university at 11 o'clock, the Rector was full of apologies. He had not received the telegram notifying him when I would arrive. He had in the meantime arranged to have a group of the professors at luncheon and they all displayed the greatest enthusiasm for the idea of an American center. The longer they discussed it, the more doubtful I became of its possibility. However, I said nothing, partly because the talk was wholly in French very rapidly spoken and partly because the Rector was to take me to the Center later in the afternoon. I motored almost ten miles from the city to a palace that had been sequestrated from an Austrian nobleman during the war. I asked how the American students were to get to the university and the Rector informed me that the government was going to establish a bus line between the palace and the university. The palace had lovely grounds and the Rector assured me that tennis courts and other means of carrying on sports were to be constructed.

There was a delightful pond in the grounds in which the Rector explained that the students might swim. The palace itself was a big building with many high-ceilinged rooms that obviously would be cold in winter. I explained to the Rector the comfortable character of our dormitories and commons but he assured me that those needs had been foreseen and that the government had set aside $75,000 to make the place ready for occupancy by the American students.

Finally, I came to the real crux of the matter. I asked the Rector how many American students he expected. He answered that expenses would be met if there were 100 but he hoped there would be as many as 150, that he had been informed there were 500 at the University of Paris. I trod on a little more dangerous ground by asking him why he thought American students would want to come to Padua. "Don't you know, Dr. Duggan, that Padua is the greatest center for the study of law in Europe?" "Yes," I answered, "but our law is a very different system of law." "But we have great scholars in all fields of learning under whom American students could study." "How many could teach them in English until the Americans learned Italian?" I inquired. He admitted that there were very few but that more would be provided, if necessary, and he inquired how the Americans understood the instruction in the vernacular in the French and German universities. I explained that French and German were taught in our high schools and colleges, and he was amazed to learn that the language of "the cradle of culture" was taught in but few institutions. The Rector was a kindly old gentleman whose feelings I did not wish to hurt and I diverted his attention to other topics.

When I arrived in Milan I wrote a note to the Minister of Education explaining why I did not think his scheme was feasible. But the whole experience was an additional evidence of the profound influence that the United States had begun to exert in foreign countries owing to the awakened consciousness of the importance of American civilization and education.

Because of a number of complications my arrival in Milan on this particular occasion was at a most unfortunate time, namely, late on Saturday night. It was unfortunate because I was almost without funds and I knew that probably no bank would be open the next day at which I might present my letter of credit. Moreover, I was due in Lucerne the next afternoon for an important conference. But the occasion provided me with a feeling of immense satisfaction at being an American. The next morning I explained my predicament to the proprietor of the hotel to which I had gone the night before and asked him whether he thought any banker in town would be willing to give me funds on my letter of credit. To my astonishment and pleasure he answered, "Dr. Duggan, I shall be delighted to lend you whatever funds will be necessary to take you to Lucerne and you can send the money back when it is convenient." When I expressed my gratitude, he added, "I have never yet rendered a service of this kind to an American who failed to keep his word."

Fascist Foreign Policy

The enthusiastic youths who formed the backbone of the Fascist party were fed with dreams of a future world order in which Italy would have a commanding place. In Rome, which all young Italians tried to visit sooner or later, visitors were surrounded with the symbols of Rome's imperial grandeur, the Forum, the Colosseum, the arches of Trajan and Constantine, Hadrian's tomb, and other inspiring symbols. Their imaginations were fired by the speeches of Fascist leaders: once more the Mediterranean was to become *Mare Nostrum;* once more the peoples on its shores opposite Italy were to fall under Rome's civilizing influence. The new school books gloried in the period of Italy's history when Rome governed the civilized world. School teachers emphasized the determination of Fascism to realize another such period of Italian glory.

The Fascist leaders, particularly Mussolini, were realists. Wherever they looked in the sphere of their immediate activity, the Mediterranean, they found obstacles to the realization of their aims under the dominion of England and France. England controlled both outlets of the Mediterranean at Gibraltar and Suez, and dominated it in the center at Malta. France had driven Italy into the Triple Alliance in 1881 by assuming a protectorate over Tunis, which Italy had marked out for herself. Moreover, both France and England had given scant attention at Versailles to the claims of Italy to share in the division of German colonies. Again, Italians were outraged at Clemenceau's ill-concealed attitude of contempt for Italy as a second-rate power. France and England were regarded by Fascists as bloated plutocracies and cowardly democracies, and they solaced themselves by repeated outpourings of contempt for the social systems of those two countries.

Mussolini was determined to get a real "place in the sun" for Italy but he was going to get it without going to war for it. Except for the Corfu incident of 1923, he engaged in no risky adventure until Japan's invasion of Manchuria in 1931 disclosed the weakness of the League of Nations and the unwillingness of its two dominant members, France and England, to resist aggression. When the Fascists determined to attack their fellow League member, Ethiopia, the League imposed sanctions which failed because of the attitude of reactionary influences in England and France. The imposition of oil sanctions, which alone could have been really effective, was delayed until German troops reoccupied the Rhineland in March 1936, and then in the excitement was abandoned.

Mussolini emerged from the Ethiopian War with thorough contempt for England, France, and the United States. Thereafter, he determined to cooperate with Hitler who had denounced the League's collective action against Italy. This cooperation became increasingly a matter of the subordination of Italy to Germany until it became a commonplace that instead of being a partner Mussolini had become the prisoner of Hitler.

When France lay in the dust in June 1940, Mussolini—like most people in Europe—expected that Britain would be compelled to surrender in a fortnight. Prepared or unprepared, Mussolini would have to get in on the winning side if he were to share in the spoils. On June 10th he delivered his "stab in the back" by declaring war on France and Britain. In October Italy attacked little Greece which was allied with France and Britain, but the Greeks were fanatically determined to defend their country and were so successful that Mussolini had to be rescued by Hitler. At the same time his invasion of Egypt from Libya resulted in his army's being driven back helter skelter by the British, who also liberated the whole of Ethiopia. The hoped-for division of French colonies was postponed till the end of the war. In the meantime Mussolini had become immersed in a terrible conflict, the outcome of which no one could foresee. As the "prisoner of Hitler" he had lost armies, territory, and prestige. Axis Italy, like conquered France, had become a camouflaged German satrapy.

The entrance of the United States into the war made a profound and discouraging impression upon the Italian people. Italian immigrants in the United States had kept the people at home informed of the enormous resources of their new homeland and of the dynamic character of its population. They gave little hope of Axis success in the war and deplored Italy's entrance into it. It is to be regretted that not the

Fascists alone, but millions of anti-Fascists must suffer bombardment of Italy from the air and invasion from the sea. But whatever may be desirable in peace, it is not possible in war to distinguish between a people and its government. With the victory of the United Nations, Italy will be rid of the Fascist gang and will probably resume the evolution toward economic and social progress which was interrupted by the advent of Fascism.

CHAPTER IX

SWITZERLAND AND DANUBIA

Switzerland—Model of Ordered Liberty

IN ALL my visits to Europe since the first World War, I never failed to go to Switzerland. I would have done this under any circumstances because of my deep interest in the continued success of the Swiss Confederation in keeping people of French, German, and Italian origin settled in distinct areas and nevertheless living in harmony and mutual respect. But naturally as a convinced believer in the League of Nations I was inspired particularly by the desire to learn how the League was meeting the great burdens and responsibilities entrusted to it in the post-war world. It is unnecessary for me to state here my conclusions as to that problem. I wish now to describe some of my experiences which led me to those conclusions. In all fairness to the League, it ought to be understood that some of my critical comments were the result of visits during the summer when the regular sessions were not being held.

The League had its headquarters in Geneva which I discovered to be a conservative, socially exclusive city, many of whose citizens did not regard the establishment of the League in their city with any too great enthusiasm. Yet some of its residents were among the most stalwart adherents of the League. William Martin, the editor of the splendid *Journal de Genève,* provided in its columns admirable résumés of the most important conferences and activities of the League and, of even greater value, courageous and critical editorials as to their wisdom. Guillaume Fatio, a banker, was indefatigable in his efforts to make Geneva an attractive rendezvous and educational center for the thousands of visitors who came to the city every summer. William Rappard, Professor of Political Science at the University of Geneva, was one of the wisest exponents of the League's place in the life of the world of today. As a member of the Mandates Commission, his courageous and searching analyses of the reports of Mandatories raised the Mandates Commission to a place of high esteem among all students of public affairs. I have always felt honored in being permitted to call these men my friends. There were others whom I also valued highly for their sane and intellectually detached attitude toward international affairs.

The International Commission of Intellectual Cooperation

I attended one of the formal openings of the Assembly of the League which, like formal gatherings generally, was a pretty futile affair. The Hall of Reformation was crowded with people of many nationalities, among them a large number of Americans. Though the Assembly was the final authority, the real work of the League was performed by the various commissions some of which, like the Opium Commission, the Health Commission, and, as mentioned above, the Mandates Commission, rendered admirable service. The United States, although it was not a member of the League, was frequently represented on its commissions. Though the United States ignored the League in the early months of its history, it soon learned that some of its own most important activities could not be carried on successfully without the League's cooperation.

One of the League commissions was the International Commission of Intellectual Cooperation composed of representatives of the various national committees of intellectual cooperation. Dr. Robert A. Millikan, President of the California Institute of Technology, was the first American representative. When he was unable to attend I usually acted as his substitute and I became well acquainted with the members of the Geneva Commission. In the early days of the League Gilbert Murray, who became permanent Chairman, represented Great Britain; Albert Einstein, Germany; Mme. Marie Curie, Poland; Paul Painlevé, France; and the distinguished botanist, Sir J. S. Bose, represented India. If the work of the Commission had depended upon these eminent representatives the situation would have been pretty hopeless because, except for Professor Murray, they spent their time and the time of the Commission in discussing projects which they had brought down from the clouds and which were usually impossible of realization. Fortunately the Commission had in its later membership such practical administrators as Sir Frank Heath of England, Professor Krisline Bonnevie of the University of Oslo, Norway; Dr. Hugo Krüss, the Director of the Staatsbibliotek of Berlin; M. G. de Reynold of the University of Berne, Switzerland; and Dr. José Castillejo, who represented the Junta para Ampliación de Estudios of Madrid, and men of like qualifications. Under the wise guidance of Professor Murray, they accomplished considerable of value.

Despite its distinguished membership, I do not think the Commission accomplished much that was really constructive. It was almost always wholly academic in its discussions and very timid in its approach to the problems it discussed. It shied away from questions of a controversial nature especially if these questions had any political, economic, or social significance. The Commission lost an opportunity to render a great service to Education by ignoring elementary, secondary, and adult education and confining its interest to the field of university work. I do not mean that the Commission did not accomplish some good work. But its work lacked significance and vitality and had little bearing upon the great problems that confronted the world, even problems of deep educational import. In its later years the Commission adopted a much more realistic attitude, partly owing to the presence of Dr. James Shotwell, who succeeded Dr. Millikan as American representative, and regularly insisted on a frank and courageous treatment of the questions under discussion.

The League treated the International Commission of Intellectual Cooperation with considerable indifference and gave it little support, either moral or financial. Lord Robert Cecil, one of the strongest supporters of the League, voiced the position of the English in opposing the establishment of the Commission as "a dangerous innovation". The French tried to make use of it as an instrument for their cultural propaganda. When they were not very successful they established and almost alone supported the International Institute of Intellectual Cooperation at Paris. The conferences of experts in the various fields of culture held at the Institute sometimes resulted in excellent conclusions, but they were seldom implemented. In fact, the chief function of the Institute seemed to be to deluge the various national committees with such voluminous reports that few members had the necessary time to read them. It is to be hoped that in a reorganized League the International Commission of Intellectual Cooperation, which ought to be not only the center of inter-cultural understanding but a stimulus to creative thinking in its field, will have more adequate support and greater prestige.

The League, Loadstone for Americans

Large numbers of intelligent Americans were strong supporters of the League and thronged Geneva during the summer. Some of them established their summer homes on the lake. Many purposeless dilettantes were also attracted because distinguished representatives from different nations were there. These Americans were highly flattered by having their hands kissed by minor officials of the different legations—a custom alien to the mores of their own country. In the early days of the League its officials were burdened during the summer by the demands upon their time and attention made by visiting Americans who wanted all kinds of information and advice and made insistent requests for tickets of admission to meetings of League commissions. Manley Hudson, Professor of International Law at Harvard, one of the strongest advocates of the League in the United States and at present a judge of the Permanent Court of International Justice, secured from one of the American foundations sufficient funds to establish the American Committee at Geneva. The Committee rendered an inestimable benefit to League officials by acting as a headquarters to provide the services formerly required of them by visiting Americans. It was also the rendezvous where residents from all parts of the United States might become acquainted with one another and plan for campaigns of education at home in the interests of a better understanding of the League's work. One of the most vital services of the Committee was as a forum at which current League problems were discussed by members of the Secretariat and representatives of the different nations that were members of the League. The Committee was for Americans an indispensable unofficial organ of the League. It always had the unfailing support of Arthur Sweetser, the only remaining American representative of high rank in the Secretariat of the League.

Geneva as an Educational Center

It was only natural that establishment of the League's headquarters in Geneva should make that lakeside capital a world center for the study of international affairs. Education has always held a place of prominence in Swiss national life. The elementary schools founded by Pestalozzi in the eighteenth century have been extended until every district, even high in the Alps, has its own free school. Illiteracy is unknown in Switzerland, and the country's intense interest in advanced education is reflected by her numerous high schools and colleges. With a population of less than four and a half millions, Switzerland supports seven universities, a federal institute of technology, and a commercial college. Prior to World War II, some two thousand foreigners studied annually in Swiss universities.

Of some importance as an instrument of education in the philosophy underlying the League and in a description and criticism of its activities was the School of International Studies of which Professor Alfred Zimmern was Director and which was carried on every summer. Professor Zimmern was one of the ablest supporters of the League in England. He was a most lucid and logical expositor of international problems. I was so convinced of this that I afterward circuited him among our colleges to deliver lectures to our students on the contentious international problems confronting the world at the time, a task he accomplished very well. He had an unusual facility for drawing out the views of the students themselves.

The School was the meeting place of men and women, especially students, from all parts of the earth, but at every session Americans formed the largest contingent. This was due partly to the fact that Professor Zimmern delivered his lectures in English, usually the only language known to the Americans, but was also due to Professor Zimmern's clear and persuasive exposition of a subject. Moreover, the issues received a comparatively fair and objective treatment unless the interests of Great Britain were involved, when Professor Zimmern obviously leaned to "virtue's" side. The "Zimmern School", as it was popularly known, became a Genevan institution familiar to thousands all over the world.

As the years passed Geneva naturally became a great center for the study of man in his political, economic, and international relations. The University of Geneva attracted students from practically all the countries of Europe for its courses in those fields, especially at its summer sessions. The Graduate School in International Affairs, of which Professor Rappard was Director, provided specialized work for a small group of advanced students who produced some excellent monographs. This was also true of the International Labor Office which government officials, advisers to great industries on labor relations and independent investigators attended in increasing numbers. One of the finest educational organizations in Geneva was the International Bureau of Education, devoting itself to the fields of elementary and secondary education. The Bureau was in communication with educational systems and particularly with individual educators of a progressive kind in every country. Its reports and statistics were a mine of information and its Director, Pierre Bovet, and its indefatigable Secretary, Miss Marie Butts, were held in the highest esteem everywhere. For most of these educational activities the splendid library building presented to the League by Mr. John D. Rockefeller, Jr., was a gift of unusual value. A unique collection of documents on all aspects of the work of the League was made available in one place and as the result of the efficient work of the American librarian, Miss Florence Wilson, the cataloguing, distribution and use of the material attained unusual value and significance. It stimulated imitation in libraries in most European countries, to the great benefit of their scholars and citizens.

Not every organization of an educational nature established by Americans lived up to its promises or possibilities. Mr. and Mrs. Alexander Hadden of New York established the Students' International Union at a fine house on the Rue St. Leger not far from the Opera House. It was visited at almost all times by students for rest, conversation, reading of magazines, teas and suppers, and general recreation. It had a board of sponsors made up of distinguished figures in international life and a local working committee to supervise its activities, composed of such eminent residents of Geneva as Professor Rappard and M. Fatio. But its administration was scarcely international or democratic. It was primarily a proprietary affair of Mr. and Mrs. Hadden in which neither sponsors nor students had very much to say. Mrs. Hadden selected the Director and usually dropped him at the end of a year—seldom by mutual consent. There was a great deal of complaint by the students at the imposed control and of dissatisfaction by sponsors at the lack of an international spirit. As time passed such sponsors as Gilbert Murray, William Rappard, and Guillaume Fatio resigned from the Board. On the outbreak of the war the Students' International Union closed, but another international student center, the *Maison Internationale,* already in existence, took its place and has carried on successfully during the war.

Several of the organizations of an educational nature that were established at Geneva after the founding of the League had in course of time appealed to the Rockefeller Foundation for grants to enable them to broaden and strengthen their activities. When the League was founded Mr. Raymond Fosdick became one of its important officials but resigned after Mr. Harding was elected President of the United States, as he felt that an American should not occupy an important political post in an international agency of which his country was not a member. But he did not lose his faith in the essential importance of the League nor his desire to be of service to it. Mr. Fosdick subsequently became President of the Rockefeller Foundation, and when I was about to go to Europe in 1930 I discussed with him some of the appeals that had been sent to me at times by various educational organizations in Geneva. He assured me that if it were possible to federate them on a sound basis, the Foundation might be interested in giving assistance for the support of such federated groups. Upon my arrival in Geneva I called together the representatives of all the interested agencies. The federation was to be set up democratically with the representatives of the different organizations in general control, but as it was impossible to secure a working agreement to that effect the scheme fell through.

Fascists and the League

When I was in Geneva in 1930 substituting for Dr. Millikan as American representative on the International Committee of Intellectual Cooperation, I had an illuminating experience which helped to explain one of the reasons for the downfall of the League. One morning while I was eating breakfast I was told that two Italian gentlemen wished to see me. They informed me that they had traveled overnight to have the interview. Then they launched into a diatribe against the League. They denounced it as an instrument to implement the power politics of France and Great Britain. They gave at length the reasons why the Four Power plan proposed by Mussolini for the solution of Europe's problems was so much superior to anything that would come out of what they dubbed the "talk club of Geneva". Now I had practically no official standing at Geneva and could not understand why I should have been approached in this manner save as a despicable attempt to sow the seeds of disunion among friends of the League. I soon showed my resentment and they left. The Italian people are not, of course, to be blamed for this questionable action but it was in full accord with the evil policy of the Fascist party.

As the years passed my admiration for the Swiss people and their government constantly increased. The threats and insults from Fascists and Nazis did not deter them from carrying on in their accustomed ways though they of necessity were compelled to move cautiously and with circumspection. The attempt of Mussolini to detach the Italian canton of Ticino from the Swiss Confederation failed completely. No part of Switzerland has been more anti-Nazi than the German area. During my last visit to Switzerland in 1938 I rejoiced at the evidences on all sides of the preparations being made to defend to the last their centuries-old freedom. During the present war Switzerland has become an enclave surrounded by the German and Italian armies, yet the proud traditions of Swiss democracy have remained unshaken. Despite numerous public threats by Nazi officials, Switzerland's press continues to report news received from all belligerent as well as neutral quarters, and its editorials on occasions have been boldly outspoken. All foreign legations are allowed to publish bulletins in the four official languages of Switzerland, and distribute them freely to anyone who asks for them. Most significant of all, perhaps, is the generous and cordial reception given by the Swiss people—at considerable personal sacrifice—to more than 13,000 war-tossed refugees from near-by countries now under German occupation.

The International Labor Organization

During World War I the workers in the Allied countries rendered loyal service to their governments and insisted that recognition of that service be made at the peace conference. Their demand received added stimulus as the result of the Bolshevik Revolution in Russia in 1917. Statesmen at the conference were anxious to prevent the Revolution from moving into the Allied countries as it had already more than wedged into defeated Germany and Hungary. Largely under American guidance, the International Labor Organization emerged as the defense instrument of Labor in the difficult years ahead. Then for twelve years we scorned it even more than we did the League and finally entered in 1934, soon to become its leading member. A "Labor Charter" was adopted by the International Labor Organization at the time of origin and this charter has since guided the Organization in its development.

The establishment of the International Labor Organization was one of the most constructive accomplishments of the peace conference. To secure the agreement of employers, workers, and governments merely to have their representatives come together and discuss the nature of possible remedies to better working conditions was an achievement in itself. These representatives soon discovered that their points of agreement were far more numerous than their points of difference, because they were nearly all animated by a sincere desire to improve working conditions in advanced industrial countries and to ameliorate the lot of the peasants in backward countries.

The I.L.O. is an autonomous organization which to a considerable extent decides upon its own membership. As soon as it was established it invited Germany and Austria to its first conference in 1919. A country like the United States may be a member of the International Labor Organization even though it is not a member of the League of Nations, and most of the countries that have resigned from the League have retained their membership in the I.L.O. This, however, is not true of Germany, Italy, and Japan, all of which were once members of the International Labor Organization as well as of the League but have now resigned from both. In totalitarian countries, where the government is everything, there are no really significant associations either of workers or of employers.

The remarkable accomplishment of the International Labor Organization during the past two decades has been largely due to its first Director, Albert Thomas, a Frenchman, and to E. J. Phelan, a Briton, now Acting Director. The Office had determined from the beginning that the splendid labor conventions and resolutions of the Organization would be founded upon factual knowledge, and its research department has accumulated the largest single collection of social and economic literature in the world. Virtually all industrial problems: hours of work, wages, contracts, unemployment, migration, labor statistics, social insurance, and many others have been carefully studied, some of them for the first time. Moreover, where adequate information could not be obtained from the study of reports, technical experts were sent afield to secure additional information, and sometimes to give advice or to render assistance that had been requested. Upon the outbreak of the second World War the Economic Intelligence Section of the League Secretariat and the International Labor Organization moved across the Atlantic, part of the former to Princeton, New Jersey; the latter to Montreal, Canada.

I had become acquainted during my visits to Geneva with some of the splendid personnel of the International Labor

Office who, as far as I could observe, discharged their functions with the Organization alone in view. During my last visit in 1938, I had the opportunity to discuss the work of the I.L.O. with John G. Winant whom I had met once before in the United States following his term of office as Governor of New Hampshire. I found him thoroughly informed about his official tasks as Assistant Director of the I.L.O. and at the same time one of the most modest of the men of vision whom I have met in Europe. It is easily understandable why he has proved his worth as our wartime Ambassador to Great Britain.

The Swiss American Student Exchange

The relationships of the Institute of International Education with Geneva and its institutions were very intimate but they were not confined in Switzerland to Geneva. Before I made my second visit to Switzerland, in 1925, after the founding of the League, Dr. Butler as President of the Carnegie Endowment requested me to discover to which city in Switzerland a library of 3,000 volumes on United States civilization ought to be presented. Similar presentations had been made to other European cities. When I first visited the public library at Zürich I was astonished at the many evidences of efficiency in its administration, so lacking in European libraries generally. My astonishment subsided when I learned that the man who served as its Director, Mr. H. Escher, had studied library economy at the New York Public Library. My recommendation to the Endowment was to present the library to Zürich and that was done forthwith.

Zürich is the largest city of Switzerland and the center of the German Swiss population. It is Switzerland's most important manufacturing city and leads a very vigorous industrial life. It is also a great educational center, having not only its own university but also the highly regarded Technische Hochschule. The Rector of the Hochschule, Dr. Arthur Rohn, became the chairman of our Swiss committee of selection in the student exchange between the United States and Switzerland. The other members of the committee were the Rectors of four Swiss universities. When I first visited Zürich, Dr. Rohn graciously invited these gentlemen to meet me at dinner and we discussed the possibility of a student exchange between the United States and Switzerland, an idea which met with their enthusiastic approval. During the discussion, our talk turned to the Swiss institutions of higher education and their function in providing for the needs of a population of four millions. I knew that the requirements for a degree, especially in scientific studies, had been progressively advanced so that the standards were unexcelled anywhere in the world. I said, "Dr. Rohn, you can't absorb all these graduates in so small a population. What do you do with the surplus?" "We export them," answered Dr. Rohn. "Where?" I asked. "To the United States and to backward regions," he answered. Wherever they went, the surplus students were welcomed because of their trained intelligence and devotion to their work. The same qualities made the Swiss exchange students welcome guests at our own colleges and universities. Since the establishment of our exchange with Switzerland, the Institute of International Education has sent almost one hundred of our students to Swiss institutions of higher education and received in return one hundred and fifty Swiss students. The Swiss exchange has been in every way satisfactory. Even after the outbreak of the second World War, Dr. Rohn continued to send students to our institutions although our government refused to give passports to United States students to study in Switzerland. Certainly when the war is over the Swiss exchange is one that we shall want to expand as much as possible.

Danubia

One of the casualties of the first World War was the Hapsburg Empire. After an existence of at least seven centuries during a considerable part of which it was the dominant European power, it disappeared almost overnight. During the fifty years preceding its fall it had been organized as a Dual Monarchy, the two parts being Austria and Hungary. The government in each division was wholly out of touch with the great forces that were determining the future of Europe. Moreover, the greatest jealousy existed between the governments of the two divisions, and the Empire was held together with difficulty. Franz Josef was the emotional cement. When the collapse came, the Hapsburg Monarchy had few mourners, even among Austrians and Magyars. But the autopsy soon showed that it had had at least one great virtue. It had been held together as an economic unit that provided free trade among the nine nationalities that comprised the Empire and enhanced the material welfare of their populations. In post-war reconstruction, that economic unity must unquestionably be reconstituted.

Austria—Stepchild of Europe

There was little hope for post-war Austria as a viable state. She had not only been reduced from 115,000 square miles to 32,369 square miles, and a population of 30,000,000 to one of 6,500,000, but she was made up of an enormous head, Vienna, with a population of 2,000,000 and a weak body with the rest of the people scattered over it. Moreover, Vienna had been a great industrial and financial city, the center of commercial relations not only of the Hapsburg Monarchy but of most of the Balkan countries also. The raw materials for most

of its industries had been imported and were now cut off and
the so-called Succession States were determined to build up
their own financial and commercial life. Again, there was not
only the greatest antagonism between radical Vienna and
the rural areas, but there was the bitterness between the conservatives and the Socialists of Vienna itself. The war had
brought Austria to ruin, and after the war unemployment,
relief, and inflation reduced her to bankruptcy. There was a
considerable popular demand in the country, especially by
the Social Democrats, for Anschluss with Germany as providing a greater economic support. France was determined to
prevent the union and under her stimulus the League of Nations granted the Austrian government a loan of 880,000,000
schillings and appointed an auditor to reorganize its finances
and budget. From that time until the Nazi invasion, Austria
led a troubled and precarious existence.

I did not visit Vienna after the war until 1925. I found it
a changed city, presenting a shabby-genteel appearance. A
great effort was made to keep the streets clean, the parks attractive, and the beautiful public buildings in good order,
but the effort was visible. Though the Viennese love of music
and drama kept the opera and theatres open, the old glamour
had departed. The former café life with its fun and gaiety
had disappeared. There was little singing and dancing, and
people looked subdued and discouraged. But many, nevertheless, maintained a smiling courage. One of my pleasantest
experiences in Vienna was the result of an invitation from a
professor of anthropology to spend late Sunday afternoon
with a group of friends riding about the beautiful forests surrounding Vienna and taking supper—which they carried with
them—in the open. These men were all well-traveled scholars
and it was a delight to listen to their tales of experiences in
foreign parts, sometimes in strange and primitive places. It
was a shock to learn, later, that this professor had committed

suicide, possibly like many others who had lost their all.

The University of Vienna had been one of the greatest universities of Europe and throngs of foreign students had studied there. The Medical School was world renowned. After World War I, neither the University nor its great Medical School could be adequately supported. The Medical School appealed to the Rockefeller Foundation for assistance to carry on and the Foundation responded in the same generous spirit that it had shown to many other institutions that had been almost destroyed by the World War. It made the grant with only one proviso: that the materials and equipment provided should be used by all students regardless of race or religion. Anti-Semitism, which had always existed in the University, had returned after the war with increased virulence.

It was sad to observe the pathetic desire of the officials of the University of Vienna to cooperate with the Institute of International Education in an exchange of students with United States institutions. They could offer nothing but tuition in return for scholarships covering board, lodging and tuition. But in association with interested citizens, they formed the Austro-American Institute of Education for the purpose of securing funds to balance the value of our scholarships. It was necessary sometimes for our students to reside in the private homes of Institute members or in the Hotel Bristol, whose proprietor was a member of the Institute and a warm advocate of the exchange. The demand for our scholarships was far greater than the supply and as the cost of transportation from Vienna was a large sum in schillings, only those blessed with the goods of this world could accept them. I regretted that some of the fine young people whom I met and whose parents had been ruined in the war were unable to come. But those who did come were usually enthusiastic about their college experiences and the American way of life.

The bitterness between the workers, who were nearly all Socialists, and the remnants of the bourgeoisie, who assured me that the Socialist Common Council that controlled the city was ruining it, was profound. They insisted that the social services that were maintained at public expense compelled them actually to sell their possessions to secure the money necessary to pay the exorbitant taxes. They were particularly denunciatory of the workers' houses that had been erected for the workingmen's families. I spent a morning visiting these houses. It was one of my most inspiring experiences. The well-lighted flats, small but equipped with baths and other conveniences, evidently filled the tenants with pride in their homes, which were neatly kept. The cellars were commodious and well-aired and equipped with iron washtubs at which I saw some women washing the family laundry and others hanging the clean clothes on lines to dry. I say it was an inspiring sight to one who had visited slum homes in Vienna as well as in other large cities of Europe and America. But I have no answer to the complaints of the bourgeois taxpayers as to the ruin such public enterprises were bringing upon them. Nothing filled me at a later time with a greater sense of outrage than the bombardment of these fine buildings by the Dolfuss government at the behest of Mussolini, who promised to protect Austria against Hitler provided the Socialist Party was suppressed. In but a few years Hitler destroyed the independence of Austria and transformed Italy into a Germany satrapy.

Czechoslovakia—Modern and Progressive Democracy

The Battle of the White Mountain in 1620, which resulted in the destruction of religious liberty and national independence of Bohemia, Moravia, and Silesia was followed by a period of reaction and persecution which almost obliterated for 150 years the peoples of those lands as a force in European affairs. It was not until French Revolutionary influences penetrated those lands that the first real attempts at revival of the national culture including language, took place. The progress of the movement became increasingly rapid among the Czechs and after the beginning of the twentieth century the Czech movement, at first for autonomy within the Hapsburg Monarchy and upon the outbreak of World War I for independence from it, was led by Dr. Thomas G. Masaryk. At the Versailles peace conference, the Republic of Czechoslovakia was born.

A great deal of criticism has been written about the creation of the "artificial" state of Czechoslovakia, of whose population 23 per cent were Germans who wanted to join the Reich. She was indeed a "nationality" state composed of Austrians, Ruthenians, Poles, and Magyars. But the majority of the population were Slavs though the Slovak division of the Slavs was made up chiefly of illiterate peasants controlled by reactionary clerics whose loyalty was doubtful. Nevertheless, the progress in the consolidation of the country due to the vision and statesmanship of President Masaryk and his Minister of Foreign Affairs, Eduard Beneš, was astonishing. In less than twenty years, Czechoslovakia had become one of the most stable states of Europe whose government was a democracy characterized by devotion to the welfare of the common people. And she had a splendid army capable of defending her national freedom.

When I arrived from Dresden at the Wilson Station at Prague it was a heartening sight for any American to see the fine statue of Woodrow Wilson opposite the station. All Czechs revere the memory of Wilson who was one of the first statesmen to be won over to the idea of a free Czechoslovakia. Another monument which I afterward visited was that of the martyr, John Huss, who has almost as abiding a place in the affection of the Czech people as Thomas Masaryk. Huss, who started the Reformation in Bohemia, was burnt at the stake in 1415, but by the time of the Battle of the White Mountain in 1620, three-quarters of the Czech people had become Protestants. Despite the fact that three-quarters of them are today Roman Catholics, owing to the success of the Jesuits in reconverting them during the Counter Reformation, Huss still remains one of their revered patriots. Unlike the Reformation in some of the German states, it was not the work of princes in Bohemia-Moravia but largely of the common people and was, moreover, something in the nature of a national movement against Austrian influence.

I had not been long in Prague when I received an invitation to visit the President at Hradcany palace, his official home. I had not seen him after he left the United States in 1918, seven years before, but he seemed to be in splendid health. We talked of his stay in the United States in the early days of the war and of the mutual friends whom he remembered. He said, "Dr. Duggan, one of the superiorities of a small country over a large one is that it enables the ruler to keep in touch with movements among the people. I know personally the influential citizens in every city and town of the Republic." One of his reflections, when discussing conditions in Central Europe, seems ironical today in the light of subsequent events. He was comparing the stability that prevailed in Czechoslovakia with the disunity in Yugoslavia due to the antagonism that existed among Serbs, Croats, and Slovenes, and predicted a stormy career for Yugoslavia. Both countries today are equally under the heel of the Nazis, yet guerrilla troops are still resisting bitterly in the Yugoslavian mountains.

The American Minister to Czechoslovakia at the time of my visit was a personal friend, Lewis Einstein. He occupied an old rambling palace surrounded by beautiful grounds, which I understand the United States government afterward bought as the permanent American legation. He had been attached to the American embassy at London before being made Minister to Czechoslovakia. His wife, who was a wealthy Greek lady, disliked the transfer intensely and did not hesitate to ventilate her feelings. I was amazed at a large dinner party at the legation, when I was seated near her, to hear her make statements regarding the Czech people which were by no means complimentary. Such conversations are sure to be repeated and I could readily understand why, though Czechs were very friendly to Americans, the American legation was not popular among them at the time.

I found that American politics reached in a mild way to Prague. The Czechs always made much of our Fourth of July, and the year I was in Prague there was a great celebration on the morning of the Fourth. Naturally the American Minister was asked to make the principal address, which he did at some length. He never mentioned Woodrow Wilson nor the League of Nations. I had been told the day before that I would be asked to say a few words. I do not know now what I had jotted down to say, but when I rose to speak my brief talk consisted of a laudation of Woodrow Wilson, the certainty of a great future for Czechoslovakia under President Masaryk and my belief in a better world order under the League of Nations. My prophecies have not come true, to be sure, but they struck a responsive chord among the Americans in Prague. Mr. Einstein gave a party to his fellow-countrymen on the grounds of the legation in the afternoon. Several of the Americans present thanked me for the specific mention of Woodrow Wilson and the League, and so did President Masaryk.

The Czech Minister of Education had put me in the good care of a high official of the Ministry, Mr. Praus, who spoke English admirably, had visited the United States, and was the soul of courtesy. He arranged a number of functions in my honor. One was to deliver an address at the Charles University on "Aspects of American Civilization." It was well attended by the student body, no doubt to hear an address in English, which most of them were very eager to learn, as much as to listen to my thoughts on American civilization. On the same evening a dinner was given for me and I had the immense satisfaction of knowing that the dinner was the occasion when the Rectors of the Charles University and of the German University sat down at the same table. It was the first time, I was told, that such a breaking of bread together had taken place.

The student exchange with Czechoslovakia was the first established by the Institute of International Education with any foreign country, and it wielded a fine influence from the beginning. Like universities in all Continental Europe, Charles University had no dormitories for students before World War I. But when I made my first visit to Prague in 1925, I had the great satisfaction of visiting the *Studenský Domov,* a combined dormitory and recreational building. My visit to the building was after the delivery of my address and it was very gratifying to be received with smiles by so many students. It was also gratifying to be assured by a number of them of the great benefit they had received as exchange students in some college or university in the United States. After the establishment of the American Institute in Prague, of which Mr. Brackett Lewis became the efficient Director, American students and visitors had a center from which American influences streamed in many ways and directions. Under the Nazis, Charles University was ruthlessly closed amid scenes of violent disorder resulting in the death of some students. Many others were sent to concentration camps. The *Studenský Domov* is now used for German military purposes and the American Institute has been suppressed. But all these activities only await the final victory of the United Nations before they are resumed. That is certainly true of the student exchange.

Mr. Praus knew that I was anxious to learn as much as possible about the condition of the German minority and their attitude toward the Czechoslovak state. He was good enough to motor me through many villages and towns of the Sudetenland. I was impressed by the transformation. Everything was in German except the names of the railroad stations and highways, and they were given in both Czech and German. Banks, schools, churches, newspapers, hotels—all were German. There was little evidence of the Czech minority of the Sudetenland, though they numbered almost 750,000, and every apparent evidence that the Germans in the Sudetenland were permitted to run their own affairs. While my guide was engaged in some official duties I had the opportunity to talk to some of the German-speaking people. I seldom failed to ask about their attitude toward Dr. Masaryk and found that it was almost always one of respect. "Masaryk is fair," one of them said to me, "but he allows the Czech politicians at Prague to send a lot of Czech boors here to govern us." That summed up the general attitude of the Sudetenland Germans. Germans have always regarded Slavs as inferiors. Under the Hapsburgs the Sudetenland people were among the German minority that controlled the country. To have conditions reversed and to have the despised Czechs in control roused the greatest resentment.

Nevertheless, I was convinced at the time that the two races would gradually find a *modus vivendi* which would enable them to live together and work for the welfare of the State. That conviction was strengthened during later visits to Europe. I believe that no other minority in Europe continued to be treated so fairly and liberally as the German minority in Czechoslovakia. Had the Nazis not deliberately planned to disrupt and destroy the Czech state and to deceive foreigners with their continuous volume of lying propaganda, I do not believe that the majority of the Sudetenland Germans of their own accord would have participated in Hitler's nefarious schemes. After the partition of Czechoslovakia, the treatment of the conquered Czechs by the Germans was of the most cruel and brutal nature. Lidice will always be a terrible memory for the Czech people. When victory is finally attained for the United Nations, one of the first crimes to be redressed is the destruction of Czechoslovakia.

Hungary—Citadel of Reaction

I went from Vienna to Budapest, one of the most beautiful cities of Europe. To sit at an outdoor café on Margaret Isle in the Danube and look across the river to the noble group of public buildings including the Houses of Parliament is an inspiring sight. The Hungarians are a very proud people and they are particularly proud of their capital, and deservedly so.

The Hungarians or Magyars are a warrior, Asiatic people who forced themselves upon the Great Danubian plain about 890 A.D., and were Christianized from Rome. The Reformation made quick progress among the Hungarian nobility because they hoped, like the English nobility, to profit by the suppression of the monasteries and estates of the Church. The ensuing Counter Reformation was not only a movement to save the Magyar people for the Catholic Church but an instrument for their Germanization, and soon Hungarian culture was practically obliterated. Among the aristocracy, conversation as well as public affairs were conducted in Latin, and the native tongue was neglected. Following the French Revolution, the nationalist movement made rapid progress and despite the reaction which destroyed Kossuth's revolution in 1848, the defeat of Austria by Prussia in the Seven Weeks' War of 1866 compelled the Austrians to come to terms with the Hungarians. But the long fight for recognition had not taught the Hungarians the virtue of toleration. They were equally adamant in their refusal to grant concessions to the minorities. They engaged in a vigorous policy of Magyarization and became the worst enemies of Trialism, the movement to incorporate the Slavs as a third division of the Hapsburg monarchy.

No country suffered a greater catastrophe than Hungary as the result of World War I. She lost two-thirds of her territory and population, and instead of being a partner in one of the Great Powers of Europe, became a state of insignificant size and importance. The hatred of the Hungarians for their neighbors who had despoiled them was intense and they never relinquished the hope and determination to recover their lost territory. When I visited the country in 1925, on the walls of every schoolhouse was a map of Hungary before World War I with the lost territories in black, under which was inscribed "Nem! Nem! Soha!" (No! No! Never!)

I was greeted very cordially by the educational officials who knew me as the person responsible for the organization of the Hungarian-American student exchange. The Minister of Education invited me to lunch with a number of his officials and afterward took me to the University and to the royal palace to see the crown jewels. At the lunch he said to me, "Dr. Duggan, the war taught us the wisdom of educating our peasants. We are engaged now in a day and night campaign of education in every village." How long the campaign was continued I do not know but I doubt that it was very long. I afterward—at the Williamstown Institute of Politics—became acquainted with Count Teleki, who was later Prime Minister of Hungary. Teleki always impressed me as a liberal and I believe that Hungary would have become one of the progressive states of Europe if he had had his way. But it was hard for Teleki or any other man of vision to wage war

against the landed magnates and the Catholic Church to secure anything like an adequate distribution of part of their
estates among the peasantry, as had been done in Czechoslovakia, Rumania, and Yugoslavia. The estates that had been
distributed in those countries had been the property of alien
aristocrats whom the new masters were anxious to eliminate.
In Hungary the estates were the property of native aristocrats. That made all the difference in the world.

The Minister of Education was anxious that I visit the
University of Debreczen in the eastern part of the country
in the company of Dr. Dennis Jánossy of the Ministry, who
was delighted to act as my guide and interpreter. As the result of the change of frontiers, Debreczen was within a few
miles of the Rumanian border. We visited the border and saw
once again the phenomenon that existed along the boundaries of nearly all Europe, the troops of two countries standing guard opposite each other with tanks and equipment
ready for immediate action. I felt sorry for the Hungarians
because the Little Entente made up of Czechoslovakia, Yugoslavia, and Rumania, all of whom had profited territorially
by the defeat of Hungary in World War I, had been organized for the very purpose of preventing the resurgence of
Hungary. This was unfair because several millions of Hungarians had been included within the frontiers of the other
states.

The first evening of our arrival at Debreczen we were present at a great demonstration in honor of Lord Rothermere,
the owner of the *Daily Mail*, who was conducting a vigorous
campaign in favor of a return to Hungary of some of her
alienated territories. The people in charge of the demonstration were very anxious to have me sit upon the speakers'
platform. This I declined to do having been only shortly before the guest of the Czech people. It was a very exciting
meeting and, judging from my friend's translations of the

speeches, not calculated to add to the spirit of neighborliness. I thought it very unfair of Rothermere to be misleading the Hungarians into the belief that Great Britain would move to secure a revision of their boundaries. He knew that Great Britain had not the slightest intention of doing any such thing.

I found the University of Debreczen to be an excellent institution. The professors whom I met were scholars in their fields and thoroughly acquainted with what our scholars were doing. I had been assigned to a professor in the medical school as host and I found him a most intelligent, attractive, and courteous gentleman who spoke English admirably, as did several of the other professors I met. I was impressed with the standard of the equipment, clinics, and laboratories of the medical school. During our discussions in the evenings I learned a great deal concerning the people of the neighborhood who are almost exclusively members of the Reformed Church. My host was a patriotic Hungarian and an advocate of Revision but he was thoroughly familiar with European history and politics and took an unprejudiced view of the situation in the Danube valley. He was a great admirer of the American people and expressed the hope that the Hungarian-American student exchange might be strengthened, a view which met with my hearty approval.

Hungary entered the present war on the side of the Axis partly because of the glamour which Germany's early brilliant victories held for the reactionary Hungarian aristocracy, but also because of Hitler's return to Hungary of a good part of Transylvania allotted to Rumania by the Treaty of Versailles. In the reconstruction following the victory of the United Nations it can be hoped that a reconstituted Hungary will become an integral part of a Danubian Confederation which would also include Austria and Czechoslovakia. If the Poles could overcome their megalomania and refrain from attempting to dominate the Confederation, their adhesion would be an immense additional strength. If such a union were modeled upon the Swiss Confederation it would in all probability be a viable state. Its economy would have a fine balance between agriculture and industry. It would have the necessary strength to defend itself against foreign aggression. And its component parts, freed from wasting their resources in military competition, could raise the standards of living and education of their peoples and contribute to the cultural life of Europe much as have other small states throughout history.

CHAPTER X

WEST TO THE FAR EAST—HAWAII AND
THE PHILIPPINES

In 1924, I was invited to become a member of the Philippine Educational Commission, of which Dr. Paul Monroe, a distinguished scholar of Teachers College, was Chairman. I became Vice Chairman. It was organized by the Insular Government to make a thorough survey of the educational system of the Islands, to discover how much had been accomplished under the American occupation and to recommend reforms. The Commission sailed from San Francisco December 27, 1924. I had always been anxious to hear the Chinese speak Pidgin English. I had read many specimens of it but had never heard it spoken. Most of the Chinese with whom I was acquainted were of the university type and spoke good English. No better place can be found to hear Pidgin English than on a Pacific liner, where all the "boys" are Chinese. The most humorous instance of its use occurred when a member of the Commission ordered poached eggs for breakfast one morning. Now the uneducated Chinese find great difficulty in pronouncing our *R*, calling it *L* instead. The boy returned and said, "No can do. Can fly. Can sclamble. No can poach. Egg no stand up." It was all entirely understandable and to make oneself understood is the primary purpose of language. The incident illustrates how one can get along with almost no use of the parts of speech other than nouns and verbs.

I believe that the use of nouns and about sixteen verbs is the chief characteristic of what is called Basic English. The sixteen verbs are naturally much overworked. The need of other verbs is avoided by the use of prepositions, thus: "to lift up" would be used instead of "to elevate", "to put down" instead of "to lower". Basic English has been very successful in preparing foreigners to use English by practically confining them to the 850 most common words. I once read a story in Basic English. It was very interesting to me as a linguistic performance and the plot of the story may have been interesting to a foreigner just learning English. But from the standpoint of literature it was poor stuff.

Our Bastion in the Pacific

All liners crossing the Pacific stop at Hawaii. Considering the increased political and strategic importance of the Pacific since the Russo-Japanese War of 1905–1906, one of the most fortunate events in our history was the annexation of Hawaii by the United States in 1898. Hawaii is now our western outpost for hemisphere defense, absolutely essential as a naval base for that purpose. Of its inhabitants, only 21,000 native Hawaiians are now left and all will probably die out soon or be absorbed, there being now 41,000 mixed Hawaiians. There are 28,500 Chinese, of a migration before American occupation; 30,000 Portuguese introduced some years ago for labor; 52,500 Filipinos; and 10,000 Americans. But there are 158,000 Japanese out of a total population of almost 425,000. Hawaii is a Territory of the United States, having a legislature elected by universal suffrage. Children of Japanese born in Hawaii are American citizens and we must look forward to the time when the Japanese may form a majority of the voters of Hawaii. Should they act as a unit they might control the legislature. However, every effort of the Territorial Government is being exerted through the schools to make them loyal American citizens and, I believe, with considerable success. The future of these young Japanese-Americans is not very hopeful. The opportunities for bright young men in the Islands are not great. Being American citizens, they have a right to come to the mainland and they do come. But they look like Japanese and are taken for Japanese, and frequently are made to feel the dislike for the Japanese that now so largely prevails in our country because of Japan's aggressive policies in East Asia. Every effort ought to be made in continental United States to avoid destroying the good effects of American schools upon these young native-born citizens.

The treacherous attack of the Japanese upon Pearl Harbor on December 7, 1941, has naturally strengthened the dislike of the Japanese upon the part of the American people. Nevertheless, the just action of our government in removing Japanese residents from the Pacific Coast area as a military measure was accomplished with a minimum of friction and ill-feeling. The wisdom of the action in the case of the 100,-000 Japanese Americans is less clear. They are native-born citizens, many of whom are of undoubted loyalty. Ought discrimination to have been imposed upon them as against other native Americans? We are at war also with Germany and Italy, but we have not removed inland any of the millions of native Americans of German and Italian ancestry who are residents of the Atlantic coast area. If such discrimination among native Americans can be made in wartime may it not sooner or later be used as a precedent in peacetime for less desirable objectives?

The Institute of Pacific Relations

Most of the countries around the Pacific have in recent years become aware of the importance of the problems that confront them in that area. I am going to digress a little to describe one way in which they have attacked the problem. One of the finest institutions with which I am associated and at whose founding I assisted is the Institute of Pacific Relations. It was composed originally of delegates from the countries bordering the Pacific: Canada, the United States, China, Australia, Japan and, because of her multifarious interests in the Pacific, Great Britain. In recent years, French, Dutch, and Russian members have been added for the same reason. It was originally a purely voluntary organization without governmental connection. Now, probably no delegation save those of the United States, Canada, and Australia is uninfluenced by official connections. Its object is to bring together intelligent representatives of the countries mentioned who have a deep interest in a wise solution of the problems that confront them. The first two conferences were held at Honolulu. After my initial visit to Hawaii in 1925 I attended the second conference in 1927 as a delegate from the United States. The American and British delegates sailed from San Francisco together and I was much impressed by the character of the British delegates. The Chairman was Sir Frederick Whyte, who had been a member of Parliament and afterwards Speaker of the House in India. Another delegate was Lionel Curtis, who was one of the authors of the Selborne Memorandum that became the basis of the unification of the South African colonies. Both were unusually able men with a thorough knowledge of international affairs and a liberal outlook upon international problems. The British delegation illustrated the usual skill of the British in preparing for an international conference by having three able secretaries: young Lord Castlereagh, a Conservative; young William Astor, a Liberal; and Malcolm MacDonald, a Laborite. I admired the way in which those three young men worked and played together. They were quite inseparable.

It will be remembered that at that time the Chinese Nationalists regarded the British as the chief obstacle to the realization of their national aims—the complete unity and independence of China—although since then they have naturally transferred their dislike to the Japanese. I shall never forget the tense situation which arose at a session of the conference when one of the Chinese delegates passionately denounced the imperialistic activities of the British in China. There ensued complete silence and the atmosphere was tense. Sir Frederick Whyte, instead of himself undertaking a reasoned defense of the British in China, said, "Mr. MacDonald is better qualified than I am to speak upon that subject." Without any hesitation MacDonald said, "I have no doubt that many of the activities described did take place. All I can say is that had the Labor Party been in power, they would not have taken place." We all joined in the laugh that followed. The tension disappeared and the conference proceeded to devote itself to the constructive projects for which it had been called.

While attending the conference, which lasted two weeks, the delegates tried to learn as much as possible about the different aspects of the Hawaiian problem. One day several of us went with the Superintendent of Schools of Honolulu to visit one of the high schools in the Japanese quarter, attended almost exclusively by young Japanese-Americans. One of those in our group was the chief of the Japanese delegation, Mr. Yusuke Tsurumi, and he was requested by the school Principal to say a few words to the students. When he finished the Principal said to the students, "Would anyone like to ask Mr. Tsurumi a question?" One young Japanese-American said, "Yes, I would like to ask him why the Japanese are so imperialistic?"

The conference accomplished an admirable work. It enabled all the delegates to learn at first hand the different views held by the various nationalities on any particular problem, such as the capitulations in China. With better understanding came greater appreciation of the difficulties involved and the conclusions arrived at were probably the best possible at the time. I feel confident that they had considerable influence on the viewpoints of some of the governments at home. The Institute of Pacific Relations held similar conferences biennially until the outbreak of the present war between China and Japan, and its reports have been invaluable for an understanding of the situation in the Pacific area.

Arrival in the Philippines

My voyage to the Philippines was, as practically every voyage to the Islands is, by way of Japan and China, but I prefer to describe my experiences in those countries when I passed through them again on my way home. This visit was my first to a tropical country and I was deeply impressed by the strangeness of the physical environment in the Philippines. The mountains surrounding Manila were to my eyes very beautiful. The trees were always green, the flowers and the foliage generally entrancing, the birds were glorious in their startling plumage, but without anything like the lovely songs of our birds; the fruits, such as papaya and mangoes with which I was unacquainted at the time, were delicious, the patient and hard-working carabaos with their immense horns, the semi-naked Igorrotes whose country I later visited—all these sights filled me with delight. And for the first time in my life I was in a place where practically everyone was accustomed to dressing in white—the upper classes in linen, the *tao*, the peasant, in B.V.D.'s.

The first night of my sojourn I spent at the Agricultural College at Los Baños, quite a distance from Manila. I was astonished to see salamanders of various sizes moving slowly about the ceiling and upper walls. In the midst of our dinner one about six inches long fell near the edge of the table and lost his tail. He might just as well have fallen into the soup. The incident caused no commotion because it is by no means uncommon. The attitude toward the salamander is very friendly because it lives chiefly on the insects it eats. I spent the evening after dinner discussing educational matters with some of the professors and went to bed really somewhat fearful. My host's house was on the edge of the jungle and I wondered whether a snake might not enter one of the many openings in the lightly constructed house. During the night I heard a noise as if someone wanted to get in. I arose to look out and there was a monkey solemnly peering in. I shooed him off and was told the next morning that I had acted wisely. Another guest had been badly bitten by a monkey which he had tried to seize. I slept more soundly the remaining nights of my stay at Los Baños despite the fact that I heard a monkey scurry across the thatched roof every now and then.

Quezon versus Wood

We arrived at a time of great political commotion, with two commanding and opposed figures in the forefront. Manuel Quezon, the leader of the Nacionalista party, had the support of the great mass of the Filipino people in his demand for complete and immediate independence for the Islands. Quezon is a Spanish mestizo and one of the most attractive men I ever met. He is a brilliant conversationalist, an eloquent public speaker and a skillful politician. His career is contemporary and identified with the history of the Philippine Commonwealth, and there is no question that future generations of Filipinos will regard him as one of the greatest of the Founding Fathers of their country. Some official Americans regarded him as unstable and unreliable. He probably resorted to some of the dubious devices used generally by a politically inexperienced colonial people trying to make its way against the power of a foreign ruling government. My personal intercourse with him was most pleasant and I found him reasonable in his attitude on difficult problems. Ten years afterward when he was visiting the United States he urged me to return with him and render a service similar to that I rendered in 1925. I became acquainted also with Sergio Osmeña, who was competing at that time with Quezon for supremacy in the political affairs of the Islands. Osmeña is a Chinese mestizo—reserved, cautious, and steady, whose word is his bond and who had the implicit confidence of the American officials. The two men afterward overcame their differences and cooperated in securing the Commonwealth of the Philippines, with Quezon as President and Osmeña Vice President.

The other commanding figure in the Islands was the Governor General, General Leonard Wood, a man of fine character and a very patriotic American. He had practically the unanimous support of the American residents in the Philippines and the support of most Americans at home in his determination that the Islands should remain under the American flag until the Filipino people had sufficient experience in self-government to justify the grant of independence. He was a man of indomitable will and unswerving integrity and worked hard and incessantly to make the American Occupation an agency for the welfare of the Filipinos. He was a forthright New Englander who did not get along well with the subtle Quezon and the politicians generally. He believed all Americans were animated by his own principles and disliked seeing any of them return permanently to the United States. Though he was very fond of the Filipinos, I think he underemphasized their contribution to the progress of the Islands.

The controversy over independence extended to all classes and even to the children in the schools. On one occasion when our Commission visited a little *barrio* school out in the country, the teacher of a class of little boys about ten years old, naturally wanting to display the accomplishments of his pupils, said in his best bamboo English, "Eduardo, deescribe dee cow." Eduardo answered, "Dee cow iss a noble beast. Dee cow has four legs, one in each corner. Dee cow geeves milk. But as for me, gif me liberty or gif me death." Obviously the spirit of the Revolution followed the flag and Patrick Henry was redivivus.

Results of the American Occupation

The volume of accomplishment in the Philippines during the American occupation has been amazing. Under the Spaniards the Islands were constantly rent by uprisings, and brigandage flourished in many of the provinces. In 1925, the excellently organized Philippine constabulary maintained a security for life and property equal to that found anywhere in the United States. Under the Spaniards individual rights were constantly suppressed and the judicial administration, like the administration generally, was corrupt. The Americans brought constitutional guarantees of individual rights, guarded by a competent and honest Supreme Court. The Spaniards left Manila a dirty, fever-ridden port. Under American administration it became one of the finest cities of the Orient in practically every respect. When the American occupation began, public health and sanitation were unknown terms in the Islands. When our Commission arrived the splendid system of medical inspection, the drainage system, the abundant artesian wells and other safeguards for health had practically put an end to the plague, smallpox, cholera and other scourges that formerly swept across the Islands. The excellent roads, the railways, the irrigation systems, the facilities for inter-island communication are all material evidences of this remarkable transformation. So are the stable currency on a gold basis and the impressive growth of trade and industry.

Better still is the record in things of the mind and spirit. No one knows just how many pupils there were in the schools of the Islands when the Spaniards withdrew, but the most generous estimate would not place the number as high as 200,000. In 1925 there existed a system of elementary and secondary schools leading to the University of the Philippines and forming an educational ladder up which 1,300,000 Filipino children were climbing. The Filipino people are devoted to the public schools, upon which no less than 27.5 per cent of the Insular revenues were then spent. This record is something that every American should be proud of. In essence it had transformed a static medieval feudalism into the beginnings of a modern progressive democracy. It had brought hope and ambition to a people that for 350 years had been kept in sterile subjection by the rigid bureaucratic regime of the Spaniards. I was proud that my country had assisted in raising this attractive oriental people, who form a Christian isle in a sea of non-Christians, to a twentieth century civilization.

The splendid practical achievements of American engineers and physicians in the Philippines have been so publicized that the equally practical accomplishments of the teachers have been overlooked. I am not now referring to the fine indirect results of their work in making better citizens and giving some understanding of the true meaning of democracy. I am referring to its direct, tangible results. For example, the Filipino people have always been great sufferers

from malnutrition and skin diseases. This is partly due to an
insufficient and unvaried diet of rice, with fish occasionally
on Sundays and holidays. They were not accustomed to a
variety of vegetables at the time of the American occupation.
One of the wise plans put into execution by the Department
of Public Instruction was to have a school garden attached to
almost every *barrio* school. The children had their individual
plots where, under supervision, they planted vegetables. On
a certain day the *Presidente* of the municipality, sometimes
even the Governor of the province, distributed prizes to the
winners in the competition for the best gardens. Much was
made of the occasion. Soon the idea was extended to home
gardens. The diet of the Filipinos still leaves much to be desired, but the public school deserves the credit for having
made an invaluable addition to it.

Wherever our Commission went we were enthusiastically
received and royally entertained. In fact the time and attention that had to be given to such entertainment seriously delayed and hampered our work. The school people always provided a fine luncheon and an exhibition afterward. Of
course, the storage of ice was hardly possible so there was no
way of keeping meat. Hence every school killed chickens the
morning of our arrival and chicken formed the chief element
of our luncheon every day. I finally grew almost nauseated at
the very appearance of chicken at a meal, and when I returned home I begged my family to omit it for a while from
our diet. The school and classroom exhibitions, which were
excellent in themselves, sometimes had humorous results.
The Spaniards some four hundred years ago imposed their
civilization upon American Indians and Malay Orientals.
There is a theory that American Indians are the result of a
migration of Asiatics to the Americas. Whether that is so is
a question but I have always regarded the Filipinos as cousins
of Latin Americans. Certainly in some respects the result of

imposing Spanish civilization upon both peoples has been similar. They both like to "speechify" and to use pompous phrases to describe simple things. On one occasion in a *barrio* schoolroom the teacher held up a picture and said, "Francisco, what do you see in dee picture?" Francisco answered, "I see dee fadder cat and dee mudder cat and dee leedle katzens." "Antonio," asked the teacher, "what does dee mudder cat do?" "Dee mudder cat gives milk to dee leedle katzens." "Juan," asked the teacher, "what does dee fadder cat do?" And Juan answered proudly and rather chestily, "Dee fadder cat defends dee honor of dee mudder cat and de leedle katzens."

English as the Medium of Instruction

It was interesting to discover, as the result of applying educational tests, the difference in the I.Q.'s of American and Filipino children of the same age. In a few subjects, for example in arithmetic, the results were higher with the Filipino children than with Americans. Generally speaking, however, the Filipino children were from one to three years behind the American children. This was particularly true in practically all language work, and naturally so. The Filipino children were very much handicapped by the fact that all instruction in the schools was in English, a foreign language to them. It was as if American children were taught everything in French. The natural query is, why was this practice followed?

The Filipino people are divided into six large language groups with many subsidiary dialects. The leaders of the people are most anxious to weld the various tribes into a united nation. Of the almost 12,000,000 inhabitants in 1925, the most politically minded group, the Tagalogs, inhabiting the area around Manila, numbered 1,850,000. If the language of this group or any other group had been made the official language, a very divisive element would have been introduced into political and social life. Moreover, there exists in no one of the languages any great amount of cultural material which might form the basis of a school system. And to provide text books and other cultural materials in even the six major languages would be prohibitive in cost and destructive of the efficiency which had been developed as the result of centralized control. The Department of Public Instruction had introduced the splendid practice of transferring teachers from one part of the Islands to another, of sending Tagalog and Ilocano teachers from the north to teach in the schools of the south, and Visayan and Bicol teachers of the south to teach in the schools of the north. This binding element in the national life was possible only if instruction were given in a common medium, namely, English.

Other reasons could be advanced for deciding that English should be the common medium of instruction and the national language. But the drawbacks were obvious. English was spoken in the school only; the native dialect was the language of the home and the street. But the chief drawback was the fact that 82 per cent of the Filipino children remained in school only through the fourth grade, not long enough to be sufficiently grounded in English to become fluent. As I have already remarked, the devotion of the Filipino people to the cause of education was evidenced in the application of 27.5 per cent of their total revenues to that purpose. Where else in the world can that be matched? But in 1925 less than one half of the Filipino children were in school. The unfortunate thing is that the Filipinos simply have not the necessary resources to meet the enormous task they have undertaken, namely, to transform themselves quickly into a united nation. I believe that a very great deal of progress has been made in nationalization in the years since our visit.

The subject of English as the medium of instruction formed part of our conversation in a visit the Commission made to the home of General Aguinaldo, the commander of the Filipino army in the rebellion against Spain and afterward in the war against the United States. He is a Tagalog, a thoroughgoing patriot, and essentially a militarist. He asked us why we were not going to recommend Tagalog as the common medium of speech, and when we gave the reasons enumerated above, he struck the table with his fist and said, "I would have said it was to be Tagalog and that would have ended it."

The Relations between Filipinos and Americans

It must have been a shock to the inhabitants of the Philippines upon the arrival of the Americans to compare the American attitude toward the different classes of society with that of the Spaniards. It had been customary under the Spanish rule for a youth attending the liceo to be followed on his way to school by a servant carrying his books. That practice did not survive the American occupation very long. Every effort was made to emphasize equality among the pupils in the schools. Unfortunately, that practice did not always extend to the relations between Filipinos and Americans. In the rural areas and small towns the relations between the two peoples were close and cordial but in the cities there was not a great deal of social intercourse. Because of the inferiority complex which has always existed in a colonial people of another race under white domination, the average intelligent Filipino felt that the Americans regarded themselves as a better folk, and the Filipinos resented it. That some justification existed for this feeling was evident from the fact that in the Army and Navy Club in Manila, only influential Filipinos were admitted. If an American officer was a bachelor, intimate friendly relations sometimes existed, but when he married that became less true and if an officer had children such relations were almost non-existent.

Generally speaking, Americans in the Philippines were held in high regard, though the disdainful attitude of some business people resulted in dislike in various places. Moreover, while the conduct of Americans generally from the standpoint of morals and manners was good, the Saturday night dances at the Manila Hotel were often accompanied by intoxication and loose conduct. The Manila Hotel is a government-owned institution and the dances were attended by Filipinos. They were not always edifying spectacles of conduct as standards of the white man for imitation by the brown man. Some delinquencies are always to be expected. On one visit to a *barrio* school I noticed a little boy with a most attractive face and beautiful blue eyes. He could hardly speak a word of English. On my inquiring of the teacher about the boy, he answered, "That is one of the products of a regiment of American soldiers stationed in the neighborhood a few years ago." The presence of the large numbers of Eurasians everywhere in Asia is the evidence of the illicit intercourse between white men and native women and the Philippines have proved to be no exception.

The Moros

It was the duty of our Committee to visit all parts of the Islands and we finally came to Mindanao and Sulu, the habitat of the Moros. When Mohamet united the Arab tribes in the seventh century in a great religious crusade for the conversion of other peoples, he did not confine his march to the West for the overthrow of Christianity, but moved also to the East, where he subdued and converted pagan peoples. This movement continued for centuries after Mohamet's death and among the peoples converted were the inhabitants of what are now the Netherlands Indies and neighboring islands, including the southern Philippine Islands. At a later time the Spaniards came from the West bringing Christianity with them and converted the inhabitants of the northern Philippine Islands to that faith. There resulted an interminable conflict between the two peoples of the same race but different faiths. The Moros have always been fierce warriors and pirates and were never fully subdued by the Spaniards. The Christian inhabitants of the northern islands could never be certain that the Moros would not swoop down upon them, destroy their towns, take back their women and children as captives to their islands and force them to become Moslems. This condition lasted down almost to the American occupation and our troops were compelled to fight some bloody battles before the Moros were finally subdued. The American army officials treated the Moros with respect and admiration and won their respect and admiration in turn. But it was always difficult to prevent the Moros from attacking the Christian Filipinos, whom they held in great disdain.

Our Commission steamed up the Cotobato River in Mindanao in the company of the Filipino Governor of the province and the American Chief of Constabulary. It was very interesting going past the dense foliage and watching the crocodiles lying in the sun. The people in the clearings along the banks wire off a large square place in the river in front of their lands so that they can bathe and be free from the attacks of the crocodiles. After an all-day trip we reached the place of Datu Piang, a villainous looking old man but very friendly to the American occupation. He passed most of the evening denouncing the Filipino Government at Manila and assuring us that if the Americans yielded to the demands of the Filipinos and granted them independence, the Moros would drive out all the Filipinos who had settled in their region during the American occupation. He insisted that Moros had never been under the control of Filipinos and never would be. I happened to admire one of his *bolos* (fighting weapon) and he promised he would give each one of us a *bolo* in the morning. I afterward learned that he had ordered some of his people to stay up all night to make them. The Moro Datu is an absolute despot. I ought to mention, however, that Datu Piang's sons developed into most progressive leaders of the Moro people. Early the next day we rode to Lake Lanao through a dense forest on the worst looking nags one would care to mount. The monkeys in the forest screamed at us and bombarded us with coconuts. We arrived at the lake in time for lunch and in the afternoon visited the local school. It was taught by a woman teacher because the Moros would never stand for a male Filipino teacher coming into contact with their young women. We found the Moro children just as bright and attractive as the Filipino children.

From Mindanao we sailed to Sulu. Sulu, though under American sovereignty, is directly ruled by the Sultan of Sulu, who is also the religious head of the Moros. One approaches the island at the capital, Jolo, a rather shabby place where houses are largely set on stilts over the water. Until the American occupation no white man dared to go outside the paling which separated the town from the interior. Yet we wandered about the whole island in perfect security. This was due not merely to the wise policy of the American administration in its observance of the customs of the people, but also to the quiet, effective, and untiring efforts of a few American men and women who were willing to exile themselves there and devote their lives to raising the standards of living of the Sulu people. The two most important figures were Mrs. Lorillard Spencer and Mr. James Fugate. Mrs. Spencer and several other American friends of the Moros established a remarkable school on the island and remained there to protect it. Mr. Fugate became its principal and saw to it that not academic subjects alone were taught but practical and technical subjects of great local value. The Moros are splendidly developed in craftsmanship and the printing of books in Arabic was one of the finest pieces of handicraft that I had ever seen. Mr. Fugate later became Governor of the Sulu province and did much for its welfare.

As can be readily understood, the Moro people are more backward than the Filipinos. However unprogressive the Spanish regime was, it was more in touch with world movements than were the Moros. But the Moros were making rapid strides under the American regime when we were in Sulu. Some young men and women were sent to school and college in the United States. In one case that had an unexpected result. The cousin of the Sultan, the Princess Tarhata, spent two years at the University of Illinois and returned a very sophisticated young woman. But when we met her in Sulu she was dressed in Moro costume, had carmine lips (like our American women today) and her teeth were black from the chewing of betel nut. She ended up in the harem of another cousin where she intrigued and was a constant storm center. She might have associated with the eleven whites on the island but preferred to revert to the customs of her own people and be one of them. That, however, is not the usual result of a Moro's sojourn at a school in the United States. He generally returns fired with the desire to share with his fellows the things that he has learned here. And he usually does it with great singleness of purpose.

The University of the Philippines

Because I was the so-called expert on higher education, I spent a great deal of my time at the University of the Philippines. The University was founded in 1910 and at first was manned chiefly by Americans, not always of the highest scholarly attainments. It pursued the excellent policy of sending talented young graduates called *pensionados* to universities in the United States to study for the degree of Doctor of Philosophy. As the independence campaign became hotter, the university undertook to get rid of the American teachers by pensioning them off. This practice was followed in the school system also, even to the extent of giving teachers a bonus provided they would return home. In the University it had an unfortunate effect. The institution was too young and had not yet thoroughly organized its standards and formed its traditions. The teachers had not yet had a sufficiently long experience in administering such an enterprise when our Commission arrived. The succession of presidents of the University, American and Filipino, was made up of mediocre men. No one was a leader. There was a great deal of friction. The Filipino teachers were jealous of the Americans and were by no means united among themselves. However, some of the departments did excellent work and the university as a whole was as good as some of the state universities in our South. The reforms I suggested for the University can be found discussed in our Report.* All were accepted but one. In order to prevent politics from influencing the administration of the University, which was an intrenched practice, I recommended the exclusion from membership on the Board of Trustees of the Chairmen of the Committees on Public Instruction of the Senate and House of Representatives respectively, who according to the Charter of the University were members. I maintained that the interests of the University could be safeguarded by the fine body of alumni. This

* *A Survey of the Educational System of the Philippine Islands,* Bureau of Printing, Manila, 1925.

was the recommendation which was not accepted by the Insular Government.

The students of the University came from all parts of the Islands and as there were very few dormitories they lived chiefly in boarding houses. Most of the students were not robust in appearance, and as the University had no gymnasium and the students did not engage much in sports, their physical deficiencies were not likely to be made good. The great majority wore glasses, not because they were necessary for good sight but because many of the students thought the glasses added to their scholarly appearance. As they had learned English from Filipino teachers who in turn had learned it from their Filipino teachers, there were times when I had difficulty in understanding their recitations. I judged that the majority of them had good memories and could reason well from the premises involved, but I did not think they were quick in perception or creative in ideas. The mortality among the students, due primarily to deficient scholarship, was very great. My sympathies have always gone out to individuals and colonial peoples who are ambitious to rise and willing to work hard in order to do so. I viewed with deep interest these young people's efforts to prepare themselves to improve their lot in the world. And I listened with emotion to the singing by these students of the patriotic hymn, "Philippines, My Philippines" written to the tune of "Maryland, My Maryland". The stanzas are as follows:

I love my own, my native land,
　　Philippines, my Philippines.
To thee I give my heart and hand,
　　Philippines, my Philippines.
The trees that crown thy mountains grand
　　The seas that beat upon thy strand
Awake my heart to thy command,
　　Philippines, my Philippines.

Ye islands of the Eastern Sea,
    Philippines, my Philippines.
Thy people we shall ever be,
    Philippines, my Philippines.
Our fathers lived and died for thee,
    And soon shall come the day when we
Shall lie with them in God's decree,
    Philippines, my Philippines.

Yet still beneath thy ardent sky,
    Philippines, my Philippines.
More num'rous sons shall live and die,
    Philippines, my Philippines.
In them shall breathe thy purpose high,
The glorious day to bring more nigh,
When all shall sing without a sigh,
    Philippines, my Philippines.

As soon as the United States assumed the sovereignty of
the Philippines, the manifold activities in which the new administration engaged created a demand for intelligent civil
servants of all kinds—teachers, field agents, technicians, clerks
and many others. The University rendered great service by
training young men and women for these posts. But by the
time our Commission reached the Islands the saturation
point for places in the government service had about been
reached. We discovered that the manual training, technical
and agricultural high schools were not nearly so popular as
the academic high schools preparing for entrance to the professions. The reason is clear. In every colonial system the subject peoples envy the rulers, who occupy the leading places
in society. When freedom and opportunity came to the Philippines with the American occupation, the Filipinos wanted
to fill the important positions in law, medicine, teaching, and
government service which formerly were largely monopo-

lized by the Spaniards. They regarded the places that might be occupied as the result of the training given in the agricultural and manual training schools as inferior. It is the same phenomenon one finds in the home countries. There are more academically-trained intellectuals than are required to meet the needs of society.

After the United States became the sovereign power the American school system was naturally the model upon which the Philippine system was organized. This was also true of higher education. Sometimes American standards were too high for Filipino resources. I had an illustration of this when I was making a study of the School of Medicine of the University of the Philippines. When the Commission was in the Philippines there was not one physician to every 10,000 inhabitants as against one to every 2,000 in the United States. What few physicians existed were concentrated in the big towns. Of the 243 graduates of the College of Medicine in 1925, 100 were in Manila alone. The Commission had no desire to suggest measures looking to a reduction of the standards maintained by the College of Medicine. But it was a question whether in the interests of unnecessarily high standards and unusual specialization, the Filipino people had not been made to suffer. The population of the Philippines is overwhelmingly rural and what the people of these small communities needed was not highly trained specialists but physicians who could treat their ordinary bodily ailments. I suggested to the Dean of the Medical School that it might be possible for the School to train two types of medical men: one consisting of graduates of an advanced course of five years as then existed and who would receive the degree of Doctor of Medicine; and another made up of men who would have a less advanced course, possibly of two years, after the completion of which they would receive the title of *practicante*. The title had formerly existed in the Islands. I suggested that in order that those composing the latter class might reside in the rural districts where their services were really needed, legislative provision might be made that only Doctors of Medicine might practice in the larger communities of a population beyond a specified number. To my suggestion, the Dean answered, "Oh, Dr. Duggan, what would the Rockefeller Foundation say?"

The University of the Philippines is not the only institution of higher education in the Islands. There are private institutions and institutions under religious control. The former can be dismissed with a word. They are money-making devices for the profit of those who organize and administer them. The scandal is that the government neither controls nor supervises them. It ignores them. When the Commission was in the Islands they were usually located in rented houses, poorly lighted and ventilated, with very inadequate libraries, laboratories and teaching materials, and with teachers of doubtful competence. Most of the work was done at night and was of the most routine textbook character. The University of the Philippines ought to be provided with sufficient funds to undertake this night work and render unnecessary the existence of the private "universities".

The institutions under religious control present a pleasant contrast to the private institutions. The best two are Silliman Institute under Protestant Mission auspices at Dumaguete in the south and the Ateneo under Jesuit control at Manila. The teachers in both are nearly all Americans; the language of instruction is English; the library and laboratory facilities are excellent, and as the representative of the Commission, I heard in both institutions some of the best conducted recitations that I heard in the Archipelago. A remarkable spirit of alertness pervaded both institutions and careful supervision for the material and moral welfare of the students was provided. Both institutions ought to receive all the support necessary to maintain and expand their work, for they are rendering a great service to the Filipino people.

The University of Santo Tomas is the oldest university under the American flag, having been established in 1600 by the Dominican Order. It has ever since been administered by Spanish Dominicans and until two years before the arrival of the Commission the language of instruction was Spanish. The chief reason for the great success of the Ateneo was that the Jesuit Order supplanted Spanish Jesuits with Americans who had excellent training in pedagogics. At Santo Tomas the teachers were nearly all Spaniards, the instruction in English was poor, the library and laboratory facilities were old and inadequate. But the university was then (1925) establishing itself upon a new site on the outskirts of Manila with a splendid group of buildings provided with modern equipment in the midst of an adequate campus. If the university were to become staffed with equally modern teachers, its future would be assured. It would then provide, with the Ateneo, the necessary competition with the University of the Philippines to advance the intellectual and professional welfare of the Islands.

Among the Igorrotes

The Commission spent its last month at Baguio, the summer capital, drawing up its Report. Summer in the Philippines, where the average annual temperature is 80° Fahrenheit, means the particularly hot season from March to June. It was delightful at Baguio, which is situated about 150 miles north of Manila in the midst of mountains more than 5,000 feet high. The scenery is beautiful and the climate stimulating. Under the Spaniards Baguio was inaccessible. It was in the country of the head-hunting Igorrotes who were fierce fighters. But the Americans forced their way through, built admirable roads, and gradually induced the natives to send their children to the newly established schools.

Baguio provided the Commission with the unusual experience of being in touch with primitive, medieval, and modern civilizations at one and the same time. One night the entire Commission—there were nine of us—were in conference as to the nature and content of our Report. We were decidedly of the twentieth century. While we were conferring we could hear the chanting in Latin of monks high above us in a neighboring monastery. They were chanting exactly as they would have done in the thirteenth century. And from down in the valley below we could hear the weird sounds of a *cañao* executed by the native Igorrotes after the death of one of the tribe. That represented primitive civilization. A *cañao* was a kind of fiesta starting with the grand wake over the death of a member and winding up with dancing and other ceremonies. The Igorrotes have different forms for the great events of life. We later attended a war *cañao* which was very exciting, but I never had a more impressive experience than on this night when events of the three civilizations synchronized.

One of the most helpful persons we met in the Islands was Dr. Otley Beyer, a remarkable anthropologist who had been in the Philippines since the commencement of the American occupation and had lived and worked very intimately with the pagan tribes of the mountain country of Luzon. He had been engaged in research everywhere throughout the Islands and because of his sincere interest in the welfare of the different peoples, especially the less civilized tribes, he was always a welcome guest. He had collected a large amount of most valuable material, some of which could nowhere be duplicated. Because of limited resources he kept this material in wooden boxes that might at any moment be destroyed by fire. Upon our return home I recommended to the Rockefeller Foundation that he be supplied with metal boxes to render his collection safe and I believe this was done.

Some of our Commission were very anxious to come into contact with the Negritos—the aborigines of the Islands, the Malay Filipinos and Moros having come as immigrants from the Asiatic mainland in the distant past. *Negrito* is Spanish for "little Negro", so called because of their small size and very dark skin. They are exceedingly shy and timid, live away from contact with other people, and wander from place to place. Their conditions of life are as low as those of the Australian bushmen. Their home is in the woods and their food what nature provides. Dr. Beyer arranged a meeting for us. The Negritos were obviously reluctant to come, but everything about them was most interesting to us. We posed for a photograph and the chief reached only to my shoulder. Like most primitive peoples, they were much taken by shining baubles. In all probability they are a doomed people, unable to withstand the pressure of modern civilization and will disappear in a comparatively short time.

Too much praise can hardly be given to the thousand teachers, chiefly women, who arrived from the United States in the third year of the Occupation. They often were stationed in isolated places in an utterly foreign environment to effect their orientation among people who did not understand them and whom they did not understand. They had to learn by hard experience to eat differently, to dress differently, and to accustom themselves to different ways of conduct. They performed their work with a singleness of purpose inspired by the desire to do a fine thing for the credit and prestige of their country. They were often lonely and homesick but they seldom failed to carry on.

The year before our arrival the Department of Public Instruction determined to have something in the nature of a summer session at Baguio, to call into conference teachers from the normal and secondary schools for the discussion of problems of administration and methods of teaching. Now the Igorrotes are an outstanding people but naturally have customs different from ours. The men's dress consists only of a "G string" and the women's upper body is naked. When the teachers arrived at Baguio they were waited upon at table by youths dressed solely in a G string. Immediately there was an indignant outcry from the outraged women teachers and a protest was sent to Governor Wood. The Governor admired immensely the physique of the Igorrotes, many of whom he incorporated into the Constabulary. However, something had to be done and it was decided that the waiters would have to wear a coat or trousers. No Igorrote will wear trousers if he can help it, so the teachers were waited upon by youths dressed in a coat and a G string! But that situation lasted only a short time.

While at Baguio, the hard work of the five months we had spent upon our program finally told upon some of us. We had risen early every day, traveled and worked in the heat without the siesta which is an ordinary part of the daily life of the Philippines and generally spent the evenings in discussing the events of the day. I finally succumbed to a prolonged attack of dysentery. It was fortunately not of the amoebic variety but simply the result of overwork under unfavorable conditions. General Wood was good enough to have me put into the fine military hospital at Baguio. I shall never forget the unending kindness of Mrs. Gilmore, the wife of the Vice Governor, who brought me delicacies of food fit for a patient suffering from my trouble. Writing my report was a hard struggle. I had a table placed next to the bed in my room and after writing for a while and often visiting the bathroom I would lie down to get up enough strength for another session with the Report. Professor Monroe had a similar but not such a hard attack and the trouble continued until we were finally treated and cured at the Rockefeller hospital in Peking.

One cannot visit the Philippines without being impressed by the extent of Chinese influence. The Chinese entered in large numbers under the Spaniards and filtered in despite the Exclusion Law under the Americans. They were to be found everywhere. Retail trade was chiefly in their hands in the large cities and no *barrio* was too small to have a store run by a "Chino". They were orderly and industrious residents. Many were rich and contributed generously to the Nationalist cause in China besides maintaining their own schools and temples. They were sometimes accused of exploiting the *tao,* but it would be impossible for them to compete in that respect with the local *cacique,* the boss of the village. The poor *tao* seldom has sufficient resources to carry him throughout the year without assistance and he must usually secure this from the *cacique* of the neighborhood and pay back at usurious rates of interest. The *cacique* is sometimes able to retain a family in economic slavery for a long period of time. *Caciquism* is one of the worst evils of the Filipino social system and it is almost impossible to eradicate it because the *cacique* often controls the votes of his locality and has himself or one of his creatures elected to the legislature.

The Place of the Friars in Filipino Life

The Filipino rebellion against Spanish rule led by Aguinaldo in 1896 was largely due to the place of the Friars in Filipino life. The rebellion resulted among other things in the death sentence for José Rizal, the George Washington of the Philippines, whose statue appears in the parks of practically all Filipino towns. He was a really noble man and in his two books, *Noli Me Tangere* and *Il Filibusterismo* may be found a description of the evil conditions which existed in the Philippines and justified the rebellion. By the time of the rebellion, the Friars had accumulated more than 400,000 acres of the best lands in the Islands and their treatment of the *tao* was as bad as that received by him from landlords generally. Moreover, the Friars were on the whole ignorant and lazy and some of them led evil lives. The rebels drove them out and confiscated their land, but when the sovereignty of the Philippines was transferred to the United States, the Church presented a claim to the American government for the confiscated lands. President McKinley appointed Mr. Taft to adjudicate the claim and he arrived at a compromise by which the Church received $7,300,000 in lieu of the confiscated lands.

In the meantime, a former Catholic priest, Father Aglipay, had founded the Philippine National Church, of which he became the head and bishop. The feeling against the Friars is evident from the fact that when our Commission was there, the Aglipay church, as it was called, numbered 1,500,000 persons. However, my belief is that like the Old Catholics founded by Dr. Döllinger in Germany after the pronouncement of the doctrine of the Infallibility of the Pope by the Vatican Council of 1871, it will gradually die out. Despite the hostility of the Filipinos, some of the more courageous Friars filtered back. I met one of them in a little town and we conversed at length about the new conditions under the American Occupation. He was very pessimistic and insisted that the introduction of American ideals and customs would result in the breakdown of family life and of Filipino society generally. When I pointed out that the Filipino seemed already to be better off and happier under the American Occupation, he made one admission: "Had we Spaniards done one-tenth of what the Americans have done in education, we would never have lost the Philippines."

The Japanese in Mindanao

When our Commission was in the Islands, only a few Japanese had settled there and these few were gathered together in the single province of Davao on Mindanao. But even then they were causing the government great disquietude, for they practically controlled the province. They evaded the law prohibiting the ownership of land by foreigners through various devices, the chief one being to register by using a Filipino. They practically owned thousands of acres, devoted chiefly to the cultivation of rice and hemp, almost all of which was exported to Japan. They had their own stores, banks, schools, and newspapers. Two steamships a week sailed to Yokohama, and the relations with the mother country were becoming closer with the passage of the years. In 1925 the Filipino leaders believed that if the Islands were given independence there would be little difficulty in obtaining an agreement among the Pacific Powers guaranteeing the neutrality of the Islands. Were the Americans to give up the sovereignty of the Philippines, I am convinced that the Japanese would take over the Islands in the course of time and Davao would naturally be one of their springboards. Since our Commission's departure the Islands have become the Commonwealth of the Philippines and are on their way to the independence for which they clamored at the time of our visit but about which they now have serious doubts. If, according to present plans, independence becomes a reality in 1946 or within a reasonable period of readjustment after the war, and our tariff rates are applied to Filipino products, the Islands are doomed. Up to the end of 1941, 80 per cent of their chief products, sugar, coconut oil, hemp, and cigars, went to the United States and 66.75 per cent of their imports came from the United States. They have practically no other market. As the result of the higher standard of living developed under the American regime through the payment of higher wages than are the rule in the Netherlands Indies and neighboring countries, they cannot compete in the cost of their products. With independence the fine democratic experiment in colonial government may perish. Within a few years after the creation of the Commonwealth the legislature, inspired by fear, had already granted to President Quezon powers that looked like the first step toward a moderate form of totalitarianism.

Military men have usually doubted that the United States could prevent conquest of the Islands by Japan in case of war. Whatever possibility did exist was lost as the result of the destruction of our naval and air forces at Pearl Harbor. But the heroic defense of the Islands by American and Filipino troops, especially the campaign of General MacArthur on the Bataan Peninsula, forms one of the brightest pages in American military history. Of much greater importance is the justification it provided for our policy in the Philippines. We prepared the Filipinos for self-government and then gave it to them. That was not the policy adopted by the Dutch in the Netherlands Indies nor by the British in Malaya and Burma. In the time of our need the Filipinos gladly rallied to our support. The inhabitants of the Dutch and British colonies in that area did not.

The Japanese now have absolute control of the Philippines. The Islands provide them with many needed agricultural and mineral products which they will unquestionably exploit to the limit. It is doubtful that they will treat the Filipinos any better than they have treated the Koreans. But Americans and Filipinos look forward to the eventual victory of the United Nations. Then the relations of the two peoples will probably be more cordial and helpful than ever before. Americans will want to assist the Filipinos to meet more adequately the severe conditions that will confront a newly enfranchised people in a chaotic world.

CHAPTER XI

CHINA AND HER PROBLEMS

I ARRIVED in Shanghai at a crucial time in the history of mod ern China. Fourteen years had elapsed since the Revolution of 1911 had overthrown the Manchu dynasty and established the Republic in the following year. Those years had been devoted by Chinese patriots to a determined campaign to secure equality for their country in the family of nations. China was the only remaining country of the Orient where foreigners still enjoyed the privileges inherent in the prin- ciple of extraterritoriality, which gave the Consular courts of foreign nations instead of the local courts jurisdiction over the lives and property of foreigners in China. She was also the only country where foreign settlements or concessions were removed from the jurisdiction of the national sovereignty. The practical and psychological evils of that situation are too well known to the student of international relations to re- quire comment. It was a situation that could not persist in the twentieth century. But the foreigner, meaning the white man, was as yet oblivious to the change that was being wrought among the people of China by the campaign of the patriots. Nothing could better illustrate that ignorance than the two signs over the gates of the park in the foreign settlement at Shanghai, "Chinese not admitted" and "Dogs not admitted".

Obstacles to a Chinese Renaissance

Who were the Chinese patriots who led the movement for independence from foreign domination? Students. Though thousands of Chinese students had studied in Japan after 1905, the leaders of the movement were students who had studied in the West, especially in the United States, or in American missionary schools and colleges in China. They had learned from their American teachers much about nationalism and democracy, the right to liberty and the pursuit of happiness. They had learned another great lesson, namely, that Western civilization was strong because it was based upon science—military science, administrative science, industrial science. These students returned home fired with a determination to spread nationalism and Western culture, especially in the field of science, in their own country and thereby free it from foreign domination. They rallied to their support the laborer and, to a less extent, the peasant. They initiated an Oriental Renaissance.

The Renaissance in Europe, introducing the New Learning, dates from the late fourteenth century; the Industrial Revolution, bringing in the factory system, from about the year 1760; the French Revolution, with its twin products, nationalism and democracy, from 1789. The latest of the three has been operating for five generations. In a single generation Western culture, the factory system, and nationalism were almost simultaneously made known to the people of China, a people wholly unprepared for any one of them. Disintegration resulted in almost every field. The abandoned temples scattered throughout the country were mute witnesses to the decay of religion. The ruined examination cells tell of the passing of the old learning upon which the moral life of the people was founded. The disappearance of the guilds, the rise of labor unions, strikes, riots and boycotts have indicated the radical changes that had taken place in the industrial life of the people. Civil war, brigandage, the freedom of the provinces from any central control and the existence of large independent standing armies under military leaders gave evidence of the political disintegration that took place after the Son of Heaven was driven from his throne in 1911. Moreover, during this generation the Chinese people did not have the opportunity to work out of their confusion in the ways they had adopted during the former crises in their long history. Then they were isolated and could use the measures with which they were familiar to restore order and stability. During the past generation they had always been subject to the interference and intrigues of foreign powers which did not consider it to their interest to have China emerge from her weakness as a unified and stable nation.

In the effort to accommodate itself to new conditions attendant upon the introduction of Western culture and institutions, China has relied chiefly upon education as an instrument. There are three systems of education at present in existence. The first consists of the very few remaining old-fashioned Chinese schools which continue to give the literary education in the Chinese classics that formed the sole method of entrance into the civil service previous to 1905. They exist chiefly in the more backward regions, are rapidly declining in numbers and will probably have little or no influence upon the China of the future.

The second system consists of the mission schools and colleges. Too great a tribute can hardly be paid to the mission schools, particularly the American schools, for their work in providing ideals and leaders for the China of today. But they are facing a new condition and must undertake a new orientation. In the first place they must now compete with the national and provincial Chinese institutions which have been founded and some of which are admirably staffed and equipped. In the second place they are facing the new and intense spirit of nationalism which pervades all aspects of Chinese life and particularly education. This means that all competition and duplication of effort among the mission colleges must be removed. It means also that they must increase the number of Christian Chinese teachers on their faculties and emphasize Chinese culture in their curricula. I met most of the leaders of education both of the mission and Chinese colleges, and all were agreed on this aspect of the matter. Indeed, some of the churchmen affirmed that if the Christian church in China is to grow it will be necessary for it to become increasingly Chinese in character.

The national and provincial Chinese institutions, which make up the third system, were having difficulty because of the uncertainty of support. At the time of my visit in 1925 the central government had neither power nor support outside of Peking. Each of the provinces was under the control of a Tuchun, a war lord. Some of these men were able administrators and were interested in education; most were concerned only with their own selfish advancement. The degree of support an institution received depended upon the favorable or unfavorable character of its location. In some institutions the salaries of the teachers were long in arrears and the equipment had been permitted to decay. Others were fairly well provided in both these respects. The National Association for the Advancement of Education in China, guided largely by the leaders of Chinese education, had a fine influence upon the development of education including guidance of student opinion and activities. The statement that the student movement is anti-foreign, anti-Christian, pro-Bolshevik and financed from Moscow is very mistaken. The student movement, like the nationalist movement generally, is primarily pro-Chinese. The Bolsheviks have unquestionably taken advantage of the ferment to further their own ends, but they are not responsible for the movement. The students, who are the head and front of the nationalist movement, in their insistence that China control her own destinies, have sometimes made unwarranted demands and have been exasperating in some of the methods they employed to realize their ends, but they are the hope of China. They have been the one sincere and earnest group in a land where selfishness and corruption are rife. They have needed wise guidance badly because in the comparatively recent past the war lords were trying to use the movement for their own ends. Fortunately today most of the younger educators are fully alive to the situation and are quite successful in their efforts at wise guidance.

Probably the most formidable obstacle to a Chinese Renaissance has been illiteracy. The Chinese are an intelligent people, but intelligent as the result of hard experience, not schooling. When I arrived in China the patriots had already begun the Mass Education Movement under the leadership of James Yen, a graduate of Yale University. Written Chinese has a sign or character for every word or sound. From the many thousands of characters, Chinese scholars selected the thousand characters (actually twelve hundred) most frequently used in the vocabulary of ordinary people as a basis upon which to work in order to reach the masses of the people. The Mass Education Movement has avoided politics and the "thousand-character" booklets are simple reading primers. But that fact has not prevented many pamphlets written in these characters from being extremely nationalistic, explaining the evil nature of the unequal treaties, tariff subjection, and extraterritoriality. Students swarmed over the entire country gathering the peasants together in abandoned temples and elsewhere to be taught the thousand accepted characters and the new nationalism.

The Kuomintang

The Mass Education Movement became one of the strong pillars of the Kuomintang or Nationalist Party. Dr. Sun Yat-sen, the Father of the Revolution, was not only a nationalist but a believer in democracy, and he hoped for great things to accompany its introduction into China. The Manchu regime was corrupt and honeycombed with grafters, but the successive regimes that followed its downfall were little better. In Chinese political life in 1925 there were pathetically few outstanding men. The majority were concerned chiefly with a scramble for place and profit. In the West the great force for maintaining restraint upon official dereliction is that of public opinion. To develop public opinion requires not only time but a literate people interested in public affairs. The Chinese were far from being such a people. The introduction of democratic political government in 1912 resulted in confusion and increased corruption. Were the Chinese true to their ancient traditions, the Manchu dynasty would have been succeeded by another. But unless all signs fail, the hope of an imperial regime died with the failure of Yuan Shih-kai to found a new dynasty in 1915.

The Kuomintang is a self-constituted oligarchy similar to the ones that control Russia, Italy, and Germany. In China local government is very democratically organized. Whether the centralized government will become so after the war remains to be seen. No one-party government has yet succeeded in becoming a democracy. However, few revolutions in history brought to the top as leaders finer men than the group of patriots who were trying to guide the destinies of China when I was there in 1925. It was a source of pride on the part of Americans that six of the ten cabinet portfolios were held by men who had received their higher education in Ameri-

can institutions. The manner in which the Kuomintang government established at Nanking confronted its difficulties
gave evidence of undoubted vision and courage among its
leaders.

The International Settlement in Shanghai

This was the chaotic China to which I was introduced
upon my arrival in Shanghai in the late spring of 1925. As so
many Americans do, I registered at the Hotel Astor until I
should decide upon a more permanent abode, and I saw there
the reproduction of a bit of New York life amid Chinese surroundings—and I did not like it. The immense quantity of
whiskey and soda consumed, the numbers of semi-naked
women dancers, often White Russian émigrés, frequenting
the dance halls, the often-riotous nature of the night life did
not make Shanghai an exemplar of Western civilization at its
best.

As is my wont when I go to any foreign country, especially
if it be a so-called "backward" country, I arranged to get in
touch with student bodies as soon as possible. I do this because in such countries I have usually found the students the
most forward-looking, sincere and independent group, as well
as the most nationalistic and patriotic. I visited St. John's
University which is under Episcopalian direction, and Shanghai College which is Baptist. I found them both pretty conservative institutions, not so strongly sympathetic toward the
nationalistic aspirations of their students as I had expected
they would be, but not opposed. The fact that the institutions
were under foreign direction did not affect the attitude of the
students who were, like the students in Chinese institutions,
strongly nationalist, anti-imperialist, and in some instances
anti-foreign. At that time it was the British who were looked
upon as the chief devils. This was partly due to their im-

mense interests in China generally and in particular to the fact that they controlled the foreign settlement in Shanghai.

Unfortunately, upon my return from Manila to Shanghai after a couple of weeks, I had a recurrence of dysentery. I consulted one of the best physicians of the city, Dr. Mac-Cracken, a relative of President MacCracken of Vassar College, of which I was then a trustee. Upon his advice I went to a private sanitarium in the hope of a quick recovery. But before I did so, Dr. MacCracken several times accompanied me through the bazaars and the great emporiums and drove me about the native city. No visitor can fail to be impressed by the place that Shanghai holds as the chief distributing center to the West for the beautiful products of Chinese handicrafts, and to the Yangtze valley and Central China generally for the manufactures of the West. Shanghai was little more than a mud flat when it was made an open port by the Chinese government after the Opium War of 1840. Like Hong Kong, its splendid condition prior to the Japanese invasion bore witness to the vision, courage, and capacity of the British.

My recollection of Shanghai will always be associated in my mind with the delightful formal dinner given by a group of Chinese scholars to the Philippine Educational Commission on its way to Manila. A formal Chinese dinner is an event in the life of any Occidental. Ours was a comparatively modest dinner consisting of twenty-three courses and lasting three hours. Some have twice as many courses and last longer. However, this bald statement sounds more formidable than the facts warrant. A course consists of a single item of food placed in a large bowl in the center of the table, sharks' fins, bird's nest soup, rice in various mixtures, ancient eggs, and other dainties following one another rapidly. Each diner had a small bowl in front of him and helped himself with chopsticks from the large bowl. I was filled with admiration at the skillful manner in which the Chinese used the chopsticks, but I was personally hungry at the end of the long dinner owing to my inability to get much from each course. During the long meal a servant went around the table with a hot towel upon which the guests wiped their fingers, in lieu, I suppose, of a finger bowl. Another servant refilled the beautiful little cups with rice wine. The dinner wound up with tea instead of our demi-tasse of coffee. During the dinner there was animated conversation, for the Chinese are a convivial people and practically all those present spoke English and most had studied in an American college or university.

Flight from Shanghai

I had not been long installed in the sanitarium at Shanghai when an event occurred which was the catalytic which unified China more than it had been up until that time, namely, the Shanghai riot of May 30, 1925. Students and laborers were engaged in a demonstration which grew out of the killing of a Chinese laborer in a Japanese factory. They were fired upon by the foreign police of the city, and some were killed and others wounded. This proved to be the Lexington of the war of independence against foreign interference which was finally won in 1928 by the unification of the country under the Kuomintang government. But the incident had an unfortunate effect upon my own movements, for the situation became so serious that the American consul-general warned his fellow countrymen that they had better leave the city at once.

Because I was more or less isolated, the notice reached me later than most Americans received it and when I applied for a first class passage on the vessel about to leave for Tientsin, I was told that there was no first class stateroom left. However, I was informed that if I bought a first class ticket I would have the run of the lounge and a seat in the dining room but only a second class stateroom. Second class staterooms are never used by foreigners, but if I was to leave Shanghai there was no alternative but to take one. I did not go down to my stateroom until I wanted to go to bed. When I turned on the light what was my horror to find the walls of the stateroom literally covered with cockroaches, some of them of great size. If I am right in my belief, cockroaches never bother human beings directly and no doubt I might have gone to bed and to sleep. But I simply could not. Instead, I spent that night and the next on a sofa in the lounge. The third day a few English people left the boat at Weihaiwai—a British leasehold until 1930—and I was transferred to a first class stateroom, which seemed all the finer because of my unpleasant experience in my former room.

The river by which one journeys from the sea to Tientsin is narrow and very winding, and it was interesting to watch the waves sent to the shores in the wash of the steamer and the alarm of the people as to the possible injury to their small boats which were badly knocked about. When we arrived at Tientsin there was the fine figure of Dr. Chang Poling waiting for me on the dock. Dr. Chang is tall and well built, like the northern Chinese generally, in contrast to the southerners. He is dignified and of aristocratic demeanor, but of very democratic feeling and principles. Dr. Chang and I had been graduate students together at Columbia University and I had conceived a great admiration and respect for him. His rise upon his return home had been rapid and he was at the time of my arrival the President of Nankai University, a private institution, which he had developed to a remarkable degree with funds secured from Chinese and American sources. Nankai was one of the most progressive institutions in all China and Dr. Chang was proud of it and particularly of its scientific laboratories donated by the Rockefeller Foundation. The student body was very patriotic, but fortunately their studies were not constantly interrupted by the parades and other celebrations which were a feature of most native institutions. I spent several days with Dr. Chang before going on to Peking, and his conversation about the future of his country, of which he was one of the most highly honored citizens, was very illuminating. Today Nankai is in ruins, bombed from the air by the Japanese deliberately, I have been assured, because of Dr. Chang's influence with his fellow countrymen. Dr. Chang is now in Chungking, where he is Vice Chairman of the People's Political Council. His university and its preparatory department are in full operation, with one section located in Kunming and the other in Chungking.

Student Attitude Toward Foreign Control

Upon my arrival at Peking I put up at the Grand Hotel, then the best hotel in the city. Dr. MacCracken had advised me to enter as a patient in the celebrated P.U.M.C. (Peking Union Medical College), built by the Rockefeller Foundation. But I was so eager to see the city which had so long been one of the greatest aims of my travels that I delayed entering P.U.M.C. for several days, and I hired ricksha men who received directions from a Chinese friend. I found the city in a turmoil, for the news of the May 30th "massacre" had been flashed everywhere throughout China. The students were in a state of constant parade and on my first ricksha drive I soon found myself surrounded by a mob of students under the walls of the Forbidden City, shouting "An Englishman." Most Englishmen just then were remaining discreetly at home. I soon convinced the students that I was an American and at once became the hero of the moment. They demanded that I deliver a speech and I told them how heartily I approved of their desire for the unity of their country and its independence from foreign control, but I urged them to advocate achieving those aims by peaceful measures. As I knew that probably not one in ten had understood my speech, I invited a committee to visit me at my hotel that evening to discuss the situation. That suggestion was immensely popular with the crowd.

When the committee arrived that night I said to them, "Do you want me to talk frankly about China's difficulties or do you want me simply to agree with your ideas and activities?" Of course they insisted upon the former alternative. Now no one at the time sympathized more heartily than I with the objectives of the Chinese Nationalists and their determination to realize them. But no one was more convinced than I that the emotional fervor of the students would lead to few constructive results unless their movement should be directed to definite and specific ends. Liberals everywhere, in China and abroad, were applauding the students and I determined to speak frankly in conformity with the view I held. I told them that I regarded many of the men in official positions in their country as grafters and corruptionists, and that one of their first objectives should be to drive them out. I said also that foreigners were undoubtedly engaged in exploiting the Chinese people but that I did not consider their exploitation any worse than that of their own war lords. I stated that instead of directing their attention exclusively to foreign interference in China's affairs, which was an entirely justified attitude, they would make more rapid headway if they curbed their own militarists also and then presented a united front to the foreign exploiters. While agreeing fully with them on the need of removing China from foreign control I described some unpleasant social conditions in their country, such as the part played by the usurer and the grasping landlord, which had forced themselves upon my attention and which I did not believe were the result of foreign control.

They were a fine group of young men and readily admitted the truth of my observations, but they had come obsessed with an *idée fixe,* namely, that foreign intervention in Chinese affairs was the root cause of China's woes. They insisted that China would never take her proper place in the family of nations until extraterritoriality was abolished, the foreign concessions returned, and tariff autonomy granted. I fully agreed with them but assured them that fair-minded people everywhere would be more sympathetic and more inclined to aid their efforts if the Chinese patriots tried also to put their own house in order. I did not convince them but they knew they had in me a sincere well wisher and we parted the best of friends.

The "Old China Hand"

It was almost immediately after the meeting with the students at my hotel in Peking that I was invited to another conference, composed of British and American residents to consider the serious situation which had arisen. It was then that I learned the difference between the attitude of the "Old China Hand" and that of the missionary in regard to Chinese problems. The Old China Hands were the men who had been in China many years as representatives of foreign banks, industries, and commercial houses or who were in business for themselves. They were in China primarily, in many instances solely, to make money and they had scant regard for Chinese susceptibilities. I met one of them on my way to the conference and said, "I suppose you're going to the meeting." "No," he answered, "I've seen lots of such disturbances. They all blow over. This one will too." At the conference the Old China Hands had but one solution of the problem, namely, to call upon the representatives of the Powers for action. That, they insisted, had always been efficacious in the past and there was no reason to depart from it in this case.

The missionary's position was very different. The missionary was in close touch with the ordinary Chinese and was confident that the present trouble could not be solved by the old methods. Moreover, he sympathized with the Chinese attitude and was aware that his teachings were largely responsible for the position taken by the students and young patriots generally. I had gone to China somewhat prejudiced against the missionary, for I believed that a civilization which had existed several thousand years before the advent of Christ was not in great need of the teachings of the Christian missionary. I left China a great admirer of the missionary. Some of them were teaching an outmoded form of the Christian religion but, I believe, most of them were actually living its finest principles. In secular things, education, hygiene, child welfare, social service, they were exhibiting Western civilization at its best. I was convinced that of all the foreigners in China they were the best friends of the Chinese people.

The Peking Union Medical College

P.U.M.C. was a gift of the Rockefeller Foundation and possesses some beautiful buildings in the Chinese style of architecture, to which laboratories, clinics, hospitalization, lecture rooms, and all the paraphernalia of a thoroughly modern medical college and hospital have been made to conform. It provided to its one hundred students of both sexes a medical education equal to the best in the United States. Its mission was the training of teachers for the various medical schools of China, not the training of practitioners, and it has succeeded in its mission. During my stay I found the treatment excellent and the atmosphere most friendly. Physicians and nurses, both Chinese and foreign, inspired confidence and good will. I was found to be on the mend anyhow and at the end of a week I was dismissed as cured, with the injunction to be careful as I had not fully recovered my strength. I was going out of the front door when there took place an incident which happened to me so often during my travels throughout the years as to strengthen my faith in the fundamental goodness of mankind. Dr. John B. Grant, one of the physicians who had been attending me, was about to enter. "Been dismissed?" he asked. "Yes," I answered. "Where are you going now?" he queried. "Back to the hotel," I replied. "No, you're not," he said. "You're coming home with me." And he brought me to his delightful home in a large compound where I was greeted just as cordially by his attractive wife. I remained with them until I left China.

I cannot adequately express my gratitude to Dr. and Mrs. Grant for their inexhaustible hospitality. Theirs was a beautiful home, kept beautiful by the large staff of servants. China is a paradise for an American housewife. Owing to the oversupply of labor she can have a staff of servants for the amount that one would cost in New York or other large American cities. Each servant has his specific function and in general Chinese servants are very efficient. The housewife is relieved of all cares, Mrs. Grant probably a little less than most and for a good reason. I once ventured to make a remark to her on the deliciousness of a pie we had been eating for dessert, and she told me how, when she was first married, she had been warned by other resident foreigners that she must turn over the running of her establishment to her servants, since they would not welcome supervision on her part such as is undertaken at home by the mistress of the house. She followed the advice until one day the dessert was so unusually delicious that she determined to go to the hitherto unvisited kitchen to compliment the cook. She did not find that all things were conducted according to her standards of cleanliness. Though she did not say so, I feel confident that there-

after she made sufficiently frequent visits to her kitchen and
no doubt to other parts of the house to be assured that it was
being managed along the lines she considered proper.

I was largely guided by Mrs. Grant in my purchases of gifts
to take home. She had exquisite taste and sometimes brought
in merchants to show the beautiful shawls, hangings and rugs
which they had for sale. Moreover, she accompanied me to
the bazaars and drew my attention to many beautiful products of handicraft in silver, copper, wood, leather and jade.
Each merchant had his booth at the bazaar for the display of
his goods. Nearly all of them spoke some English, though
sometimes only of the Pidgin variety. On my first day at the
bazaar I received an amusing lesson in Far Eastern bargaining. I admired especially a beautiful bronze dish that might
be used for a variety of purposes. Mrs. Grant said, "It is really
worth $15. The man will probably ask you as much as $40
but don't give a cent more than $15." I inquired of the mer-
chant the value of the bronze and sure enough he said, "Forty
dollars." I offered him $15 and he dismissed me with a look
of scorn. Before I reached the end of the aisle, however, I felt
a tug at my coat and he said that though to do so would mean
a complete loss, he would let me have the bronze for $30. I
repeated my offer of $15, which he again rejected and I went
my way among the booths looking at other merchants' goods.
I could feel that he was watching me and in about five minutes he appeared in front of me and assured me in the name
of all his ancestors that by letting the bronze go for $20 he
would be risking bankruptcy. I wanted the bronze badly and
was tempted to yield, but I knew that the eye of Mrs. Grant
was upon me and I remained adamant. When a little later he
saw we were about to leave, he came forward and in broken-
hearted accents let me have the bronze for $15. Except for
the presence of Mrs. Grant I would certainly have paid twice
as much.

Tsing Hua and Yenching

Among the most pleasant experiences I had in Peking were my visits to several of the educational institutions. When as the result of the success of the Kuomintang in unifying the country, the capital was removed in 1928 from Peking to Nanking, which had been the capital in former days, the removal had no effect upon the position of Peking as the cultural center of China. The number of educational institutions, museums, and temples, not to mention the Forbidden City, would keep an intelligent visitor engaged for months in their study. My limited time precluded my going to the many I should have liked to observe, but I was fortunately able to visit some of the most important. I went first to Tsing Hua College, the Boxer Indemnity college, founded with more than $10,000,000 in gold which was returned by the United States to China as part of the share of the United States in the indemnity imposed upon China by the Western powers because of the Boxer rebellion. The buildings of this institution were in every respect equal to any to be found on an American campus, the teachers were of a high scholarly type and the students were carefully selected from all parts of China upon a basis of merit. Tsing Hua was setting a fine standard for all government institutions. This was possible because the Board of Trustees was composed of Chinese and Americans devotedly supervising the expenditure of the funds without regard to anything but the maintenance of a college of the highest rank. I felt proud that it was my country which was responsible for the existence of this splendid institution. Today the campus and buildings of Tsing Hua are used by the Japanese army as barracks.

My next visit was to Yenching, the American university of which that fine scholar and administrator, Dr. Leighton Stuart, was the moving force. It is a very beautiful architectural group, uniting Chinese styles with modern building methods and equipment. In order that Yenching should be a cooperative enterprise it had a Chinese scholar as Chancellor and a majority of the faculty was Chinese. Dr. Stuart was President. The University was highly regarded by Chinese and foreigners alike and not only provided a fine undergraduate education but carried on research of great value in various fields of Chinese culture. When the Japanese took over Peking they showed by constant pinpricks their annoyance at Yenching's effort to carry on, regardless of the Japanese occupation. However, though they considered it really a center of Chinese patriotism, they did not venture to close the institution until after December 7, 1941. The North China Union Language School had just been incorporated into Yenching at the time of my visit. It was organized to instruct teachers, missionaries, and diplomats in the use of that difficult language, Chinese. The School, under the efficient administration of Mr. William B. Pettus, was rendering a service of unusual value to both the Occident and the Orient.

My repeated visits to the Forbidden City left me always with a feeling of sadness. It was impossible of course that the Forbidden City should have been continued into the twentieth century as a symbol of an outmoded and decadent way of life. The feeling of sadness is not relieved by a visit to the Summer Palace, some ten miles from Peking. It was beautifully built at enormous expense by the old Empress Dowager, Tzu Hsi, at the very time when the Empire was on the verge of collapse. One finds it difficult to conceive of the utter futility of the life of the imperial court, confronted at that time by impending danger and with practically no one among the Manchu aristocracy of sufficient calibre to make even an attempt to avert disaster. This situation was repeated, however, only six years later in the collapse of the Russian Czardom and for similar reasons. Corruption is no respecter of races.

While I was at Peking the Dalai Lama arrived there, having fled from Tibet before a column of British soldiers advancing from India. It was arranged that he should receive a group of Americans. As he knew only Tibetan and none of his people knew English, what he said had first to be translated into Chinese and then into English. This strange personage is deeply revered by the Mongols particularly. They swarmed about the place where he was staying and knocked their heads upon the ground before him whenever he appeared. At our reception each of the Americans held out his hands, upon which the Dalai Lama placed a fine piece of blue silk cloth at the same time offering a prayer. I noticed that the lace on his cuffs was considerably soiled and that his costume generally was not in keeping with his fine physique or his religious position. However, if what he said was what the interpreters translated he must have been an intelligent man. He spoke of the evil of war and the good fortune of the United States in being located between two great oceans. And he concluded by asking us to convey his respects to our President.

Though I had by no means fully recovered my strength I determined to visit the Great Wall, one of the most remarkable structures ever made by man. It is a three-hour railroad journey from Peking. It was begun in 221 B.C. and is about 1,400 miles in length. In some places it is as much as 22 feet high and 20 feet wide. It was built regardless of mountain heights or swamps to keep out the barbarians of all races. As I painfully climbed to the top and stood upon the Wall and gazed out upon the immense plain to the north, inhabited only by wandering Mongols, I found it difficult to conceive how the Wall, when well defended, could ever have been scaled or its gates rushed by tribesmen armed only with swords and spears. But it proved to be only a slight obstacle to Japanese cannon during the present war.

Glimpse of Japan

My stay in Japan was intensely interesting but too brief to justify a separate chapter about it. It was long enough, however, to enable me to hear a great deal concerning the vital needs of that country. Nevertheless, after making allowance for the very difficult problems that confronted the Japanese people—the need for *Lebensraum*, and the possibility of a Malthusian catastrophe—the invasion of China seems to me not only completely unjustified but an atrociously immoral proceeding. Certainly, when one considers the congestion of population in eastern and central China, the need for having living space in order to avoid a Malthusian catastrophe *in China* is very obvious.

If the Chinese have been endeavoring for twenty years to rid themselves of the domination of Western powers, it was not to allow themselves to be ruled and exploited by the Japanese. The event has proved the great unwisdom of the Japanese action. As the result of almost seven years of bloody warfare in which probably a million Japanese and several million Chinese have lost their lives, Japan is no nearer the conquest of China than when she began this "incident". The resurgence of the Chinese people during the past five years forms a glorious page in the history of human freedom. It is estimated that 50,000,000 people laden with such belongings as they could gather together trekked on foot to the open spaces of their Far West. It was the story over again of the pioneer expansion to our own West only this time crowded into a few years instead of taking several generations. Patriots dismantled factories to carry machinery with them and set up munition plants distant from Japanese armies. Scholars and students took books and laboratory materials to improvise universities in order to maintain academic life. The "Incident" unified the Chinese people as never before in modern history. Nationalists and Communists, despite their mutual suspicions and resentments, combined to withstand the invader. The Chinese people opened their eyes to their own capabilities and to the great resources of their country and were started upon a path of development which will probably mean a finer life for the common man and a nobler career for the Chinese nation.

The Japanese have one characteristic in common with their allies, the Germans, namely, an inability to understand the psychology of other peoples. They failed miserably in their attempt to force friendship upon the Chinese during the "Incident" and to enlist them in the "East Asia Co-Prosperity League". They were no more successful in rallying Indians and Chinese to their crusade with the slogan, "Asia for the Asiatics". Indians and Chinese know well that the slogan properly interpreted means Asia for the Japanese. And no longer do the Chinese expect to have their country dominated, through direct or indirect devices, by foreign governments. They have set their course toward full emancipation.

World War II accomplished for the Chinese patriots in their relations with Great Britain and the United States what World War I did for them in their relations with Russia, voluntary yielding of extraterritoriality. The Germans were compelled to yield it at that time and the Japanese will be compelled to give it up when the United Nations win this war. Then one discrimination deeply resented by the Chinese people will finally be removed.

There remains one action entirely within the competence of the United States, and only the United States, which the Chinese greatly desire, namely, repeal of the Exclusion Act. That would bring China under the general provisions of the Immigration Laws of 1924 and 1929. Under those laws only 110 Chinese would be admitted to this country each year. Surely a population of 135,000,000 could absorb 110 persons annually without dangerous conseqences! Although it is Japan that has always been most vocal in its protest against the Exclusion Act there is no doubt of the deep resentment that China feels toward it. For the United States thus to recognize racial equality would gratify a proud and sincere ally, would move toward implementing the Atlantic Charter, and would nullify the Japanese propaganda as to the hypocrisy of that document.

The Lost Supremacy of the White Man

An epic no poet has yet adequately sung is contained in the story of the ascent of the white man, from his little habitat in Western Europe to the overlordship of practically the whole earth. Beginning with about the year 1500 he conquered all of North and South America, Africa, Australia, and a large part of Asia, and dominated the regions which he did not annex. Moreover, during this period of his rise the white man developed a civilization which he considered superior to that of the men of any other color despite the fact that some ancient civilizations antedated his own by thousands of years. While the average white man welcomed people of color from other lands into his country, admitted them to his institutions of learning and even to his home, he resented any suggestion that they were his equals. Moreover, he made evident his faith in the superiority of his own civilization by sending missionaries into benighted lands to convert the inhabitants to a belief in his religion and way of life.

During the four hundred years which elapsed between the start of this period of expansion and World War I the white man almost exterminated the red man, reduced the black man to slavery, and lorded it over the brown and yellow man. He maintained his supremacy by force. He was enabled to do this because of his knowledge of science and its applications, science being his chief contribution to civilization. In developing the resources of old and settled lands his primary object was self-enrichment. Whatever gains accrued to the natives were a by-product.

The speedy development of commerce and industry, and the rapidity of transportation resulting from new scientific discoveries and inventions in the nineteenth century caused a large increase in the number of white men settling in the lands of colored peoples. Many of these men, relieved of the restraints of their home environment, led lives not at all in conformity with the precepts of the white man's religion as expounded by his missionaries. The same ease of movement enabled many of the ablest and most intelligent men of color to visit and study in the lands of the white man. What they saw in the way of poverty, ignorance, and oppression raised serious doubts as to the value of the white man's civilization.

The Boxer Rebellion was really the first notice to the white man that the political principle upon which his own life was founded, namely, nationalism, had begun to take root among backward and colored peoples. Up to that time the political doctrine of nationalism, i.e., loyalty to a group with common traditions, ideals and aspirations usually expressed in a common language, was almost unknown among them. The Japanese were the chief exception. The average Chinese was seldom interested in what took place even in the neighboring province and had only at intervals conceived of China as an entity. The average white man resident in China had regarded him with disdain because of what he considered his lack of patriotism. He was soon to regard him with outraged feelings because of his excess patriotism. The victory of the Japanese over the Russians in 1905, the first instance in modern times of the defeat of a nation of white men by a nation of colored men, had profound repercussions throughout all lands inhabited by so-called "backward" peoples. Nationalism spread among them like wildfire. At first it was everywhere a different nationalism from that of the West. Nationalism in the West was aggressive; in the East it was defensive. In the West it aimed at territorial expansion or economic exploitation or cultural superiority. In the East it aimed to enable a country to determine its own destiny, to retain control of its economic resources for its own benefit and to save itself from being placed in a position of international inferiority.

Effect of World War I upon White Supremacy

When World War I broke out in 1914 the supremacy of the white man was unquestioned. He expected colored peoples to admit it, and with few exceptions they did admit it. White men had engaged in fierce competition among themselves for supremacy in areas which would provide them with raw materials and markets; but joined together as they were by the cohesive power of race superiority, they presented a united front as against the colored man. The first World War spelled the doom of that superiority. Seldom is attention directed to the remarkable phenomenon of the great change in interracial orientation, a change which in less than two decades brought a downfall in the white prestige which it had taken more than two generations to build up.

In World War I white men of different nations not only engaged in slaughtering one another; they called in the despised black and yellow men to assist in the process. If it were worth while to call in "backward" peoples like Indians and Arabs to cooperate in activities of war, why not in activities of peace? Positive promises in this direction were made. "Self-determination" was promised. Hopes ran high. But the peace conference impressed the "backward" peoples with the belief that the promises were made as a war measure to win a victory. The failure of fulfilment was regarded as a moral betrayal, an additional indictment of the white man's civilization. Moreover, the superiority of the white man had hitherto rested largely upon an economic foundation. He was better off than the colored man in all the necessities and luxuries of life. But the war reduced many white men to the economic level of colored men. In China a beggar is an outcast. One may throw him a copper to get rid of his importunities, but he receives no consideration as a person. Imagine the effect upon white prestige when hundreds of White Russians, driven from their country by the Bolshevik Revolution, were found in the streets of Chinese cities with outstretched hands begging of the yellow man for bare subsistence.

Unfortunately the white man had not appreciated what was taking place in the minds of "backward" nations and colored peoples during the World War and he attempted to restore the *status quo ante*. His awakening was startling. Amritsar, where in 1920 British Indian troops fired upon a mass meeting and killed inoffensive protestants, was as a fire alarm in the night throughout the whole of India. Amritsar, before the World War, would have been an incident resulting in little more than sullen anger upon the part of Indians. Not so in 1920. From Amritsar dates the weakening of British control in India. The riot of May 30, 1925 in Shanghai, in which protesting students and laborers were shot down by the foreign police, as I have already mentioned, became the Lexington in the Chinese struggle for independence from foreign domination. All over Asia the different peoples were heartened by Turkey's revival in their determination to get rid of the white man's control. The Turks had been able to throw the Treaty of Sèvres, which dismembered their country, into the waste basket, to dictate the Treaty of Lausanne which put an end to foreign interference in their domestic affairs, to rebuild their country upon a thoroughly national basis, to eradicate many old abuses, and to introduce reforms which put them upon the path toward becoming a modern progressive state. The Turks achieved their freedom by fighting and their international equality by peaceful negotiations at Montreux. But the Indians and Chinese had learned to use peaceful methods of coercion as efficacious as warlike methods, namely, the boycott and passive resistance. Neither the individual Chinese nor the individual Indian is a good customer for foreign goods but the potential purchasing power of the combined population of the two countries, equaling almost half that of the entire earth, is enormous. The white man's domination throughout the world was based upon force. Force is largely powerless against the boycott and passive resistance.

Until today the colored man, in Asia at least, considered himself the inferior of the white man in force alone. Now he considers himself equal in that and in most other respects, and superior in some. For this change in attitude the white man has only himself to blame. He has never known when to yield. The renascence of "backward" peoples was always accomplished in the face of contemptuous disbelief on his part. He shows greater respect today for peoples of another color but they regard the change as forced, not voluntary. The white man in the world of today is really on the defensive. In his own lands he is trying to maintain his racial integrity by means of exclusion laws. In his international relations he is not yet ready to admit racial equality even in principle. The request of the Japanese delegation at the Peace Conference to have some expression of that principle embodied in the Covenant of the League of Nations met with a prompt and absolute refusal. But the attitude of the white man today toward colored peoples is very different from the soulless exploitation of the pre-war period. His actions are no longer those of an overlord. The growing respect of the white man for the accomplishments of colored peoples may eventuate earlier than now seems possible in a real acceptance of the principle that evaluation of men should depend upon no other test than that of worth.

Nothing that has been said above is intended to depreciate the marvelous contributions of the white man to civilization and to the welfare of colored peoples. The social organization of tomorrow will everywhere be based upon the science and material equipment of the Western world. "Backward" peoples have learned to appreciate the place in life of personal hygiene, public health and sanitation, and medicine. Roads and railroads, the telegraph, telephone, radio and electric light are rapidly becoming essential elements in their daily lives. Moreover, the white man's influence has been very effective in securing a different status for one half of the human race, women, wherever he has come into contact with other peoples. Foot-binding has been practically abolished in China, the veil has been torn from the faces of women in Turkey, and the institution of purdah in India whereby women are kept in seclusion to the detriment of their physical and mental health is crumbling. There is no justification for a pessimistic belief in the downfall of Western civilization. Reasons might readily be adduced to justify a belief in its more general adoption. But one contribution of the West most highly prized today by peoples of other regions is found not in the domain of matter but of spirit, viz., the sanctity of personality, and the white man has yet to demonstrate his belief that personality knows not race nor color nor religion.

CHAPTER XII

LATIN AMERICA AND OUR GOOD NEIGHBORS

To the Spanish Main and Beyond

IN 1931, Institute affairs directed me to South America, and when my good friend, Dr. Leo Rowe, the Director of the Pan American Union, learned that I was going there, he arranged that I lecture on American Civilization at some of the universities of the West Coast. I afterward lectured at the universities of the East Coast also. When another friend, Edgar Ricard, one of Mr. Hoover's right-hand men in carrying on Belgian, German, and Russian relief during and after the first World War, learned of my intention, he suggested that as Mr. Hoover had gone around South America during the period between his election to the Presidency and his inauguration, he might be willing to make suggestions about my visit. I had met Mr. Hoover once and though I did not expect him to remember me, he received me at the White House at Mr. Ricard's suggestion.

In the midst of our discussion about aspects of my visit, Mr. Hoover asked, "In what language will you deliver your lectures?" I answered, "In English. I don't know Spanish." The President expressed his great regret at that fact and assured me that the value of my lectures would be reduced fifty per cent by my delivering them in English. He expatiated on this point to such an extent that finally I said, "All right, Mr. Hoover, I'll deliver the lectures in Spanish." "I thought,"

said the President, "that you said you didn't know Spanish.
"That's true," I answered, "but I still have sixty days befor
I sail."

I returned home to New York, consulted my friend, Pro
fessor Federico de Onís of Columbia University, and secure
the services of a young Spanish teacher to give me lesson
The teacher came to my house every morning at nine o'cloc
for fifty days and drilled me in the pronunciation of the Spar
ish language. He did more. He translated my five lectures int
Spanish. After the first two weeks, each morning I read alou
to him one of the lectures and he corrected my mistakes. A
the end of the fifty days he assured me that I read them ver
well and that I should be understood easily by any Spanish
speaking audience. This view was confirmed by my readin,
the lectures aloud to Spanish-speaking friends.

I felt fairly confident of success because I knew that th
Latin American professors followed the practice of the pro
fessors in Continental Europe in reading their lectures to
their classes instead of discussing the subject with them, as i
customary with us. Everything went well. As my teacher ha
prophesied, the audiences evidently understood and appeare
interested. Alas, at every university where I lectured, incon
siderate people came up to me after the lecture to discus
various points! However, I had learned the military prin
ciple of the strategic retreat and always had at my side a na
tional who could speak English as well as Spanish. Moreove
the upper classes in Latin America nearly all speak French
and when absolutely necessary I fell back on *mon faibl
français*.

Nor was the need of discussing the lectures the only ob
stacle I met. My first lecture was at the Instituto Nacional a
Panama, now the University of Panama. When I had finishe
the lecture the courteous Rector said, "Dr. Duggan, I notice
you speak Castilian Spanish." "Yes," I replied, "I try to; tha

was what I was taught." "I wouldn't if I were you," he answered. "Most Latin Americans don't try to and will smile at
your doing it and might think you affected. It would be as if
a Middle Western audience in your country listened to an
English professor talking with his Oxford accent. For example,
we do not refer to this institution as the 'Instituto Nathional'
but pronounce it as a Frenchman would, the 'Instituto Nacional'." It was good advice. Only in a few places somewhat
removed from the current of affairs, like Bogotá, did I find
much use of Castilian Spanish. I gladly confined my efforts to
Latin American Spanish. Moreover, just as at home, I encountered a good many corruptions in speech. When I reached
Buenos Aires I found there many people calling "calle"
(street) "caje", and referring to their ex-President Irigoyen
as "Irigoshen". Buenos Aires has a large foreign population:
Italians, Basques, Englishmen, Germans, and others. It may
be that this fact explains the variation.

Big Business and Latin American Rapport

I flew from Panama to Barranquilla, where I stayed two
days with the representative of the Standard Oil Company.
I had expected to go up the Magdalena River to Bogotá, a
long and tiresome trip of some ten days or two weeks, provided the boat did not get stuck on a sandbar. He suggested
the possibility of my flying from Barranquilla to Barranca
Bermeja, far up the Magdalena and the center of the Standard's oil fields in Colombia. I gladly accepted, for I had been
greatly impressed by the engineering feat of piping the oil
from that place in the midst of a tropical forest to Cartagena,
where I afterward observed the process of pumping it into
ships for export.

It took only a few hours for the courteous representative of
the Standard Oil and myself to fly on a hydroplane to Bar-

ranca Bermeja, where we landed on the river. From the dock
a railway and a motor road lead to the oil fields, a distance
of five miles. There I found an astonishing settlement, a
place of about 2,500 inhabitants, of whom about 500 were
foreigners, including Americans, Englishmen, Germans, and
others. In the settlement were two schools for children, one
for instruction in Spanish and the other for instruction in
English, and a Catholic and a Protestant church. There was
good provision for recreation, including tennis courts and an
excellent moving-picture theatre. There was a savings bank
and a general store for the purchase of anything from a needle
to a set of furniture—and at fair prices. The agent there
showed me his accounts and explained the rate of wages re
ceived. As far as I could see, the people of the settlement
were contented. They were obviously better clothed and
probably better fed than the other workers in the neighborhood.

Now, my liberalism is sufficiently old-fashioned to be always suspicious of Big Business. I know something about the
evil practices of the corporation pirates in the early days of
American penetration in the Latin American countries,
about the bribing of their politicians and the financing of
revolutions. I was acquainted not only with the tirades of
American radicals familiar with Latin America but with the
fine study of the history of the machinations of the Standard
Oil by Ida Tarbell. But, as I have already said, this book is a
statement of my own experiences and impressions, and certainly at Barranca Bermeja I saw no evidence of coercion of
workers, nor cheating nor unfair practices generally.

I arrived in South America nearly two years after the beginning of the economic depression of 1929. The depression
had hit Latin America particularly hard. Many Latin Americans blamed us for a great part of their troubles, especially
for withdrawing practically all credits after having, before

he depression, almost begged them to take loans. The attitude of Latin Americans toward the United States had stiff-
ened considerably and Latin American students in particular
were bitter in their denunciation of "Yankee imperialism".
Since then American corporations have tried in various ways
to conciliate the governments and peoples of Latin America,
but with only partial success. In fact, I am of the opinion
that now, instead of American corporations taking unfair
advantage of Latin American governments, the reverse is
true. Our State Department is sometimes hard put to defend
even the just interests of American corporations.

One of the best plans adopted by American corporations
to increase the good will of the Latin American peoples toward them is to bring bright young South Americans to the
United States and employ them in the home offices so that
the young men will learn the corporation's methods while
they are at the same time learning English. They are then
given places in the offices located in their native lands. This
is an excellent idea, for these young men are almost invariably friendly to the United States upon their return home
and remove some of the prejudices against Americans which
are based on ignorance.

Part of the road from Barranca Bermeja to Bogotá was very
precipitous and circuitous, and along it the automobile I had
hired moved so rapidly as almost to fill me with terror, but
the chauffeur took it with the greatest *sang-froid*. Bogotá is
situated at a height of some 8,500 feet surrounded by mountains. It is quite isolated and except for the fact that it is the
capital of the country would be out of the current of national
affairs.

I delivered one of my five lectures on American civilization
at the National University and it seemed really to interest the
students. Most of the students had queer notions of United
States civilization but probably no queerer than the views held

by students in the United States concerning Colombian civili
zation. Colombia is one of the few Latin American republic:
where democracy has taken real root. The prolonged perioc
of Conservative control was broken in 1930 by the victory o
the Liberals. Led by the new President, Dr. Olaya Herrera
they introduced many progressive measures. Later undei
Presidents López and Santos the separation of Church anc
State, the improvement of educational facilities, and the con
struction of many new roads were evidences of the reformin;
spirit. While some resentment remains over the Panama Cana
incident of 1903, I found most of the Colombian people witl
whom I came into contact happily disposed toward the Unitec
States. I would have liked to stay more than a few days in th
city because of the kindly attitude of its citizens, but I wa;
due in Lima within a week. When the boat arrived at Callao
I was met by a representative of the embassy and a repre
sentative of the university and taken by them in an auto th
short distance to Lima.

Vis-à-Vis Student Opinion

I had one very interesting personal experience at Lima
Arrangements had been made to have me deliver lectures a
the University of San Marcos, the oldest university in Soutr
America, older by eighty-five years than Harvard. But shortl)
before I arrived the dictator, Leguía, had been driven from
power. There had been a revolution in the university alsc
and the students were largely in control. They had elected ;
new Rector, Dr. José Encinas, whom I found a delightful
man. I told him I feared that the arrangements for my lec
tures might have fallen through but he assured me that the)
held. I said to him, "Dr. Encinas, would it be possible for m(
to meet about twenty of the most anti-imperialist, anti
American students in order to discuss relations between Peru

nd the United States?" "Yes," he answered, "there will be
o difficulty. The men who represent the student body on the
Jniversity Council are the most anti-imperialist and anti-
American students. I'll invite them. But yours is a rather as-
onishing proposal. Would you mind my being present at the
neeting? I would like to see what happens." I assured him I
vould need him because of my poor Spanish. It chanced that
 professor of history, Dr. Víctor Andrés Belaunde, was also
present. He had been exiled in the early days of the Leguía
egime, and I had circuited him among our United States
olleges and universities to lecture on Latin American affairs.

 I should note here that university students in South Amer-
ca are thoroughly familiar, because of their deep interest in
olitics, with the evil practices formerly pursued by some of our
conomic exploiters in that continent. But their resentment
t "Yankee imperialism" had been kept at fever heat by the
ccasional pilgrimages made around South America by such
cholars as Manuel Ugarte and Alfredo Palacios of Buenos
Aires. They delivered vehement protests against the attempts
f the Colossus of the North to control the destinies of the
Latin American peoples.

 So behold us, the three men at one end of the table, myself
etween Dr. Encinas and Dr. Belaunde, and about twenty
tudents along the sides! I began by explaining why I was
here. I said I had come to learn as much as I could of their
ivilization so that I might go back to my own country better
ualified to interpret it to my own people. I finished by say-
ng that before I returned, however, I would like to know
hat they thought of my country. Immediately there was an
utburst. One student shouted "Wall Street", another "the
Monroe Doctrine", another "the Panama Canal steal", an-
ther "the Platt Amendment". Each one gave voice to his
 articular *bête noire* in our relations with Latin America. The
piritual atmosphere was very low but nevertheless I had a

delightful time. I said to the student who had shouted "Wall Street", "Do you think we Americans are in love with Wall Street? We hold most of the views you have of Wall Street. Do you think it is fair to condemn us all for what you think are the evil traits of a few?" To the student who had shouted "the Monroe Doctrine" I said, "There is no doubt that the United States engaged in some imperialistic adventures under the pretense of the Monroe Doctrine. But the record isn't all bad. When President Cleveland invoked the Monroe Doctrine in the dispute about the boundary line between Venezuela and British Guiana, he was challenging the most powerful empire in the world to protect a small and weak country. And though the Monroe Doctrine was not invoked when Napoleon III sent an army to Mexico to set up an empire under Maximilian during our Civil War, its spirit was. The invasion was called off when our President, after the war, mobilized veteran troops near the Rio Grande. That was what really saved Mexico." So I went around the table discussing in the frankest manner with the students each of the topics mentioned. And as we discussed, the temperature rose and we parted shaking hands most amicably. Needless to say the whole affair would have been impossible without the linguistic assistance of the Rector and Professor Belaunde.

During the week at Lima while I was delivering my lectures, I was informed that a Convocation of the University was to be held to which Mr. Deering, the American Ambassador, and I were invited. What was my surprise and delight when there was conferred upon me the honorary degree of Litt.D. Moreover, I learned afterward that this action was taken upon the motion of the student members of the University Council. I have a number of honorary degrees but none I value more than the one conferred by the University of San Marcos. I have often wondered whether ulterior motives would enter as much as they sometimes do into the conferring of honorary degrees by our own colleges and universities if representatives of the student body had a voice in the selection of persons to receive them. I remember meeting one day on the street in Baltimore my old master, Frank Goodnow, after he had become President of Johns Hopkins. I asked him how the campaign for additional funds in which the university was just then engaged was making out. He answered, "Not so happily," and then jokingly, entirely jokingly, he added, "An LL.D. for a hundred thousand, Duggan."

Shades of Inca Civilization

While I was at Lima, I did not fail to visit the Inca Museum that contains relics of Inca civilization which have been dug up since that civilization was destroyed by the *Conquistadores*. The Museum was under the supervision of the distinguished archaeologist, Dr. Tello, who afterward took me out to the immense graveyards at Pachacamac and in a few minutes dug up a partial skeleton. He did this to demonstrate what had been happening in recent decades. The peasants of the neighborhood had become aware of the treasures in the graves and took to archaeological research on their own. This proved so profitable in the early days, as the result of sales to rich tourists, that the graves were in ruins by the time of my visit.

Before leaving Lima I was asked to deliver a lecture at the little university of Cuzco. As I was going to Cuzco anyhow to see such remains of the Inca empire as are still in existence there, I gladly agreed. I flew across the Peruvian desert to Arequipa in the company of a delightful gentleman by the name of Carlos Gibson, one of the many descendants sprung from unions of nationals and Englishmen whom one finds all over Latin America. He put himself to considerable inconvenience to serve me and took me to the place where practically all foreigners who visit Arequipa stay, namely, at Quinta Bates. ("Quinta" means a small estate, usually with kitchen garden and orchard.) Mrs. Bates, a charming old Scotch woman, had developed in the course of time an admirable inn on Anglo-Saxon lines. The food, the rooms, the refreshing bath with plenty of hot water, the lovely garden were all thoroughly British. The old lady had a cold when I arrived and she insisted on my having a glass of "whoskey" with her. Now I like wine but I do not like hard liquor and when I saw the size of the glass of "whoskey" poured out for me by Mrs. Bates my heart sank. I unquestionably lost caste with her when she saw the small amount I swallowed.

During my brief stay at Arequipa I inquired whether the Shippee-Johnson expedition had been seen there, and was informed it had. This expedition had been organized by the American Geographical Society to take aerial photographs of the Andes. I have forgotten whether it was my good friend, Dr. Isaiah Bowman, the Director of the Society, or his able assistant, Dr. Raye R. Platt, who gave me letters of introduction to the expedition, should I come across it in my travels. Imagine my delight when on the evening of my second day at Arequipa there appeared at Quinta Bates an aviator belonging to the Shippee-Johnson expedition. I presented my letters of introduction and told him I was bound for Cuzco. He said, "It will take you two days and a night to go there by rail but if you want to fly with me over the Andes at an altitude of 16,000 feet, we shall leave here tomorrow at 10 A.M. and arrive there in three hours." I gladly accepted the invitation. Next morning we left the beautiful, snow-clad Mount Misti behind us at Arequipa on our flight over the Andes at an altitude almost 1,000 feet higher than Mont Blanc! The aviator pointed out to me the old Inca trail between the mountains with some of the ruined block houses, still visible. The flight was one of the most thrilling experiences of my life.

Reflections on the Status of the Indians

When we landed at the rather primitive airport some distance from Cuzco, the Indians—Peru is about 20 per cent white, 32 per cent Mestizo, and over 45 per cent Indian—from the neighboring fields crowded about the airplane peering at us as we descended from the cockpit. As I drove from the airport to the city I saw reproduced several times a picture of Palestine as described in the Bible in the days of Christ, namely, groups of Indians threshing their grain with the flail and winnowing it by throwing it into the air for the wind to blow away the chaff and let the grain fall to the ground. As yet the machine has invaded remote Latin America to but a slight extent.

I had hardly arrived in Cuzco when I received a courtesy call from the Mayor and the Rector of the little university. They assumed I knew no Spanish, which was practically true. They knew that they knew no English. That was absolutely true. So they brought with them the Rector's daughter who was supposed to know English, and that was only relatively true. But she began well. She said, "I saw your picture in the paper this morning." "Did you?" I answered. "Is it as homely as I really am?" "Yes," she answered, and was obviously quite unaware that a "no" would have been equally devastating. An English woman who was standing near by, highly amused, said, "What a mean thing to string an innocent girl in that way!" The girl was fortunately unconscious of any intention on my part to have fun at her expense, for I afterward overheard her say to her father, "Es muy simpático, el Yanqui."

From Cuzco I several times went out into the surrounding country to visit some of the Indian villages. If the picture

presented in Prescott's *Conquest of Peru* is at all accurate
the fall in the status of the Indians since the Conquest is de
plorable. They live in hovels, in unsanitary surroundings
ignorant of hygiene, devoid of medical assistance, illiterate
and intensely suspicious of strangers. For four hundred years
they have been exploited by Church and State. The Church
did a noble work at first in protecting them. But Peru was a
long way from Spain, the voyage took months, the discipline
of the local clergy was hard to maintain, and by the end of
the sixteenth century the Indians were practically without
protection. I could readily appreciate the origin of the sad
plaintive, melancholy music and songs of the Indians of the
Altiplano. A fine young American research scholar whom I
met on the ship that carried me to Peru, told me he was going
to the Altiplano to make records of the sad tunes of the Inca
Indians. I have since been told that they have been pub
lished, but I have not heard them. In the United States, pres
ervation of the Negro spirituals by securing records of them
before their disappearance is an undeniable contribution to
our civilization. The plaintive tunes of the Inca Indians were
the product of the same cause as were the Negro spirituals
—slavery. It is to be hoped that those tunes may some day
occupy a place in West Coast civilization similar to that
which the spirituals do in ours. That is not true today.

Though the revolution of 1930 which ended the Leguía
regime was the result chiefly of economic causes, it was has
tened unquestionably by the propaganda of the proscribed
Aprista party whose leader, Haya de la Torre, was in exile
One of the planks of his platform of reform was the enfran
chisement of the Indians, to be secured primarily through
education and their incorporation into the national life of
the country. Practically nothing has been accomplished in
this respect, for the Apristas have continued to be an illegal
party and few others are interested in improving the condi

ions of the Indians. Haya de la Torre, who was the idol of he students, was also the bitter enemy of "Yankee imperialsm". However, because of the adoption by the United States of the Good Neighbor policy, in the face of the greater evil of totalitarianism he has become a strong advocate of hemisphere solidarity.

Bolivia Indigenista

I can well understand how and why the Indians of the Altiplano became sun worshippers. It is difficult for anyone who has not visited the region to realize the part played by the sun in the life of the inhabitants. The penetrating cold that falls upon the Altiplano as soon as the sun disappears is most depressing. The revitalizing influence which accompanies its rise is very marked. My own experience testified to this. We Americans read with considerable pride of the way in which our fathers frequently walked miles to and from school in order to get an education. I do not know how far the students of the University of Bolivia at La Paz must walk, but they certainly suffer hardships of another kind. I delivered one of my lectures to them in the first period of the day when the sun had been up only a short time. I lectured wearing my overcoat and was filled with sympathy as I watched the students trying to take notes with their hands red from the cold. I could but wonder how they pursued their studies after sunset.

I was fortunate enough to be invited to be the guest at La Paz of the American Minister, Mr. Edward Feeley, whose residence was furnished with one of the few central heating plants in the city. My stay in his home is one of the pleasantest memories of my visit to South America. I must briefly digress here to express my admiration for our ambassadors, ministers, and consular officials in Latin America. I found them intelligent, efficient and courteous, always speaking the language of the country in which they were stationed. This is in marked contrast to the political hacks who were frequently sent to the South American countries before World War I in payment for political services at home.

Bolivia is the most Indian of all the Latin American countries. The Indians number more than 50 per cent of the population. They have become race-conscious but they have not yet found the leaders to galvanize them into action as have the Indians of Mexico. They too lost their lands to the *Conquistadores* in the sixteenth century and a few of their leaders have followed with keen interest the efforts of the Cárdenas government in Mexico to create *ejidos* out of great landed estates. It is also significant that Bolivia was the first South American state to follow the example of Mexico in expropriating the property of foreign oil companies. Bolivia was part of the Inca Empire, as were Ecuador and Peru and a portion of Colombia. The whole area to the south of our southwestern boundary down to Chile is still inhabited mostly by Indians, whose ancestors lived under communal conditions. The poor, illiterate Indian peon knows little of the history of his people during the past four hundred years, but tradition plays a part in his life as in the life of all subjugated peoples. It is interesting to speculate as to what might happen if race-consciousness were revived in that enormous area. However, outside of Mexico, there is little evidence of its existence yet. The stimulus will have to come from others than Indians, and few others want to change the *status quo*.

Strains and Stresses That Make Up Chile

As I had hoped to see somewhere a country in process of revolution, I was unfortunate in arriving in Chile shortly after the Dictator, Ibáñez, had been driven out. The students of the University of Chile took an important part in the driving out process. I was again impressed, as at Lima, with the political influence of the student body and their radical program. One of the influential administrators of the University arranged for an interview with the president of the students' association and I have seldom heard anywhere as frank talk even among faculty members. In discussing the aims of the students, the young president turned to my companion and said, "For example, you, Professor X, are an excellent teacher of your subject but you are no good as the Director of the ——— Institute, and you have got to go." And go he did!

All the countries of South America are favorably disposed to the assimilation of white immigrants. This has been true of Chile ever since the country won its independence. The first President, and a good one, was General O'Higgins, whose name indicates his ancestry and to whom the finest monument in Santiago was erected. But it is Englishmen in Chile who best illustrate the assimilating process. They did not usually settle in colonies but as individuals who threw in their lot with the country and became citizens, married among the upper classes, and often assumed places of leadership. Persons with names such as Edwards, Foster, Mackenna, and Simpson have in many cases been Chilean citizens for several generations. They speak excellent English and are very proud of their British ancestry but are even prouder of their Chilean citizenship. The Germans are more prone to settle in groups and do not assimilate so readily. But it is not only Englishmen who remain proud of their ancestry. I asked our ambassador to Chile, Mr. Culbertson, to give me an introduction to a conserative leader of the Church with whom I might discuss religious conditions, and he gave me a letter to Mr. Silva Vildósola. Mr. Vildósola, who had just retired as the editor of Chile's chief newspaper, *El Mercurio*, told me that there had recently arrived in Santiago a number of

American students, all Jews, who wanted to study medicine at the local university. He said he could not understand the reason considering that in the United States were some of the finest medical schools in the world. He hoped it was not due to anti-Semitism. "It is true," he continued, "that I am a pillar of the Church, but I am of a family of Jews driven out of Spain by Philip II and I am as proud of my Jewish ancestry as of my Catholic religion." Suppose Hitler had heard him! Spanish Jews who became Catholics were called "Marranos", and I have met them in several other parts of the world where they had settled and had sometimes become influential.

I paid a visit to Mr. Alessandri, who had recently been voted out of the presidency of Chile and was at a later time voted in again. At that time he was the leader of the radicals, and spoke with great frankness and with what I thought moderation about Chile's social problems. First of these problems was the position of the *inquilino,* i.e., the peon, which had changed little for generations on the great estates of central Chile. The peons were practically bound to the soil and dominated by the landowner. It was difficult to bring about improvement of their condition because the political control of the country was largely in the hands of the old land-owning families. Alcoholism, and the extreme poverty and wretched living conditions of the urban poor are also major problems. A problem having at times international repercussions was the relation of the Chilean workers in the nitrate fields and copper mines to the foreign, chiefly United States, industrial corporations. These workers and the *rotos* of the cities are much more radical than the peons on the estates. They have been influenced by Communist propaganda and often go on strike. Legislation on industrial relations in most of the South American countries is usually very favorable to the workers. Nearly all the industrial corporations are foreign owned and controlled and no native objects to their footing the bill in industrial conflicts. And, of course, such legislation makes the government popular with the workers.

World War I forced upon the consciousness of all people, as never before, the fact that scientific invention may be applied to destructive as well as constructive purposes. The scientific discovery of synthetic nitrates during the first World War almost ruined Chilean economy. Up to the time of that discovery Chile had been the chief source of nitrates for fertilizing purposes in peace and explosive purposes in war. Her export tax on nitrates had furnished most of the revenue of the government and had enabled the *hacendados,* the great landowners of the central valley who controlled the government, to maintain their semi-feudal social system. But with the revenue from nitrates drastically reduced, in turn diminishing foreign exchange for the purchase of manufactured goods from abroad, the Chileans were of necessity driven to manufacture for the home market. These manufactures are only in their infancy, but already a small middle class and a larger working class have developed in Santiago and elsewhere, forming an opposition to the *hacendados* and their peons whose votes the *hacendados* control. The latter have been compelled to tax themselves to a certain extent, but there are still other resources which enable them to avoid the drastic taxation which would otherwise be necessary, viz., the huge mining interests and the slowly recovering nitrate interests, both of which are practically wholly foreign controlled. But the lines of battle are slowly developing, the *hacendados* forming the core of the conservatives, and the adherents of industry and mining together with the professional classes, the opposition. And in the forefront of the reforms demanded by the latter is the break-up of the great estates.

I found the Chileans a most attractive people, virile, alert, and progressive. Though they inhabit one of the smaller states from the standpoint of population they lead a vigorous cultural life and send students to United States colleges and universities under the auspices of the Institute of International Education far beyond their proportion according to the number of people. All three institutions of higher education, the National University, and the Catholic University at Santiago, and the independent University at Concepcion, do excellent work.

One of the best influences in Santiago in developing a better understanding between Chile and the United States is Santiago College for Women. When it was established in 1886 as a secondary school comparable to a liceo, it was probably the first institution in Latin America to give women a vision of a broader and deeper life. It was chartered by the Regents of New York State and has recently been elevated to the status of a Junior college. It made its way to success against much local prejudice at first, but it is now largely attended by the daughters of the socially elect. Its success is chiefly due to the remarkable work of its Directora, Miss Elizabeth Mason, formerly Dean of Women at Goucher College, Baltimore. Miss Mason was aware that a woman's college in Chile would need to be more conservatively administered than the average woman's college in the United States, and moved forward cautiously. Today the scholastic, physical, recreational, and character-building activities of the College are as high as those of any Junior college in the United States. The result is that Santiago College has made a deep impression upon the life of Chile and its Directora has become one of the most respected and admired educators of the country and beloved by the alumnae of the institution.

Chile owed a good deal of her progress to the opening of

the Panama Canal in 1914. Up to that time the whole West Coast of South America was largely out of touch with modern movements. The Canal awakened the region by making it easily accessible to western Europe and the eastern United States. The Latin Americans generally hold the view that the Canal was obtained by the United States through shady and imperialistic measures. Certainly I doubt the morality of some of the measures and I have always regarded the $25,-000,000 afterward paid by the United States to Colombia, because of the secession of Panama, as "conscience money". The Canal is but another illustration of the problem that has always bothered decent men, namely, ought men seek to realize a desirable objective by dubious means? There can be no doubt of the remarkable service rendered not only to the people of western South America, but to the people of the whole world, by the building of the Panama Canal. It seems to me, however, that we were all becoming rapidly convinced of the great need of the Canal and that its early building was inevitable. Theodore Roosevelt was perhaps in too great a hurry when he "took" the Canal. When I am visiting a foreign country I do not like to have to discuss an action of my own country of which I cannot be proud.

Over the Andes to Argentina

I left the beautiful capital of Chile with real regret. As the train ascended to go over the Andes to Argentina and as I watched the city disappear in the valley surrounded by snow-capped mountains, I was filled with admiration. It was a fine sunny day; but, alas, when we arrived at Los Andes, the last stop before going over the mountains, it was pouring rain and very cold! It must not be forgotten that the seasons in South America are reversed. It was August but it was still winter there. Word had been telegraphed down from the crossing at the top that the railroad was blocked with immense drifts of snow and that there would be no train service until the way could be cleared. No one could say how long the wait would be. Not long before, the Prince of Wales (later Edward VIII) had been forced to wait a week. Rooms in the nice little inn at Los Andes were very cold and the only method of heating was to have a brazier brought in. This I did, but after nearly smothering from smoke I fled. The rain ceased the next day and it was warmer. During the remaining two days of our enforced stay at Los Andes a Chilean student who was on his way to a United States university and I explored the surrounding country in one of the funny little *cabriolés* drawn by a very bony horse. Our third night we had a great celebration with wine and song in which everybody, natives and foreigners, participated. An Englishman and I sang "Annie Laurie" and "Drink to Me Only with Thine Eyes" and all the others sang la, la, la, as we all do when we do not know the words. The Chileans sang more hilarious songs to which the Englishman and I la, la, la'd. Then we told stories and jokes to one another in Spanish and English which practically none of us understood but at which we courteously laughed with great gusto.

The next morning we began our ascent on the railroad, and passed under the top through a tunnel banked high at the entrance with snow and ice. The whole scene crossing the mountains was unforgettable, and the railroad is a testimony to the courage and foresight of the Chilean and Argentine peoples. The descent on the Argentine side was quite rapid and we soon reached Mendoza, the center of the Argentine wine country. The next morning I walked to a lovely park outside the city to see a fine statue of San Martín, who made the almost incredible march across the mountains, liberated Chile, and aided in consolidating independence for the Spanish colonies in South America.

In Argentina

The ride across the Argentine plains resembles traveling across the Russian steppes or our own prairies. All are dusty and tiresome rides. The country is wholly flat and unattractive. One is glad to see on the horizon every now and then an *estancia* surrounded by tall trees which serve, I suppose, to give shade and to break the wind. One can understand why the cattle barons who own thousands of acres of these fertile lands prefer Buenos Aires or Paris as a place of residence. The cattle barons form the ruling caste in Argentina, despite the existence of liberal groups in the large cities and radical and socialistic elements in Buenos Aires. Fortunately, the *Ley Sáenz Peña* passed in 1912 secured the secret ballot to the Argentine people. It serves as a slight brake upon the control of the landed magnates who naturally form the conservative element in the country as they do everywhere in Latin America, if not in the entire world.

Buenos Aires is the second largest Latin city in the world, being surpassed only by Paris. It has a population of two and a half millions, one-fifth of the entire population of Argentina. I do not think it is as beautiful a city as Santiago in Chile or Rio de Janeiro in Brazil. It resembles an American city of the first class, with some beautiful public buildings and many fine private residences. I think the Opera House is the finest opera house I have ever seen. There the great German, Italian, and French operas are frequently performed, at which the most notable European artists are heard. The people of Buenos Aires resemble ourselves—alert, vigorous and aggressive. It is a cosmopolitan city like New York with many immigrant groups. About one quarter of the population of Argentina is either Italian or of Italian ancestry, but I did not hear as much Italian spoken on the streets as one does in

New York. I had a good many friends in Argentina because I had been responsible for bringing to the United States quite a number of students upon scholarships, and also some visiting professors. My friends were very kind to me and did a great deal to make my visit a success. I was particularly indebted to Judge Alfredo Colmo of the Supreme Court of Argentina and to Dr. Enrique Gil, a distinguished lawyer who introduced me to the chief clubs and took me to the cattle show, which is the great Argentine social event of the year, like the Horse Show in New York.

I was very anxious to spend a few days at an *estancia* and Dr. Gil secured an invitation for me from a gentleman who was of the third generation of an American family that had settled in Argentina. I spent a good part of a day traveling by rail to his place and when he met me at the station he asked, "Did you notice the name of the last station before this one?" "Yes," I answered, "I was quite surprised." The name was Duggan. "Did you notice the people who got off there?" "Yes," I answered, "I thought they were a very nice looking lot of people." "Well, Dr. Duggan, they have the same name as you but they differ in one important respect. They are very rich and I presume you, as an American professor, are not." Those Duggans had an enormous estate. Among the family are some of the celebrated polo players who come to New York every year and almost invariably win the games from the American players. It seems that about a hundred years ago their ancestor landed at Buenos Aires intending to settle to the south, in Buenos Aires province, but was persuaded by an Irish priest to go to the north where land could be obtained for almost nothing. The family gradually extended its holdings until now they are among the richest people in Argentina. One of those Duggans married the most beautiful woman in Argentina, and after his death she became the wife of the Marquess of Curzon.

My host was a charming gentleman who drove me around his estate and explained its administration. He was particularly proud of a beautiful little Catholic chapel erected for the family and for workers on the estate. His ancestor, who had emigrated to Argentina, was a Protestant. He was probably an intelligent person who, finding no Protestant church in which to worship, attended Catholic services and in course of time became a Catholic. This has been true of a large number of early Protestant settlers. The reverse process often happened with early Catholic immigrants to the United States who settled in remote rural regions where no Catholic churches were to be found. Such change in either direction would be natural for people of a deeply religious nature but not of a strictly sectarian attitude.

Argentine Attitude Toward the United States

Most Englishmen I met in Argentina were usually of a fine class, intelligent, courteous and proud of their ancestry. They frequently inter-married with the Argentines and became patriotic citizens. In Buenos Aires they numbered about 25,000 and many of them live in a purely English suburb called Hurlingham. They control a good deal of the foreign commerce and first-class retail trade of Buenos Aires. They have a fine Anglo-Argentine cultural center at which distinguished Englishmen of letters and publicists make addresses to audiences composed not only of Anglo-Argentines but of the intellectuals and the socially elect among the native Argentines. The English have been in the past a popular group of foreign descent with the *estanciero* class. I had personal proof of this shortly after my arrival in Buenos Aires. André Siegfried, the author of *America Comes of Age,* and I have been good friends for many years. It so happened that we began lecturing at the South American universities at the same time

and frequently crossed each other's path. That happened at
Buenos Aires and we were both invited to spend Sunday at a
delightful home in the suburbs. At dinner I was seated at the
hostess' left and M. Siegfried at her right. The conversation
gradually turned to the interesting question of racial and national characteristics. The hostess closed the discussion by saying, "My own view is that the finest type of man in the world is
an English gentleman." It was not the most tactful thing that
might have been said when a French gentleman sat on her
right and an American on her left, but it did reflect the general attitude of the socially elect at that time among the Argentines. With the passing years I believe a much more
critical attitude has become general.

When Argentina was cut off from Europe during World
War I, she turned to the United States for most of her sup-
plies of manufactured goods, but not for all. She started her
own industries and today provides most of the textiles, shoes,
clothing, glass, cement, furniture, beverages and other consumers' goods. With the passage of time many Argentines
became convinced that their country would never become the
great power of their dreams unless they became self-sufficient
through industrialization. They have practically no coal, iron,
or other minerals and not enough oil for their needs. But
neither Italy nor Japan has these requisites for industrialization. Both those countries, however, have large populations
and though exports of manufactured goods are essential to
their position as great powers, the domestic market is of primary value. Argentina has a population of only 13,000,000
and outside of Buenos Aires most of the people have a low
standard of living. It is questionable, therefore, whether it
will ever be able to develop a self-sufficing industry, as in fact
few countries have. But the movement toward industrialization has awakened the agricultural interest in their own defense. The landed magnates who furnish the millions of tons

of grain and the thousands of tons of meat for export do not intend to relinquish their control of government to the *porteños* of Buenos Aires. And outside of Buenos Aires and a very few other large cities, Argentina is still living in the nineteenth, not the twentieth century.

Education in Argentina

I shall write more fully of education in the Latin American countries at the close of this chapter, but I wish to say a special word here about education in Argentina. The Argentine educational system is one of the best in Latin America and in the early days was influenced by our own education. Few people in the United States know of the splendid career of one of Argentina's most notable presidents, Domingo Faustino Sarmiento. In the late 1840's while returning from an educational mission which he had undertaken in Europe at the request of the Chilean government, he became a friend of Horace Mann and an admirer of his educational ideas. As President, he introduced into Argentina from the United States a considerable number of normal school teachers imbued with Mann's principles. The result was a reorganization of Argentina's system of elementary education which put it at once in the forefront of Latin American school systems. Sarmiento was afterward appointed Minister to the United States and became a great friend of Lincoln. While returning to Argentina he was elected President. He is justly regarded as one of the finest figures in the history of the American republics.

One educational experience in Buenos Aires made a deep impression upon me. My good friend, Dr. Ernesto Nelson, who was in charge of the work in secondary education, invited me to the Normal School of Living Languages. In this school children begin learning English, French or German in the ABC class, learning not only to read it but to write it and especially to speak it. Practically all the instruction is in the language studied. They continue this practice until the close of their secondary school career. I spent an entire morning at the school, visiting the various classes. The group that interested me most was the graduating class, whose members were destined to become teachers of English. When I entered the room the students, all girls, were engaged in discussing George Eliot's "Mill on the Floss". They were not only discussing its literary values but the philosophy behind the ideal of life presented, and the discussion was all carried on in admirable English. Not a word of Spanish was spoken.

Now the teaching of modern languages in our country is one of our major educational failures. The number of schools and colleges from which students graduate who can speak or even write a foreign language is so small as to be negligible. In some American colleges it is possible for a student to begin a foreign language one year, a second foreign language the next year, and even a third the following year. Moreover, the student can in many schools and colleges drop the study of a foreign language at the close of almost any year. A reading knowledge may be obtained, though even that is not always accomplished. The explanation of this is not far to seek. We are a country of immense area inhabited by people who habitually speak only English. There is no feeling of a need to know foreign languages. It is altogether different in the countries of Europe west of Russia. The largest of them, Germany, could fit inside Texas, with plenty of room to spare. The inhabitants of some of the smaller European countries could not travel in any direction for a hundred miles without crossing a frontier. A knowledge of foreign languages is, for them, a necessity. With more than a million students in our colleges and more than eight millions in our secondary schools, it may be impossible to demand that everyone teaching a foreign language must have lived a year, or at least spent a summer vacation, in the country of the language which he teaches. In most of our states persons of foreign birth may not teach in publicly supported educational institutions until they have become citizens. Hence competent teachers of foreign languages are not easily found for our public schools and colleges. But at least we might adopt some modification of the Argentine plan for students looking forward to teaching a foreign language as a career.

This discussion of language teaching leads naturally to some mention of the splendid work that is done at Buenos Aires by the Instituto Cultural Argentino-Norteamericano, whose president is the distinguished scholar, Dr. Cupertino del Campo, the former Director of the Museum of Fine Arts at Buenos Aires. The aim of the Instituto is the fostering in all possible ways of cultural relations between Argentina and the United States. It is well housed in an excellent building for its purposes, has a fine library, primarily of books on American civilization, and provides lectures and musicales for its members. It forwards its objective with excellent films secured from the various departments of our federal government and from private agencies. One of its most important functions is to teach English, and today there are more than 3,000 persons studying English under its direction. Sections are organized at different places in the city, one for business men, another for physicians, still another for engineers, etc. The Instituto is the Argentine Center from which a large number of our scholarship holders come north to study in American universities. In the last few years similar cultural institutes have been established in the capital and the chief cities of each of the larger Latin American republics.

It is impossible to overestimate the influence of the movies in the spread of a knowledge of English in the Latin American countries. To help in understanding the story there are always captions in Spanish, or in Portuguese when American movies are shown in Brazil. But the people are very prone to watch for idioms in English. I was watching a movie one night in Buenos Aires in which an actor used the words "very well", which were naturally translated "muy bien". I overheard a young girl on the seat in front say to her neighbor, "Did you get that? 'muy bien' is 'very well' in English." No doubt she picked up other English expressions in the same way.

Though university life in Latin America is devoid of sports, that is not true of life generally. In Argentina, tennis, football, polo, Jai Alai, and other sports are freely engaged in. Sunday afternoon is a time for thousands to turn out to attend soccer football games. The Latin Americans have not so good a sense of real sportsmanship as have the Anglo-Saxons, probably because sports form a more recent ingredient in their civilization. At football games not only are opprobrious epithets in frequent use but fist fights often take place, as was true in the earlier history of baseball in our country. I attended a football game at one of Buenos Aires' big stadia and witnessed a phenomenon wholly new to me. When a speaker makes an address to an enormous audience in our country, if the people present approve, they not only clap and stamp but whistle. Now while I was in Argentina the campaign for the presidency was going on and naturally candidates liked to take advantage of every possible opportunity to advance their cause. A football game was a splendid opportunity, and at this particular game General Justo, the candidate of the conservative elements, was introduced "to say a few words". The few words were colorless enough but he was received with a whirlwind of whistling which I took to be a form of approval. I was astonished when my companion, General Justo's own son, informed me that it was an emphatic form of disapproval.

I spent a month in Argentina visiting various sections of the country and becoming acquainted with the different attitudes toward life of people in the different sections. Even in the more remote places new ideas and mores were creeping in and causing friction. I made similar observations during short visits in Paraguay and Uruguay, before sailing to Brazil.

Paulistas and Other Brazilians

Santos is the great port from which most of the coffee crop of Brazil is exported. It is not an attractive city and upon arriving there I did not tarry but went directly to São Paulo, the greatest manufacturing city south of the Rio Grande. It has a population of more than a million people including a large colony of Italians, smaller numbers of Syrians, and other foreigners. As so often at home, I was struck by the prominent part played by many of these foreigners in the busy life of the city. Most of them had been poor peasants or workers at home, but given an opportunity to put their native abilities to use, they had risen to places of influence. Many of them, unlike the majority of Brazilians, are good technical workers and they control to a large extent the varied manufactures of the city.

São Paulo is the capital of the state of that name, and there the great coffee planters control the political and social life of the state. Brazil is a federation with some of the features that existed in North America before the adoption of the Constitution in 1789, and the chief political problem for a long time has been states' rights vs. federal control. São Paulo resembles the Virginia of our early history, which dominated our political life during the first thirty-five years of our republic. São Paulo, however, has much greater power and influence in Brazil than Virginia ever had in the United States. The second great state of the Brazilian federation is Minas Geraes, and during the past generation it had been customary for a Paulista president to be succeeded by one from Minas Geraes. When in 1930 the Paulista President, Washington Luis, tried to secure the succession of another Paulista, Minas Geraes obtained the support of the third most important state, Rio Grande do Sul, and staged a revolution which put Getulio Vargas of Rio Grande do Sul in the Presidency. São Paulo did not yield, however, and two years later civil war ensued, resulting in the defeat of the Paulistas. In contrast with what happened in the Reconstruction period following our Civil War, the State of São Paulo was speedily restored to its place in the federation. Under President Vargas the unitary state has become dominant. When his term of office expired he assumed the dictatorship, overthrew the constitution and replaced it by one with strong centralizing tendencies. As long as he has the support of the army, the dictatorship will probably last.

I found the influence of the United States to be quite pronounced in the city of São Paulo, and it was a good influence. One of the finest medical schools and hospitals in the world was being aided there by the Rockefeller Foundation, and its Director, Dr. de Paula Souza, was one of the influential men of the community. And it is not only in São Paulo that the Foundation has rendered splendid service to the people of Brazil. As the result of its researches and field work in cooperation with the Brazilian government, one of Brazil's greatest plagues, yellow fever, has been stamped out. The Foundation cooperates with the medical authorities of the country in many other ways. One of its best activities is the bringing of well-selected research students in medicine and public health to the Rockefeller Institute in New York, where they receive admirable training.

São Paulo is the seat of Mackenzie College, an American institution chartered by the Regents of the State of New York. It is supported chiefly by the tuition fees of the students but receives some contributions from friends in the United States. It gives the regular academic instruction of an American college, but wisely appreciating the need in Brazil of a more practical education, it emphasizes technical instruction and has an admirable engineering school. The college has always tried to conform to the requirements of the Brazilian educational system and because of the fine results of the education it provides, its graduates receive professional degrees similar to those given to the graduates of State institutions.

French vs. American Cultural Influence

Accompanied by the Commissioner of Education of São Paulo, I undertook the all-day rail journey to Rio de Janeiro. We were met at the station by the Rector of the University of Rio and a group of professors and officials, nearly all of whom had secured their graduate instruction in the United States. I knew some of them personally and all of them as a result of correspondence. They formed the real progressives in the higher education of Brazil. They were all pro-American and devoted to the political, social, and educational ideals of the United States. This was not true, however, of the Rector, who in his intercourse with me did not disguise his love of and preference for French culture. It is hard to over-estimate the influence of the French Revolution upon the Latin American peoples in their reaction against the absolutism of Spain. French philosophical ideas, French political principles, French literature, French civilization and culture became the sources from which the Latin Americans drew inspiration, especially during their formative years. Practically all members of the upper classes speak French fluently and French books are found in every cultured home. When children are sent abroad to be educated, in normal times they go to France. Sorbonne professors deliver lectures in French Institutes, which are found in many of the large cities of Latin America. All this is particularly true of Brazil, and when I lectured in Rio de Janeiro it was in French. Most Brazilians do not speak English and though they do understand Spanish they do not like, as a matter of pride, to be spoken to in Spanish. When a foreigner does not understand their native tongue, they prefer to be addressed in French.

The Brazilian system of education is not so good as the Argentine. Outside of a few large cities like São Paulo and Rio de Janeiro, the teaching staff is not well trained and the equipment is poor. The fine group of progressive scholars mentioned previously begged me to associate myself with them in drawing up a prospectus for a training school for teachers which was much desired by the Minister of Education. They thought the occasion of my visit would make opportune an appeal to the government for a grant of funds for that purpose. We spent almost a week in drawing up a plan for the school—the curriculum, the standards for the teaching staff, the needs of the technical library, the qualifications for entrance, the scholarships to be competed for throughout the country, in short, every proper requirement of a good teachers' college. Then, the Director of the Dom Pedro II Liceo, Dr. Delgado Carvalho, who was influential with the government, and the Minister of Education accompanied us on a visit to President Vargas. The President was enthusiastic and sent at once for the Minister of Finance, who stated that the treasury could not afford to spend the considerable sum needed for the establishment of the school. The President insisted that the money must be forthcoming and our group left the conference quite jubilant. Alas, the school does not yet exist! This was but one example of the lesson I learned in Latin America, viz., that a promise made by a politician in favor of an important activity is not necessarily to be relied upon. That is true in our own country also, though probably to a less extent.

A Great United States Ambassador

When I arrived in Rio de Janeiro I found I was to be the guest of Mr. Edwin V. Morgan, the American Ambassador to Brazil, whom I did not know. Mr. Morgan, who was a wealthy man, had been Ambassador to Brazil for twenty-one years when he was retired in 1933. He occupied a fortunate diplomatic post, for throughout its history Brazil has been a loyal friend to the United States. He was greatly loved by all Brazilians, for he had made himself almost one of them and was far better informed as to the history, geography, resources, literature and institutions of Brazil than any but a few Brazilians. He had a place in the diplomatic history of Brazil similar to that of Mr. Bryce and M. Jusserand in the diplomatic history of the United States. Before he died he repeatedly expressed his wish to be buried in Brazil and was buried in the summer capital of Petropolis. The Americans in Brazil were not so enthusiastic about Mr. Morgan as were the Brazilians. The business interests maintained that in matters of controversy he looked out for Brazilian interests as often as for American.

The fact was that Mr. Morgan was intensely interested in Brazilian culture. His knowledge of it was profound. When he took me to visit the Foreign Minister, he drew my attention to a large and beautiful rug in the ante-room and named the distant place, which he had himself visited, where it was woven. Then he showed me a magnificent escritoire and dilated upon the wood from which it was made and the forest from which the wood came. We made a circuit of the room so that Mr. Morgan could show me the pictures on the walls. He knew every detail of their history and value. It is easily understandable why the Brazilians loved him.

The Color Line in Brazil

A great deal is written in our magazines about the lack of color prejudice and the non-existence of a color-line in Brazil. Certainly there exists no legal discrimination as in some States of our country. But it is a fact that at all the social gatherings I attended no Negroes happened to be present. Indeed even at such a semi-social and public gathering as my lecture at the embassy, I saw only one Negro, whom I afterward met and found to be a fine scholar and gentleman. However, if there be any distinction in Brazil between people of different races and colors it is by no means so openly declared as with us. I was taken one day by a university professor across the bay from Rio de Janeiro to Nichteroy to get a good view of Rio, and I happened to mention the alleged non-existence of race discrimination in Brazil. Probably as a kindly warning to prevent my saying anything that might hurt a sensitive person, he said, "You know, Dr. Duggan, I have Negro blood in my veins." I should not have known it. There was no indication of it in the color of his skin or the appearance of his features. I wonder how many persons in our country with Negro blood in their veins would publicly avow the fact if it were not at all evident. The problem of large masses of Negroes and whites living in the same community has received different solutions in Brazil, the Caribbean area, and the United States where that condition exists. The prominent Brazilian sociologist, Gilberto Freyre, has made a thorough study of it for Brazil. It ought to be similarly studied in the other areas.

I like the Brazilian people immensely. To me they resemble the French more than does any other Latin American people. They are kindly and courteous and few have any of the aggressive qualities of the Argentines or ourselves. Perhaps they are not sufficiently endowed with the determination to exploit wisely the immense resources of their great country. It is larger than the United States, excluding Alaska, and has a population of over 40,000,000—about one-third of the population of the whole of Latin America. We Americans boast that for more than a hundred years we have had an unfortified frontier between our country and Canada. It speaks well for the peaceable character of Brazilian statesmanship that Brazil borders every one of the South American countries save Chile and Ecuador, and has had no war with any one of them since the Paraguayan war of 1865–1870. Brazil seems destined to play a great rôle in the future of the southern continent.

Reflections Homebound

I bade good-bye to André Siegfried on the dock at Rio de Janeiro, he to return to France and I to the United States. I thought he seemed saddened by the obvious increase of our cultural influence and the recession of French cultural influence in Latin America; for he is frankly not an admirer of our civilization. As I sailed home I could not but reflect upon the relations of our country with the Latin American republics. At the time (1931) they were certainly bad. The imperialistic policy pursued by the United States in the Caribbean during the previous twenty years, and the insistence that only we had the right to a voice in the interpretation of the Monroe Doctrine, caused the United States to be regarded in

Latin America with suspicion, distrust and resentment. Fortunately, two years subsequent to my visit President Franklin Roosevelt dedicated his administration to the Good Neighbor policy and at successive Pan American conferences the patience, the obvious sincerity, and the broadmindedness of Secretary of State Cordell Hull won the Latin Americans to cooperation. Today our relations with the Latin American countries are founded upon a spirit of mutual good will. Nothing could have been more fortunate, because the totalitarian wave that swept over practically all Europe might have engulfed Latin America or certainly parts of it, had the old attitude of distrust and dislike toward the United States persisted. Instead, our State Department has attempted to develop a policy of hemisphere solidarity with a large degree of success due to the cordial cooperation of the great majority of the Latin American republics. It may eventually prove, however, that some of the Latin American countries are not impervious to Fascist propaganda.

The Western Hemisphere, in the large, is made up of only two great civilizations: the Iberian (Spanish and Portuguese) and the Anglo-Saxon.* Although these two civilizations are now united in a most important resolve to make this hemisphere a haven of peace and to arrange for its adequate defense, they differ from each other in many ways. I should mention here that I know of no two highly civilized countries which differ more in language, race, religion, traditions, legal systems, and attitude toward life than France and England. Moreover, no two have had a longer history of mutual conflict. Yet a common danger knit them together and the alliance was only dissolved by force, by the German conquest of France.

* I am not losing sight of the some 1,000,000 French descendants in Haiti and the 3,500,000 French Canadians of Quebec. But as an element of the population of this hemisphere they would of necessity abide by the decisions of the other 250,000,000.

It is true that all the nations of the New World seem now to realize that they are confronted by a common danger which threatens to destroy their peace and retard the development of their immense resources. Hemisphere solidarity is unquestionably their best safeguard. But hemisphere solidarity is primarily dependent upon mutual understanding and there is very incomplete understanding between the two parts of the hemisphere, the Anglo-Saxon and the Latin American. Each is very ignorant of the civilization and culture of the other and that ignorance must be overcome. The chief remedy is personal contact. It is hard to understand people with whom one has never come into touch. Personal contact on a large scale is difficult. Throughout history the lines of travel have been east and west, not north and south. Until war commenced in 1939 citizens of the United States and Latin Americans voyaged to Europe to visit the monuments of the civilization which are their common cultural heritage. Moreover, it takes twice as long to travel from New York to Rio de Janeiro or to Lima as it does to go from New York to Europe, and it costs correspondingly more. Hence, though the scenery of some parts of Latin America is equal to anything in Europe and though the remains of ancient civilizations such as the Mayan, Inca and Aztec are deeply interesting, it cannot be expected that our tourist traffic with Latin America will ever assume anything like the dimensions of our tourist traffic with Europe. Nor is Latin American tourist traffic with the United States likely to become as great as its traffic with Europe. The political tensions of the past few years and the present war, however, have turned many tourists to the Latin American countries and that movement may increase with time.

Commercial and financial relations are bound to expand, but they do not necessarily lead to better understanding. Next to personal contact the most important remedy is wider and deeper cultural relations. The more that students and teachers from the Latin American countries study and teach in our institutions of education and the more they become familiar with the great strides we have made in music, literature, art and the higher things of life generally, the more will they remove the misconception existing among many in Latin America that our civilization is but a brutal materialism devoid of spiritual values. And the more that United States students and teachers visit the countries of Latin America and become aware of the vigorous and progressive civilizations that are developing there, the more will they help to destroy the attitude of disdain and superiority which so many North Americans have held in the past. What has been said of students and teachers is equally true of publicists, journalists, men of affairs, and professional men.

It is unfortunate that at present so few in the upper strata of Latin American society speak English with any degree of fluency. It is equally unfortunate that so few of our distinguished scholars and men of affairs can speak Spanish, Portuguese or French fluently enough to deliver lectures or addresses in those languages. It is noticeable, however, that the language obstacle is rapidly being overcome. This is true in the field of literature also. In 1939 the most influential publishers in the United States cooperated to send to South America three libraries of their most important publications, to the number of 2,500 volumes—one library to Rio de Janeiro, another to Buenos Aires, and a third to Montevideo. The books so generously donated were put into the public libraries of those cities and already are being widely read.

Although a person catches the spirit of a work of foreign literature better when he reads it in the original, in most cases he will secure a knowledge of it faster if he reads it in a good translation into his own tongue. During the past few years some of the finest masterpieces of American literature have been translated into Spanish and Portuguese, and some masterpieces of Spanish-American and Brazilian literature have been translated into English. One of the most efficient agencies for the spread of a knowledge of United States civilization among the Latin American peoples is the *Reader's Digest*. It translates its articles into Spanish and Portuguese, and adds a few in each issue by writers in Latin American countries. It now has attained the amazing circulation in Latin America of more than 1,000,000.

Europe and the Americas

Since the United States gained its independence it has developed a new civilization, based upon England's but different from it and, as Europe has learned in recent years, not a provincial imitation of English civilization. The same thing is true of the countries of Latin America since they became independent of Spain and Portugal. The prophecies of Spengler and Keyserling as to the downfall of Western civilization probably apply nowhere, not even to Europe. They certainly do not apply to the Western Hemisphere. Europe may be old, tired, and pessimistic. The Americas are young, virile, and optimistic; theirs is a new land with vast natural resources to be developed and great empty spaces still to be filled. Despite differences in race and civilization the people of the United States have much in common with those of the Latin American countries. Some thinkers in both continents believe in the possibility of the development of a new civilization in this hemisphere, with Latin elements contributed by Latin America and Anglo-American elements contributed by the United States, a civilization founded upon those inherited from Europe but different from them. The realization of any such possibility is very distant. In the meantime, the peoples of the United States and the Latin American countries can learn to know and understand one another better, to respect and admire the culture and civilization of one another more fully, and to cooperate in enterprises for the improvement of themselves and of humanity.

The University in Latin America and in the United States

The great interchange of students and teachers between the United States and the Latin American countries that has taken place in increasing numbers in recent years naturally suggests making a comparison between the systems of higher education of the United States and of Latin America.

The students of Latin American countries, many of whom are sons of politicians, are intensely interested in politics and in the conduct of government. Generally speaking, Latin American students are far more radical than our students and sometimes cooperate with workers in labor strikes and other forms of workers' movements which are productive of better social conditions. Politics with them takes the place of athletics with us and they not only have a deep interest in the political and social problems that confront their countries but they actually know a great deal about such problems. The university, its professors and students, wield more influence in the political and social life of a Latin American country than with us. The government always gives careful consideration to the probable attitude of the university upon any new policy and the views of the university professors and students upon a political situation carry great weight with the people. In a number of the universities the students have secured representation upon the university council.

Until recently our college students have not been seriously interested in the political, economic, and social problems that confront our country. Since the beginning of the recent economic depression, however, there has been a gratifying change in that respect. Moreover, the establishment of student councils in all our best colleges is a splendid step in preparing students for participation and leadership in the life of a democracy. In some colleges the entire control of student activities, including the matter of discipline, has been turned over to the student councils. In others, they participate even in the organization and administration of the curriculum. As in life generally, this situation is to a great extent a matter of atmosphere and morale. For unfortunately student politics in some of our colleges is characterized by the worst features of manipulation that exist in our municipal politics.

When Latin American students consider a situation intolerable in a university because of the presence of an utterly incompetent professor or a political rector, they go on strike and the university is shut down until the *persona non grata* is removed or a compromise reached. By means of the strike, students have also sometimes initiated and carried to a successful conclusion movements for modernizing antiquated courses and methods of instruction. But students go on strike for other reasons and sometimes their interference in public affairs has been admirable. Most of the revolutions of 1930 began in student uprisings. In Santiago de Chile they led the movement against the Dictator Ibáñez in 1931. When Ibáñez resigned as the result of the strike of physicians, engineers, teachers and finally labor, the provisional government wisely kept the *carabineros* in their barracks because they had been his favorites and had fired upon the people. For three days the students helped to maintain order. They directed traffic and rendered other services to the government in a most helpful manner. There was no such looting in the city as there had been in Boston in 1920 when as the result of the police strike, the citizens were without protection. The episode is one of which Chileans may really be proud. Unquestionably the fall of the Machado regime in Cuba was as much the result of student activity as of any other single factor. In this case, after having tried for more than two years the ordinary methods of agitation to secure necessary political reform, the students formed a secret organization and resorted to terroristic activities.

But not all student strikes are of this admirable kind. Some are caused by an insistence upon interfering in matters of university curricula and administration, owing to such demands as that an unpopular professor be dismissed, a vacation extended, an examination superseded, or courses duplicated or eliminated. In some universities the regular work is frequently interrupted and the university shut down for months. This is sometimes followed by sympathetic strikes in the other universities, secondary schools and even primary schools of the country, lasting until the dispute in the original strike has been settled—nearly always to the satisfaction of the students. Some of the dictators who feared student uprisings have closed universities even for a year or longer. It is obvious what a hindrance this is to a student's education, especially in a professional faculty. In the United States if a student were to return home and announce that he was on strike, his father would probably tell him that his education was ended and that he must earn his own living. But that is just where the difference in attitude toward life is shown. In the Latin American student's home, going on strike would be considered part of the individual's independence. Furthermore, the patriarchal tradition is still so strong that no one would consider expecting a student to earn his living under the circumstances described. In fact, few opportunities exist to enable him to do so. The only way that a young man can secure the coveted title of "Doctor" and a place in official life is by graduating from one of the faculties of the national university. Very few private universities are empowered to grant degrees. This has, at least, the advantage of preventing ill-equipped institutions from imposing badly trained graduates upon the public, as is still the case in the United States.

Political professors and even politicians outside the university are sometimes behind student movements. Certainly politics ought to be driven out of educational affairs and particularly university affairs. A people that witnessed a few years ago the dismissal of an upright superintendent of schools on the demand of a political demagogue who happened to be Mayor of Chicago, or the dismissal of professors from their chairs in the state university by a stupid governor of Mississippi, understand that need. But those occurrences are not usual in the United States and bring a storm of disapproval and usually retribution upon the offenders. It is not so in most of the Latin American countries. The peoples of those countries might, in fact, profit by our experience in this matter. In addition to arousing public opinion to the necessity of the independence of the university, some of our states have adopted two measures that go far to take our state universities out of politics, though by no means all the way out. These universities have been placed under the control of a Board of Regents which is usually made up of well-known citizens who serve entirely outside of the state government and are assured a definite tenure. Minimum support has been provided for the universities by allotting a certain number of units in every dollar raised by public taxation for university purposes exclusively. These provisions appear in state constitutions and can be changed only by vote of the people. Unfortunately, such ideas are alien to the Latin Americans, and tradition plays a much larger part in their civilization than in ours.

How the product of the Latin American university compares with our own is difficult to say. It is almost like comparing incommensurable quantities. The critic of the American college insists that the student is lacking in intellectual discipline and is too much "spoon-fed". I believe that is largely true. Moreover, there can be no question that the American college student pays too much attention to athletics and extracurricular activities generally. But at least these teach him the necessity of self-effacement, of cooperation, of accepting defeat gracefully. The friendly and even intimate relationship that exists between teachers and students in a well-organized American college is also one of the finest aspects of American higher education. And fortunately, the aim of character building in most colleges has survived the cynicism of the decade after the World War. The American ideal of training body and mind, and not only intellect but will and emotions as well, is an approach to the old Athenian ideal of the "rounded" man as the objective of education.

The *liceo, colegio,* and university in Latin American countries present a sharp contrast in these respects. Those institutions pay little regard to the students' physical, moral or social welfare. They are places of intellectual discipline only. They emphasize the student's individualism and he is already individualistic by racial and social inheritance. It is probably true that at twenty-one the Latin American has a keener intellect, knows more, and has a far more mature outlook upon life than the North American of the same age. He is probably possessed of more polish and social grace. But it is doubtful whether he has as much initiative, creative spirit, sense of responsibility, and consideration for inferiors.

The Latin American university is almost everywhere a national institution directly under the control of the government, which provides practically all of the budget. Universities are not autonomous as we understand educational autonomy in the United States. Lacking even the partial autonomy of our state university under its separate Board of

Regents, the Latin American university often becomes a pawn in the play of national politics. A distinguished official of one of the countries said to me in the course of a conversation, "There is little in common between your country and mine, but there is one thing: we both have politicians to take care of. Your government is so big with so many departments and bureaux that you can provide for them rather harmlessly. We have to put some in the university."

The Latin American university is always located in a city, always the capital city if there is but one university in a country. Moreover, its main building and center of administration is likely to be on the principal avenue along which surges the daily life of the people. The building is often a converted monastery and still preserves its cloistral appearance and arrangement. Other parts of the university are frequently scattered about the city in buildings made over for university purposes. There are no dormitories, no campus, no shady walks, no commons. The students live at home or, if they come from other parts of the country, with relatives or in boarding houses. There is no gymnasium, athletic field or tennis court, because athletics form no part of university life. Nor is there any chapel. Religion is generally excluded from the curriculum and though most professors and students are nominal Catholics few participate in religious activities. There is always a central hall for educational gatherings, public addresses by visiting celebrities, and student agitation. There is seldom any social center for there is little social intercourse. The university is a place for intellectual discipline and political activity. The feeling of loyalty toward Alma Mater which is so strong a characteristic of the American alumnus seldom exists among the alumni of the Latin American university. Hence the generous gifts which an American university receives from its graduates are almost unknown in Latin American countries.

The Latin American university does not attempt to equip the student for life in the broader sense. It is practically everywhere organized as a vocational institution to provide for the professions and the government service. It is essentially, therefore, a loose collection of professional schools, generally free to the graduates of the *liceo,* the secondary school. Except in the most progressive countries, it is fair to say that the chief aim of the average graduate of one of those faculties is to secure a government position. It is a question whether the objective of very many American college graduates, namely, of preferring to go into business to make money is much nobler than that of securing an easy berth in a government job. The Latin American political objectives will, to a certain extent, explain the astonishingly large number of candidates studying law or medicine. In Buenos Aires the number of students studying medicine at the university was 4087 in 1941. Argentina, moreover, has three other universities with medical faculties. The fact is that a large part of the students do not intend to practice their profession. Graduation from one of the faculties gives the coveted title of "Doctor" which marks a man at once as above his fellows. In our "practical" civilization the title carries little weight outside college walls. The graduate of a university faculty in Latin America may finally land in a small government job in a provincial town, but he is a somebody. Money is just as highly regarded in Latin America as in the United States, but it hardly has the place in public esteem that honors have. The situation just described is roughly parallel to that which obtains in the graduate schools of our own great universities. They are to a considerable extent filled with students who seek the degree of Doctor of Philosophy not as an evidence of competent scientific research ability, but for its usefulness in their quest for a job of teaching in a college.

University teachers in Latin America in the faculties of

law, medicine, and engineering are nowhere full-time professors, and even those in the faculties of letters, science, and education are often engaged in professional work. The theory is that a man so engaged is better qualified to teach the subject. The salaries of such professors, because they teach only part time, are not large except in the most advanced universities. However, they are fair for the few lectures the men give. In fact, many of the professors in the universities hold their positions as a matter of prestige and give little attention to their teaching duties.

Chiefly because of the slower economic development of Latin America, scientific education, so necessary in the commercial and industrial life of today, has made little progress compared with that in the United States. The libraries, laboratories, apparatus, and general equipment which are necessary for scientific instruction and are found in practically all of our universities are to a large extent missing in all but a few Latin American universities. The lecture method is everywhere the prevailing method of teaching. Our discussion and quiz methods are conspicuous by their absence. Science cannot be taught by the lecture method alone, and in any field this method lends itself readily to slipshod work. In some of the Latin American institutions there is fine teaching in science, but it is not typical. The result of this attitude has been that young Latin Americans who have come to the United States for advanced technical training have usually found themselves handicapped by a lack of necessary scientific preparation and of acquaintance with laboratory methods. The great economic expansion that has taken place in the more advanced countries of Latin America since the first World War is causing a demand for greater emphasis upon practical subjects and methods in the educational system. Moreover, this movement has received stimulus from the policy of the large American corporations that are active in those countries, in employing properly qualified natives in preference to foreigners. This is not the result of pure altruism, however, because some of the Latin American governments do not allow foreign corporations to operate unless they agree to employ a certain number of qualified nationals for high positions and usually all the required laborers.

The liberal education provided by the faculties of philosophy and letters and by the law schools, which in many countries are the real liberal arts colleges, is very effective along the lines which the Latin Americans themselves admire. This is shown by their extraordinary versatility and their keen interest in and knowledge of literary and artistic subjects. They consider that these are the real values of life rather than the more material and social ones which are stressed in the United States.

American influence is exerted to a considerable extent through American schools in the Latin American countries. They are to be found in practically every capital and in many other large cities. Many are private-adventure schools of poor standards, but some are highly regarded and nearly always well filled with students. Their popularity is due primarily to the fact that, though they are seldom equal to schools of the same grade in the United States, their methods of school organization and teaching are usually more modern, their equipment more up-to-date and, aside from actual information imparted, their standards of attainment are higher than those of the local schools. Moreover, they attempt to give a rounded education, looking after physical welfare and character training as well as intellectual discipline. Their success has sometimes been pronounced, and many people prominent in social and political life send their children by preference to these schools rather than to national schools or Church schools.

Though there are also a considerable number of German,

British, and French schools scattered about Latin America, they have not encountered the opposition of the Church as have the American schools. This opposition is due to the fact that most American schools started as adjuncts to Protestant missions and although some of them are now independent organizations and receive little or no financial support from mission boards in the United States, all of them are still regarded by the Catholic Church as mission schools. The Church naturally looks upon these schools as agencies for proselytism and wherever one is established the local bishop usually issues an annual denunciation of it. It is hard to believe that proselytism was not the prime reason for their establishment, despite denial by those in charge of the schools. Observation of the work of some of them, however, disclosed no evidence of a deliberate attempt at it or of much place for it in the daily routine. The teachers of some of these schools are sometimes inferior to those in similar institutions in the United States, partly because of the difficulty of retaining teachers over a considerable period of years and partly because of the lower salaries they receive. Nevertheless, they are apparently making a real contribution to the welfare of the communities in which they are established.

The denunciations of the bishops apparently have little effect upon the prosperity of the strong schools and colleges, and their existence has stimulated the establishment of better Church schools in some places. That the Church can maintain schools equally good is made evident by the splendid work accomplished by the Catholic University of Santiago, one of the very few private universities in Latin America. It has fine scholars as teachers, excellent equipment, and a progressive spirit and outlook. The Catholic University at Lima has become popular in conservative circles because of the radical character of the student body at San Marcos. If the Church in Latin America wishes to compete successfully with the American schools already established there, it would do well to secure teachers who are familiar with American educational methods and ideals. They might be selected from the many nationals who have studied in American institutions or from American teachers who speak Spanish or Portuguese. After the American occupation of the Philippines the Church adopted this policy there with excellent results. Americans have much to learn from other nations in many fields of thought and endeavor, but despite the imperfections of their school system they have much to give in the field of education.

CHAPTER XIII

THE QUEST FOR HEMISPHERE SOLIDARITY

In 1929 Franklin Roosevelt and I were colleagues on the Board of Trustees of Vassar College. One day in the spring of that year after a meeting of the Board Mrs. Roosevelt, who had been waiting for the close of the meeting, asked whether she might give a lift in her auto to any member of the Board who was going in the direction of New York City. I wanted to make a visit at Scarsdale, about twenty miles from the city, and gladly availed myself of the offer. On the way down we discussed Mr. Roosevelt's chances of success in becoming the Democratic nominee for the Presidency, a development I earnestly wished. We had not gone many miles before we stopped at the estate of Henry Morgenthau, Jr., to have afternoon tea. Henry Morgenthau, Sr. had been a trustee of the Institute of International Education for many years but I had never happened to meet his son. I saw at once the intimate friendship that existed between the Roosevelts and the Morgenthaus, which was obviously of long standing.

At that time I lived in an apartment house in Sixty-fifth Street, three doors from the Roosevelt home. Sometime afterward Mr. Roosevelt invited me over for a talk. We discussed the campaign for the nomination briefly, and then Mr. Roosevelt asked, "Do you know Sumner Welles?" I answered, "No," but stated that I had read Mr. Welles' book, *Naboth's Vineyard,* and found it very worth while. "If I am nominated for the Presidency and am elected, I shall rely largely upon Sumner Welles as my adviser on foreign policy," said Mr. Roosevelt. From that day to this Mr. Roosevelt has to a great extent relied upon Sumner Welles for advice upon foreign affairs. I afterward became acquainted with both Mr. Hull and Mr. Welles and have greatly admired their ability.

I had long been aware of the suspicion and distrust of the United States maintained throughout Latin America. My visit to the countries of South America in 1931 confirmed my belief. I regard the pronouncement and implementation of the Good Neighbor policy as one of the outstanding successes of American diplomacy. The three men, Roosevelt, Hull, and Welles, who have been the builders of that policy deserve unstinted gratitude from their fellow countrymen. One can readily imagine what might have happened in this war period had the former attitude of resentment toward and mistrust of the United States prevailed in Latin America.

From the standpoint of foreign policy it is also most fortunate that the Roosevelt administration has been retained for three successive terms, because ever since 1933 many influential Latin Americans have wondered whether the Good Neighbor policy was fully supported by the North American people as well as by President Roosevelt's administration. Most of them now realize that this program has received the active endorsement of leaders in both major political parties in this country, and has really become an established policy of the United States.

The Seventh Pan American Conference was due to be held at Montevideo in 1933. President Roosevelt established the setting for the success of the conference through a speech made two months after his inauguration. In that speech he eschewed intervention by the United States in the internal affairs of any Latin American country. The Latin American peoples have always regarded that principle as a *sine qua non* for harmonious relations with the United States. At the conference the modesty, urbanity, and obvious sincerity of Mr. Hull moderated the suspicion with which some bitter representatives of the Latin American countries viewed the United States. He did not adhere rigidly to formalities. Unlike the procedure at former Pan American conferences, Mr. Hull did not expect the chairmen of other delegations to wait for the chairman of the United States delegation. He visited the others first. The American delegation went to Montevideo determined to sense the attitude of the Latin Americans toward the problems which concerned the nations of the hemisphere as a whole. For the first time in many years the United States delegation was cordially received by the Latin American delegates.

One day while preparations for the conference were being made, Mr. Hull, with whom I was discussing another matter, said to me, "What do you think we ought to do with the Platt Amendment?" "Repeal it," I answered. "I am glad to hear you say so. That's my view." "What attitude do you think we ought to take with reference to the Monroe Doctrine?" "Make it a basis for collective rather than unilateral action," I answered. Again Mr. Hull stated that that was also his view. Now I knew that my name had been mentioned as a possible delegate to the Conference and because of the way in which my views on two of the major topics that might be considered conformed to those of Mr. Hull, I was hopeful of being selected. Mr. Hull had told me that there would be but six delegates and all but the sixth were of necessity predetermined, namely, himself as Chairman of the delegation, the American Ambassadors at Montevideo and Buenos Aires, an authority on economic relations with Latin America, and a distinguished Republican. Before a final decision could be made, the embattled cohorts of the various women's organizations marched upon Washington with a demand that one representative be a woman. Miss Sophonisba Breckenridge of Kentucky, who had always been deeply interested in Latin American affairs, displaced my chance, if there had ever been one, of going to Montevideo as an official delegate.

The Division of Cultural Relations of the State Department

As described in Chapter II, the Institute of International Education was founded as a private organization without any governmental affiliations. This fact secured for it a great deal of the respect and confidence with which it has been regarded in foreign countries, especially in the so-called "backward" countries. It was generally conceded that its activities were carried on without any political or nationalistic motives and for cultural purposes only. Our State Department had always looked with favor upon this attitude of the Institute because it conformed with its own policy of refraining from propaganda of any kind in foreign countries. However, this policy placed the United States at a disadvantage in making its civilization and culture known in foreign lands. In the Latin American countries, for example, France, Germany, Italy and, to a less extent, Great Britain repeatedly—in some cases annually—sent distinguished scholars to lecture in the universities. After Hitler had been in control of the German government for three years, the Germans developed a regular program of sending Nazi professors to the Latin American countries and inviting groups of Latin American students to study in Germany at German-government expense. Americans finally waked up to the wisdom of having in their Department of State a division similar to that maintained in the foreign offices of other major powers, which would give general oversight to our educational and cultural relations with other nations.

In 1938 I was invited by the State Department to attend a

conference of some fifteen persons to consider the formation
of a Division of Cultural Relations within the Department.
Mr. Hull opened the meeting to explain the general purpose
of the new division, after which the conference was turned
over to Mr. Welles who presided during the consideration of
the agenda. Both gentlemen emphasized the point that although the new division was to consider our cultural relations with all countries, nevertheless because we had hitherto
neglected developing those relations with the Latin American peoples as against the European, and also because the
German drive in Latin America was developing more and
more into an anti-American movement, the new Division
would devote its attention at first to our cultural relations
with the Latin American republics. Dr. Leo Rowe, the Director of the Pan American Union, was naturally the first
person from whom Mr. Welles asked an opinion. It was very
gratifying to me to hear Dr. Rowe state that no organization
in our country had done more than the Institute of International Education to further our cultural and educational
relations with Latin America, especially in the exchange of
students and teachers, and to listen to Mr. Welles reply that
the State Department was deeply appreciative of what the
Institute had already accomplished in the republics to the
south of us.

At first the new Division followed the policy that had
hitherto been maintained of merely giving moral support to
private agencies engaged in cultural activities with the Latin
American nations. But at the Inter-American Conference for
the Maintenance of Peace held at Buenos Aires in December
1936, a convention had been adopted, Article VIII of which
provided for the annual interchange of one professor and
two graduate students between the various republics of the
Western Hemisphere that ratified the convention. The Directors of the three great scholarly organizations, the Na-

tional Research Council, the Social Science Research Council and the American Council of Learned Societies, and the Director of the Guggenheim Foundation were invited to become members of a committee to implement Article VIII of the Buenos Aires Pact. The Department added the Professor of Latin American History at Goucher College, who also represented women, and the Professor of Political Science at Bryn Mawr, who had been one of the American delegates at the Buenos Aires conference. Mr. Hull appointed me as chairman of the committee. At all the meetings of the committee representatives of the Division of Cultural Relations and of the Office of Education were present to advise. Thus the first step in governmental support of cultural relations with foreign countries was undertaken.

The Coordinator of Inter-American Affairs

At the Havana conference of Foreign Ministers in July 1940, the information presented by delegates from some of the Latin American countries showed that German propaganda in those countries was not only very anti-United States but deliberately directed to attacking the democratic ideal of social organization, and to fostering totalitarian ideology. Hence, although we were not at the time participants in the war, our government with the approval of all Americans—isolationists and interventionists—determined to undertake measures to uphold our influence in the Latin American countries and defend the democratic against the totalitarian way of life. Therefore President Roosevelt on August 16, 1940, appointed Nelson Rockefeller Coordinator of Commercial and Cultural Relations between the American Republics. His title was afterward, on July 30, 1941, changed to the more appropriate one of "Coordinator of Inter-American Affairs". That Mr. Rockefeller should have been appointed coordinator of commercial affairs is wholly understandable. He had become a very successful young executive and administrator in New York City, and his experience in business could be expected to enable him to grasp quickly our commercial and financial relations with the Latin American countries. But he was practically unknown in the field of educational and scholarly affairs. Moreover, only two years had passed since the State Department had organized the new Division of Cultural Relations with the particular aim of developing those relations with the Latin American countries. It is true that the new Division had not accomplished much outside the United States and had exerted only a moral influence within the United States. But this was almost wholly because it had been provided with practically no funds, whereas the Coordinator received an allotment of a substantial amount from the President's emergency fund. Nevertheless, the Division of Cultural Relations and the Coordinator's Office at once cooperated in the most friendly and helpful manner and in 1941 both organizations were adequately provided with funds by Congress to carry on their activities. Mr. Rockefeller, with whom I had a slight acquaintance before his appointment, proved to be not merely an efficient administrator but a man endowed with imagination who was very desirous to learn the various fields of his difficult assignment and to obtain advice from specialists in those fields.

In October 1938 Mr. Hull had appointed an Advisory Committee to the State Department on Cultural Relations with Latin America, and I was included. The committee met several times a year to plan ways and means of making the United States better understood among the Latin American peoples and the Latin American republics better known to our people. Every agency that might help to accomplish the purpose was considered: the radio, moving pictures, newspapers, libraries, translations, visits of distinguished statesmen and men of affairs, and interchange of artists, musicians, scientists and technicians. I was the adviser on the extension of the program of the interchange of students and teachers.

Immediately after his appointment as Coordinator, Mr. Rockefeller attended a meeting of the Advisory Committee to explain his objectives and the methods whereby he hoped to accomplish them. In essence these were to use every legitimate device to promote the integration of the American republics into a unity that would be a solid support for hemisphere security against the propaganda of the Fascist powers. There were so many similarities between the programs of the two organizations that several of Mr. Rockefeller's aides were invited to attend the meetings of the Advisory Committee and participate in its discussions. They did attend regularly and it was largely the decisions which were made at those meetings that were afterward implemented. To those meetings experts in all the fields pertinent to the purposes of the Committee were invited to give the latest available information.

Because of the more than twenty years' experience of the Institute of International Education in the field of student and teacher exchange, it was natural that the Coordinator should select the Institute to be his agency in the administration of that part of his program. I found Mr. Wallace Harrison, Mr. Rockefeller's right-hand man in carrying out the cultural activities of the Coordinator's Office, and his associate, Kenneth Holland, to be men of broad vision and human qualities. They have been very successful in realizing the cultural objectives of the Coordinator's program. This success is largely due to the happy and cooperative relations that existed between them and Mr. Charles Thomson, Chief of the Division of Cultural Relations of the State Department.

It was natural that Mr. Rockefeller, a young man of thirty-three, should select for his chief aides other young men with many of whom he had become acquainted at college or in busi-

ness. Most of them were wide awake, loyal, devoted to the job—
and inexperienced. It was this inexperience which explains
some ventures of the Coordinator's Office which brought it
into conflict with other agencies of the government or resulted in its undertaking enterprises in Latin American countries which did not at first add to the prestige of the Office.
Many self-seekers who wished to attach themselves to the
Coordinator's Office—some with and some wholly without any
experience in Latin American affairs—presented wild schemes
of a wholly unrealizable nature. Few were accepted, and with
the passage of time and greater experience most obstacles
were overcome. I regard the work of the Coordinator's Office
as of unusual merit in helping to advance hemisphere solidarity.

Vice President Wallace was added to the Advisory Committee in the fall of 1941. I had already become acquainted
with Mr. Wallace and awaited with interest his attendance at
the first meeting after his appointment. He was asked to give
his views and said, "This is a committee on cultural relations. Perhaps you will not include what I am going to say
in the category of cultural relations, but I believe that to
teach the poor women of Latin America how better to take
care of their babies and to give them some knowledge of good
diet and personal hygiene is a form of culture." His entire
talk was devoted to practical suggestions concerning such
things as improved methods of farming and technical training
looking to better standards of living. He was very emphatic
in insisting that the spread of democratic ideas should not be
overlooked. It was a discourse that would naturally come
from a farmer statesman from our agrarian West. Though
the Advisory Committee had not conceived of its work in Mr.
Wallace's terms, his statement appealed to its members.

The money allotted to the Institute by the Coordinator's
Office and the Division of Cultural Relations of the State De-

partment, to expand the interchange of students and teachers with the Latin American countries, was distributed in the form of scholarships secured competitively on the basis of merit. It enabled bright and ambitious young men and women of the middle and underprivileged classes in Latin America to study in our institutions of higher education. Without this assistance, financial restriction would have prevented most of these students from coming to the United States. It unquestionably had a real influence in helping to spread the democratic spirit in the Latin American countries. My own experiences with the élite in those countries had not given me the impression that they were deeply interested in the spread of democracy among their people. They were among the class in control and, generally speaking, did not favor sharing that control. However, as mentioned before, the visits to the United States made by some of them upon invitations given by the Division of Cultural Relations of the State Department and by the Coordinator's Office had a great influence in removing from their minds the belief that had hitherto prevailed among many of them that ours was a mechanized and materialistic civilization devoid of spiritual elements.

In Latin America as everywhere the future belongs to youth, and now when it seeks education abroad Latin American youth is turning by preference to the United States, realizing that today it is probably the most wealthy, most powerful, and most influential nation on earth. The present war has intensified this conviction. Latin American youth, both most friendly toward and most critical of the United States, recognizes also that to a great extent the United States will set the standard and pace of social evolution in the next generation. We are interested in Latin American youths not because they are already well disposed toward the United States, but because they hold the key to the whole future of Latin

America and hence of Western Hemisphere solidarity. Our universities, foundations, and educational organizations should be interested in the opportunity to select from the fine, earnest, mature students who because of economic considerations could come here only upon fellowships. Everywhere are to be found returned graduate students teaching in the institutions of Latin America, enthusiastic over their studies in our universities and strong advocates of a better understanding with the people of the United States. This is equally true of the few professors and scholars who have lectured in our universities.

In recent years, and especially during the present war, United States civilization has rivaled the French and is now rapidly becoming the dominant foreign influence in Latin America. Our language and our attitude toward life follow in the wake of our business, our movies, our newspapers and magazines. In several of the South American countries English has already supplanted French as the required foreign language in the secondary schools. Repeatedly in the home of a cultured family the father would state that he, his wife and his elder children had been educated in France but that he was sending his younger children to universities in the United States. "The immediate future is yours," he would say, "the more distant future is ours. We must learn what has made you strong and great." I do not wish by any means to imply that no Latin American students are going to French universities. Although the movement has now been stopped of necessity by the war, the advent of peace will doubtless again be a signal for Latin American students to renew their work in France. But the number is and will be small compared to the more than two thousand Latin American students who studied in United States colleges and universities in 1942–1943.

Administering the exchange scholarships was not without

difficulties. The scholarships allotted under the Buenos Aires pact provided that the holders should know the language of the country to which they were to go. The knowledge of English upon the part of the students chosen by some of the Latin American governments was very inadequate. Some knew practically no English; others had evidently received the scholarships as the result of political or social influence. In certain cases governments were very dilatory in sending the lists of applicants from whom the successful candidates were to be chosen. The result was that students were sometimes unable to arrive in the United States until after the beginning of the academic term, a tardiness which handicapped their progress and sometimes disturbed the administration of the host colleges and universities. Few of these difficulties arose in the administration of the scholarships provided by the Division of Cultural Relations and the Coordinator's Office. I believe that this was due primarily to the fact that the work was carried on by unofficial agencies in our own and the Latin American countries.

On the United States side the difficulties usually resulted from an excess of zeal. All our institutions of higher education favored the movement to develop closer cultural ties with the Latin American countries and cooperated admirably in making the exchange a success. Many of them provided tuition scholarships for Latin American students. Some organized special courses at their summer sessions designed to acquaint the Latin American students with United States civilization. Practically all of our first-class colleges offered courses on Latin American history and institutions and expanded the teaching of Spanish and Portuguese. Some, however, organized programs of studies which were far beyond the means at the disposal of the Division of Cultural Relations and the Coordinator's Office. A few offered schemes of a grandiose character which it would have been difficult to realize under any conditions.

One difficulty that arose had been wholly unforeseen by the Institute of International Education. For more than twenty years it had been administering exchange scholarships with foreign countries without encountering any religious question. Shortly after the establishment of the Coordinator's Office, however, a German-born Roman Catholic educator, who had spent several years in Latin American countries, visited the Institute to discuss the possibility of the establishment of United States schools in the Latin American countries with money provided by our government. He presented a carefully worked out program which had attached to it the names of some prominent United States Catholic educators. I thought the method of organization and administration of the proposed schools admirable until I read the following paragraph:

"The schools are non-denominational: this means that the schools are not under the rule or control of any Church and that students of all religious denominations may attend the North American schools. However, the schools will also seek the approval and moral support of the local Church authorities, which are the Catholic Bishops. For, as an exponent of cultural rapprochement the organization is well aware of the fact that cultural activities have a predominantly spiritual content, which in the case of the Latin American culture means the Catholic religion. Any approach to cultural relations with Latin America which would ignore this religious link, would be doomed to failure, whereas any approach by way of the common bond of the same faith, provides not only the basis of a ready understanding of the cultural background of Latin America, but it also eliminates the danger of being met with skepticism, suspicion or even open antagonism. For this reason, the guidance, direction and majority of personnel will always have to be Catholic, i.e., Americans belonging to the Catholic faith."

Considering that there is a strong anti-clerical movement in some of the Latin American countries, I could readily imagine the resentment its adherents would have to an apparent attempt to take sides in a domestic issue were the United States government to establish schools in those countries under clerical control—even though the people of Latin America are overwhelmingly Roman Catholic. Considering, moreover, that the Roman Catholics number only one-sixth of the population of the United States, I could also imagine the resentment among the non-Catholic population at the use of public funds supplied by all the people were they to be devoted to such sectarian purpose.

The Catholic educator asked for my approval for his program. I told him that as presented I disapproved. He later returned with a modified scheme which provided for non-sectarian control of the proposed United States schools. It is a question whether the United States government ought to engage in such an enterprise despite the fact that nearly all the other great powers have established their own schools in Latin American countries. There are already a large number of private schools in Latin American countries under the auspices of United States citizens. Many of them are not of high standard. Some are very good but in almost every instance these are under denominational auspices. The logical thing for our government to do would be to subsidize the good schools. But to do so would almost certainly introduce sectarian controversy. If our government is to undertake to establish United States schools in Latin American countries, the only wise plan to follow is to establish an impartial committee made up of well known educators and able administrators to control and supervise the work of the schools.

The anxiety caused by the visit just described was not lessened by the later activities of one of those whose names were attached to the memorandum as sponsors for the plan, namely, Father Joseph Thorning. Father Thorning suggested upon several occasions that Catholic institutions in the United States were largely ignored in the placement of Latin American scholarship holders coming to the United States for purposes of study. This charge appeared at times in the press and might readily have misled its readers as to the real facts of the situation. As I was the responsible head of the organization that administered the exchange of students and teachers between the United States and the Latin American countries, I wrote the following letter to the *New York Times* of April 12, 1942, in order to give wide publicity to the facts:

To the Editor of The New York Times:

There has been belatedly brought to my attention a statement in THE NEW YORK TIMES of March 8, made by Father Thorning, based upon a complete misconception of the activity carried on by the Coordinator of Inter-American Affairs in the matter of the exchange of students between the United States and the Latin American republics. Father Thorning implies that there has been discrimination against Catholics and Catholic institutions in the selection and placement of students under the Inter-American cultural exchange program. This is wholly contrary to the facts.

Let me first give a preparatory word: Since its foundation in 1919 the Institute of International Education, of which I am Director, has brought almost 2,500 students on scholarships from European countries and sent a similar number from the United States to those countries. It developed a *modus operandi* founded upon scholarships, personality, linguistic ability and adjustability which produced results highly satisfactory to university authorities in our own and the foreign countries. By the time the Office of the Coordinator of Inter-American Affairs was established in 1940 the Institute had also brought some 300 Latin American students upon scholarships to our country.

It was not unnatural, therefore, when the coordinator undertook to expand the student exchange between the United States and the Latin American countries, to request the Institute to be the agency administering the exchange. The Coordinator acted upon precedent in that the State Department had already requested the Director of the Institute to be the chairman of a committee to administer the exchange of students and professors under the Buenos Aires pact of 1936.

The selection of the Latin American students to receive scholarships is made by a committee of selection in each country, organized usually by the rector of the local university or by a distinguished scholar, but always with the approval of the American Minister or Ambassador. The committee, whose chairman and secretary are nationals, usually numbers not more than seven of whom two are Americans to insure that in each case some members are familiar with the American system of higher education. The Institute of International Education has absolutely nothing to do in the choice of the personnel of the committee. The committee makes the preliminary choice among applications for scholarships and sends only the few best to the Institute, which makes the final choice solely upon the basis of the credentials presented.

In the placement of Latin Americans, as of all foreign students in our institutions, the Institute's first consideration is the field of study of the student. The Latin Americans have for long regarded our country as the best place to study scientific, technical and practical subjects. We may wish the desire were more widely diffused among other fields of study, but we must undertake to fulfill, if possible, the requests of the students. Agriculture, engineering, medicine, journalism, library science and architecture have been the fields in increasing demand by Latin American students. Of the 222 Latin American students brought to this country by the Institute this year fifty-eight were students in those fields. It happens that there are very few schools or departments specializing in these branches among our Catholic institutions. I think that the availability of institutions as a chief consideration is shown by the fact that of the fourteen students wishing to study our methods of social service six were placed in schools of social service attached to Catholic institutions.

The second consideration in placing a student is the preference for study in a particular institution expressed in his or her application. In a number of cases, however, it is not possible to satisfy this preference, because many applications are made for the few institutions well known in Latin America. Unless the institution is of obvious inadequacy in the field of study—a very unusual occurrence—we do not interfere with such choice. We are always glad, however, to serve with information or advice when we are asked for it.

The third consideration is the degree of cooperation upon the part of the various institutions. For the purpose of student exchange, the Institute of International Education is only an administrative agency. It established the practice twenty years ago of requesting our colleges and universities to provide scholarships for foreign students in exchange for scholarships provided in the foreign countries. Our institutions responded admirably and in the year before the war there were almost 100 on the accredited list of the Association of American Colleges that made such provision. In January of each year we distribute a questionnaire to all colleges and universities on the accredited list requesting:

1. Whether the institution will provide one or more scholarships for the ensuing academic year.

2. Whether it will be a full scholarship covering tuition and maintenance or a partial one.

3. Whether the college has any preference as to the nationality of the student.

4. If the college has no preference as to nationality, whether it will permit the Institute to make the choice. This we do in order to give opportunity to students from as many countries as possible to become acquainted with American civilization.

The Coordinator of Inter-American Affairs provides a full scholarship only for the Roosevelt scholars coming from each of the twenty Latin American republics and for the twenty United States Roosevelt scholars going to the Latin American countries this year. The Coordinator provides only maintenance for some of the other students. The Division of Cultural Relations of the State Department provides travel grants for some of the students. In order to relieve the government of some of the financial burden, but especially in order to retain the fine spirit of cooperation developed among our institutions of higher education, the Institute gives preference in placing all foreign students, including Latin Americans, to institutions providing at least a partial scholarship. This seems to us to be a very fair arrangement.

The selection of United States graduate students and professors for exchange with the Latin American countries under the Buenos Aires pact is made by a very able and efficient committee of five, of whom I happen to know that at least one is a Catholic. Moreover, the State Department is represented at each meeting of the committee by one of its staff who is also a Catholic. Either of those gentlemen will bear witness that the question of religious faith has never entered into the discussions of the Committee. The choice was always made solely on the basis of merit.

The same thing is true of the choice of the United States Roosevelt scholars. The country has been divided into ten geographical areas, from which two students are chosen by committees of selection on the basis of scholarship, personality, language ability and adjustability. The partial scholarships provided by the Coordinator are allotted by another committee consisting of five members. I do not know the religious faith of all the members. I do happen to know that one of them is a Catholic.

In the case of all scholarships administered by the Institute of International Education the application blank contains a question as to the religious faith of the applicant. This has been put in because embarrassment sometimes, though seldom, arose in sending a religious misfit to an institution. Of the sixty United States scholars chosen to go to the Latin American countries this year, eight did not answer the question. Of the remainder, thirteen—or 25 per cent—stated they were Catholics. This ratio of Catholic to non-Catholic students selected is higher than the ratio of Catholic to non-Catholic elements in the United States population as revealed in the 1940 census, and is also greater than the ratio of Catholic to non-Catholic institutions of higher learning on the accredited list.

It is possible that Father Thorning is anxious that the faith of the students from Latin America brought here on scholarships should be properly safeguarded. If that is true, his anxiety is not only belated but unnecessary. During the past twenty years we have sent hundreds of scholarship holders from such Catholic countries as France, Italy, Hungary and Czechoslovakia to our institutions of higher learning and we have yet to hear of any with whose faith there has been any attempt to tamper. I feel confident that the same condition holds with the Latin American students brought here on scholarships now provided by the Coordinator and the State Department.

Because of the difficulties of transportation and the activities of enemy submarines, it is probable that there will be a smaller exchange with the Latin American countries during the next few years. In any event, I am anxious that all our people, of whatever faith, may be assured that this student exchange activity is carried on with fairness and without discrimination. If Father Thorning or any one else can indicate a way whereby greater impartiality and objectivity may be obtained, he can be assured it will receive most careful consideration.

STEPHEN DUGGAN.

New York, April 6, 1942.

Historical Obstacles to Hemisphere Solidarity

The recent emphasis which has been put on Catholicism in inter-American relations has underscored several significant differences between Latin and Anglo-Saxon America. Every nation reflects the interplay of the two forces of geography and history. These forces are so different in Latin America and the United States as to give rise to difficulties in integrating the nations of the Western Hemisphere in a common attitude toward hemisphere solidarity.

The United States was founded by rebels—by men who rebelled against religious persecution or economic discrimination in Europe. Puritans in New England, French Huguenots in New York and South Carolina, German Lutherans from the Palatinate in Pennsylvania, English Catholics in Maryland, all sought religious freedom in the New World. They were later joined by Ulster Presbyterians outraged by the destruction of their industries in the north of Ireland as the result of a deliberate policy of the British government to favor English agriculture and industry. Moreover, there was a steady infiltration of Catholic Irish from the south of Ireland, whose feelings toward Great Britain were those of extremist rebels. The population from which a new civilization was to be developed in the United States was made up of people of a variety of races and beliefs, not the kind of population that would readily submit to coercion from without or agree to the establishment of a state church. Diversity was the dominating characteristic. As has been stated in Chapter IV, in the seventeenth century, the mother country was the scene of a great struggle between King and Parliament, which was not concluded until the Revolution of 1688 gave the supremacy to Parliament. This had hardly been accomplished when Great Britain engaged in a second Hundred Years' War with France for colonial and maritime supremacy. During these two centuries the mother country could not give continuous and unremitting attention to the colonies and the colonists developed their own self-governing institutions and were able to consolidate their control of their own affairs.

Geography smiled upon the English colonies. They were almost all situated in the temperate zone where the climate was bracing and invited vigorous activity. The natives, who were hunters and fishermen, retreated before the colonists or were killed off. The colonists brought their women with them and did not intermarry with the natives. As their numbers increased their children moved west and built homesteads in the free land. When the Revolution took place, the United States was inhabited to a large extent by an independent, vigorous and self-respecting yeomanry. After the Revolution, the attempt on the part of the Hamiltonian plutocracy to develop an aristocratic caste system of society in the new republic was prevented outside the slave states by the political sagacity and strategy of Jefferson and was finally destroyed by the victory at the polls of the Jacksonian democracy. Successive generations thereafter saw a moving frontier, peopled by pioneers, all equal because all were working out their own salvation. Necessity compelled them to administer their own affairs and democracy became their form of political organization.

In all these respects, the story of the settlement of Latin America was entirely different. For several centuries previous to the discovery of America, Spain had been the scene of a religious war between Christians and Moslems. The war was characterized by religious fanaticism, personal bravery, and relentless cruelty. During its prosecution national and religious uniformity was considered essential to success, and the men who came out of the long struggle as the Spanish nation's honored and trusted leaders were the warrior and the priest. The war ended in the very year that Columbus discovered America. The marvelous tales that soon came back from the new lands concerning their people and their wealth induced the hardy warrior seeking riches and glory and the priest seeking the salvation of souls, to sail west in considerable numbers. Not primarily farmers seeking homes in a new land but, after the conquest of Mexico by Cortes, military adventurers looking for gold and silver; not peoples from a half-dozen countries speaking different tongues and observing different customs but all Spaniards speaking but one tongue; not a diversity of religious sects fleeing from persecution but all devoted to one faith—such were the people who founded the Spanish colonies in the new world—all Spaniards, all Catholics, all obedient subjects of one form of government, absolutism. Uniformity, not diversity, was the dominating characteristic. And what was true of the Spaniards was true only to a slightly less extent of the Portuguese.

From the standpoint of location, geography was not kind to Latin America. Three-quarters of Latin America is in the tropics. The colonists in the Caribbean area and Brazil had not only to withstand the extreme heat, the humidity, and the venomous insects of the tropics but their vitality was reduced by the existence of such tropical diseases as malaria, yellow fever, dysentery, and hookworm. After the Indians of those regions had been killed off by disease and excessive work, the colonists imported Negroes from Africa and built their civilization upon the institution of Negro slavery, as did the planters in the southern colonies of the United States. On the West Coast of the hemisphere from the Rio Grande to Cape Horn altitude provided a climate that permitted the establishment of a flourishing white man's civilization. But the Spaniards found there Indian agricultural civilizations whose people were not nomadic but settled upon the soil. These they conquered and enslaved. They appropriated ownership of the soil and as elsewhere were relieved of the necessity to work.

Moreover, after the conquest of Mexico in 1520, the early discoverers and explorers from Spain and Portugal were *conquistadores,* not settlers but conquerors, who brought practically no women with them. They cohabited freely with the native Indian women and later with imported Negro women. The consequence was that the resulting population and civilization were respectively mestizo, the product of the union of red and white people, or mulatto. The pure white population increased but little because comparatively few new settlers came from Europe. In a mestizo civilization everywhere, manual labor has been regarded as the badge of the inferior, the mestizo imitating the white man in that respect. The result in Latin America has been that an aristocratic caste civilization grew up, with the Indian and Negro ignorant, despised, and exploited, at the bottom of the scale; the average mestizo everywhere was little better off, but the successful mestizo shared rulership and the professions with the white man and scorned to be considered either Indian or Negro. Even in the southern regions of South America where the population is wholly or predominantly white, partly as the result of Spanish heritage, partly because of the distribution of land in great estates, society is aristocratically organized.

In the United States geography and history determined

that the independent colonies would form a united country despite the diversities that existed. The thirteen states were all situated east of the Alleghenies and though communication by land was slow and difficult, water communication was frequent and fairly rapid. No colony was isolated from the others and business relations among the colonies were well developed. The long experience in self-government had developed a political ability that surmounted the obstacles to unity with comparative ease. The United States began its national career as a real republic and with all the elements present for the development of a vigorous democracy. Its history since is the story of increasing national independence, individual liberty and equality, self-government and democracy.

Political Obstacles

These factors were non-existent in Latin America. The colonies there covered an enormous area and were separated from one another by mountain chains, jungles, and deserts. There was no business interchange of any importance between the vice-royalties of Mexico and Peru. Despite their unity in language, religion, and customs, the colonies separated into states upon the basis of the administrative divisions that had existed under Spain, and as the boundaries of these divisions were vague, wars between the states were at first frequent. Inexperienced in administering their own affairs, familiar only with government from above, these states naturally became dictatorships, whose ruling personnel changed frequently as the result of civil wars. Despite the efforts of patriots in their struggle for freedom, of writers and of idealistic men of action like Bolívar, the Latin American countries began as republics in name only and the elements of democracy were practically non-existent.

Hence the political organization of the Latin American states has always been dictatorship or at best oligarchy, and that is what it remains today. It is nowhere a democracy in our sense of the word—with the possible exception of stalwart little Costa Rica, which has long taken pride in the fact that it has more teachers than soldiers, and more recently Colombia, Chile, and Uruguay. Democracy to the average Latin American means a republican form of government. Democracy is essentially a middle-class institution dependent upon the existence of public opinion. In the United States anyone below the middle class hopes to advance into it and public opinion is largely secured by the existence of the public school. In few Latin American countries does a middle class exist. Neither does public opinion, as we understand it, for public opinion is largely a matter of literacy, and illiteracy prevails to a very large extent in most of the Latin American countries. Dictatorship in Latin America means control of the political life of the country by one man and his adherents. It does not mean control of all aspects of the life of the people such as exists under totalitarian governments. There are strong groups in some of the Latin American republics that believe in totalitarianism, but it is doubtful that they could secure sufficient power to make that form of social organization a permanent condition.

Economic Obstacles

Economically, hemisphere solidarity is confronted with great difficulties. The economy of the United States is of a varied nature. Though primarily industrial it is also extractive, i.e., agricultural and mineral. The economy of the Latin American countries is almost wholly agricultural and mineral, usually limited to only one or two major products. In favorable years there is a great surplus. The chief source of income of Cuba is the export of sugar; of Brazil the export of coffee; of Uruguay and Argentina the export of grain and meat; of Chile the export of copper and nitrates. The economy of the United States and that of the Caribbean countries of Latin America are complementary. They send us sugar, coffee, bananas, oil; we send them in return manufactured goods and processed food products. But the economy of the United States and those of the countries of the temperate zone of South America, viz., Argentina, Uruguay, and Chile are competitive, and the resultant economic antagonism has sometimes made it difficult to achieve full harmony between those countries and the United States. There is no market in the United States for their meats and grain because they compete with our own. Therefore, until recently Argentine meat has enjoyed no sale in the United States. During the present war, moreover, inter-American shipping difficulties have seriously complicated the bringing to the United States of many products from all the southern countries of South America.

Often Americans complain of the lukewarmness toward hemisphere solidarity shown by the Argentine government. But many Argentines have not been convinced that Hitler will lose the war. If he does not lose, and continues to control continental Europe, they have no desire to offend their best customer. It may fairly be assumed that hemisphere solidarity would not survive a Nazi victory, and that unless some better international economic organization is established for the postwar world than now exists, it may not survive even a Nazi defeat.

Germany was one of the largest customers for products of the southern South American countries. As these countries are not highly industrialized they gladly accepted German manufactured articles in return. It soon appeared that by the use of the same devices as Germany used in the case of the Danubian and Balkan countries, namely, exchange controls,

quotas and blocked marks, Germany might be able to dominate some of the Latin American countries economically and
in all probability begin attempts at indirect political control.
Then the words of the Monroe Doctrine, finally transformed
in 1940 at Havana into a multilateral pact, would be rendered futile: "The political system of the allied powers (the
Holy Alliance) is essentially different from that of America.
. . . We should consider any attempt on their part to extend
their system to any portion of this hemisphere as dangerous
to our peace and safety." Nazi totalitarianism as a political
system is a far more deadly danger to the nations of this
hemisphere than were the anti-republican principles of the
Holy Alliance in 1823. The safety and security of all the nations of the entire hemisphere depend upon their unity and
solidarity, not only militarily during the present war but as
far as possible economically after the war.

Recent Industrial Developments

When we were building up our industries after the Civil
War we borrowed immense sums from Englishmen and
Frenchmen and other Europeans. But it was American individuals and corporations that did the borrowing, not the
United States government. When in the spendthrift days of
the 1920's, the Latin Americans started to develop their resources, it was not usually Latin American individuals who
borrowed in Wall Street but Latin American governments.
In the world depression which took place in 1929 most of
those governments discontinued payment of the interest on
the loans. They said they could not pay, and they were right.
Moreover, they did not understand why they should be asked
to pay back the millions they borrowed from the United
States when Great Britain, France, and Italy did not pay
back the billions they borrowed from the United States.

American corporations have invested immense sums of money in Latin American utilities of many kinds such as electric lighting, telephone plants, street railways, and harbor improvements. At first this was done in a form of unquestioned exploitation. That period has fortunately passed away. But when a patriotic Peruvian student learns that the principal railroads of his country are the property of and operated by British interests, that the electricity, light and power system in Lima and Callao is owned by Italian interests; that the largest petroleum company is Canadian, that the mines are in the hands of Americans, and that the great sugar interests are German, he naturally asks himself, "What do *we* own in our country?" Hence the desire on the part of extremists to expropriate foreign properties, a desire already realized in the case of oil in Mexico and Bolivia. Thoughtful Latin Americans realize that if they are to develop the resources of their countries the necessary capital must come largely from foreign sources. But thoughtful people in any country, even if in the majority, do not always make decisions contrary to the desires of a militant minority.

Under the stress of the war conditions of today, however, industrial activity has been greatly augmented in Latin America, particularly in Argentina, Brazil, and Chile. The United States has been buying in those countries immense quantities of materials needed for the military effort. The Latin Americans cannot use the increased exchange for the purchase of needed consumers' goods because the United States is not producing enough of these for its own people. The result has been that those countries have themselves turned to the production of consumers' goods in greatly increasing quantities so that they bid fair by the end of the war not only to supply the needs of their own people but also the needs of neighboring nations. Inter-American trade among the Latin American republics has been almost non-existent in the past. What worries Latin American statesmen is whether the new industries can be maintained after the war in competition with the United States and the European countries, when the latter cease manufacturing for war purposes and turn to the production of consumers' goods.

Obstacles of a Social Nature

As Bismarck once remarked, it is the imponderables that sometimes count most. If we are actually to realize the Good Neighbor policy we must understand the civilization and culture of the Latin American peoples. Every civilization is organized into institutions: the family, the school, the church, the government, and others. What is the nature of these institutions in the Latin American countries and how do the Latin Americans regard our institutions?

The Family—In our civilization marriage is based upon romantic love and the man and wife meet upon a basis of equality, certainly theoretically. Latin American civilization is a man-made civilization in which the woman has an inferior status. Until marriage she is under her father's control and after marriage under her husband's. In the family she has a high and honored position but as a mother, not as a woman. In our civilization the individual is the unit. In Latin America it is the family, and the family is a very closely knit and exclusive unit. With us the son or daughter leaves home to seek his or her own fortune. Not so in the Latin American home. There separation takes place with difficulty and usually in sorrow, though the growth of apartment life in large cities has a tendency to lessen control by parents. Chaperonage here is practically dead; in Latin America it is a very real institution. Divorce here is easy and frequent. Divorce in Latin America is difficult and infrequent and the Latin Americans wonder at the place enjoyed by the divorcée in our society. American movies picturing the night club life of our cities, in which unchaperoned young women play a part, fill Latin American conservatives with alarm. They fear our influence will help to disintegrate the family.

The School—Our civilization has a fundamental social ideal: equality of opportunity. Our school system is founded upon that ideal. All children must go to school and the elementary school is the favored part of the educational system. The Latin Americans do not have that ideal and the ruling classes do not want it. They believe society should be organized to put control not in the masses of the people but in the social and intellectual élite. Hence, the favored institution is not the elementary school for the masses; it is the liceo, the secondary school, the school for the socially elect. Except in a few progressive countries like Mexico, and especially in a number of the large cities, little has been done in the elementary school to make it attractive to the masses. Health education, manual training, and vocational courses have received little attention. The children of the workers usually leave school very early. Even in an educationally advanced country like Argentina which has the lowest percentage of illiteracy among all the countries of Latin America, namely, 20 per cent, only 11 per cent of the pupils who enter the first primary grade go on to the sixth grade and in the rural areas many do not go to school at all. The causes of this unfortunate situation are poverty and a social system in which manual labor is held in low esteem. The educational conditions in the cities of Argentina are much better.

The liceo in most of the Latin American countries is conservatively organized and administered. It has a rigid curriculum with few modern subjects, its methods of teaching are old fashioned, and extra-curricular activities are practically unknown. To pass the examination and secure the *bachillerato* is the chief aim, memoriter work is the chief method, and the percentage of failures is very high. Obviously the liceo is not a strong agency in the development of a middle class, the necessary foundation of democracy.

The Church—The great mass of people in the United States is of the Protestant religion; an even greater percentage of the people of Latin America is Roman Catholic. True Christianity consists in a proper balance between faith and works. In the United States the emphasis is increasingly upon works, and Protestantism is characterized by a reduced emphasis upon faith. In Latin America there is no such attitude, unquestioning faith is the desideratum and a belief in the miraculous prevails almost everywhere. The Higher Criticism has no place in Latin America and the loss of religious faith in the United States following the researches of the Higher Criticism makes the Catholic Church in Latin America very distrustful of Protestant influence. Enormous philanthropy is practiced in the United States but it is largely in the form of social agencies of various kinds not necessarily connected with the Church and it has the aim of making the underprivileged self-supporting. Charity in the form of actual almsgiving plays a very minor rôle. In Latin America that form of charity is considered a virtue and the agencies of social amelioration are practically always agencies of the Church. In short, the Church in Latin America regards Protestantism with distrust as a disintegrating influence upon Latin American culture, in which religion plays so large a part. The Church in some countries is state supported, is a bulwark of the *status quo,* and has seldom favored democratizing influences. Among the conservative classes Americanism is identified with those influences. In some countries, therefore, the Church is anti-democratic and anti-American.

Generally speaking, the Latin Americans on the whole do not regard us as *simpático.* Our philosophy of life is that of the pragmatist. We ask of an idea, "Does it work?" Their philosophy is that of the traditionalist. They ask, "Does it conform to our ways of doing things?" If not, then "Why change those ways?"

International Obstacles

The international relations of the United States with the Latin American countries after the Mexican War of 1846–1848 became increasingly bad and were not relieved until the advent of the Good Neighbor policy, begun in the Hoover administration, and expanded and transformed by Mr. Roosevelt. It cannot be expected that ten years of the Good Neighbor policy will remove from the minds of the skeptical in Latin America the impression made by unfriendly acts in the past. This is particularly so when German agents have used all kinds of measures to organize Fifth Columns among people of their own race and among Latin Americans who are opposed to United States policy.

Pan Hispanism is one of the strongest obstacles to good relations between the United States and Latin America. The name antedates World War I but the movement at that time had few adherents in the Latin American countries outside the most conservative intellectual circles. In fact it had little vitality until Spain fell under the control of the Franco regime. Then nationalist fervor in Spain demanded a renascence of Spanish prestige and culture in the lands which were once Spanish colonies, that is, in Latin America and the Philippines. Large sums of money were allotted by the Franco government to Falangists, who began a strong propaganda in the Latin American countries. The Falangists are anti-democratic and anti-American. Spain has as yet remained neutral in the war and has taken charge of the affairs of Germany, Italy, and Japan in the Latin American countries that have severed diplomatic relations with the Axis powers. The result has been that Spanish embassies and legations in the Latin American countries have become to a great extent centers of intrigue against the principle of hemisphere solidarity. In spite of this, Pan Hispanism has not made great headway in Latin America. Brazil, with half the population of South America within its borders, looks askance at it. Most of the Spanish American countries, especially the stronger ones, are very nationalistic and patriotic, and proud of their national cultures. They have no more desire to be under the cultural domination of Spain than have the people of the United States to be under the cultural domination of England.

The Difficulty of Hemisphere Defense

The military obstacle to hemisphere solidarity is a most serious one. When President Monroe proclaimed the Monroe Doctrine in 1823, George Canning, the British Secretary of State for Foreign Affairs, issued a similar declaration. It must frankly be admitted that the tacit acceptance of the Monroe Doctrine by European countries depended more upon the existence of the British fleet than upon our Declaration. Community of interest upon the part of Great Britain and the United States in maintaining an open door in the Latin American countries for freedom of trade binds them together today to prevent domination of the southern continent by the Axis powers.

The doubt of the Argentine government as to the ability of the United States to guarantee both its economic and military security is perhaps sufficient justification for its noncooperative attitude toward hemisphere solidarity. However, no one can read the proceedings of the successive Pan American conferences and of the more recent emergency meetings of the Foreign Ministers of the American republics without a feeling that many Argentines are not enthusiastic about hemisphere solidarity anyhow. Hemisphere solidarity means the enhancement of the prestige of the United States, the greatest exponent of that policy. Argentina has looked forward to being regarded as the spokesman of Latin America vis-à-vis Anglo-Saxon America. Few other Latin American republics regard her as such, and she naturally does not view with a happy eye their granting the United States the use of air fields and naval bases even for use only during the war.

The Future of Hemisphere Solidarity

Hemisphere solidarity has not yet been realized. It may not be realized during the war. Can it be realized after the war? The statesmen who will construct the peace must consider in the light of experience, reason, and common sense what is practicable politically, economically, and psychologically. The trend of international thinking at present is largely in the direction of the establishment of regional federations with some kind of limited control by a superior organization to prevent conflict. No single pattern of organization can be expected to apply to all regional federations. What would be wise for a European federation would not necessarily be best for a regional federation of the Western Hemisphere. In Europe there are five great powers and a large number of smaller powers. In the Western Hemisphere there is one great power, whose military and economic strength is much greater than that of all the other nations of the hemisphere combined. In Europe, whether there be one general European federation or more than one regional federation, each will probably be fairly closely organized and the central organ may have considerable power of control. Europe will finally put an end to the *liberum veto*. That bad principle of allowing the adverse vote of a single member of the Polish Diet to prevent the adoption of an absolutely essential action was the primary cause of the destruction of Poland in the latter part of the eighteenth century. The *liberum veto,* which allowed even a weak and backward state to prevent unanimous action in the Assembly of the League of Nations, was a subsidiary cause of the failure of the League.

The overpowering position of the United States in the Western Hemisphere will probably prevent the organization of a regional federation similar to those projected for Europe. Little is read today in Latin American publications about the Colossus of the North. That does not mean that the fear of the immense power of the United States has been removed in the Latin American countries. It exists in every Latin American nation, not only in Argentina. It is shown in the hesitancy of even friendly nations to permit United States soldiers in association with national troops to man naval bases and airfields that are constructed by American funds awarded under the lend-lease program. The United States has shown a scrupulous regard for its commitments under the Good Neighbor policy. It is providing badly needed aircraft and munitions to strengthen the military defenses of nearly all the Latin American countries. It is undertaking well-planned economic measures not only to help those countries tide over the loss of their markets in Europe during the war but also to build up their industries for the post-war period. The great majority of the Latin American nations, as a *quid pro quo,* have responded admirably to the need of the United States for products necessary to the conduct of the war and which they can supply.

The United States is admittedly looking after its own security as well as the security of the Latin American countries. All this cooperation would be futile were it to cease at the end of the war. If the new world order is to be organized upon a basis of regional federations, it is likely that the Western Hemisphere would be generally regarded as one of the federations. The necessities of the situation will require that it be a looser form of regional federation than that of Europe. It may be that the growing practice of consultation among the governments of the Western Hemisphere on matters of major policy might suffice. It would not suffice if the practice of unanimity is followed as it was attempted at Rio de Janeiro in January 1942. If even a loosely constructed regional federation is to be viable, no one member can expect to possess a *liberum veto*. It has repeatedly happened at conferences of representatives of the American republics that agreements receiving the approval of all the other states have had to be whittled down before being accepted by Argentina. And this unanimity has been sought despite the regulation that decisions should be made by majority vote. Majority rule would not affect the autonomy of states nor justify interference in the domestic affairs of states. The conventions agreed upon at the Pan American conferences are not always implemented and they will not be implemented unless the democratic principle of majority rule is followed. So far, much good has been accomplished at these conferences by conventions and resolutions bearing on the common interests of the American republics and it may be that experience will show that a closer form of regional federation would be undesirable or unnecessary. But Rio de Janeiro was an impressive lesson of the weakness of the "inter-American system" when confronted by a world emergency.

What Place Canada?

Thus far attention has been directed to the relations between the United States and the Latin American nations. The status of Canada in hemisphere solidarity has been omitted. Canada is not a member of the Pan American Union and thus far has never indicated a desire to become a member.

It is a member of the British Commonwealth of Nations and is very loyal to Great Britain as was manifested by its voluntary declaration of war against Germany. Hemisphere solidarity is not possible without Canada's cooperation. If the post-war world order provides a regional federation for the Western Hemisphere, Canada must be included. Her orientation in recent years has been increasingly toward cooperation with the United States, despite the Ottawa Agreement. During these war years it has been made entirely evident that her security depends upon military collaboration with the United States and that has been given unstintedly. It must be equally obvious that in the post-war world economic considerations will direct her to increased cooperation with the United States. In the post-war world there would be no difficulty in her becoming a member of the Pan American Union and sharing the responsibility in the attempts that are being made to organize the Western Hemisphere. There would be no reason why she should not remain a member of the British Commonwealth of Nations. It is entirely likely that in the new world order a country may of necessity be a member of more than one regional federation. Despite her geographical position in one hemisphere and her political affiliation in another, Canada presents a lesser obstacle to hemisphere solidarity than does Argentina.

What of Caribbean Colonies?

There remains one matter for consideration. Can hemisphere solidarity, or rather hemisphere security, be realized if non-American countries retain colonies in the Western Hemisphere in the post-war world? Where is the security of the Western Hemisphere most likely to be endangered? The Canal Zone is the weakest link in the system of defense. One cause of its weakness is the existence of some of the strategic

European colonies in the Caribbean. The French island of Martinique has been causing us anxiety in the present war. Hemisphere security will not be fully assured until strategic places in the possessions of European powers in the Caribbean are transferred by purchase to the inchoate federation of American republics or to the United States. This does not mean that the United States should take over entire islands where the people are deeply attached to the British or French or Dutch connection and would dislike the change because of what they believe to be our unfair attitude toward Negroes. Furthermore most of them present distressing economic problems and can exist economically only because they have access to highly protected markets in the mother countries. With our already existing obligations to Cuba and Puerto Rico it would be much more difficult for us to give them tariff preferences. The suggestion is only that points of real strategic importance should be purchased, such as the small area on the island of Antigua yielded to the United States for ninety-nine years.

One source of danger in the Caribbean was removed during World War I by the purchase of the Virgin Islands from Denmark, now "protected" by Germany. The action suggested above is therefore in conformity with precedent. Moreover, when Britain signed the Kellogg Pact she stated, "there are certain regions of the world the welfare and integrity of which constitute a special and vital interest for our peace and safety. . . . Interference with these regions cannot be suffered." She meant Gibraltar, Malta, and Suez, protecting her life line to India and the Far East. Britain has recognized the special interests of the United States in the Caribbean in various ways. It is time for us now permanently to safeguard those vital interests in cooperation with the other nations of the New World by realizing the policy suggested.

CHAPTER XIV

THE UNITED STATES AND THE
POST-WAR WORLD

THUS far this book has undertaken but little conjecture. In this final chapter there must of necessity be conjecture because it is concerned with the future and no one can foretell what will happen even in the immediate future. We are in the midst of war and the war has compelled the United States and its allies to engage in cooperative activities of immense importance and with excellent results. It can be hoped that the pattern may be carried over into the post-war world and that the experience will indicate methods of cooperation of equal value in a time of peace. In any event the United States will probably participate in making decisions concerning concepts like sovereignty and activities such as preventing aggression. Common sense would dictate that a study of those concepts and activities be made now in the light of our traditions and historical experience and while the feeling of the need for unity among the United Nations is strong. It ought not be left to the exigencies of the situation at the close of the war.

The Period of the Armistice

The terrible destruction of life and property and the mounting hatred of Germans resulting from the plundering and bestial treatment of the defeated nations by the Nazi government can hardly have other effect than a condition of chaos in the world generally, but in Europe especially, when the Axis nations lay down their arms. The demand for revenge upon the German people by the outraged nations of Central and Eastern Europe caused by the activities of the Gestapo is entirely understandable and will be difficult to control. But to permit mass murder of Germans because of the terrible crimes of the Nazis would not only be futile but repulsive to Americans. Nor is it necessary in the interest of justice. The people of every subjugated nation know who the Nazi terrorists and murderers in their midst have been. There would be little difficulty in bringing them to trial and punishment immediately upon the establishment of the armistice.

The first consideration in realizing a proper program of control by the United Nations would be the restoration and maintenance of order. This must be accomplished at first by the Armies of Occupation. In some cases such as Norway, Belgium, and the Netherlands the responsibility could be transferred to the governments in exile. In others, greater difficulty would be encountered. In the case of Germany and Italy there are no governments in exile. It is a question how returned political refugees would be regarded by the people of those countries. The refugees will have been in exile for several years—in some instances as much as a decade—and out of touch with the course of events at home. Those who have been compelled to remain at home and endure the terrors of Nazi and Fascist control might resent refugee participation in national or even local government. Some persons among the resident population will probably have won the confidence of the people generally and might be regarded by them as their natural leaders. When the Nazi and Fascist regimes have been destroyed by the occupation, and complete disarmament of Germany and Italy accomplished by the United

Nations, the occupying powers would naturally turn to those persons for advice and assistance. But for a considerable time administrative control would have to remain with the occupying powers.

The United States has already undertaken to train temporary administrators in the language, history, and national psychology of each country and in the changes in the form of administration that will probably be essential. As described in Chapter II, a splendid opportunity presents itself here to utilize some of the several thousand exchange students from the European countries who have studied in the United States during the past quarter century under the auspices of the Institute of International Education and have become familiar with the English language and our way of meeting difficult situations. Of even greater importance are the more than two thousand American students who have studied in the European countries and who have learned the languages and attitude toward life of their peoples.

Unquestionably the most exigent problem that will confront the administration in every country is the problem of relief, of providing food, clothing and shelter for starving people. Relief will require trained workers such as nurses and social workers with a knowledge of nutrition, and experienced teachers because the school will have to be the situs of most relief activities. The British have already had a remarkable experience in undertaking activities of this nature at home. In all probability relief agencies will everywhere be welcomed and it can be hoped that the aid will be extended in a spirit of humanity and not of charity, of service and not of condescension. It ought, moreover, to be done without political motive. The contrast between methods of conducting necessary activities by totalitarian and democratic regimes will probably be enough to strengthen the latter in the good will of the people. And as control by the democratic powers will be accompanied by a considerable degree of free speech, a free press, and a free radio, popular respect for democracy will in all probability be strengthened.

The most difficult problem to solve is the re-education of the Nazi mind, especially the minds of the young who have been subjected for a decade to an education thoroughly corrupt in its spirit, objectives and methods. For the first time they will have other and fairer sources of information, and with intelligent and considerate teachers from among nationals, and to a much less extent from the ranks of the democracies, it can reasonably be expected that they will take a truer view of the Nazi and a fairer view of the democratic regimes. It cannot be too strongly emphasized that re-education in Germany must be under the leadership of German anti-Nazis and not enemy aliens however forbearing and moderate. The rôle of the latter should be to provide sympathetic advice and assistance. The rôle of education—and especially international education—in the post-war world can hardly be over-emphasized. If, as the spokesmen of the democracies reiterate, this war has as one of its principal objectives the exaltation of the "common man" in life rather than the state, education for world citizenship to enable him to exercise a more direct influence on international affairs is essential. Since educational institutions in many European countries have been destroyed or have degenerated, the responsibility of the United States for assisting in the training of foreign leaders for post-war reconstruction—for our own "peace and safety"—is obvious.

The countries upon whose financial resources the call must chiefly be made to carry on the work of relief and rehabilitation are the United States and Great Britain, particularly the former. However, many other nations can share in the effort —Argentina and Brazil, for example, can contribute much grain and meat. The citizens of the United States and Great

Britain have been compelled to bear staggering burdens of taxation for destructive purposes during the war. Will they be willing to continue to do so for constructive purposes after the war? Certainly humanitarianism would suggest an affirmative answer. But so will every instinct of prudence. The productive machines of both countries are now geared to the greatest extent to manufacturing instruments of war. At the moment of the armistice that ceases. Factories will become idle and men unemployed unless machinery is at once converted and workers directed to the production of goods needed to keep men alive instead of putting them to death. Lend-lease is one of the most important agencies in enabling us to win the war. It can be as potent an instrument in organizing markets among the destitute millions in all quarters of the globe for the goods they need and we can produce.

World-Mindedness

If there has been any lingering belief that an important happening in any part of the world can fail to have repercussions over the entire world, the events of the present war ought to remove it. Today there are but few states in the whole world not included among the combatants. The day of localized war between major powers, as illustrated in the Franco-Prussian War of seventy years ago, is probably gone for good. This war is global not only in its battles but in its consequences. The export trade of neutral Argentina was temporarily ruined. The industrial life of neutral Sweden was brought almost to a standstill. The people of neutral Spain are still starving. To understand this war one must study a globe, not merely a map.

Unless the peace is to be merely an armistice between wars, during which both sides will feverishly continue to rearm, the peace must also be global. It will decidedly not be global unless it is planned now by men who really know the fundamental causes of war, who are sufficiently objective to work for their removal, and who have vision enough to foresee at least some of the probable obstacles to a durable peace. There are few such men in any country and there is of course no certainty that they will be the architects of the peace. With the continuance of the war there comes the increased hatred and desire for vengeance fatefully reminiscent of Versailles. Wisdom would dictate that the armistice be made for a long enough period, possibly four or five years, to enable the world to become stabilized and reconstruction undertaken before calling a peace conference. Such an intermission would enable passions to cool and reason to reassert itself.

It would be futile to attempt today to draw a detailed blueprint of such a world order. But there are certain aspects of life that must be safeguarded if any new world order is to meet the needs of mankind. Men must be permitted to live their daily lives in peace and not be dragged from their homes and families to fight and possibly die for causes in which they have no reasonable interest and to which they may even be bitterly opposed as is true in some European countries today. Men in one part of the globe must be able to carry on their business with men in another part of the globe without interference. Mankind must be guaranteed protection of the characteristics that distinguish it from the lower forms of life: the right to speak and write and do and believe what one chooses so long as the practice does not interfere with the possession and practice of the same rights in others. And it must be understood that these rights are the heritage of mankind simply as men—not merely of advanced as against primitive men. The new world order of the democratic nations must banish the imperialisms that have hitherto exploited primitive mankind.

The form the new world order may take will be determined largely by the events and the outcome of the war. It may be a union of all peoples similar to the League of Nations but an improvement upon the League. It may be in the nature of regional federations or councils with a superior council to prevent conflicts among them. It may take other forms. The peace and the new world order will depend to a great extent upon the amount of preparation undertaken by scholars, publicists, and statesmen of the United Nations in the solution of the long-term problems that are outstanding and of a relatively permanent nature. Some of them are briefly considered in this chapter. Of even greater importance is the morale of peoples at the end of the war. If their first consideration is a hasty return to "normalcy", or if they have become utterly war worn and apathetic, there will be little hope of a wisely planned world order. But if they are determined that not national-mindedness as at Versailles but world-consciousness is to prevail in the building of the new world order, mankind may look forward with hope to an era of peace and understanding. It will require a great and continuous educational campaign to make world-mindedness prevail over national-mindedness, because the spirit of nationalism is deeply rooted in all countries.

How Much Sovereignty Will Remain?

The theory of sovereignty predicates the absolute freedom of the state to control its internal affairs and to determine its external relations with other states. In Western civilization the theory, though not formulated at the time, was practically realized in the Roman Empire. With the dissolution of the Empire all evidences of the modern concept of sovereignty disappeared. During the Middle Ages two powers, the Papacy and the Holy Roman Empire, struggled for supremacy in Europe, but because of the rise of feudalism the authority and control of each were vague, ill defined, and not generally acknowledged save in words. The theory of sovereignty as understood today had its origin in the Renaissance with the gradual establishment of such nation states as France, Spain, and Great Britain. With the publication of Grotius' *De jure belli ac pacis* in 1625, sovereignty in the modern sense became a definitely established principle of international law. The sound principles formulated by Grotius were repeatedly violated by monarchs like Louis XIV and Frederick the Great and particularly by Napoleon, who ignored the principle of the equality of states and destroyed the independence of those states that interfered with his organization of Europe into something similar to the Roman Empire.

The overthrow of Napoleon restored the practice of basing the relation of states upon treaties which recognized their independence and equality regardless of size and strength. The unification of Germany and Italy and the revival of national states in the Balkan peninsula placed increased emphasis upon the idea of the absolutely independent state. That idea reached its apogee in the peace treaties at the close of World War I, which revived some dormant nation states and established others with the same attributes as the states already in existence. The organization of a League of Nations with some slight limitations upon the sovereignty of its members failed among other reasons because, except in a few matters of procedure, decisions required unanimous consent. A decision of vital importance might thus be prevented by the vote of a weak, backward state. Sovereignty might thereby be reduced to an absurdity. The situation resulting from the failure of the League provided aggressor states with the opportunity to attain their unlawful objectives and brought about the present war. Certainly any new world order will require greater restriction on the sovereignty of states than existed under the League of Nations.

The Atlantic Charter to which the United Nations are officially committed states that "They wish to see sovereign rights and self-government restored to those who have been forcibly deprived of them." There can be hardly any doubt that the smaller states look forward to regaining their prewar status in which their "sovereign rights" enabled them to exist as theoretical equals of all countries—but in actuality only upon the sufferance of their great and powerful neighbors. This may be a hopeless dream, because whether Briand's ideal of a United States of Europe will be realized or a federation of regional European areas will result, an incessant campaign must be maintained if the small states are not to be confined to mere formal independence and autonomy in internal affairs. The trend of international thinking today is largely in the direction of the establishment of regional federations with some kind of limited control by a superior organization to prevent conflict. What those regional federations will consist of will be determined by the course of events, but it must be assumed that federations will vary in organization to meet the requirements of different local conditions and backgrounds. All these problems are still in the domain of speculation, but it is wise at least to realize their existence before the need of actually attempting to solve them arises.

It does not seem likely that mankind will submit to another blood bath with its accompanying destruction of human, natural, and industrial resources. But the problem of sovereignty must be faced realistically. The nation state is the unit of political organization today and it will unquestionably survive this war. The relations between nation states will no doubt remain on a treaty basis as they have been in the past, but the future treaties will probably be enforced. The limitations on sovereignty will be those which experience has shown to be the minimum essential to a regime of peace, security, and justice. Such a regime cannot exist if a sovereign state can judge its own controversies and go to war to enforce its judgments; it cannot exist if each nation can determine its tariffs and economic policy generally without regard to the effect of its policy upon other nations; it cannot exist if minority populations and even its own citizens are denied ordinary human rights. To be assured of the maintenance of a new regime where these conditions will be observed will require modifications in the existing international order that will be very difficult to attain: an adequate world police force to prevent aggression and secure the observance of treaties, a body to obtain modifications in outmoded treaties and laws whose existence causes antagonism and conflict, a carefully organized non-partisan international court with judges having sufficiently long tenure and compulsory jurisdiction in clearly defined types of disputes.

Fortunately, mankind has had almost a generation of experience with the League of Nations. Some of its organs, such as the International Labor Organization and its non-political committees, attained great success and served mankind admirably. They should be retained and other organs be reconstructed so as to meet the needs of new world conditions. All these changes will make a great demand upon the abilities and statesmanship of the leaders of nations. Mankind looks forward with hope that a long-term view of the necessary limitations upon sovereignty will be taken and that action will not be determined by emergency needs and by aroused passions.

Maintaining Peace Throughout the World

Whatever form of world order may result from the present conflict, keeping the peace among the constituent nation states will probably be its most difficult problem. In the evolution of humanity from families to tribes, from tribes to city states, and from city states to national states, the problem of keeping the peace had to be faced and solved. The query naturally arises, will there be unusual difficulty in keeping the peace in the event of a development of national states into regional federations such as have been envisaged?

In the evolution of humanity mentioned above there existed undoubted loyalty to family, tribe, and city state respectively, but that loyalty is as nothing compared with the loyalty to the nation state of today. In the long progress from primitive life there have slowly developed standards of conduct for the individual which are not accepted as applying to the state. Hence whereas the citizen within a national state accepts as a matter of course the state's police power as the instrument which is to prevent conflict between individuals, he is hostile to any attempt on the part of a supra-national organization to exercise police control over his state. Even when his country is clearly in the wrong, his leaders find little difficulty in convincing him of the necessity of rallying to the national standard.

The ideal solution of the police problem would be to place control in the hands of a power which had the confidence of the regional members and the necessary strength and capacity to enforce law and order. However, it can be assumed that this ideal solution will not be realized. National mistrust, jealousy, and fear are too great obstacles. There will have to be some form of voluntary pooling of forces and of control, and this is an undoubted weakness, as is almost every kind of condominium. But it is not necessarily a fatal weakness. The fatal weakness is lack of will as was shown repeatedly by the League of Nations.

Now we must be realistic. When the war ceases it will be a tremendous task to bring order out of the chaotic situation that will probably prevail. The states that have succeeded in maintaining freedom in the world—Great Britain, the United States, Soviet Russia, and China—will be the states that have the will and strength and ability to carry through that task. It seems obvious what their first step must be: to disarm Germany and her allies so thoroughly and to exercise such a degree of control over them that there can be no possibility of another secret rearmament such as took place in Germany after the last war. The task of policing the world, which must be prolonged until stability has been secured, will not only take time but will be very costly to the taxpayers of the United Nations, particularly of Great Britain and the United States, who probably would alone have the resources to finance the work. The taxpayers of those two countries would be no more willing to have their governments play the part of policemen indefinitely than other states would be to have them do so. Hence the importance of having some associating contingents from other states in the police work at the earliest practicable moment.

When the armistice period has come to a close the four states will have to organize a peace conference as promptly as conditions permit to undertake the Herculean task of organizing the new world order in such a manner as to justify men's belief that it will inaugurate a period of peace, security, and justice. This can be accomplished only if the disarmed Axis powers participate in the movement. As a practical matter the maintenance of peace would probably fail unless provision were made for the continuance of the inter-Allied war machinery into the peace situation.

It seems equally obvious that the four states mentioned above must eventually undertake measures to disarm themselves as promised in the Atlantic Charter. One of the fatal misfortunes of the period after 1919 was the development of a conviction among the defeated powers that France and the Little Entente had no intention to keep the promise of a reduction of armaments. The disarmament should be slow enough, however, to be consistent with the maintenance of control by the four leading allies. No state should be deprived of the right to use the force which is now the only means of securing justice for itself unless other means are provided of assuring justice for it. In other words provision must be made for "peaceful change". It is obvious how immensely difficult and complicated the problem of policing the world will be and how far removed from this speculation the reality may be.

World Economic Organization

In time of peace the United States consumes more rubber than all the rest of the world together. Its economy demands an adequate and continuous supply. As up to the present it could not produce rubber it had to secure its supply from abroad—almost wholly from the plantations of British Malaya and the Dutch East Indies. During the Coolidge administration, the President made a vigorous protest against the British attempt in Malaya to limit drastically the production of rubber so as to raise the price to the consumer. This British attempt at regulation failed because the Dutch plantations in the Netherlands Indies increased their production to take advantage of the increased price. Rubber is here used to illustrate the anarchy resulting from monopoly control of a commodity of international need coupled with the power of a sovereign state to determine the amount of supply. Cotton might have illustrated the evil equally well. The reduction of cotton-raising acreage by the United States stimulated the increase of acreage devoted to cotton production by Brazil, Peru and other countries, some of which were not so favored by nature for producing this crop as is the United States. Americans have long been convinced of the need of national regulation of unfair trade practices and have laws to prevent them in the domestic market. Similarly a sound economic world organization will require some degree of control of international economic competition.

Despite Mr. Coolidge's protest the United States would probably have paid the higher price of rubber had the British plantation owners' scheme succeeded—at least until our own entrepreneurs could develop new sources of raw rubber. The United States was rich enough to afford the increase and it is a nation that believes in law and order in international affairs. But there were and are other nations not so complaisant. All the so-called "Have Not" nations, afterward transformed into the Axis, came late upon the international scene as economic competitors with states that earlier had secured control of essential raw materials denied by geography to the Have Nots. The latter were determined to have a share of those natural resources, if not by peaceful means, then by measures of force. In fact the raw materials were wanted in anticipation of a war effort.

Nor was the problem of raw materials all. The Axis powers maintained that in order to stifle competition, access to markets was denied them. Tariffs prevented such access to a certain extent but tariffs were imposed by practically all countries. They themselves imposed tariffs upon imports. They insisted that what was outrageous was for some colonies of European countries to be administered as closed preserves of the mother countries. It was certainly true that the French colonies were regarded almost as extensions of the mother country from which foreign economic penetration was practically excluded. But even in more liberally administered colonies, such as those of Great Britain, the use of the coinage and banking system of the mother country, the purchases for government services and public works, and the indirect methods of favoring business with the homeland put the Axis states, they maintained, at an unfair disadvantage. It is true that the Japanese in Korea and the Italians in Libya followed the same practices, as had also the Germans in their former African colonies. But these facts were disregarded in the propaganda program. That it was possible for great powers to be excluded from the enormous colonial domains of such disdained little countries as Belgium, Portugal, and the Netherlands, filled with natural resources which they ardently coveted, seemed to the Axis wholly inadmissible.

Economic "penetration" was the method first adopted to accomplish the desired change. For example, with countries whose products found a ready market in Germany, such as the nations of the Danubian area and the Balkans, barter arrangements were made. Those countries sent their agricultural and mineral products to Germany and took in return manufactured goods. The deal was mutually satisfactory at first, because in most cases the German market was the most profitable for the countries indicated and Germany was greatly assisted in securing the necessary raw materials to carry on her covert rearmament. But gradually such totalitarian devices as exchange controls, blocked marks and quotas were introduced and enabled Germany to dictate prices and quantities. The Danubian and Balkan countries gradually found themselves in a condition of economic semi-slavery, unable because of their commitments to Germany to sell in free markets and often compelled to accept goods from Germany which they did not want. It was but a step from economic semi-slavery to political interference and final domination. The previous chapter described the attempt of the Germans to realize a similar program with the Latin American countries. These methods will continue after the war unless we can bring economic as well as military war under control. Otherwise each state will be forced by the danger of war into totalitarianism. Indeed, it is a question how far inevitable centralization of governmental powers during this war is going to carry us anyhow toward totalitarianism.

The illustrations of economic maladjustments reviewed in the preceding paragraphs emphasize the lesson that the welfare of nations depends very largely upon their economic cooperation. Self-determination and self-sufficiency must have a lesser rôle in the post-war world. Given the creation of a World Trade Commission to secure such cooperation, its decisions would be valueless unless they could be implemented by a body having sufficient authority and strength to command obedience. The corollary to that conclusion is the need for some restriction upon the sovereignty of states. Debasing the currency in one nation to undersell competing nations can result only in economic deterioration in all nations. The imposition of a tariff by a sovereign state regardless of its effect upon others has sometimes resulted in the destruction of an industry in one of them. The effect of an international situation where such action can be taken is to drive the victim nations to search for *Lebensraum* in order to secure control of raw materials and of markets. The almost inevitable result is physical conflict.

Economic cooperation even under the aegis of a supranational body would be immensely difficult. But just as progressive countries have learned that national welfare demands proper provision for citizens who have been made underprivileged largely by their environment, similarly world society must be so organized that nations made underprivileged by geographic factors shall receive necessary assistance if the international organization is to be one of peace, security, and justice.

The Future of Colonies and Mandates

A colony in the modern meaning of the term is an area in one region of the world under the control of a state situated elsewhere. The primary motive for the control has always been trade profit, but the spread of religion has been an important reason for the extension of colonial dominion. At first colonies were regarded as sources of tribute and later of trade. At all times the chief function of the administration of a colony has been the maintenance of order to facilitate economic exploitation. The native has always been subjected to the needs and wishes of the governing element. When it was felt that colonies did not "pay", as was the view of many Liberal statesmen in England in the middle of the nineteenth century, the wish was often expressed that the mother country rid herself of her colonies. That attitude, however, did not survive the program of the imperialists led by Joseph Chamberlain, Cecil Rhodes, and Rudyard Kipling toward the end of the century. Nor has it since been held by any Power having colonies.

Colonies were considered profitable for a great variety of reasons. They were sources of raw materials for the industries of the mother country and were markets for her manufactured goods. They were places for the investment of surplus capital. As mentioned before, the use of the monetary system of the mother country, the placing in the metropolis of orders for equipment for road building, port improvement, transportation systems and the thousand and one requirements of governmental administration were of great benefit to the citizens at home. Colonies offered careers for "younger sons" and others in both civilian and military fields. Colonies provided *Lebensraum* for surplus population—a thesis of doubtful validity. More recently the importance of colonies to furnish bases for land, naval, and air forces needed for the protection of lines of commerce and for the extension of the power and prestige of the mother country has been emphasized. Some American military and naval officers have expressed the view during the war that the defeat of Japan should result in the acquisition by the United States of Japanese Mandates in the Pacific.

It can be readily understood, therefore, why Powers without colonies should regard with envy those who have them. It can be even more readily appreciated why Germany should so deeply resent the expropriation of her colonies by the victorious Allies in 1918. It would have been inconsistent with the idealistic promises made during the war by the Allies for them simply to have divided up the German colonies among themselves. Hence there was invented the principle of mandates, a principle up to that time unknown to international law.

When one of the Allies was granted a mandate for a former German colony, the mandatory power did not acquire sovereignty over the mandate. It has ever since been a moot question where the sovereignty over the mandate resides. The administration of the mandate was placed wholly in the mandatory but the mandatory was committed to making an annual report to the Mandates Commission of the League of Nations, which had the right to question the representative of the mandatory. Moreover, all the members of the League of Nations were put upon an equality with the mandatory as regards trade and commerce. Article 22, section 5 of the League Covenant prohibits the training of natives for other than police purposes and the defense of the mandate. Obviously, all these commitments of the mandatory are legal limitations upon its sovereignty so far as concerns its mandates.

The mandate system reflects the weakness of the League itself, namely, the inability to implement decisions. The Mandates Commission was not given power to make independent investigation of the statements in the mandatory's report, probably a difficulty inherent in the circumstances. But the result has been that the sole means at the disposal of the League for compelling the proper execution of the mandate is the force of public opinion. The British mandatory has observed its commitments best, the Japanese worst. The Japanese have tried to exclude foreigners from their mandates and have observed great secrecy in their administration. In the meantime they have fortified them to the greatest possible extent.

What will be the probable attitude of the United Nations toward colonies and mandates when the war is finally won? The mandate system is so distinctly an improvement over the colonial system that many political scientists advocate the extension of its principles to all colonies. They would place the supervision over colonies as well as mandates in the central agency of the new world order that is to be organized, with the addition of direct power of investigation and sanctions for breach of trust. That would mean practically the transfer of the colonies to the new collective organization—something that is not likely to take place. The reasons given above for having colonies will hold in the post-war world as strongly as they did in the pre-war world. Moreover, to shift the actual administration from the experienced officials now in control would be a serious risk. If the new world order would establish agencies that could secure equitable distribution of raw materials and access to markets, the demand for colonies on the part of the Have Not powers would be largely met. It would be a forward step in the removal of international jealousy were vacancies in the civil service in mandates to be filled by examination open to peoples of every nationality. This is a policy not likely to be adopted by any state entrusted with mandates, however, unless powers with no desire to administer foreign territory—such as the United States, which refused to accept a mandate over Armenia after the first World War—recognize their responsibility to become mandatories as executors of a public international trust.

According to the Covenant of the League of Nations, the

mandate system has for its objective "the well-being and development" of the peoples of the mandates. That ought to be the objective for colonies also. The intent repeatedly expressed at League meetings was unquestionably that the natives of mandates should be trained in self-government and that the economy of the territory should be gradually brought under their control. That is a big order. Vested interests in the meantime will have been formed in the mandates and it will not be easy to secure agreement upon the part of the mandatory's civil service to prepare native people to take over their jobs. Success will depend upon the will really to achieve the aim. Similar aims have been realized by the British in Egypt and in the former mandate of Iraq. It is noticeable that with the approach of victory for the United Nations idealistic statements about colonies and mandates are less frequently heard from people within states possessing them. These people emphasize that the experiment in self-government by the Filipino people was a success because of the continued political and economic connection with the United States. A similar connection will probably be necessary between the Netherlands and her Indies colonies and between Burma and Great Britain if success in those areas is to be attained. But a greater degree of control by the native populations must be assured.

Peaceful Change Through Supranational Legislation

Almost every advanced national system provides for the right of the individual to use violence in self-defense and also establishes laws, courts, and administrative agencies to protect him in the exercise of that right if investigation shows that he was justified. One of the evidences of wishful thinking in recent international affairs was the movement to "outlaw" war, incarnated in the Kellogg-Briand Pact, which

provided no mechanism to do for states what national governments do for individuals. Moreover, practically all nations
recognize that the law of life is change, and therefore they
have made laws to rid themselves of conditions which if un-
changed will lead to revolution. Similarly, if no provision is
made for changing outworn treaties and unfair conditions in
international affairs, war is inevitable.

The new world order may be a federation of regional
federations and its control limited to what is absolutely
necessary to maintain peace, order and justice throughout the
world. The American federal Constitution specifies a minimum of powers to be granted to the central union government, while all the rest are to be exercised by the states. As
the world order and the regional federations which may be
set up will in all probability be very loose associations as the
result of compromise, it is not likely that any central authority will be entrusted with as strong powers as is true in the
American system. Nevertheless, with the passage of time they
will require interpretation and modification which in turn
means courts and legislatures.

In order that the views of the people of each state should
have a more direct bearing upon regional decisions, the legislature of each state should be associated with the executive
in selecting the representatives to the regional legislative
body. Provision would have to be made to prevent the
swamping of the legislative body by the number of representatives elected from a single great state or from a few
states on a proportional basis. If there should be established
a regional European federation, Germany should not have as
many representatives as France and Great Britain combined
simply because she has as large a population. Elements other
than mere numbers must be taken into consideration, including recent history. It is the United Nations who must decide
what the organization and composition of the legislative as-

sembly shall be but, it can be hoped, with a due regard for fairness.

One of the advantages of regional federations is that their existence would avoid the intrusion of problems of an intimately regional nature into the discussions of a world council constituted for the purpose of regulating and administering interests which transcend regional boundaries. One of the defects of the League of Nations was that, though theoretically universal, it was primarily a European organization devoted to attempting to solve European problems. The representation of the various regional federations in a world council presents unquestioned difficulties. It could not be on the basis of population. Other factors, such as the maturity of political development, the richness of industrial activity, the progress of social welfare and education, would have to be considered. In these respects a Far Eastern regional federation could not compare with a European federation. The determination of numbers of representatives would again be a matter of compromise, and the method of appointment would almost of necessity be left to the regional federation. The important matter would be to emphasize the objective, namely, unity and cohesion of the regional federations.

The Place of Courts in the New World Order

Disputes between nations can be settled by law or by force, by an appeal to reason or by a test of physical power. Disputes settled according to law may render justice to the small as well as to the large nation. In an appeal to force, the small nation can hope for little or no justice. To the individual, law means a command of the sovereign power, disobedience to which may bring painful consequences. To the nation, this is not true because there is no world sovereignty to issue commands. The law controlling the relations among nations, international law, consists primarily of custom and agreements voluntarily entered into by the various nations. These are binding upon the parties at the time of their acceptance and may eventually become binding on other nations by general acquiescence. International law may in part be incorporated into municipal law. This has happened in the United States to the extent of incorporating treaties into the Constitution as "the law of the land". In the history of most countries there have been times when municipal law has been partially or wholly ignored, as was true in our South during Reconstruction. So there have been times in the history of the relations between nations when international law has been partially or wholly ignored. The past decade has been such a period. A time of chaos within a country or among countries has always been followed by the reassertion of law. That can be expected to be the case after the prevailing period of chaos.

To the individual the term *law* immediately suggests a concept *court,* a body set up to decide disputes between individuals. In international law the persons corresponding to individuals in municipal law are nations, and until the formation of the League of Nations there had never existed an international court except the Central American Court of Justice, which was of only eight years' duration, 1908 to 1916. If world reorganization after this war is to take the form of a federation of regional federations, then each regional federation would require its own supreme court. The present World Court, i.e., the Permanent Court of International Justice, would then be relieved of considering purely European controversies and would devote itself to deciding controversies between the federations or between countries in different federations. Its almost exclusive attention in the past to European controversies militated against its supposedly universal character.

The United States has been throughout its history one of the strongest advocates of the judicial settlement of international disputes, but because of the Senate's insistence upon its prerogative to pass upon every treaty the United States has never yet ratified a treaty of compulsory arbitration. Though the United States did not join the League of Nations, provision has since been made for its adherence to the World Court upon an equality with the members of the League. Since the establishment of the Court every President and every Secretary of State has urged upon Congress our adherence to the Court. In the light of the increasing need for international cooperation in all fields of human activity, it can hardly be doubted that the United States will become a member of a revived World Court.

Intercultural Understanding

Humanity in its long uphill climb from barbarism has developed different civilizations and cultures which for centuries were isolated from one another by various geographic factors. The different races among men developed views of life usually based upon a theory of the superiority of themselves over all others. One race considered itself "chosen" of God; another maintained that it was the "celestial" kingdom ruled by the Son of Heaven. With the very slow and gradual growth of understanding the sharpness of those differences tended to fade. But until modern science, through improvements in transportation and communication, had reduced the world to physical unity, the belief in the spiritual unity of mankind received very little attention. The Christian teaching of the brotherhood of man did not prevent Christians themselves from assuming that they were the holders of religious views superior to those of any other people. As nearly all Christians were white people, this belief easily led to the conviction that white peoples were superior to colored peoples. The transition to the exploitation of colored peoples, the acceptance of the "white man's burden", and the adoption of the philosophy of imperialism formed a natural sequence. That was the pattern of social thought in our world when the first World War began in 1914, and it had been only slightly modified by the time the second World War broke out.

It is generally assumed that revolutionary views are today in process of formation and acceptance almost everywhere. But it is as possible for revolutionary changes, in fact any changes, to be retrogressive as well as progressive. The acceptance of the doctrine of race superiority in Germany is a case in point. So is totalitarianism. Both are opposed to the objective of the present revolutionary movement: economic security with freedom for the individual. The first activity in the international education of today, therefore, is to make that fact clear as the primary distinction between the totalitarian and democratic conceptions of life. The corollary to that thesis is inescapable. A true humanism cannot admit discrimination founded upon race, color, or religion. The victory of the democracies ought to mean that within a nation equality of opportunity should prevail and that in the competition of individuals advancement ought to depend only upon merit and ability. To that end not only in the educational but also in the economic field men of good will should try to remove obstacles to the realization of human welfare and security for the common man. And a similar principle holds true in the field of international relations. A world organization founded upon the maintenance of peace and justice must guarantee the independence, economic opportunity, and cultural autonomy of all nations regardless of size and stage of development. In the international as in the national field, to the principle of self-help ought to be added the principle of service to the deserving.

Americans like to think—and with some justification—that they exemplify these principles better than most other nations. Their great Declaration of 1776 is the embodiment of those views and was proclaimed for all mankind. It states, "When in the course of *human* events. . . ." It affirms, "the inalienable rights of *man*"—of all men. It was made necessary out of "a decent respect to the opinions of *mankind.*" So strong was the feeling of the new nation that it was dedicated to the welfare of human beings that the Declaration was soon followed by the adoption of a Bill of Rights guaranteeing freedom of speech, of the press, of assembly, and of worship— of the things that make for the dignity of man. And the content of education in the schools and colleges of the early period of our history was devoted to a consideration of the nature, accomplishment, and destiny of the human being as embodied in literature, ethics, religion, and history, in other words, in the humanities.

Later American experience justified the faith in the principles of the Declaration. The almost forty millions of immigrants who have come to our shores since the organization of our government in 1789 have been absorbed with only little difficulty, have learned to live together in peace and generally have assimilated the democratic attitude toward life. We held and they learned from us that the essential meaning of life is to be found in the ideas that unite men, and not in those which divide them. The Civil War was fought to maintain the union of the states and naturally resulted in a strong emphasis upon the nation as being first in the affection and loyalty of our citizens. As the years passed nationalism as a cult was exalted to the same high position that it had attained in Europe. It reached its apogee in World War I. Thereafter democracy was no longer interpreted in the humanist spirit of the Declaration but in the nationalist spirit of Americanism. One might be in reality very undemocratic provided he was not "un-American".

The movement away from humanism and toward materialism was greatly strengthened by the important part played by science in the civilization of the nineteenth century and by technology in the twentieth. Science deals primarily with matter, not persons; with facts, not moral judgments; and its method is essentially that of analysis. Its achievement was remarkable in discoveries and inventions which provided materials to increase the welfare of all mankind. Because of the maldistribution of these materials, however, the increase was comparatively small—out of all proportion to the possibilities. The growth of the influence of science and its methods upon men's thinking was amazing. In the course of a short time it was difficult for a new subject to obtain a hearing unless it was dubbed "scientific". The method of rigid scientific analysis was taken over in the study of the humanities and social sciences which thereby lost their moral fervor. One cannot apply the technique of laboratory experimentation to the life of a human being, as to a guinea pig, without endangering human values. The evils of the world demand the passing of judgments upon them if the "inalienable rights of man" are to be preserved. The totalitarians mocked moral judgments. The disillusionment and cynicism resulting from the first World War have caused many to fear that the democracies have lost a measure of faith in the principles of the Declaration which required moral judgments. The absence of them is partial explanation of the chaos in which we live today.

Americans are sometimes accused of regarding education as the panacea for all ills. That charge is an exaggeration, but it is true that they are thoroughly devoted to education as the best basis for a civilized life within a nation and among nations. They had shared the hope that the International Commission of Intellectual Cooperation of the League of Nations would provide the vision and leadership for a program of education and culture among the nations. And they hoped that this education and culture in turn would provide for the spiritual welfare of individuals and peoples in a way similar to that by which the International Labor Organization provided for their material needs. That hope failed. But forward-looking men and women in the United States and in some other countries of the United Nations are now insisting that any world order—if that should fortunately become a reality—having for its objectives the freedom of the individual and the autonomy of nations will fail unless an International Education Organization is provided to spread a knowledge of the ideals and cultures of the different nations among one another and an understanding of their problems and difficulties.

The third chapter of this book was devoted to a consideration of foreign contributions to American culture and education, and to the influence of Americans upon foreign cultures. Americans are ready to admit the deficiencies of their civilization, but they believe that the basic ideals of that civilization are the hope of the world. No organization such as the Institute of International Education can devote itself to a nobler work than to spread a knowledge of these ideals, not by means of propaganda but by cultural association and cooperation. It is to that end that the Institute of International Education has labored, and labored as a pioneer.

THE END

INDEX

451

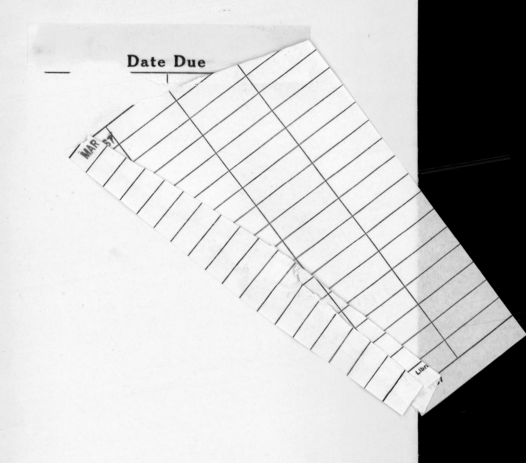